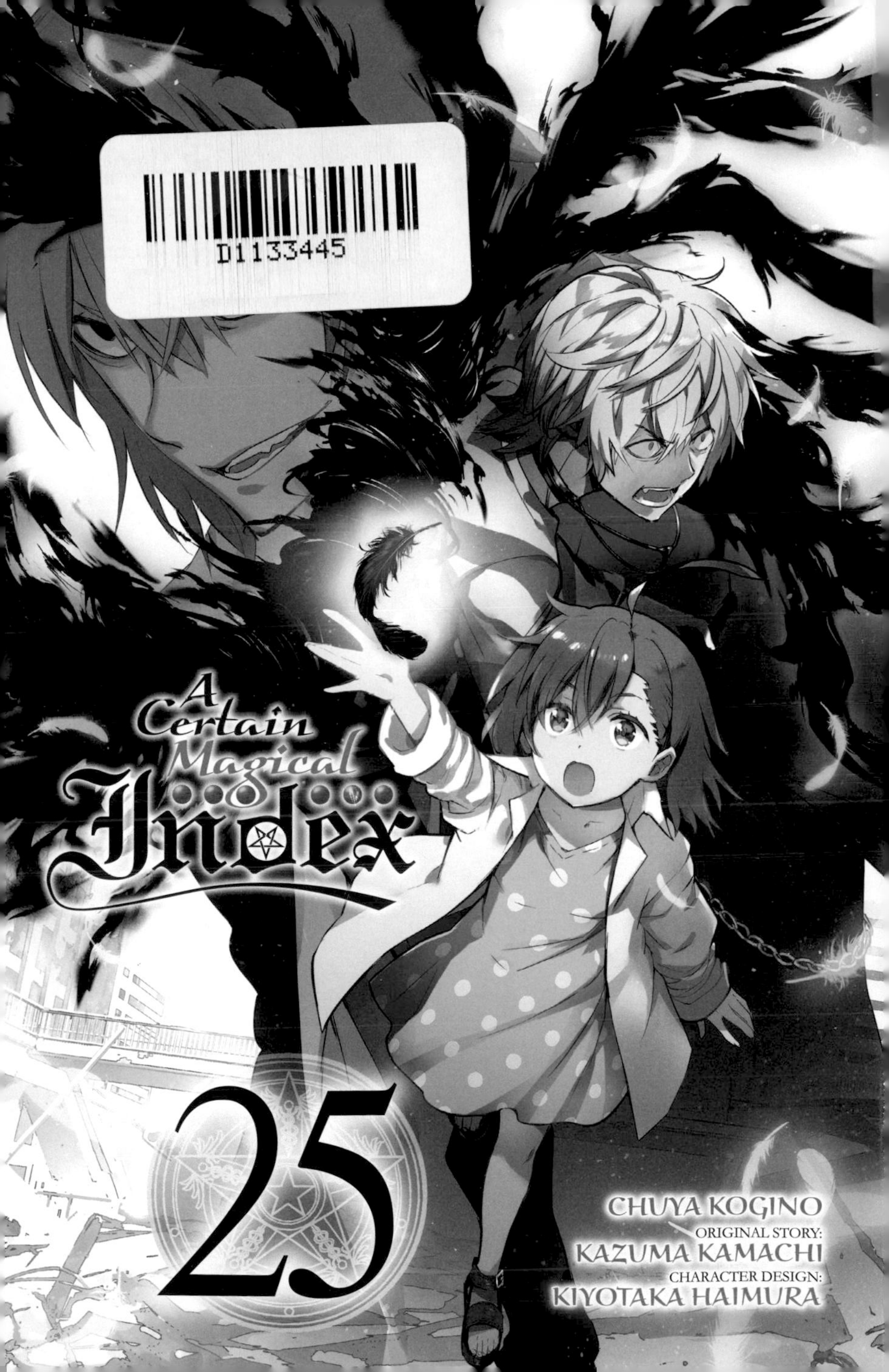
A Certain Magical Index
25
CHUYA KOGINO
ORIGINAL STORY:
KAZUMA KAMACHI
CHARACTER DESIGN:
KIYOTAKA HAIMURA

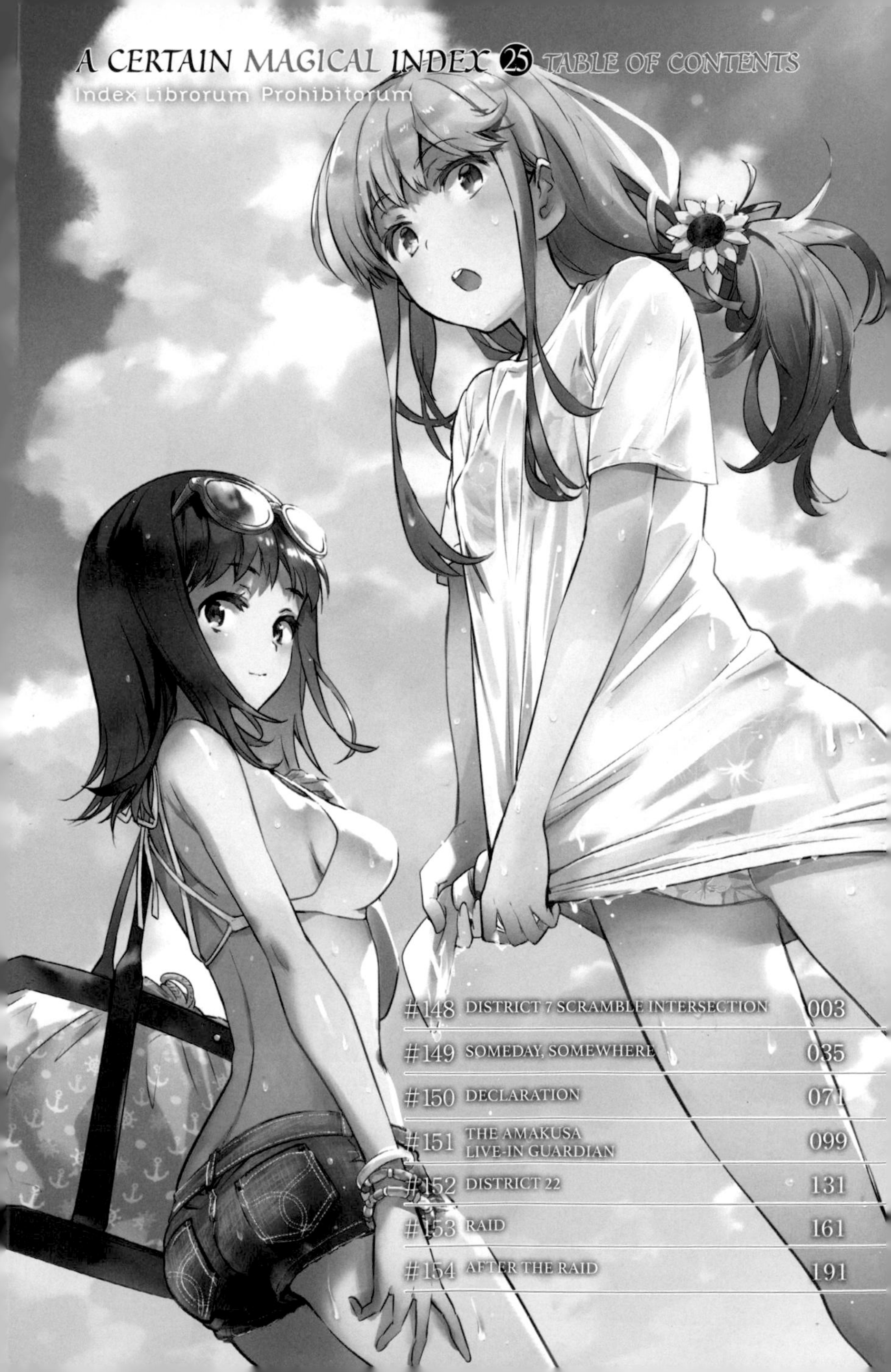

A CERTAIN MAGICAL INDEX 25 TABLE OF CONTENTS

Index Librorum Prohibitorum

#148 DISTRICT 7 SCRAMBLE INTERSECTION

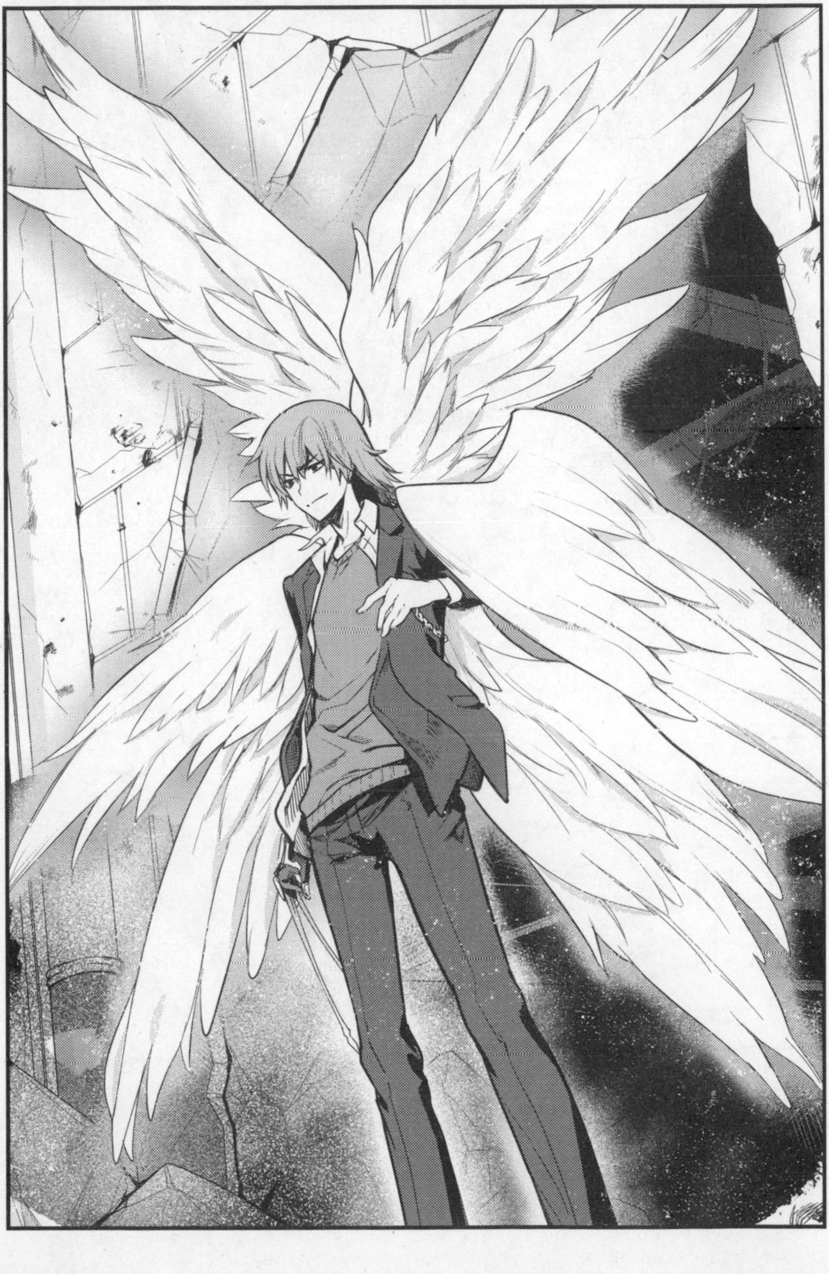

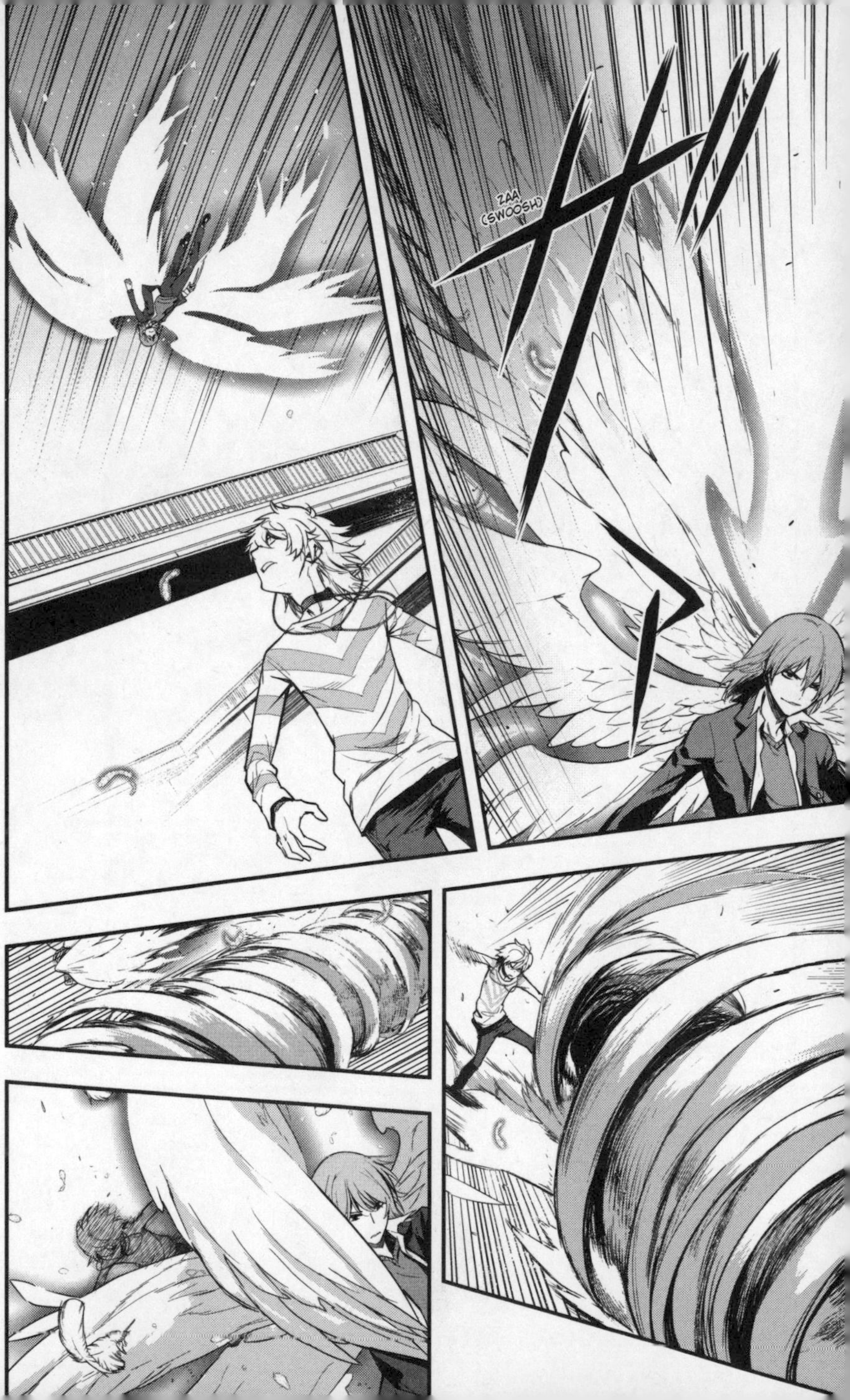
ZAA
(SWOOSH)

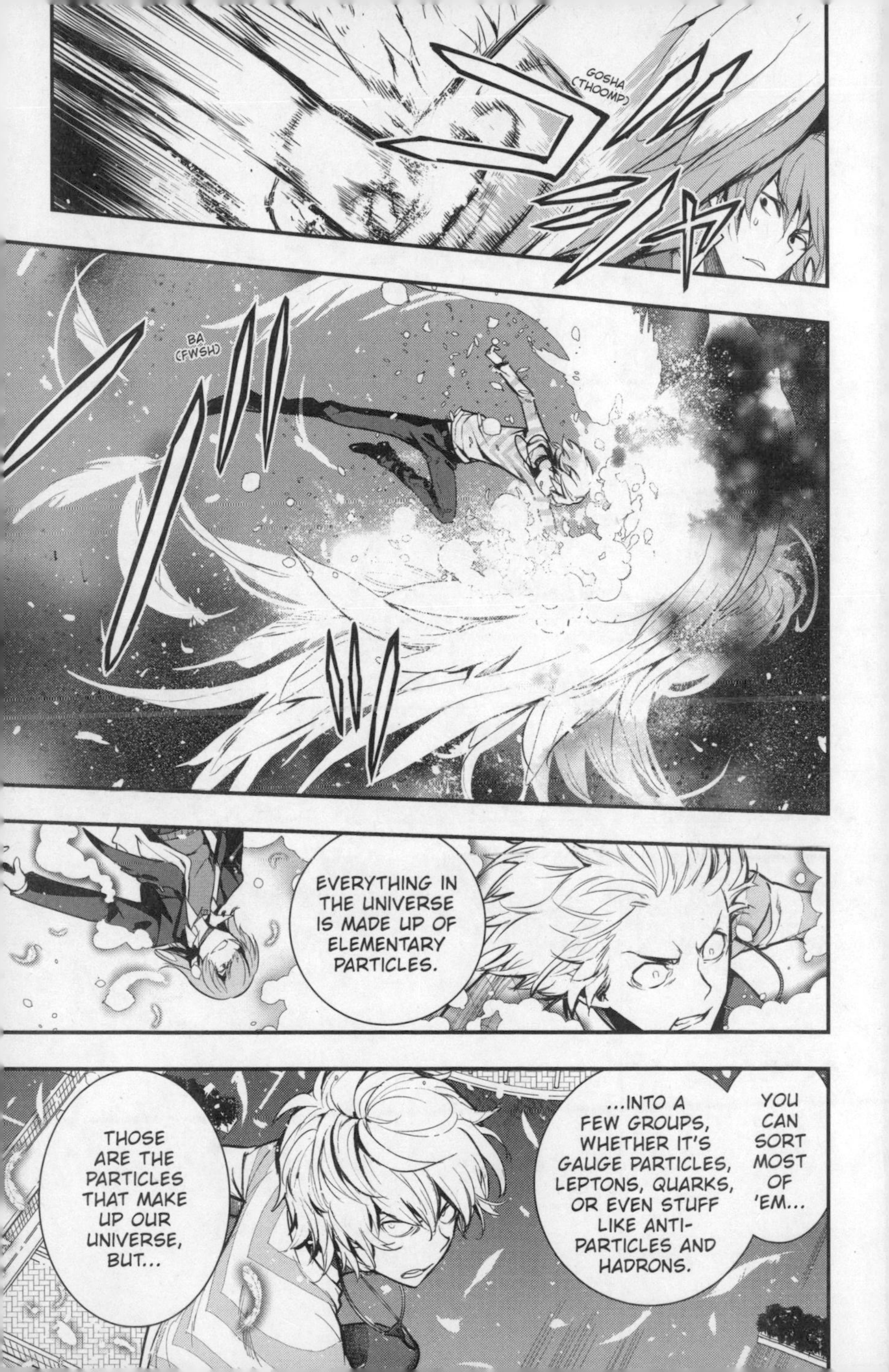
GOSHA (THOOMP)
BA (FWSH)
EVERYTHING IN THE UNIVERSE IS MADE UP OF ELEMENTARY PARTICLES.
YOU CAN SORT MOST OF 'EM...
...INTO A FEW GROUPS, WHETHER IT'S GAUGE PARTICLES, LEPTONS, QUARKS, OR EVEN STUFF LIKE ANTI-PARTICLES AND HADRONS.
THOSE ARE THE PARTICLES THAT MAKE UP OUR UNIVERSE, BUT...

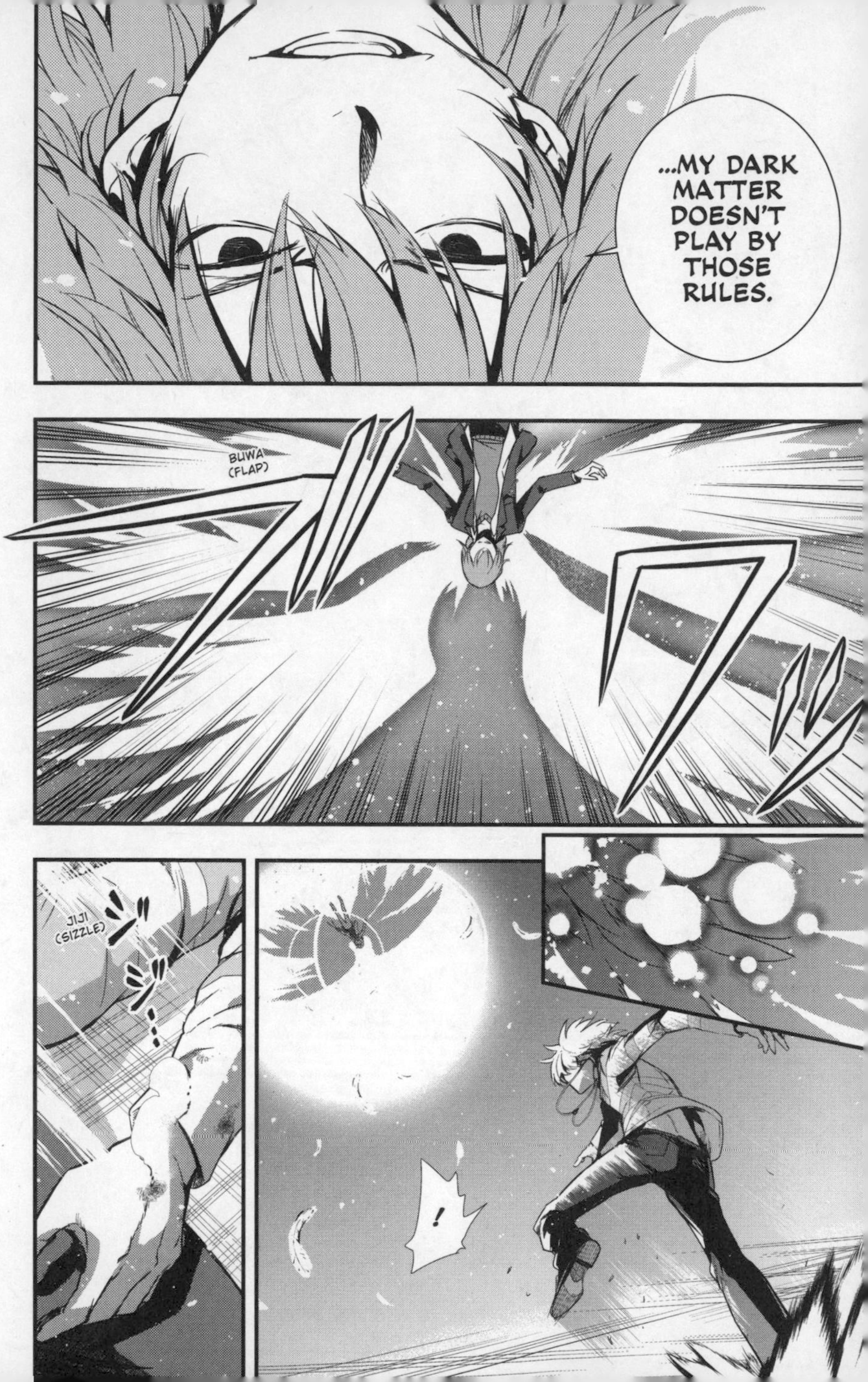
...MY DARK MATTER DOESN'T PLAY BY THOSE RULES.
BUWA (FLAP)
JIJI (SIZZLE)
!

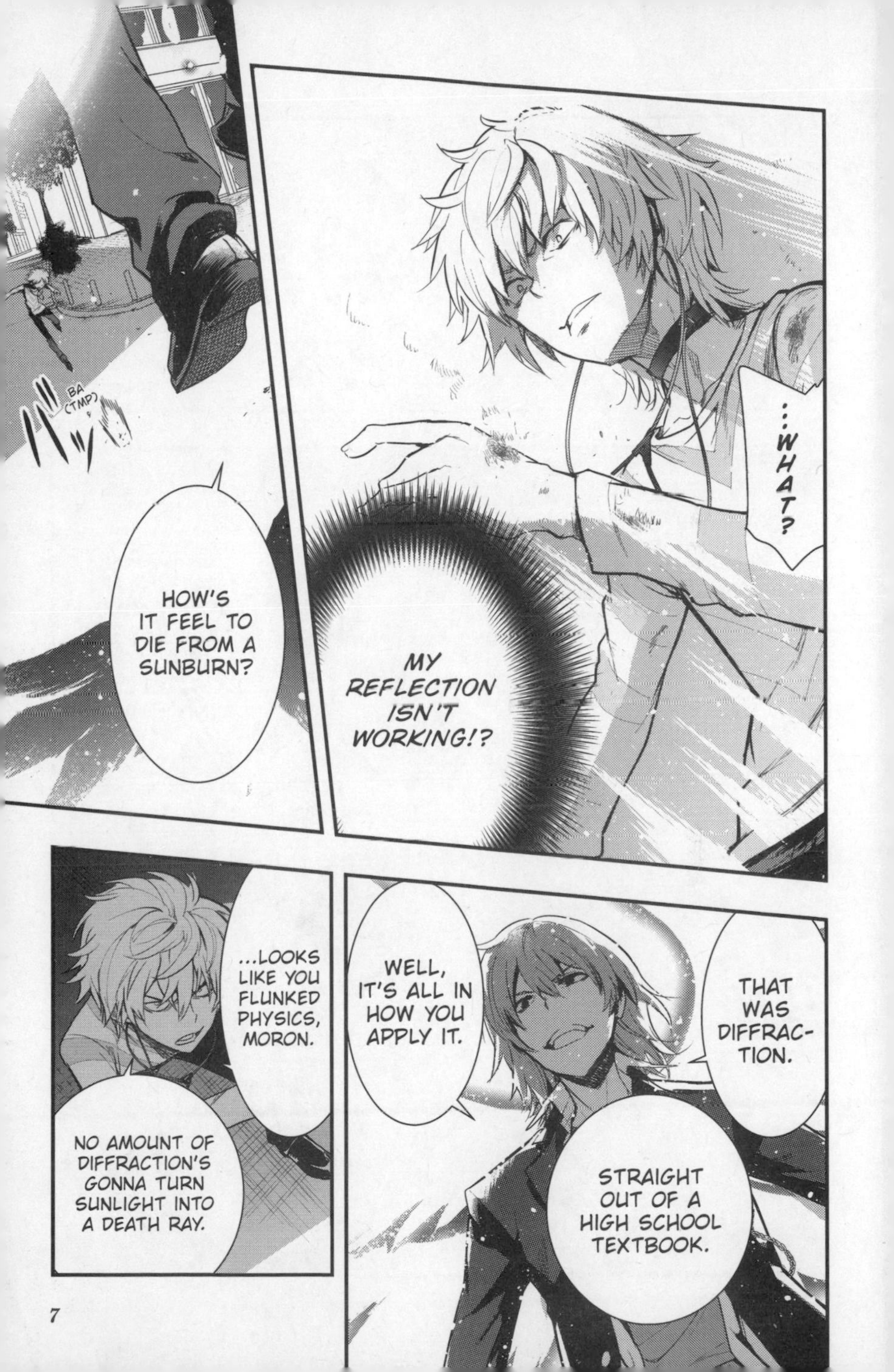
...WHAT?
MY REFLECTION ISN'T WORKING!?
BA (TMP)
HOW'S IT FEEL TO DIE FROM A SUNBURN?
THAT WAS DIFFRAC-TION.
WELL, IT'S ALL IN HOW YOU APPLY IT.
STRAIGHT OUT OF A HIGH SCHOOL TEXTBOOK.
...LOOKS LIKE YOU FLUNKED PHYSICS, MORON.
NO AMOUNT OF DIFFRACTION'S GONNA TURN SUNLIGHT INTO A DEATH RAY.

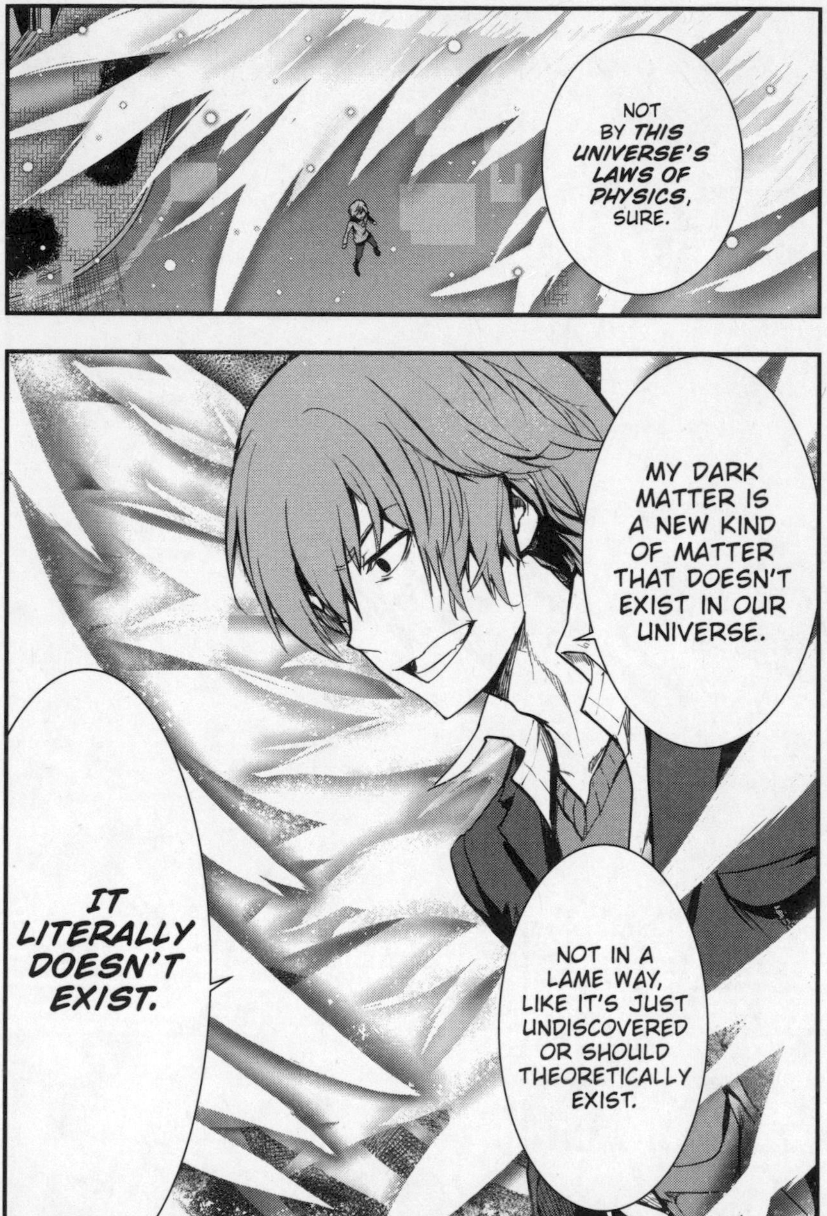
NOT BY THIS UNIVERSE'S LAWS OF PHYSICS, SURE.
MY DARK MATTER IS A NEW KIND OF MATTER THAT DOESN'T EXIST IN OUR UNIVERSE.
NOT IN A LAME WAY, LIKE IT'S JUST UNDISCOVERED OR SHOULD THEORETICALLY EXIST.
IT LITERALLY DOESN'T EXIST.

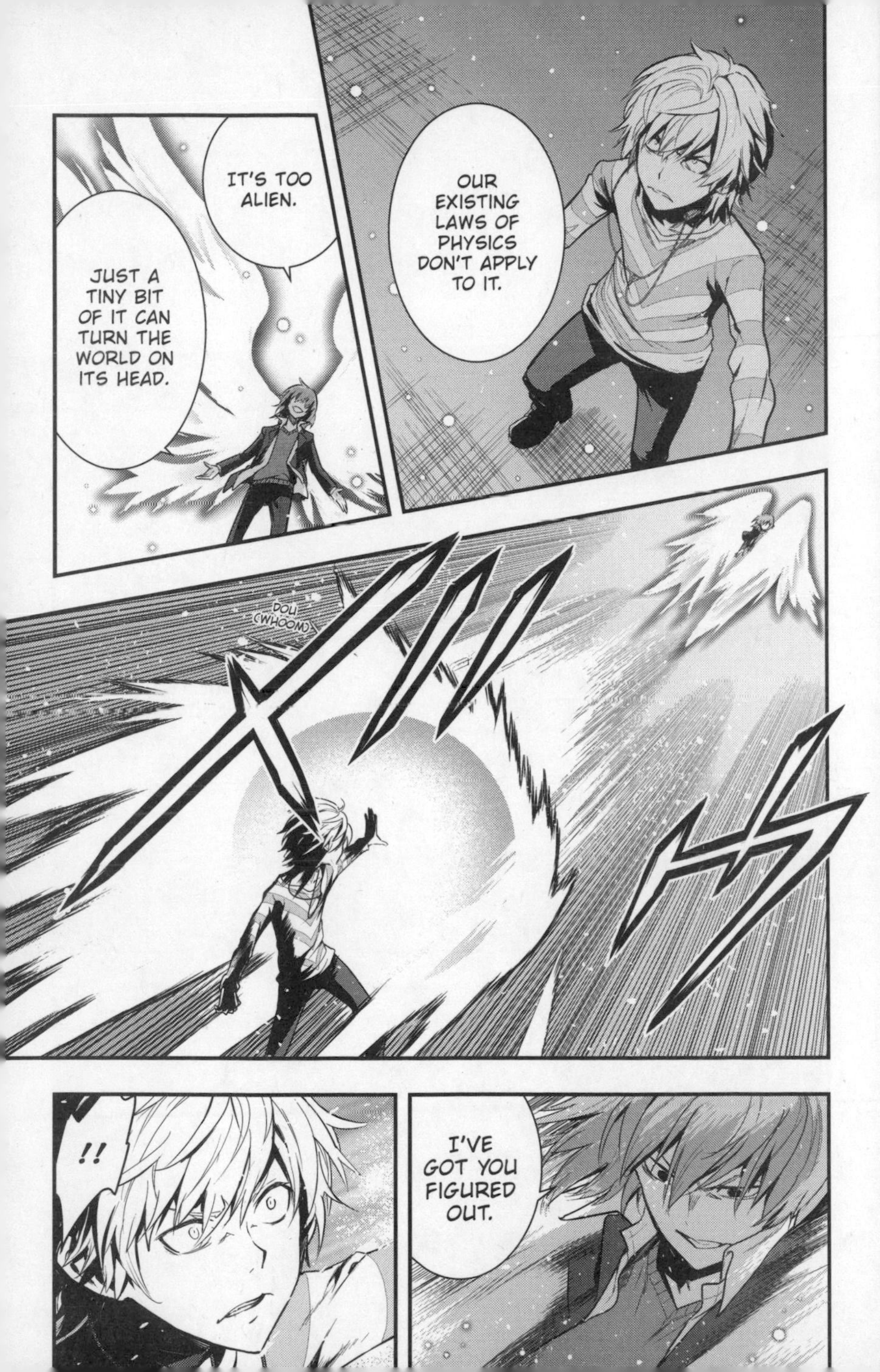
OUR EXISTING LAWS OF PHYSICS DON'T APPLY TO IT.
IT'S TOO ALIEN.
JUST A TINY BIT OF IT CAN TURN THE WORLD ON ITS HEAD.
DOU (WHOOM)
I'VE GOT YOU FIGURED OUT.
!!

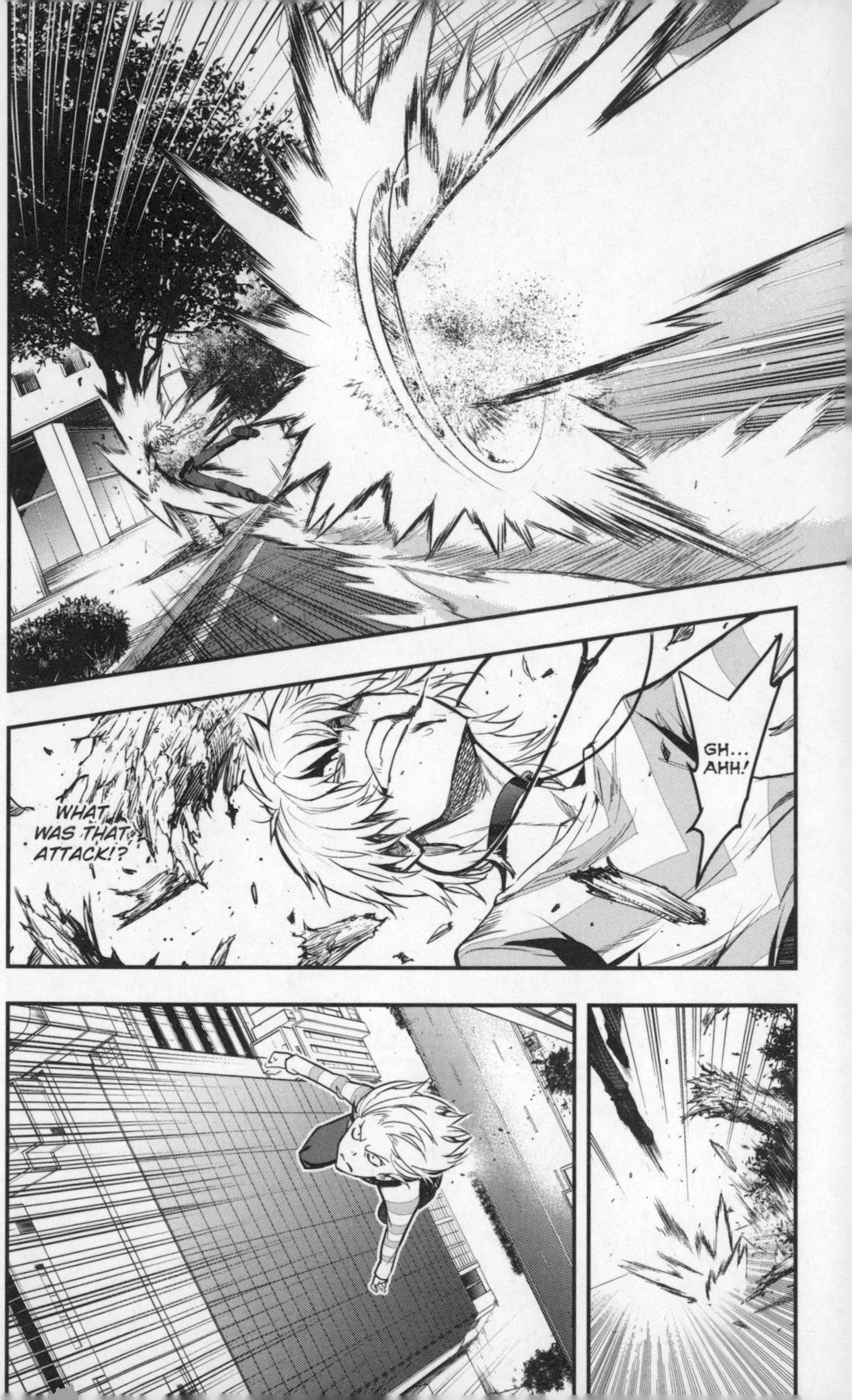
GH... AHH!
WHAT WAS THAT ATTACK!?

ACCELER-
ATOR...

YOU SAY
YOU REFLECT
EVERYTHING,
BUT THAT'S
NOT QUITE
ACCURATE.

GYURU
(TWIRL)

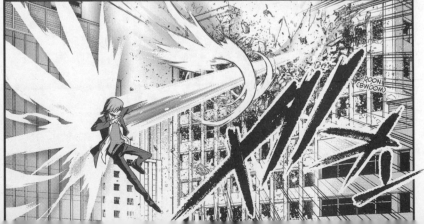

DOON
(BWOOM)

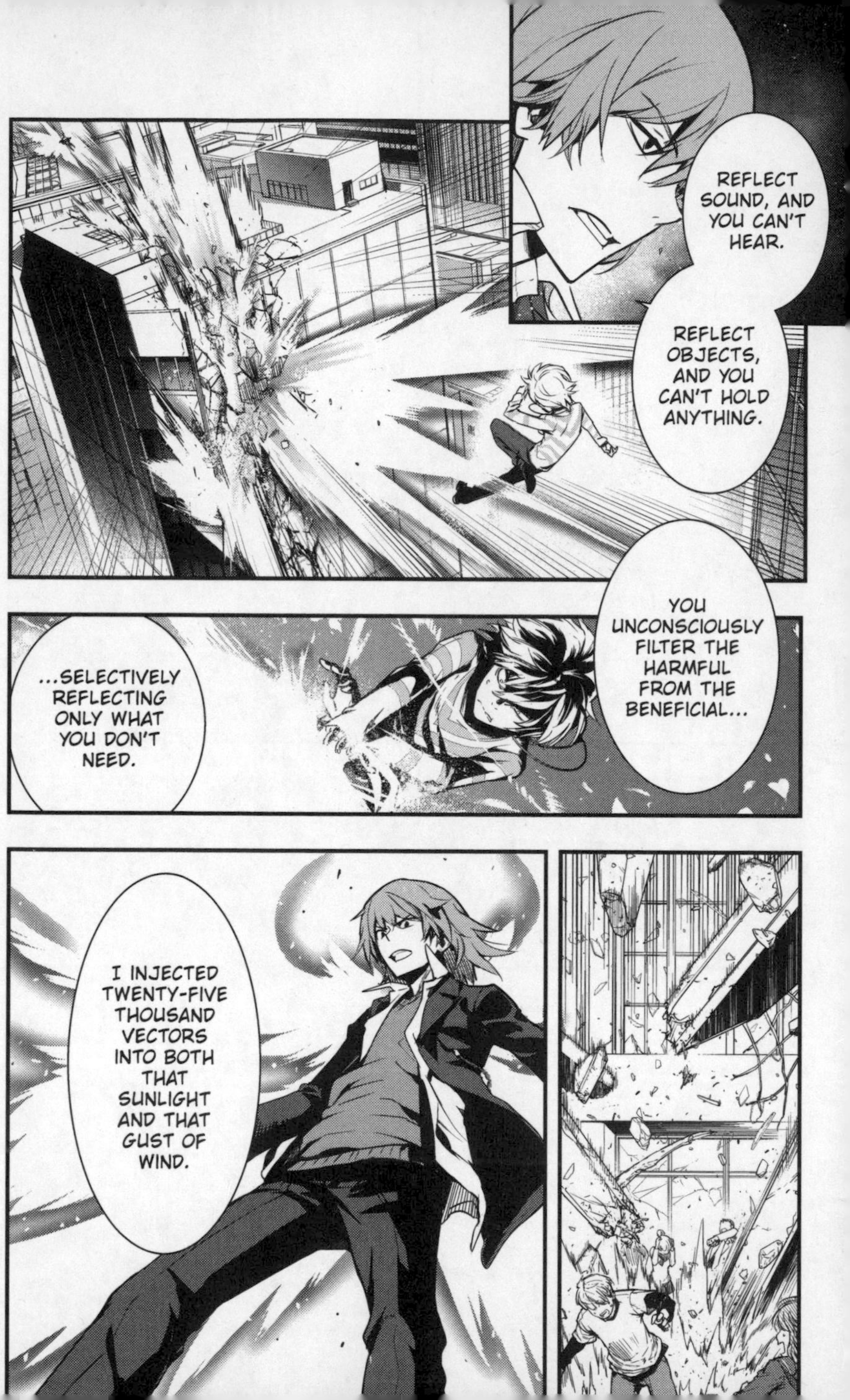
REFLECT SOUND, AND YOU CAN'T HEAR.
REFLECT OBJECTS, AND YOU CAN'T HOLD ANYTHING.
YOU UNCONSCIOUSLY FILTER THE HARMFUL FROM THE BENEFICIAL...
...SELECTIVELY REFLECTING ONLY WHAT YOU DON'T NEED.
I INJECTED TWENTY-FIVE THOUSAND VECTORS INTO BOTH THAT SUNLIGHT AND THAT GUST OF WIND.

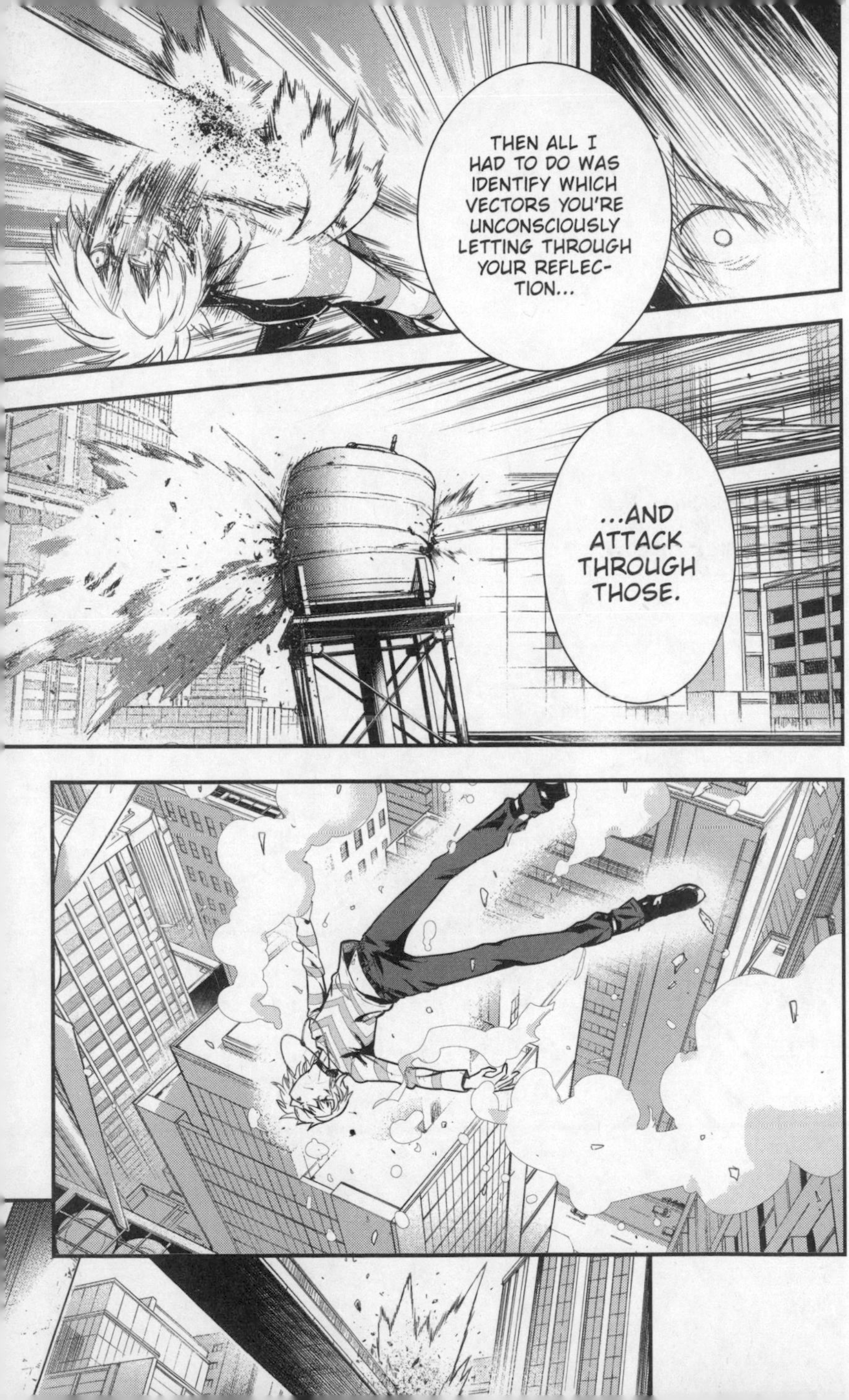
THEN ALL I HAD TO DO WAS IDENTIFY WHICH VECTORS YOU'RE UNCONSCIOUSLY LETTING THROUGH YOUR REFLEC-TION...
...AND ATTACK THROUGH THOSE.

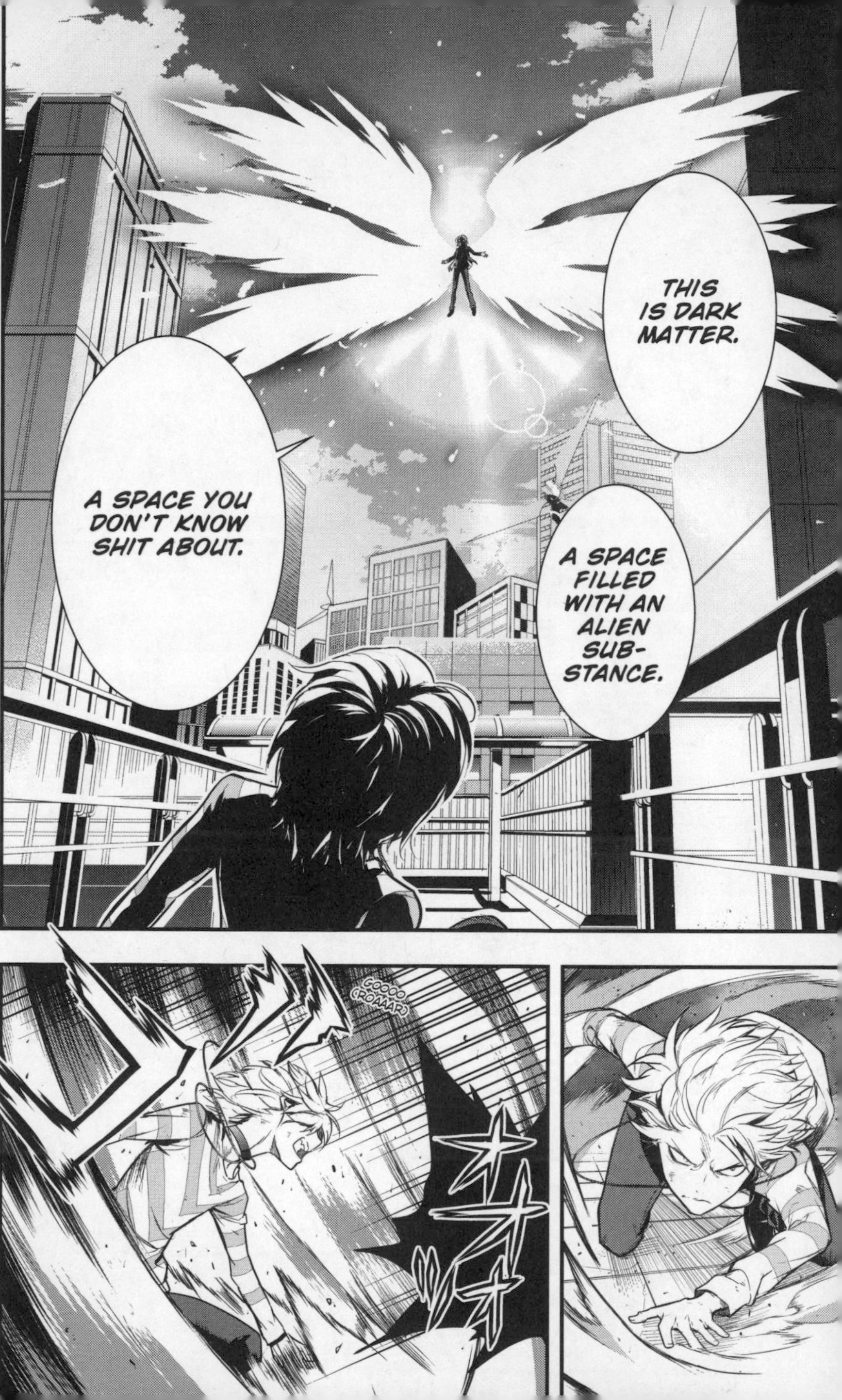
THIS IS DARK MATTER.
A SPACE FILLED WITH AN ALIEN SUB-STANCE.
A SPACE YOU DON'T KNOW SHIT ABOUT.
GOOOO (ROAAAR)

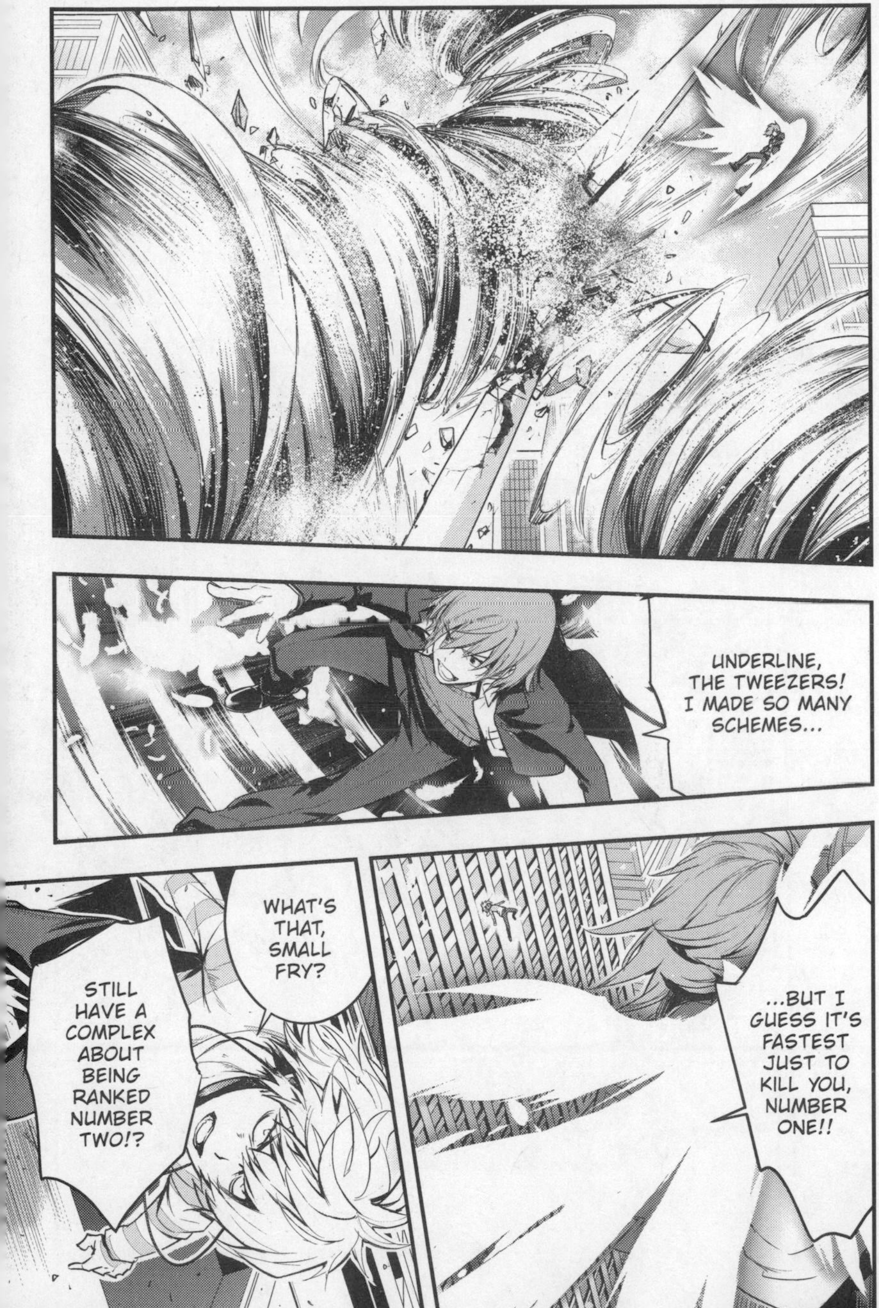
UNDERLINE, THE TWEEZERS! I MADE SO MANY SCHEMES...
...BUT I GUESS IT'S FASTEST JUST TO KILL YOU, NUMBER ONE!!
WHAT'S THAT, SMALL FRY?
STILL HAVE A COMPLEX ABOUT BEING RANKED NUMBER TWO!?

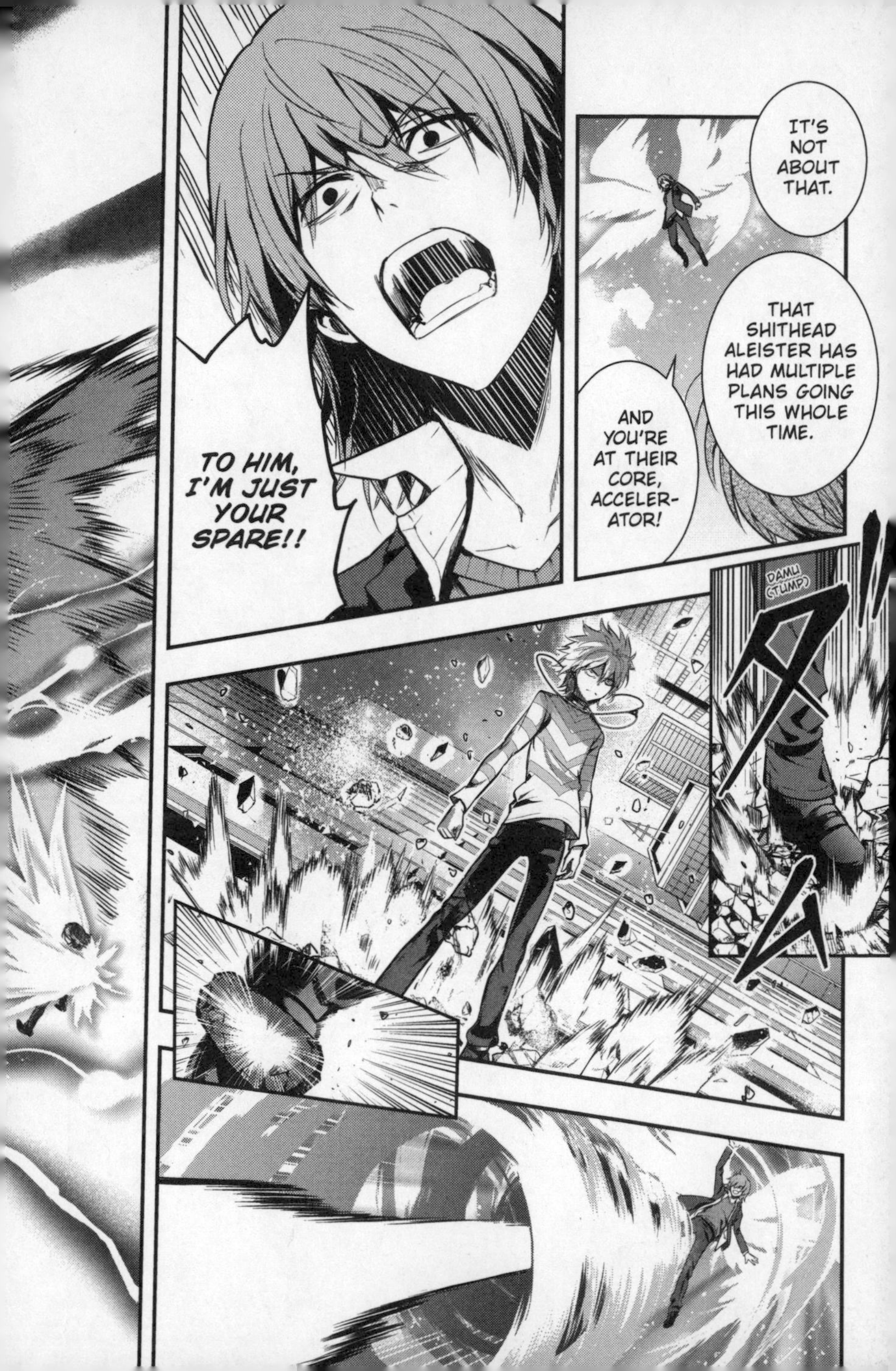
IT'S NOT ABOUT THAT.
THAT SHITHEAD ALEISTER HAS HAD MULTIPLE PLANS GOING THIS WHOLE TIME.
AND YOU'RE AT THEIR CORE, ACCELER-ATOR!
TO HIM, I'M JUST YOUR SPARE!!
DAMU (TUMP)

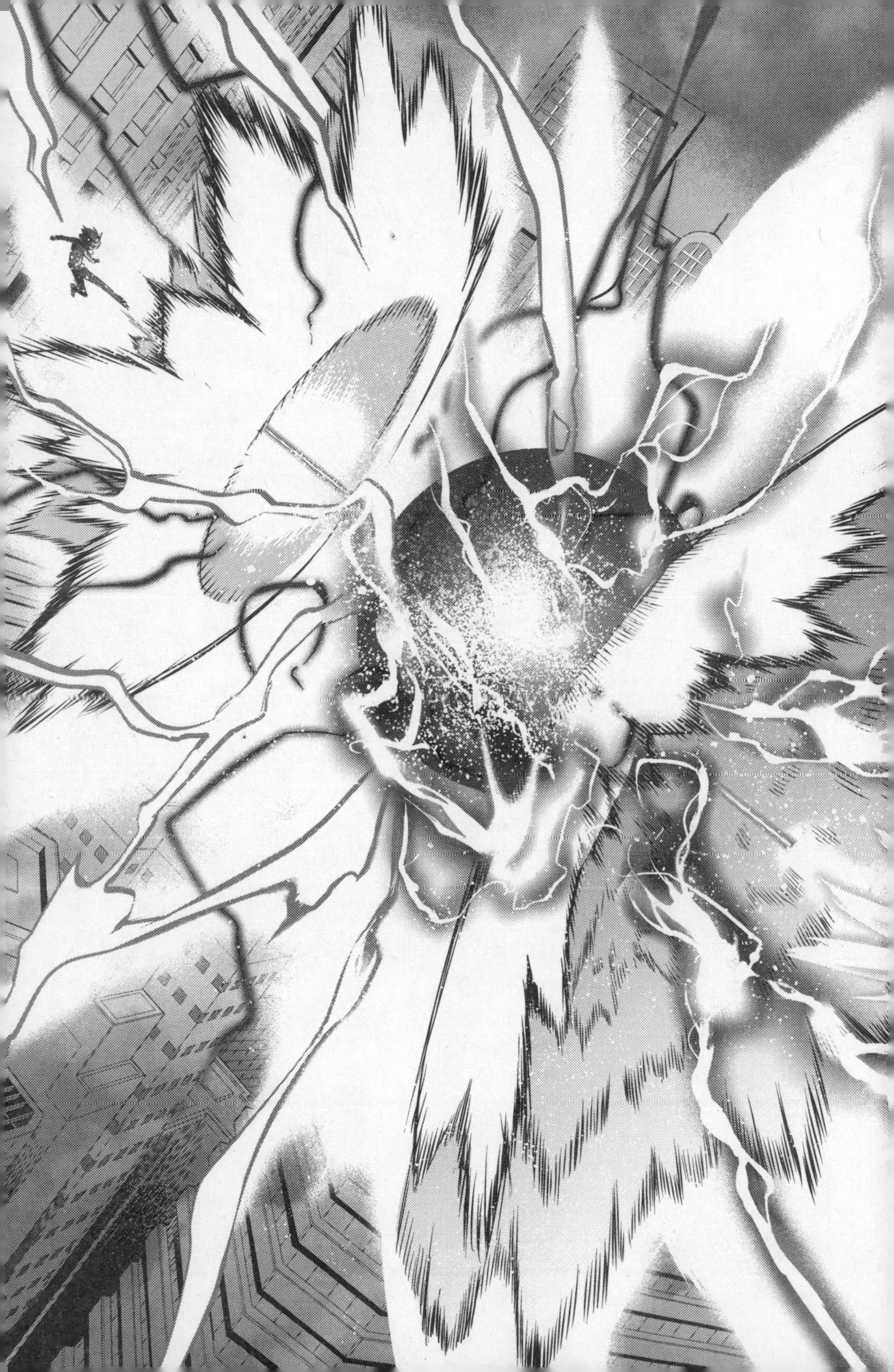

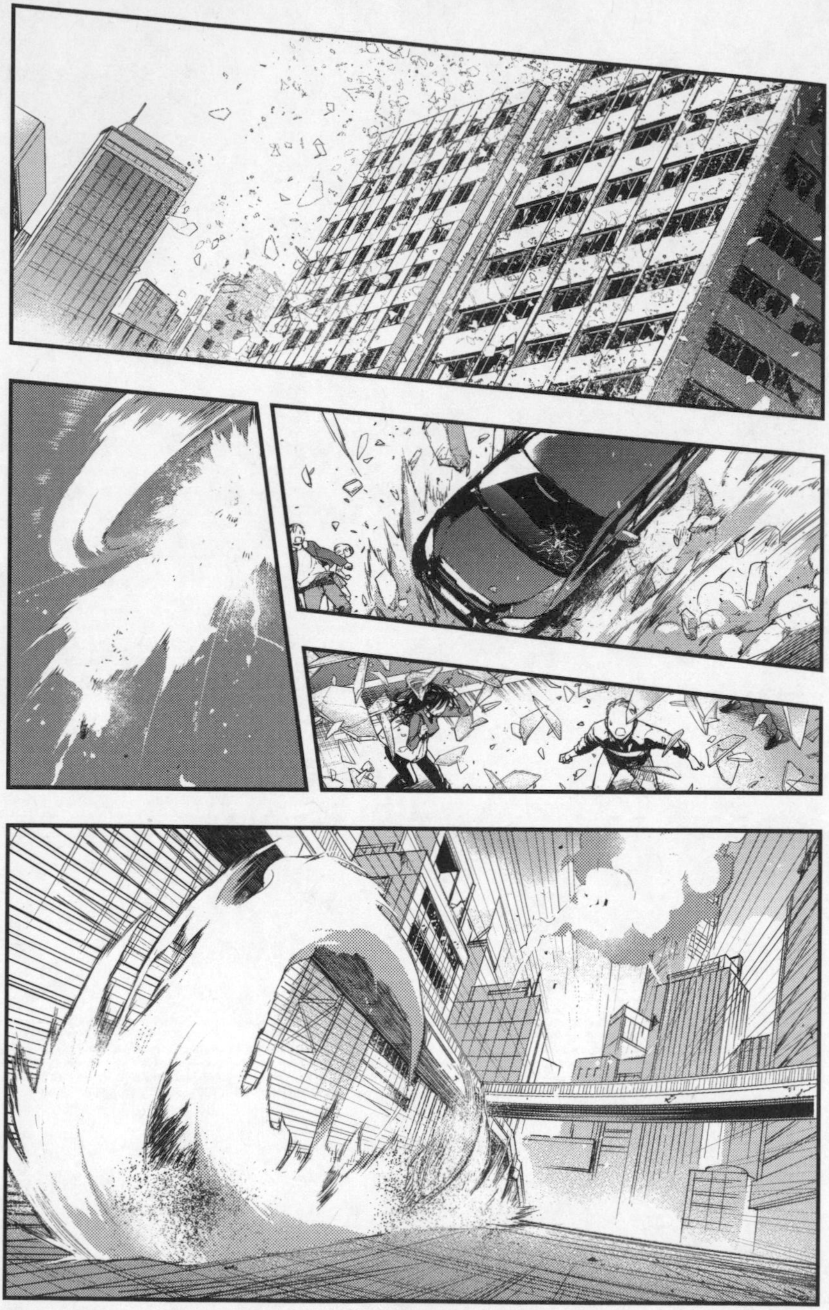

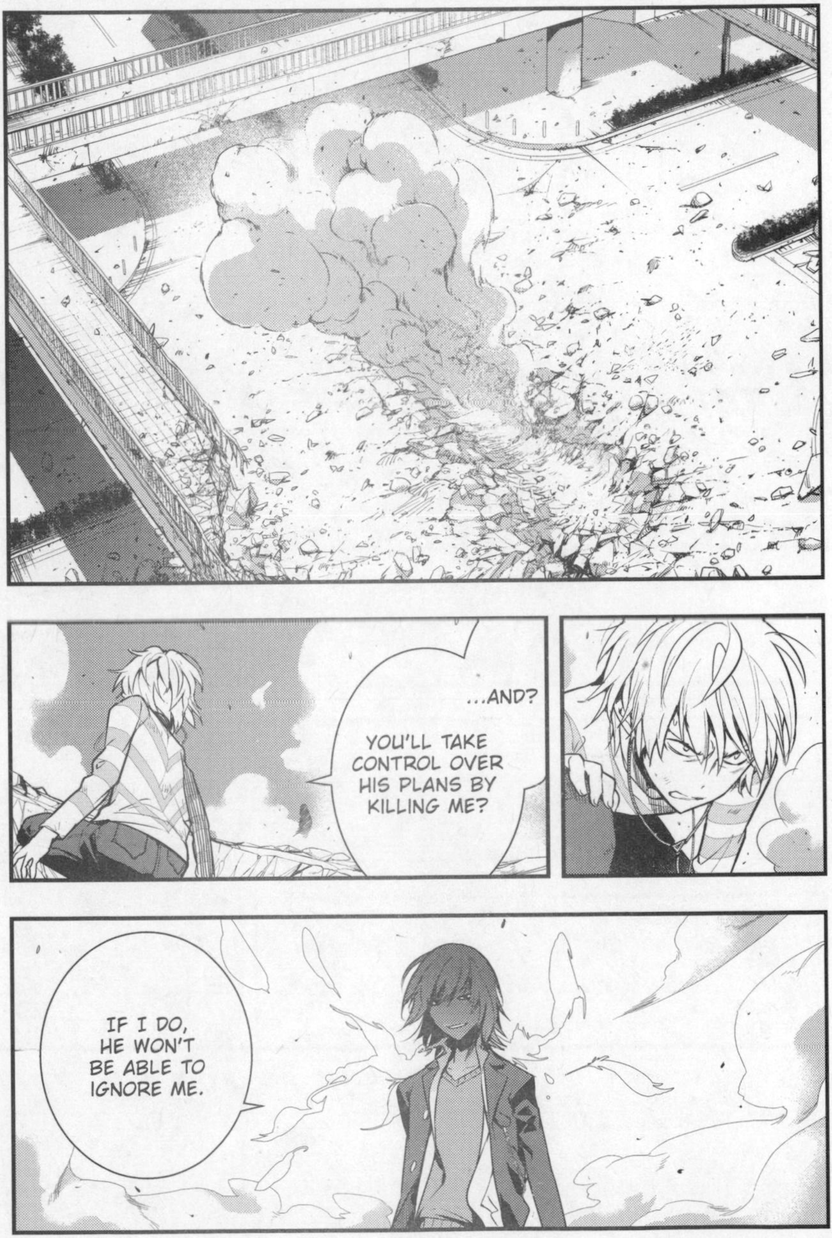
...AND?
YOU'LL TAKE CONTROL OVER HIS PLANS BY KILLING ME?
IF I DO, HE WON'T BE ABLE TO IGNORE ME.

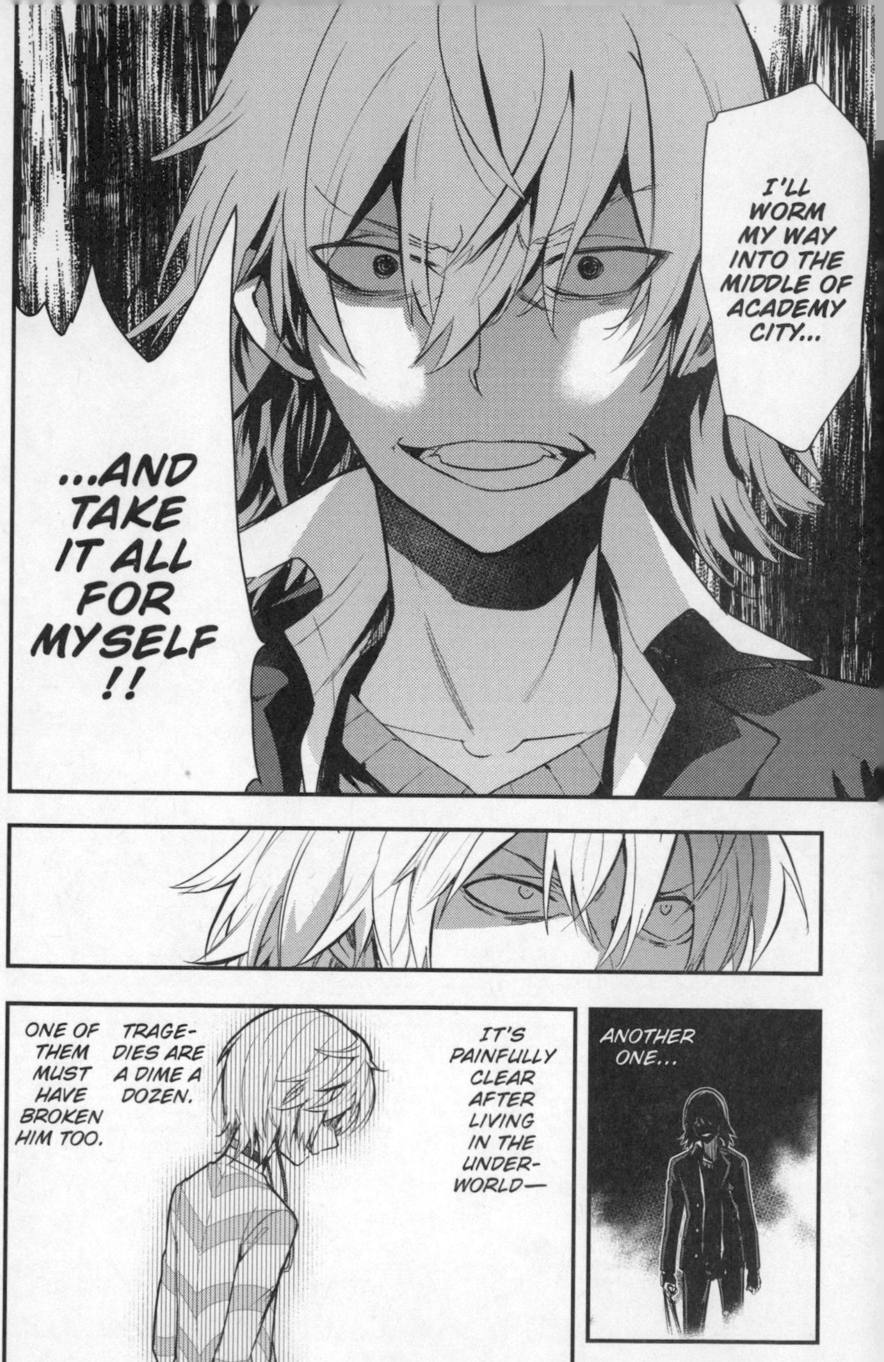
I'LL WORM MY WAY INTO THE MIDDLE OF ACADEMY CITY...
...AND TAKE IT ALL FOR MYSELF!!
ANOTHER ONE...
IT'S PAINFULLY CLEAR AFTER LIVING IN THE UNDER-WORLD—
TRAGE-DIES ARE A DIME A DOZEN.
ONE OF THEM MUST HAVE BROKEN HIM TOO.

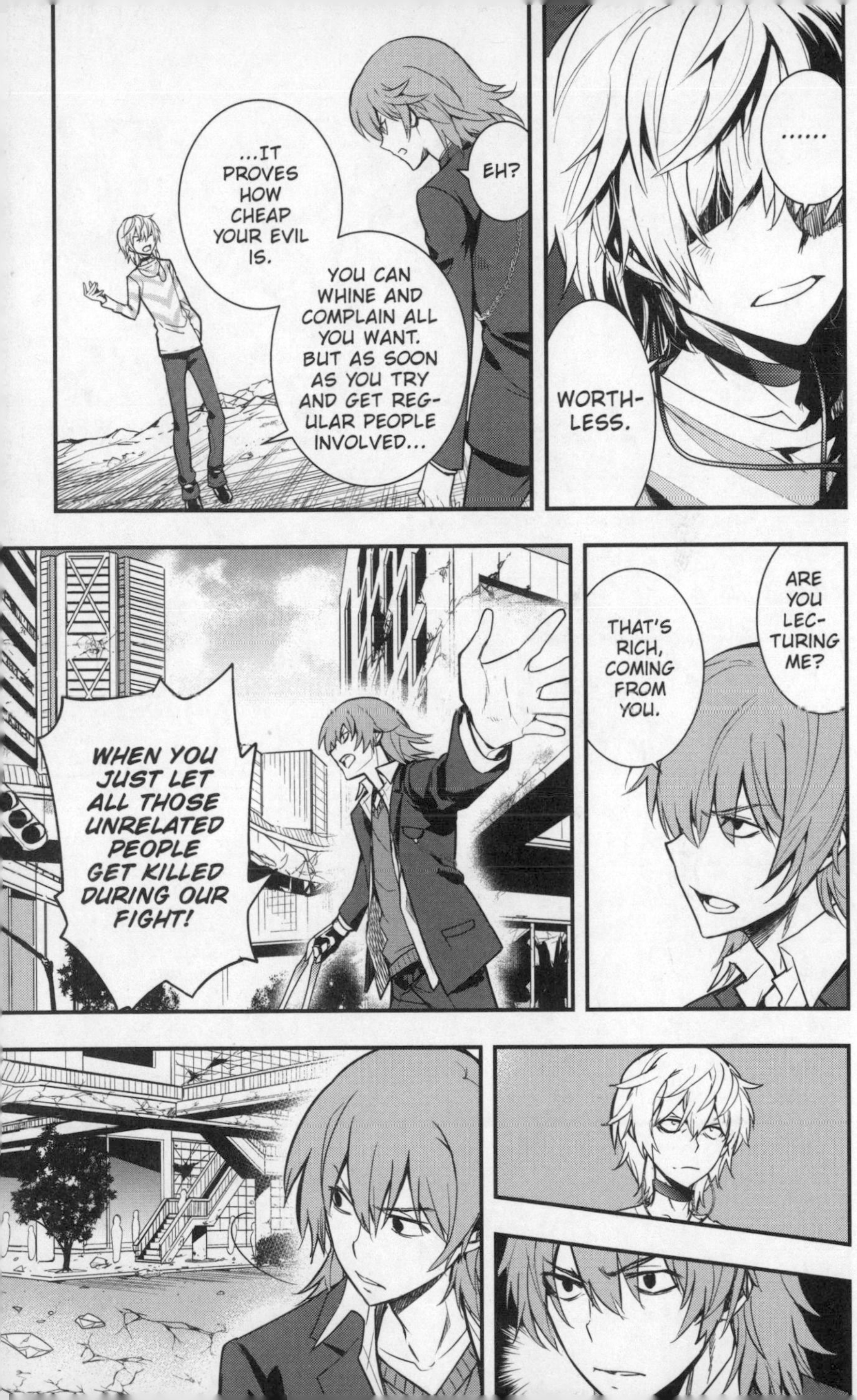
......
WORTH-LESS.
EH?
...IT PROVES HOW CHEAP YOUR EVIL IS.
YOU CAN WHINE AND COMPLAIN ALL YOU WANT. BUT AS SOON AS YOU TRY AND GET REG-ULAR PEOPLE INVOLVED...
ARE YOU LEC-TURING ME?
THAT'S RICH, COMING FROM YOU.
WHEN YOU JUST LET ALL THOSE UNRELATED PEOPLE GET KILLED DURING OUR FIGHT!

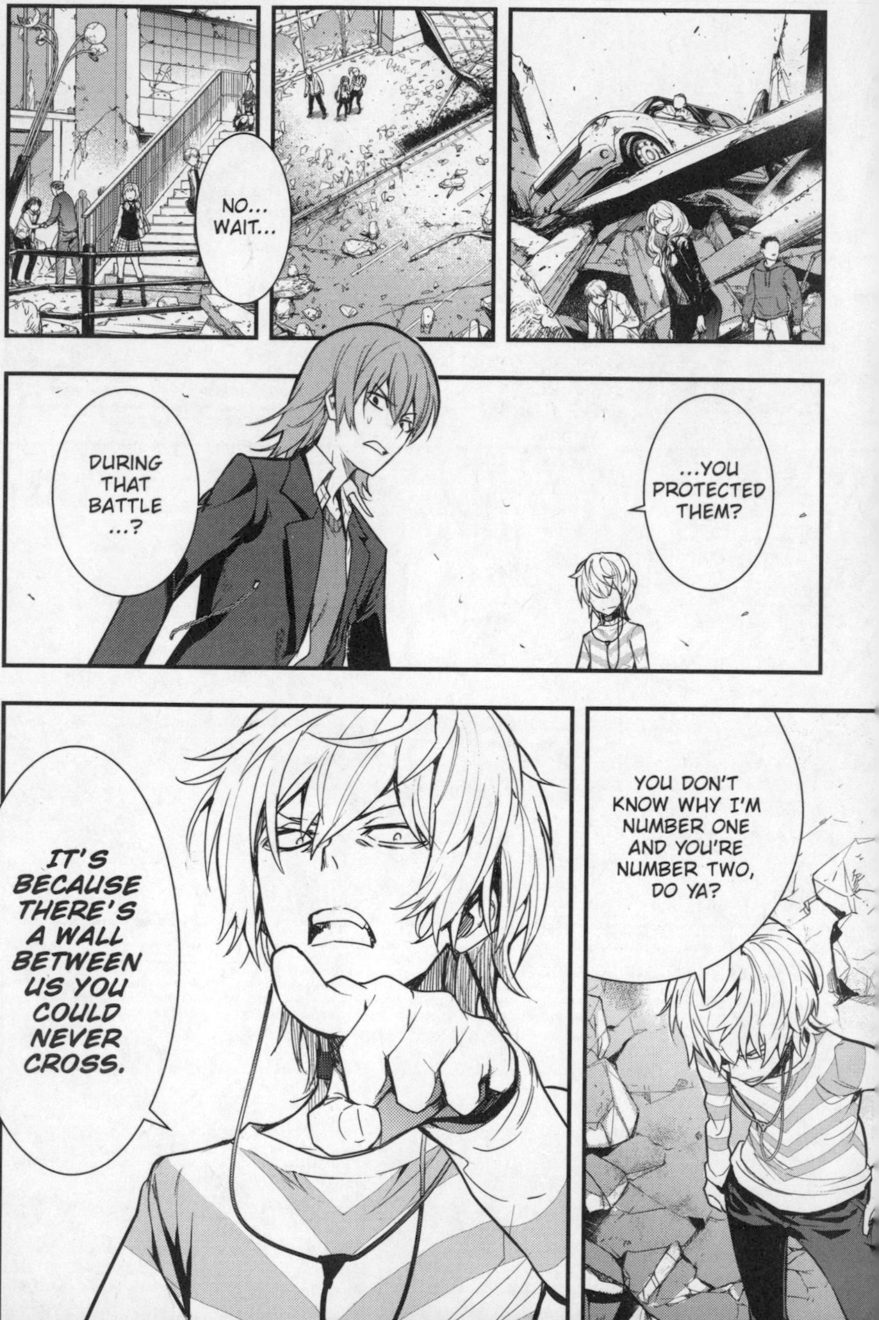
NO... WAIT...
...YOU PROTECTED THEM?
DURING THAT BATTLE ...?
YOU DON'T KNOW WHY I'M NUMBER ONE AND YOU'RE NUMBER TWO, DO YA?
IT'S BECAUSE THERE'S A WALL BETWEEN US YOU COULD NEVER CROSS.

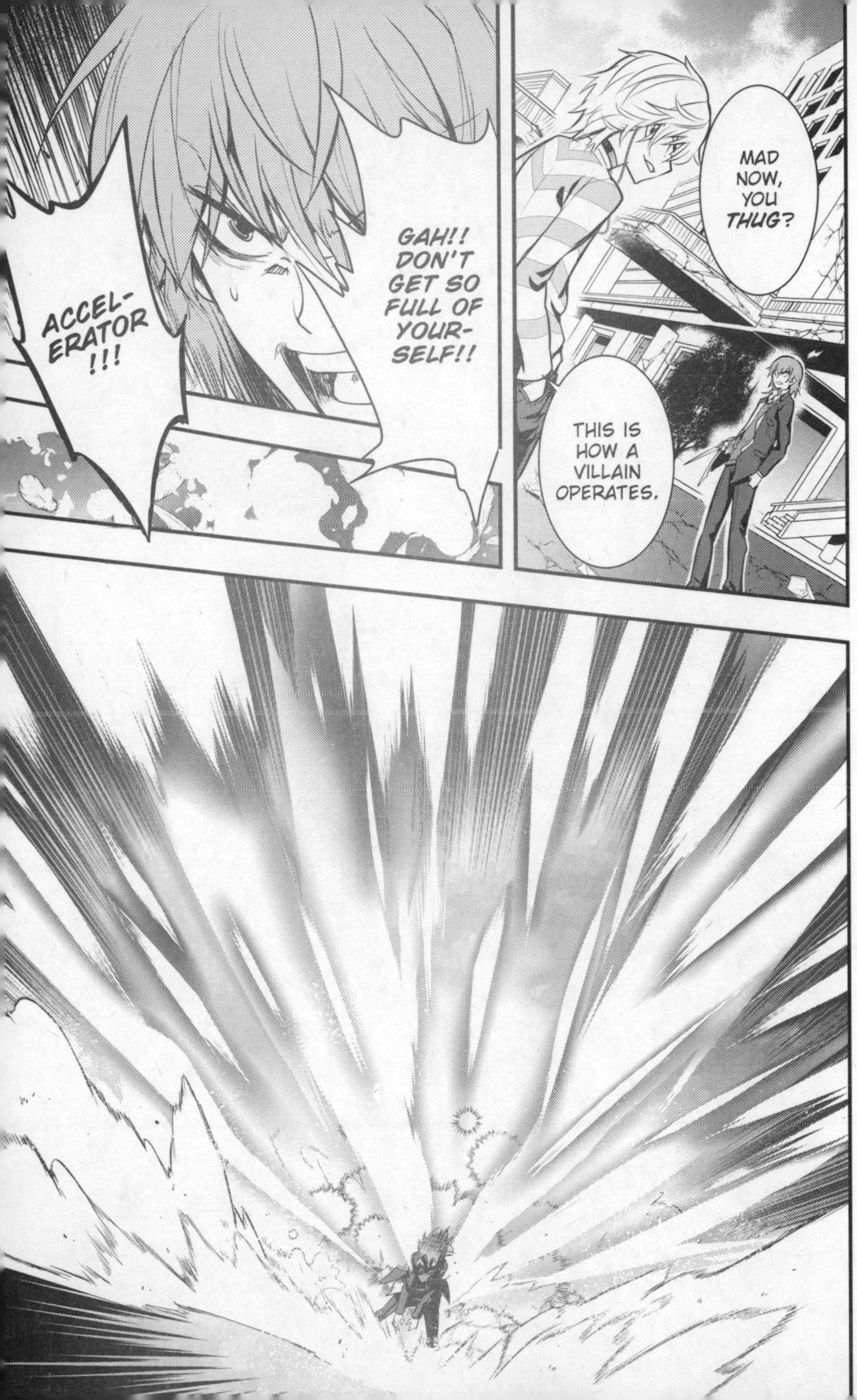
MAD NOW, YOU *THUG*?
THIS IS HOW A VILLAIN OPERATES.
GAH!! DON'T GET SO FULL OF YOUR-SELF!!
ACCEL-ERATOR!!!

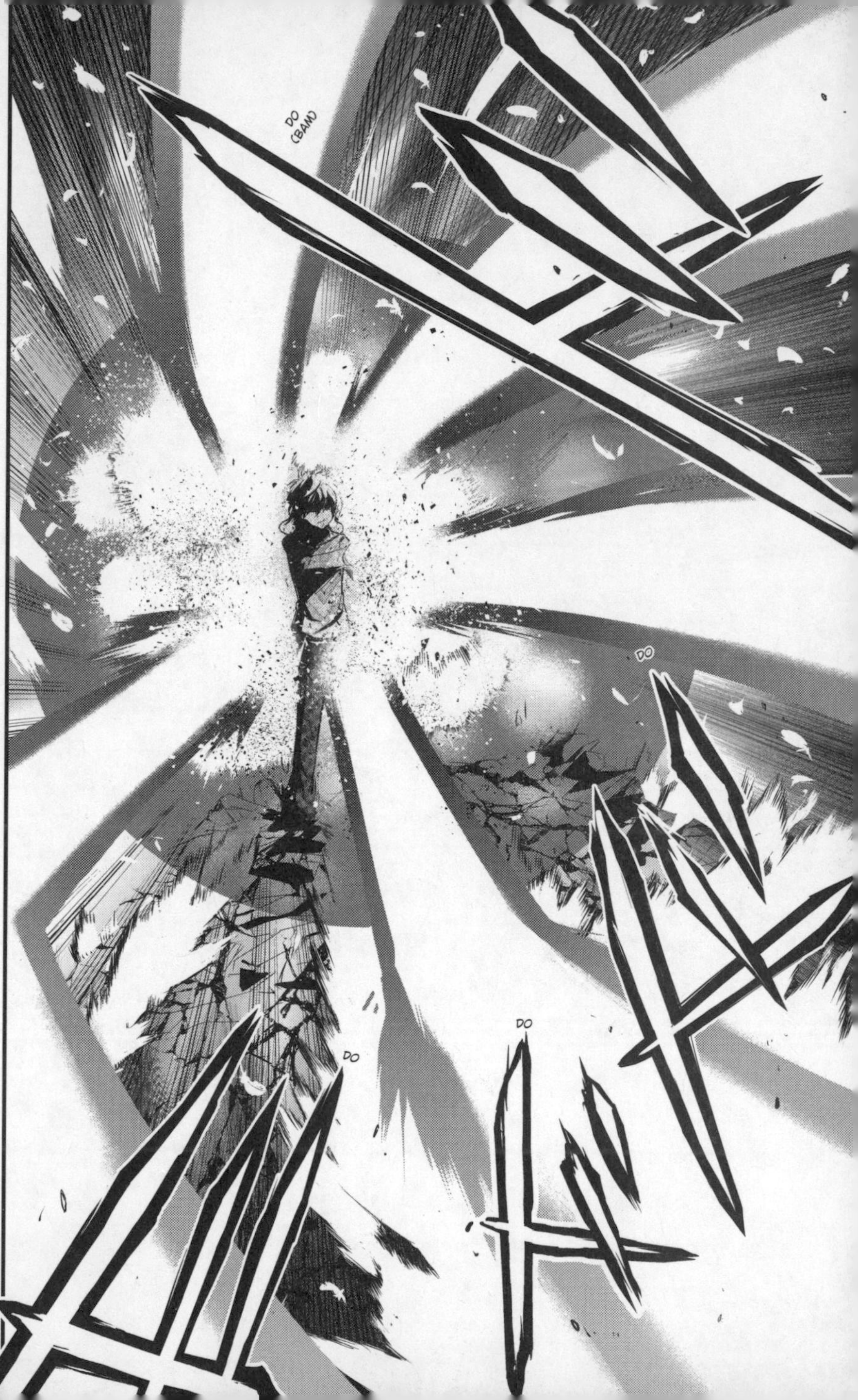
DO
(BAM)
DO
DO
DO

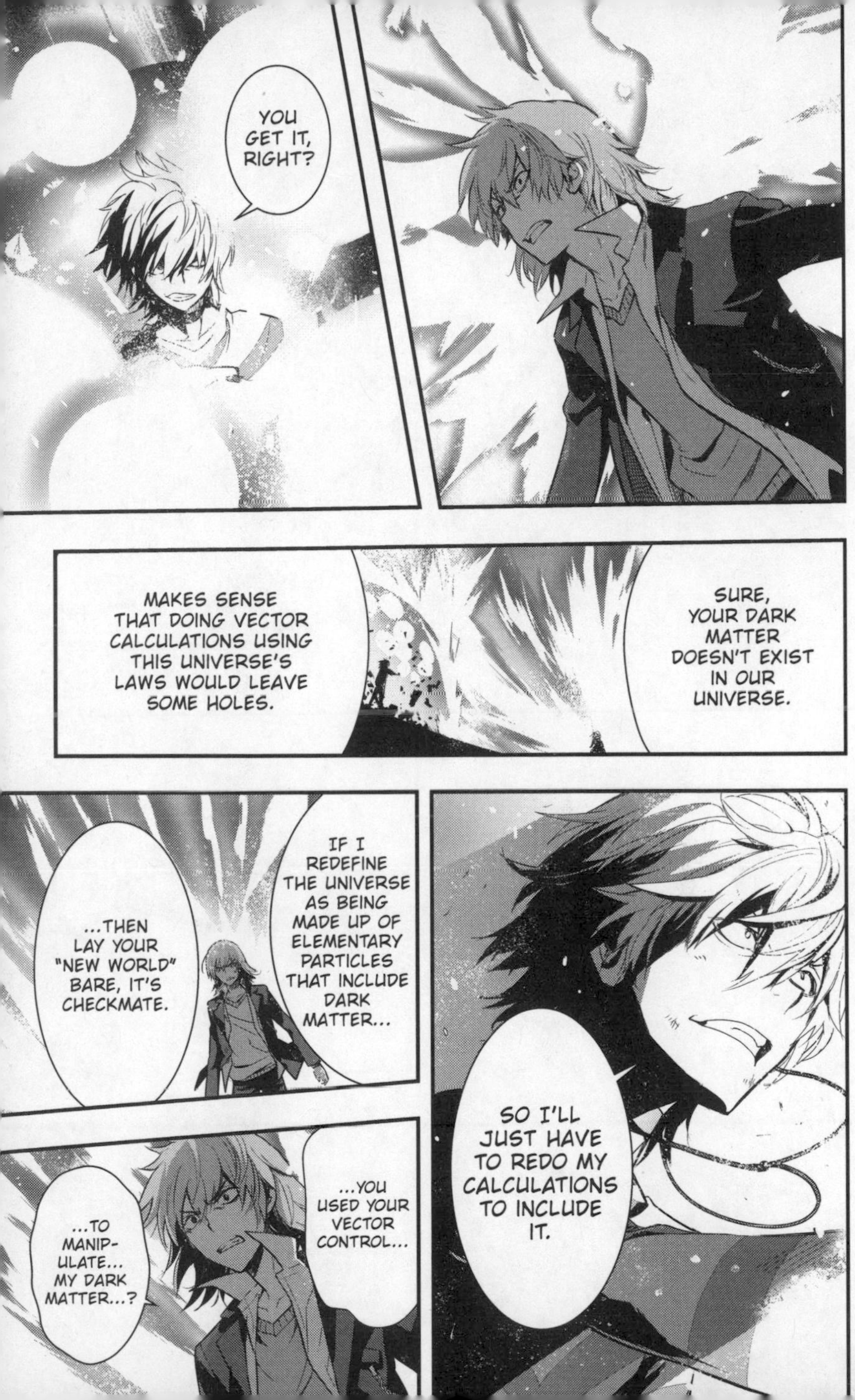
YOU GET IT, RIGHT?
SURE, YOUR DARK MATTER DOESN'T EXIST IN OUR UNIVERSE.
MAKES SENSE THAT DOING VECTOR CALCULATIONS USING THIS UNIVERSE'S LAWS WOULD LEAVE SOME HOLES.
SO I'LL JUST HAVE TO REDO MY CALCULATIONS TO INCLUDE IT.
IF I REDEFINE THE UNIVERSE AS BEING MADE UP OF ELEMENTARY PARTICLES THAT INCLUDE DARK MATTER...
...THEN LAY YOUR "NEW WORLD" BARE, IT'S CHECKMATE.
...YOU USED YOUR VECTOR CONTROL...
...TO MANIP-ULATE... MY DARK MATTER...?

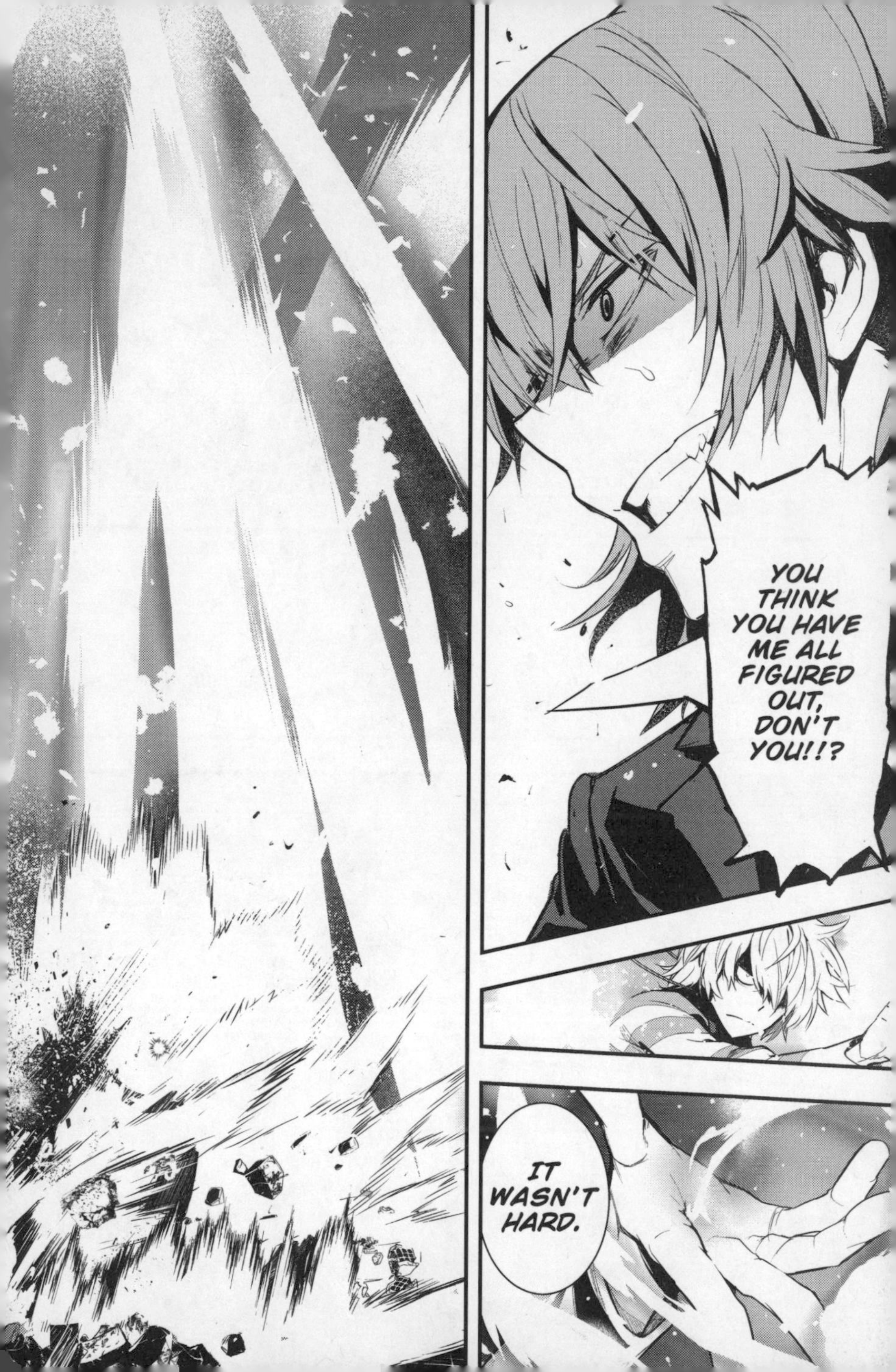
YOU THINK YOU HAVE ME ALL FIGURED OUT, DON'T YOU!!?
IT WASN'T HARD.

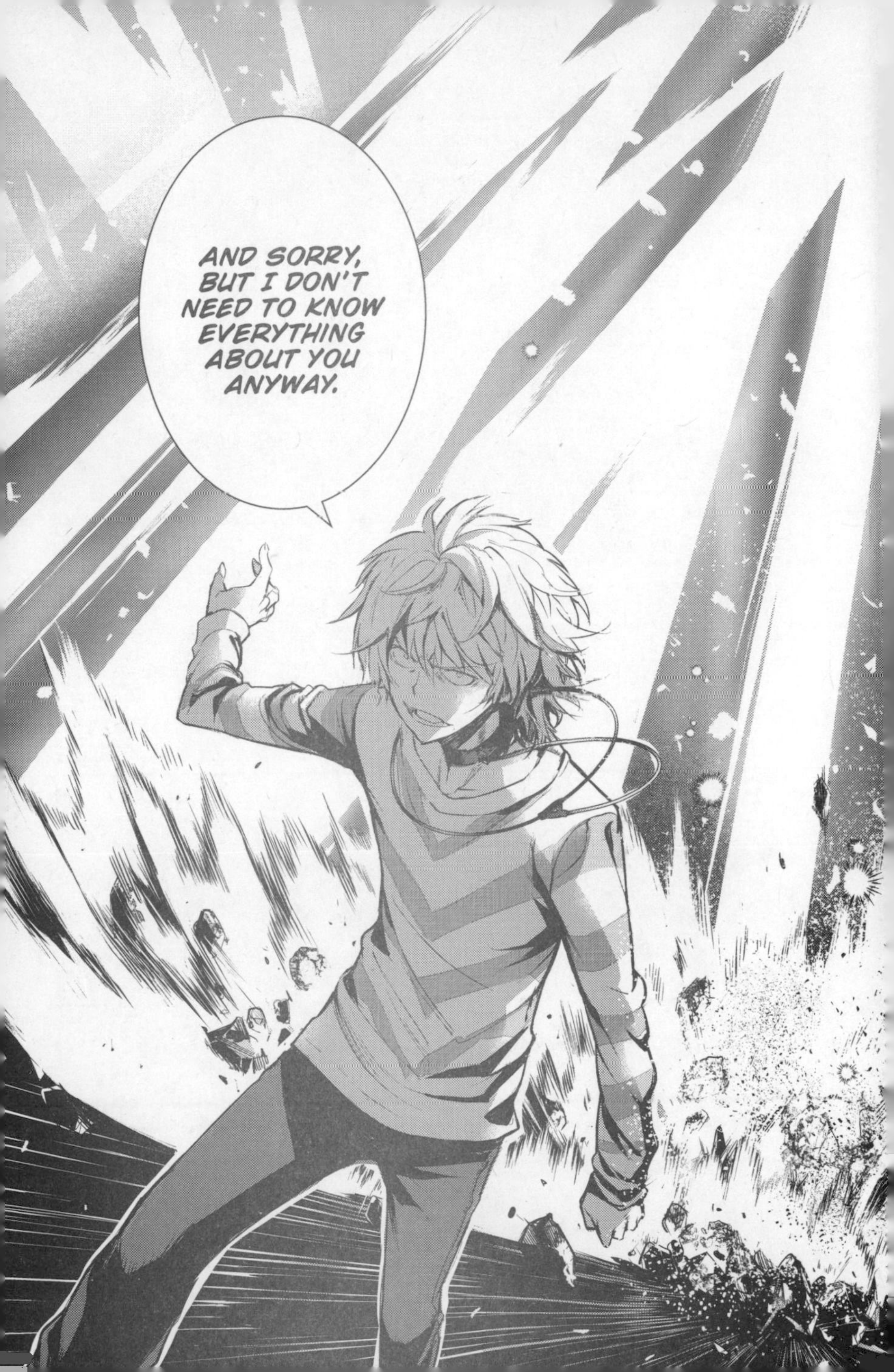
AND SORRY, BUT I DON'T NEED TO KNOW EVERYTHING ABOUT YOU ANYWAY.

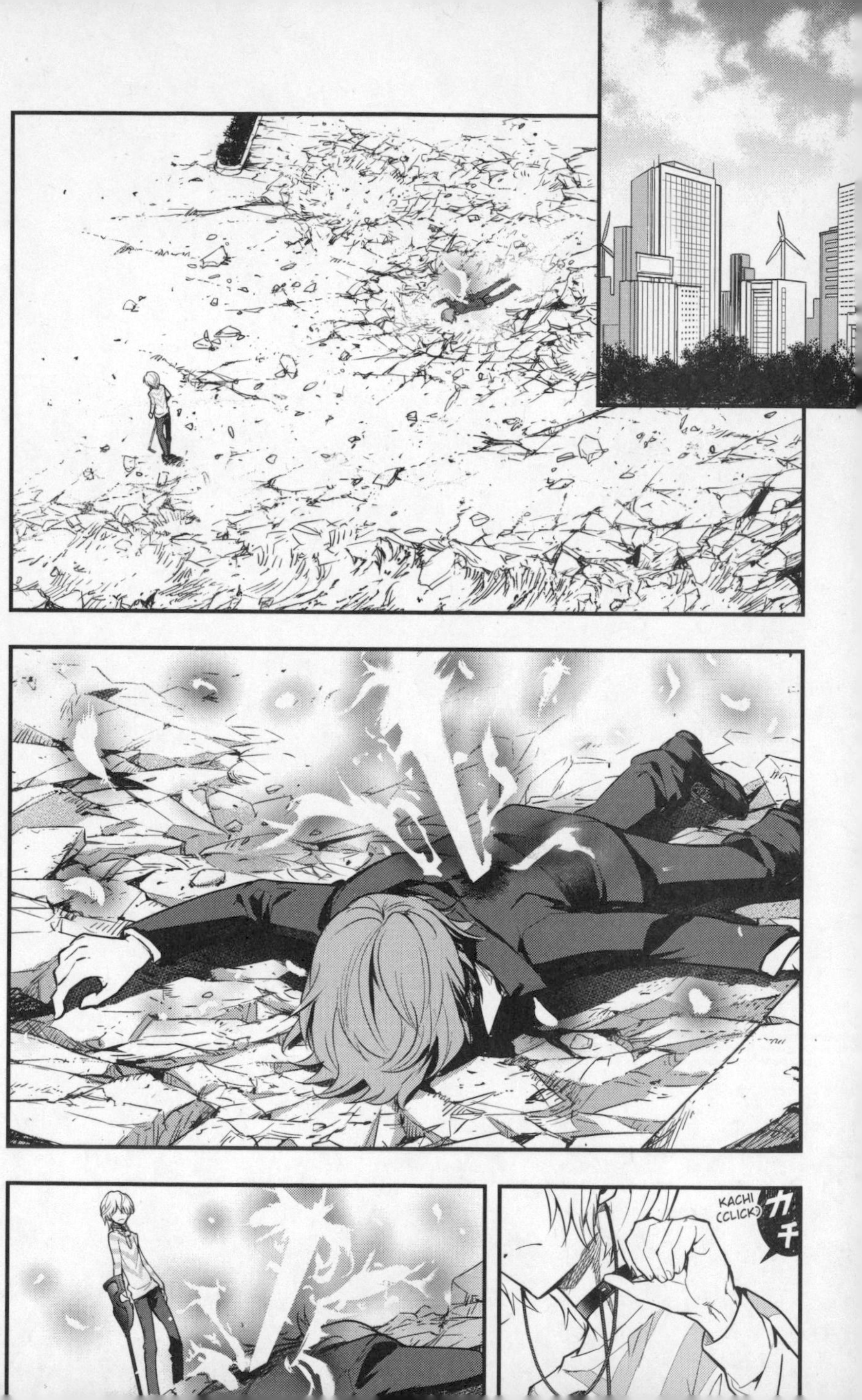
KACHI (CLICK)
カチ

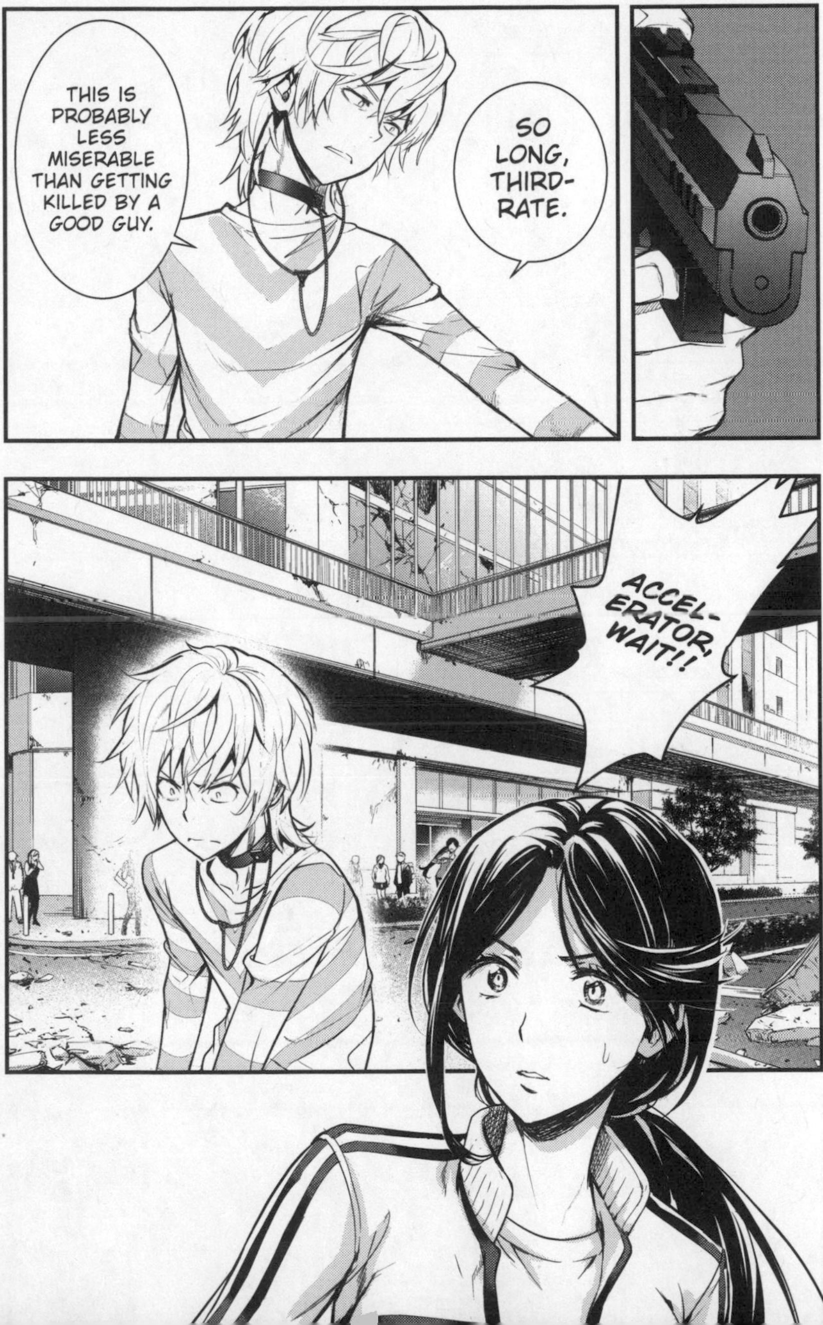
SO LONG, THIRD-RATE.
THIS IS PROBABLY LESS MISERABLE THAN GETTING KILLED BY A GOOD GUY.
ACCEL-ERATOR, WAIT!!

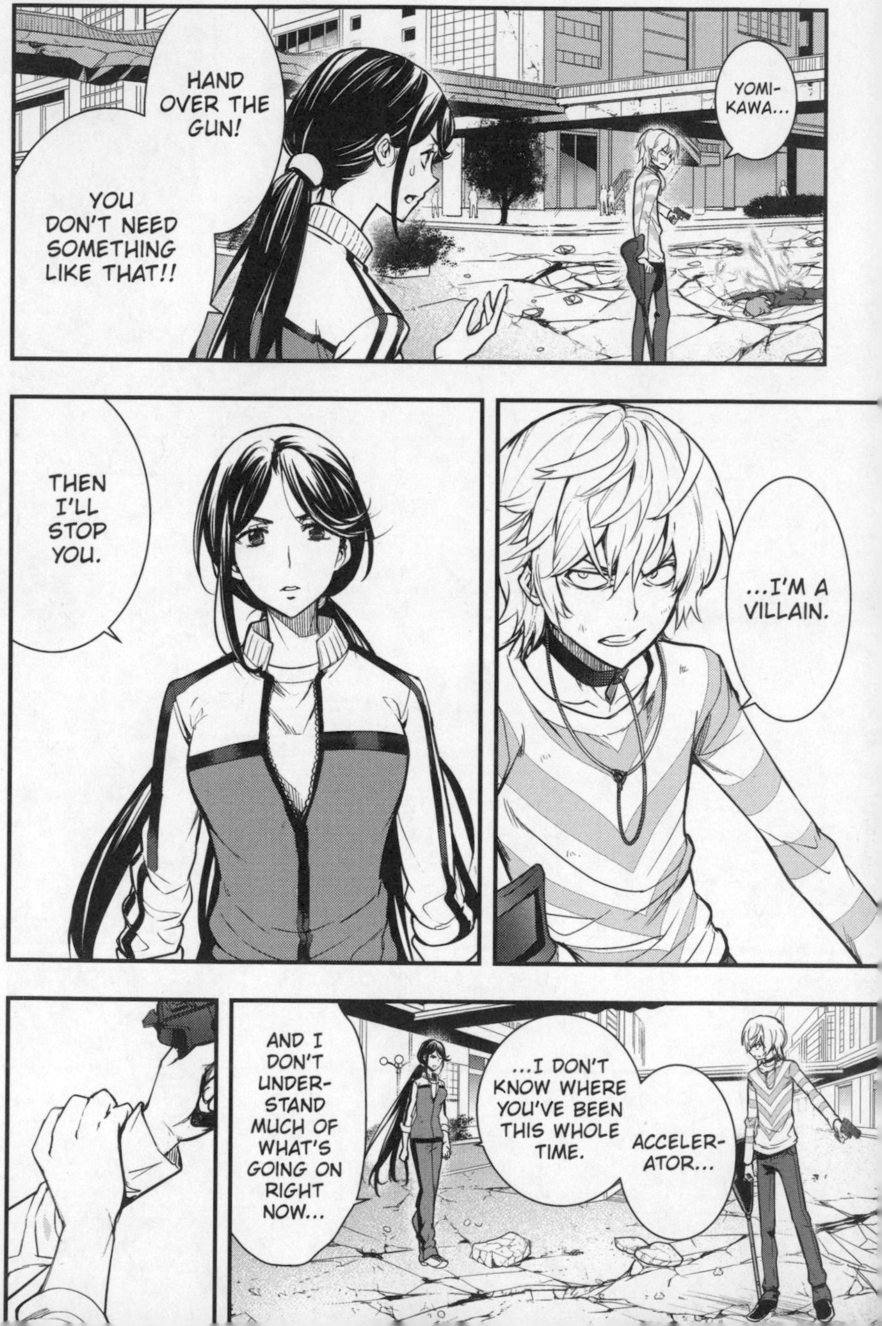
YOMI-KAWA...
HAND OVER THE GUN!
YOU DON'T NEED SOMETHING LIKE THAT!!
...I'M A VILLAIN.
THEN I'LL STOP YOU.
ACCELER-ATOR...
...I DON'T KNOW WHERE YOU'VE BEEN THIS WHOLE TIME.
AND I DON'T UNDER-STAND MUCH OF WHAT'S GOING ON RIGHT NOW...

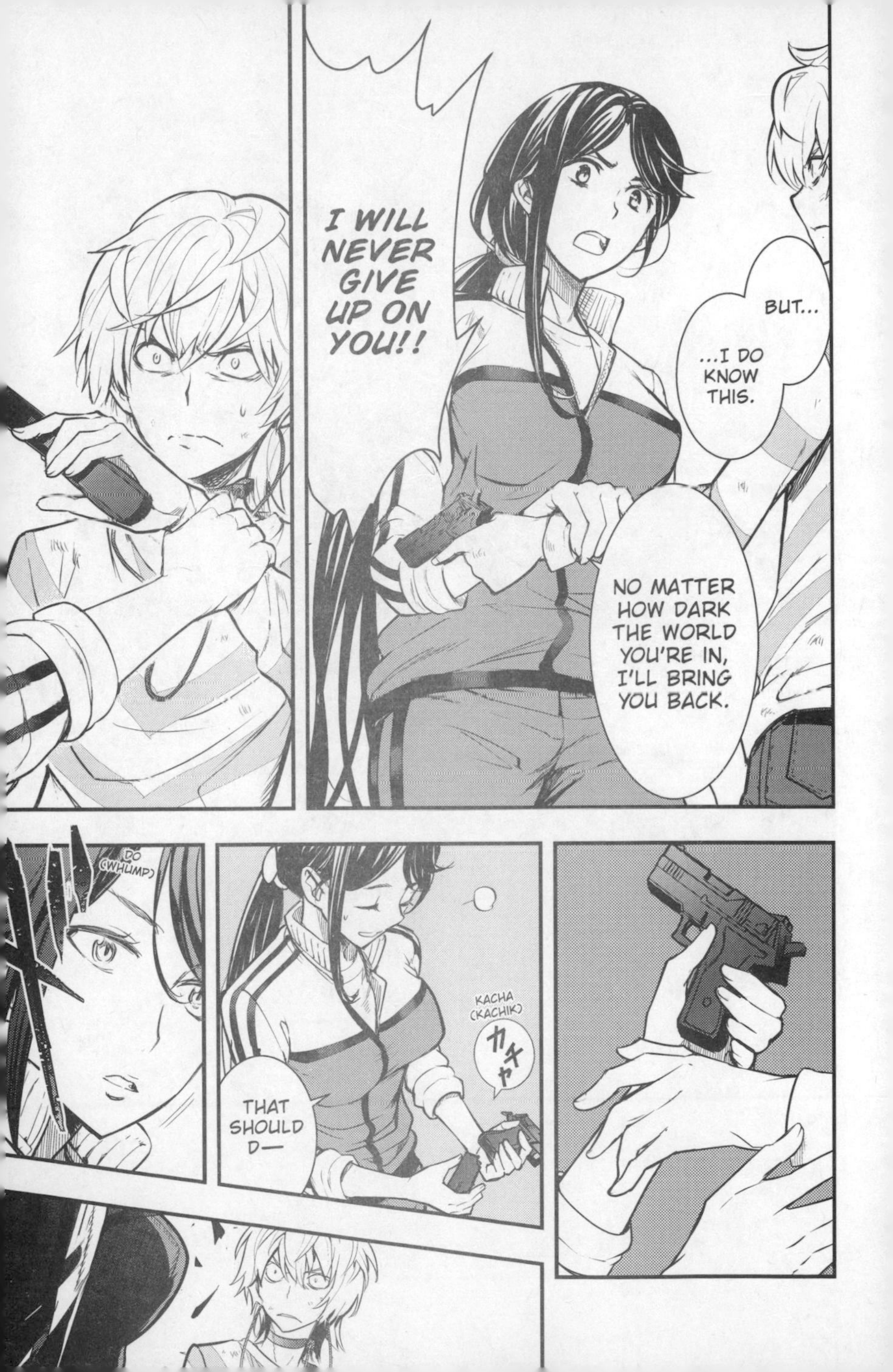
BUT...
...I DO KNOW THIS.
NO MATTER HOW DARK THE WORLD YOU'RE IN, I'LL BRING YOU BACK.
I WILL NEVER GIVE UP ON YOU!!
KACHA (KACHIK)
カチャ
THAT SHOULD D—
DO (WHUMP)

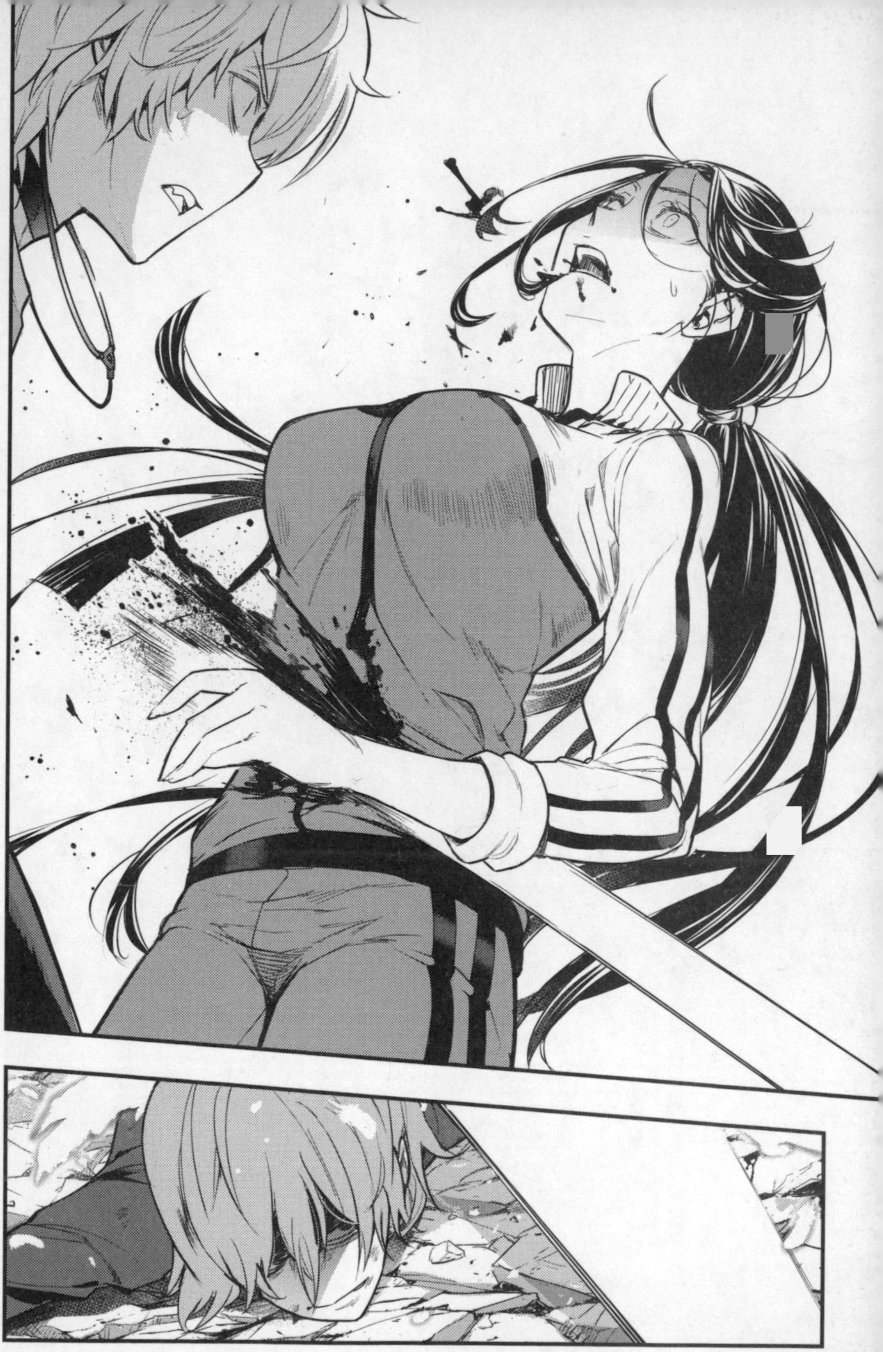

A
Certain
Magical
Index

A Certain
Magical
Index

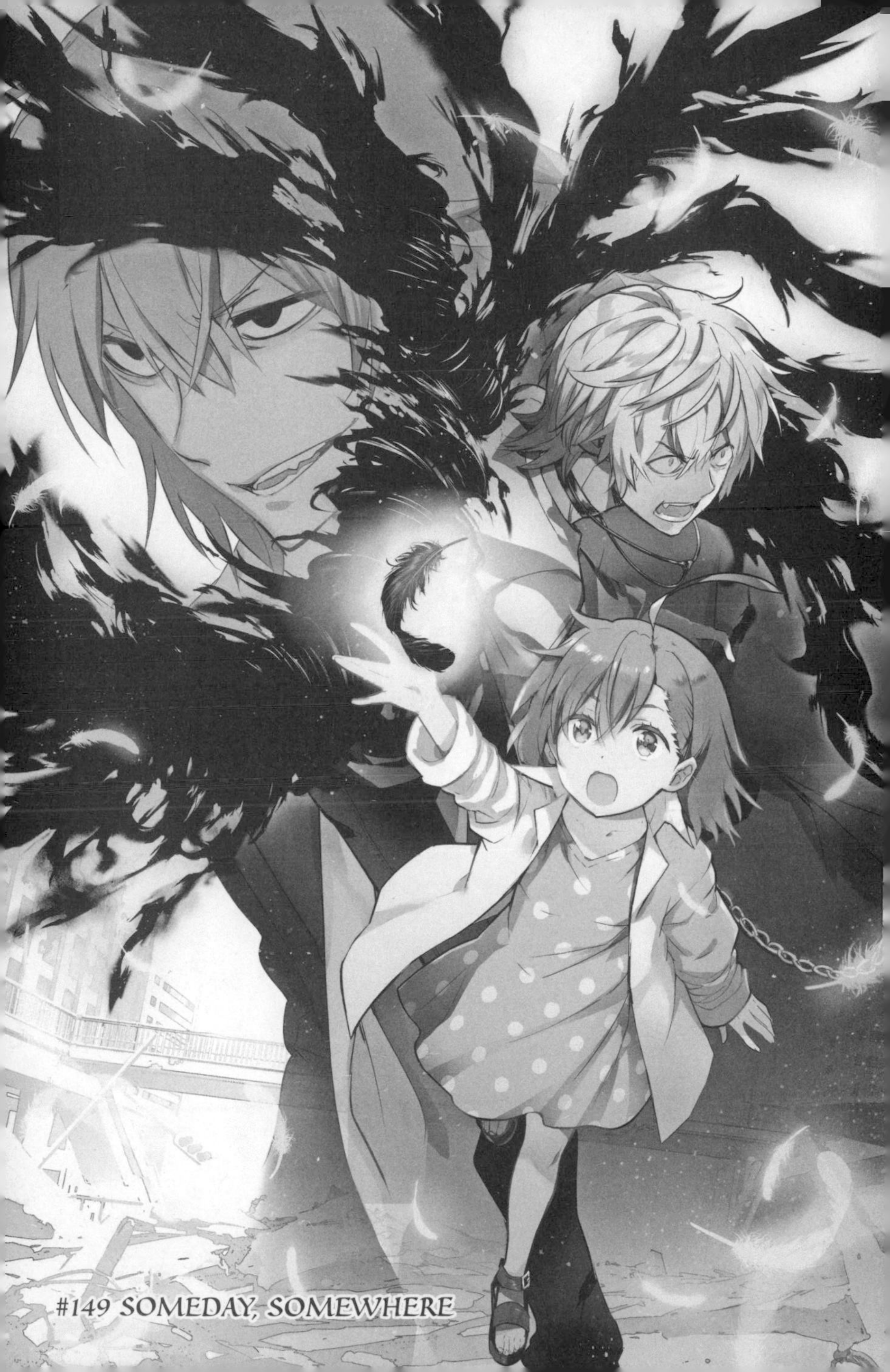
#149 SOMEDAY, SOMEWHERE

A Certain Magical Index

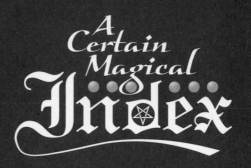

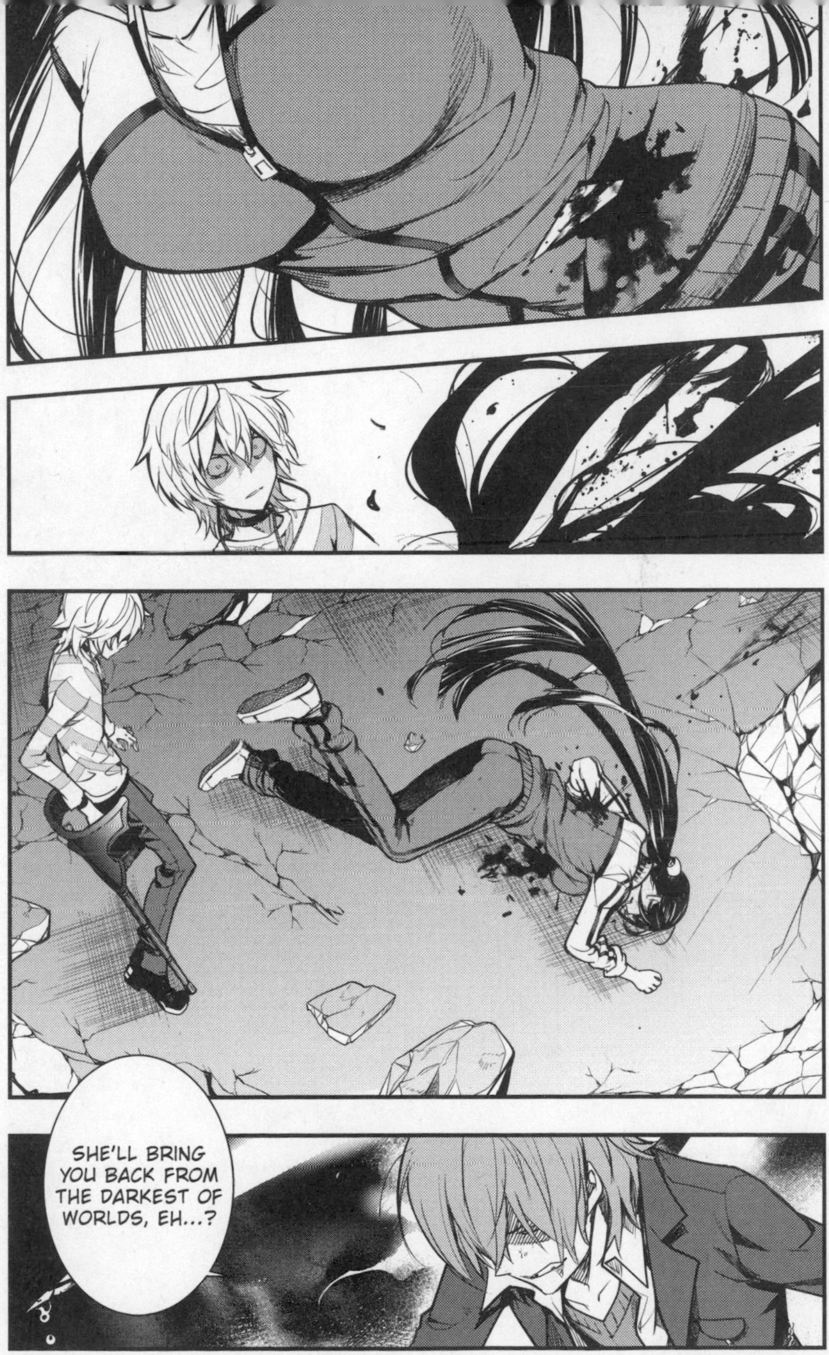
SHE'LL BRING YOU BACK FROM THE DARKEST OF WORLDS, EH...?

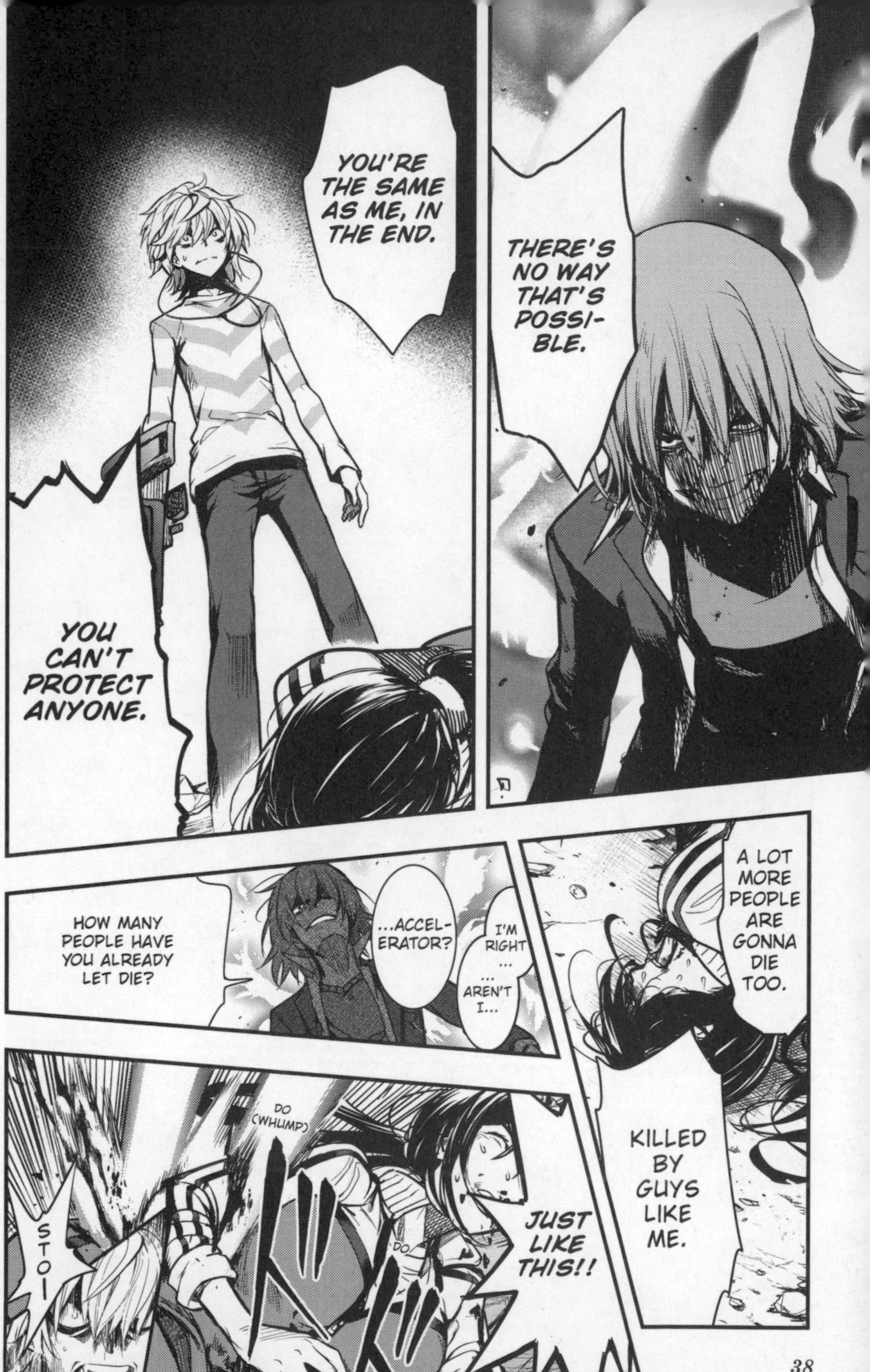
THERE'S NO WAY THAT'S POSSI- BLE.
YOU'RE THE SAME AS ME, IN THE END.
YOU CAN'T PROTECT ANYONE.
A LOT MORE PEOPLE ARE GONNA DIE TOO.
KILLED BY GUYS LIKE ME.
...ACCEL- ERATOR?
I'M RIGHT ... ... AREN'T I...
HOW MANY PEOPLE HAVE YOU ALREADY LET DIE?
DO (WHUMP)
JUST LIKE THIS!!
DO
STO!

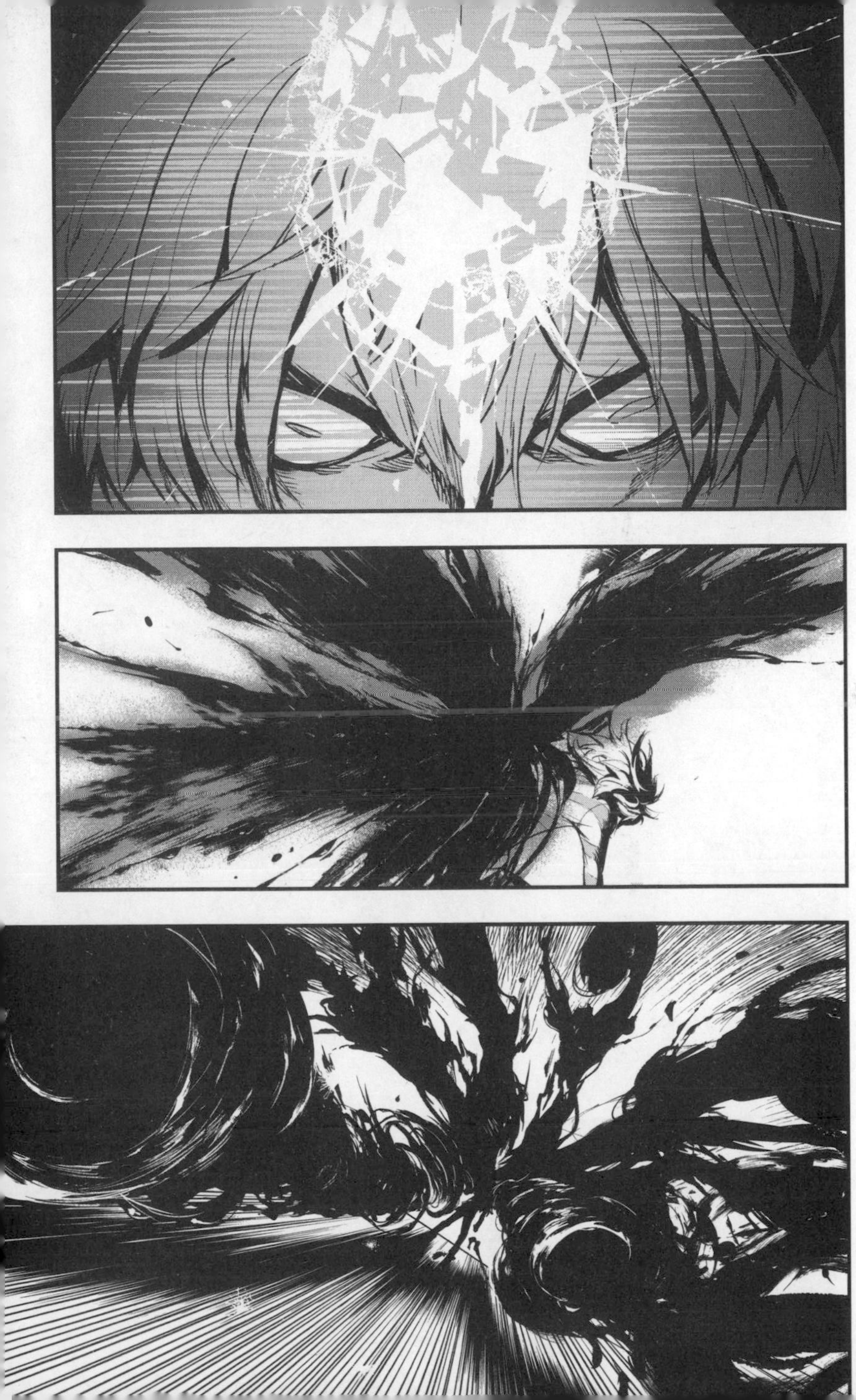

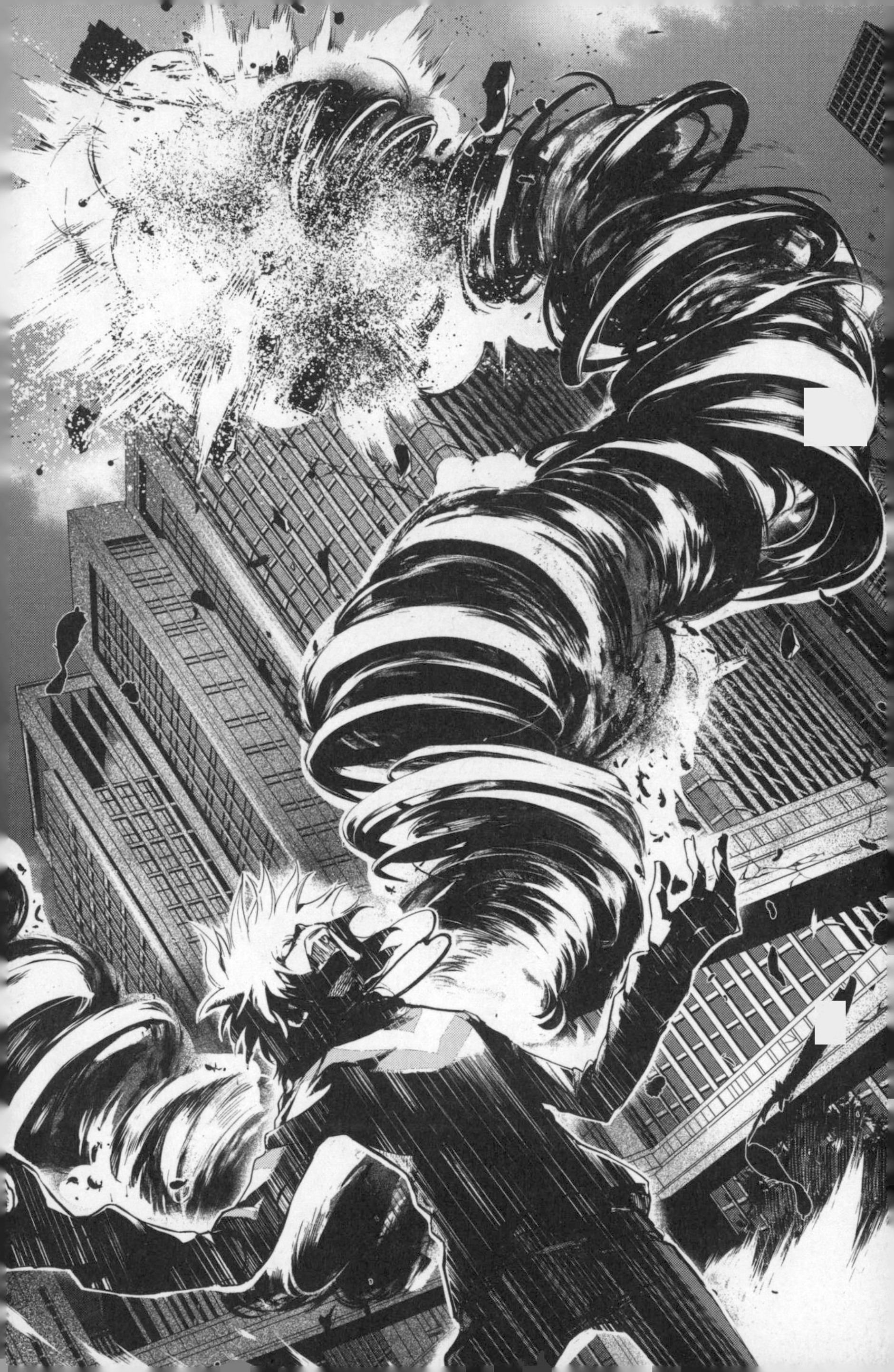

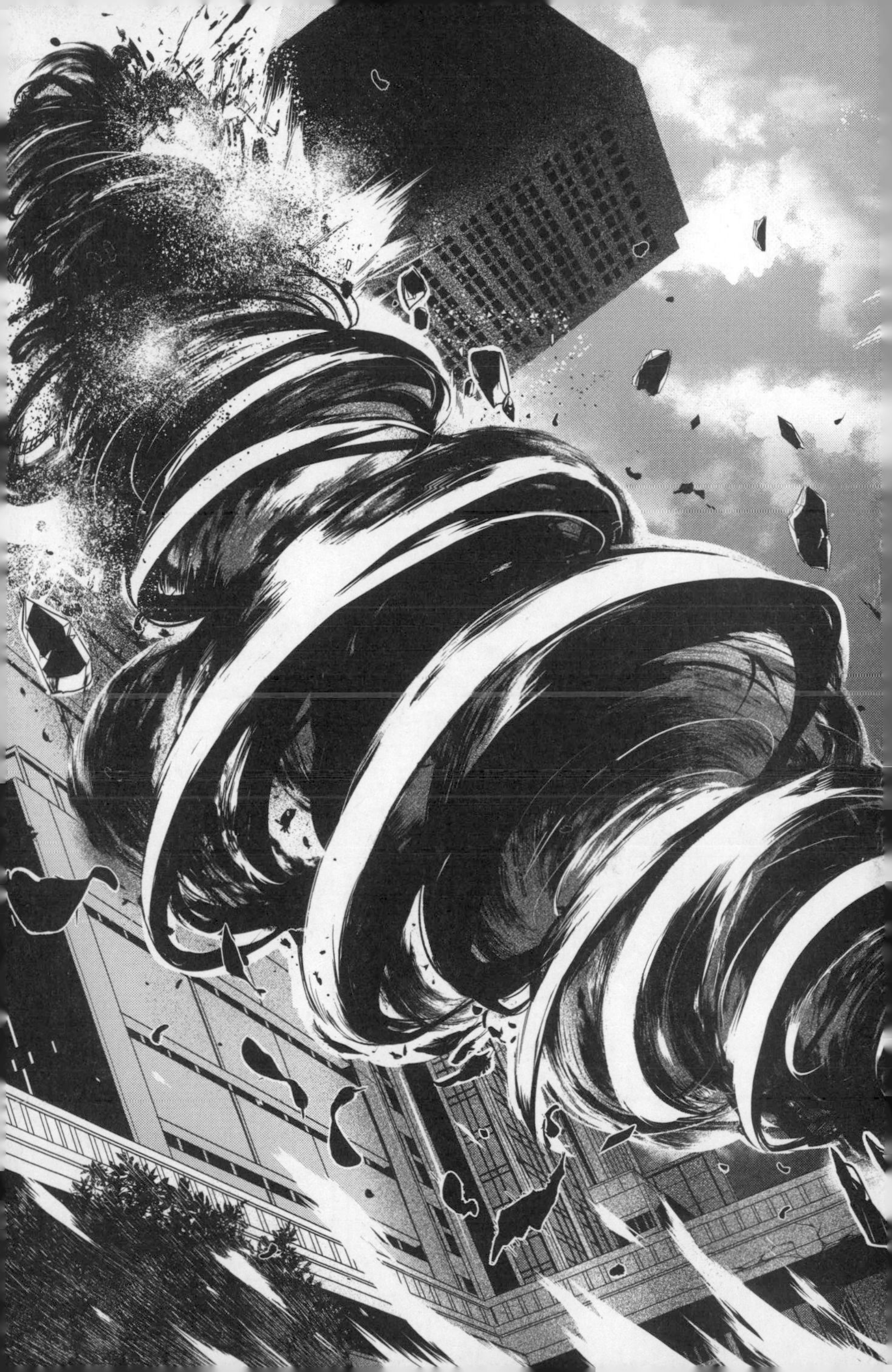

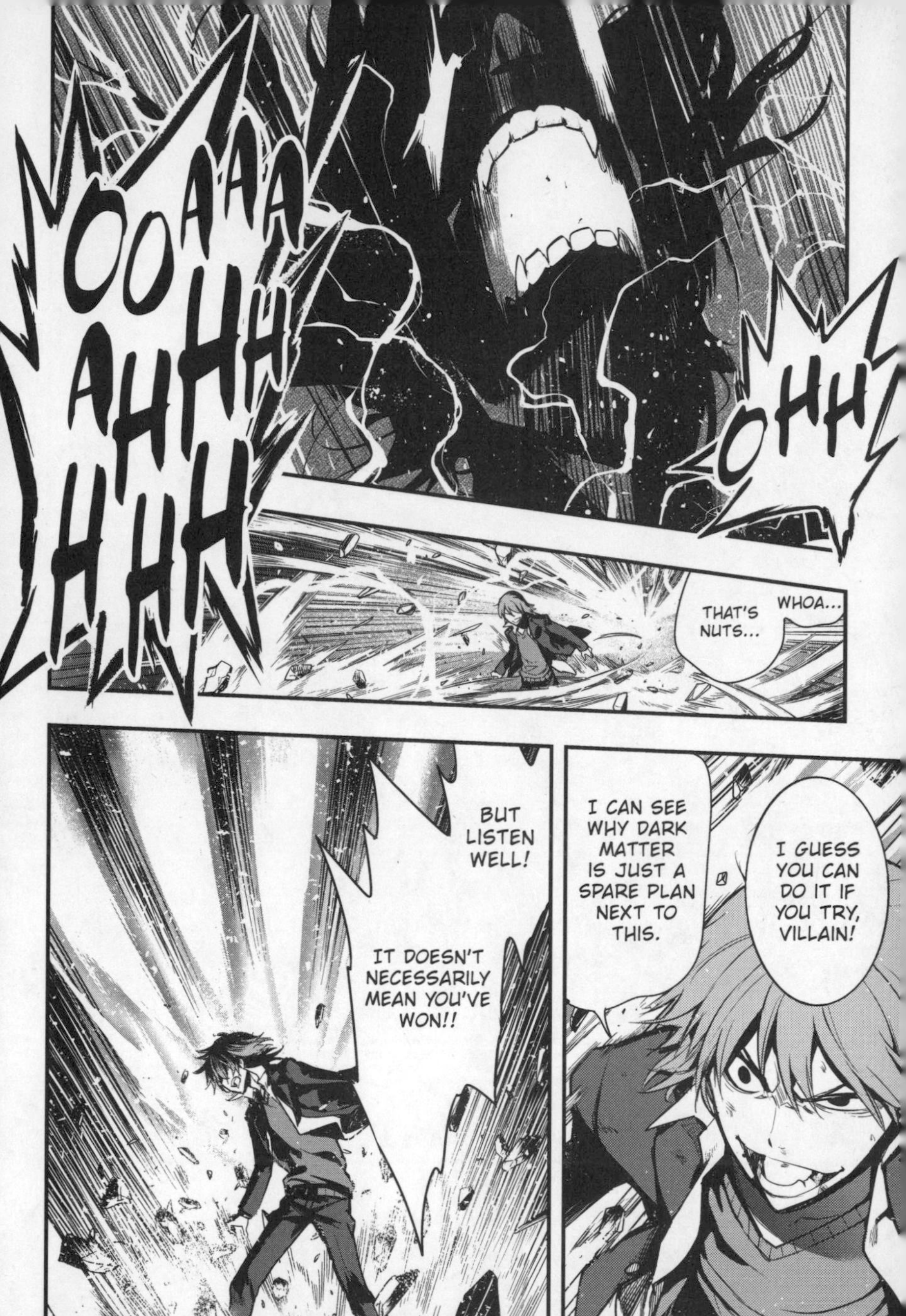

OOAAAAHHHHHHHH
OHH
WHOA...
THAT'S NUTS...
I GUESS YOU CAN DO IT IF YOU TRY, VILLAIN!
I CAN SEE WHY DARK MATTER IS JUST A SPARE PLAN NEXT TO THIS.
BUT LISTEN WELL!
IT DOESN'T NECESSARILY MEAN YOU'VE WON!!

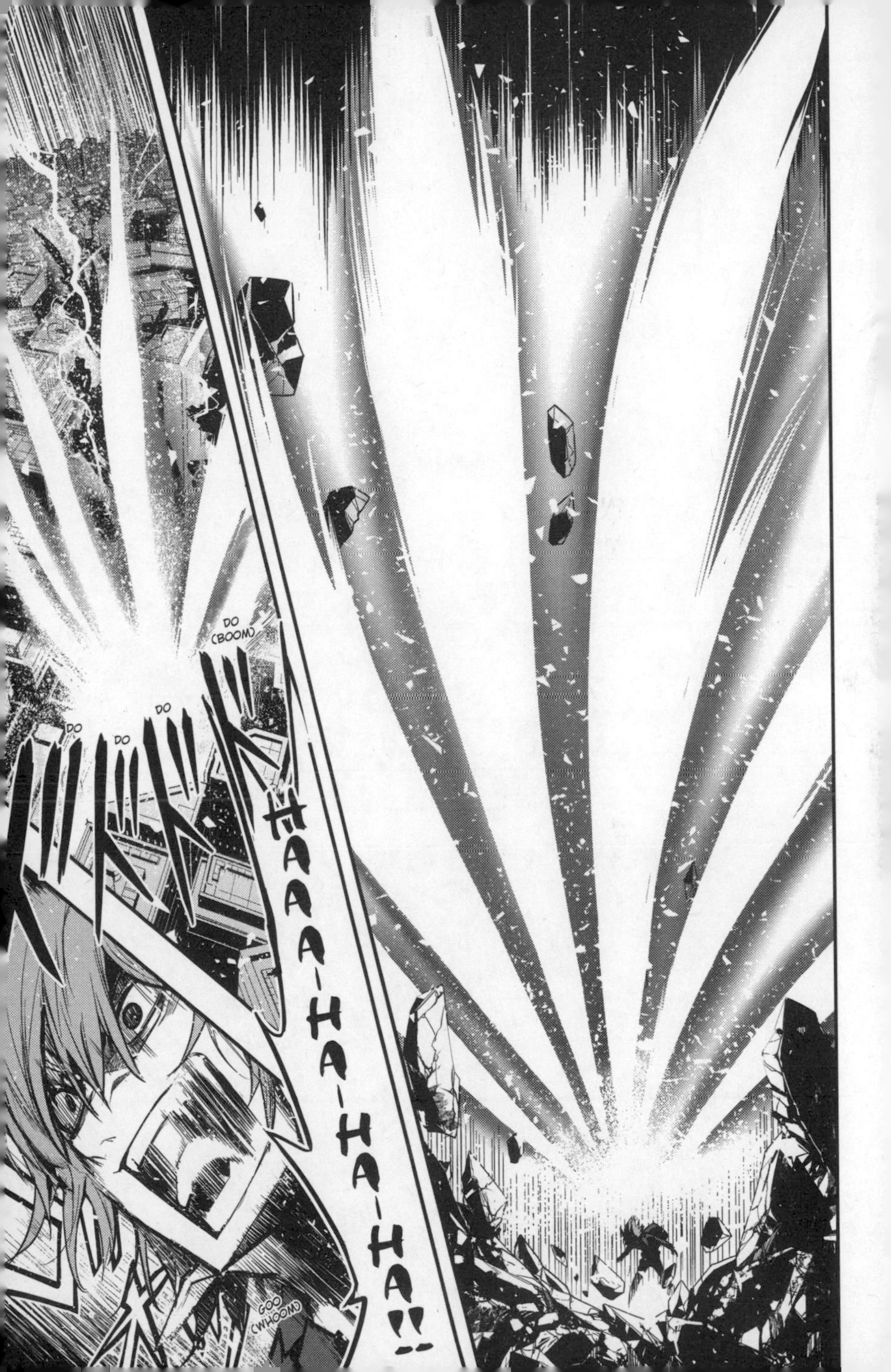
DO
DO
DO
DO (BOOM)
HAAAA-HA-HA-HA-HA!!
GOO (WHOOM)

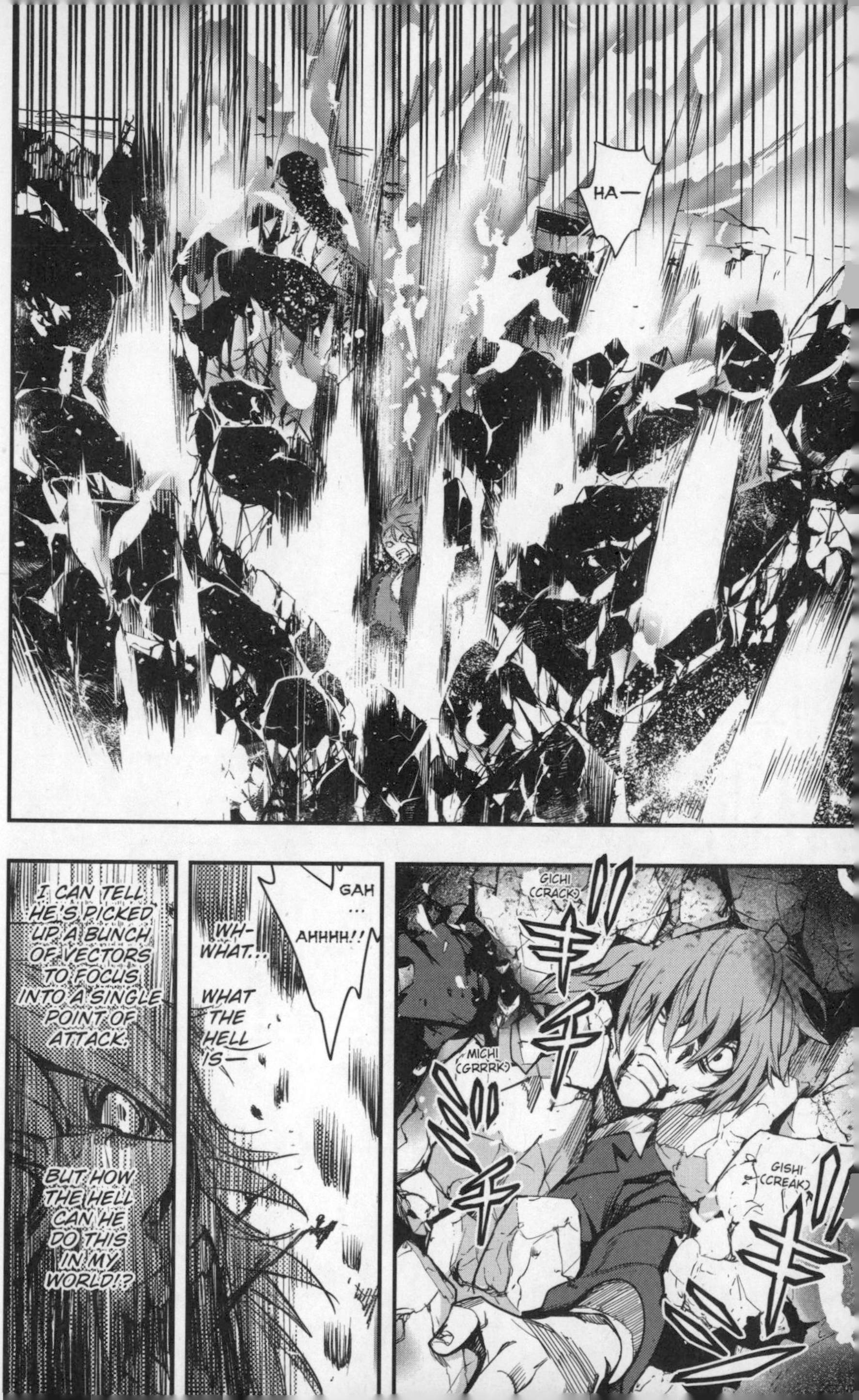
HA—
GICHI (CRACK)
MICHI (GRRRK)
GISHI (CREAK)
GAH ... AHHHH!!
WH- WHAT...
WHAT THE HELL IS—
I CAN TELL HE'S PICKED UP A BUNCH OF VECTORS TO FOCUS INTO A SINGLE POINT OF ATTACK.
BUT HOW THE HELL CAN HE DO THIS IN MY WORLD!?

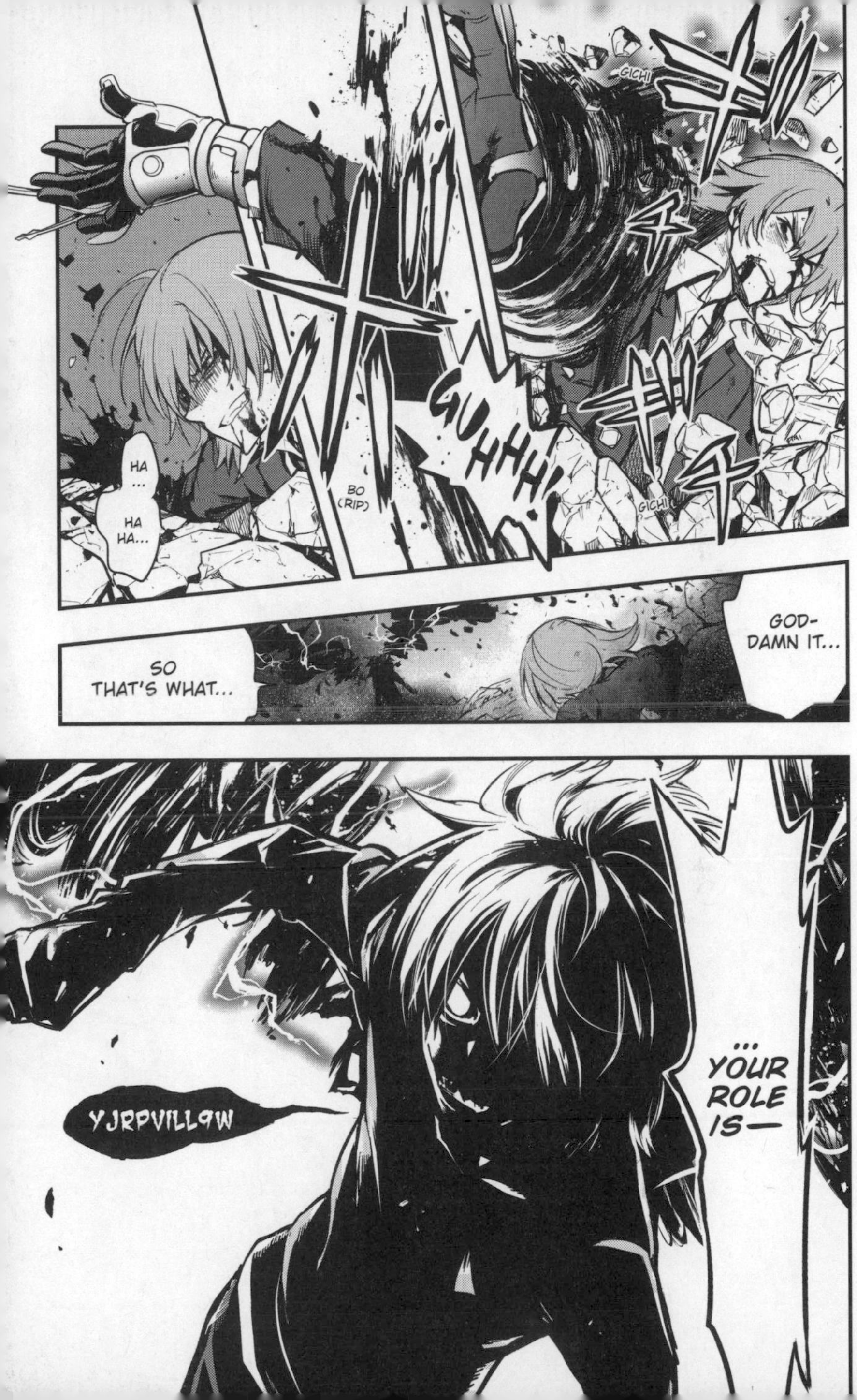
GICHI
GICHI
GUHHH!
BO (RIP)
HA ... HA HA...
GOD-DAMN IT...
SO THAT'S WHAT...
... YOUR ROLE IS—
YJRPVILL9W

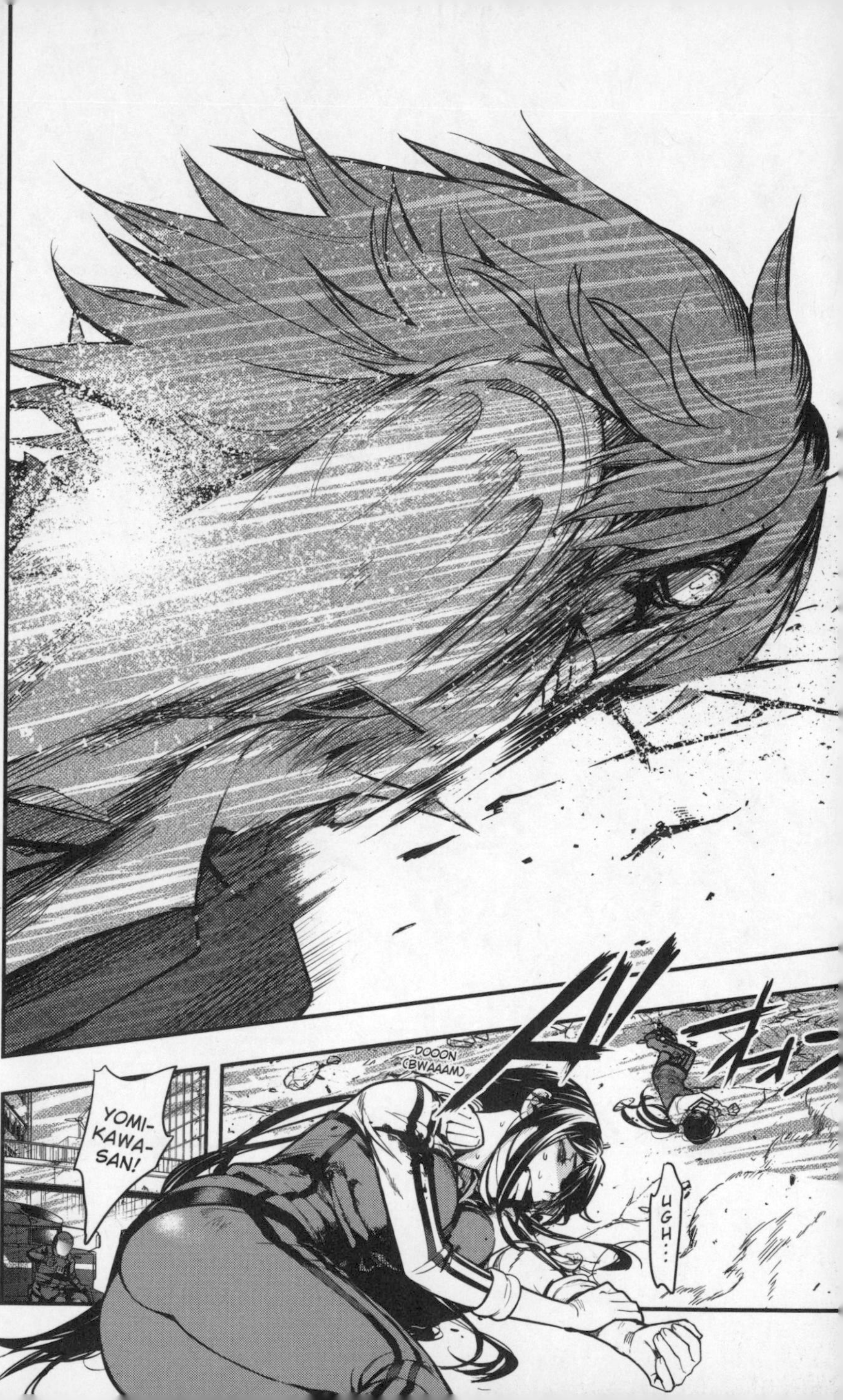
DOOON (BWAAAM)
UGH...
YOMI-KAWA-SAN!

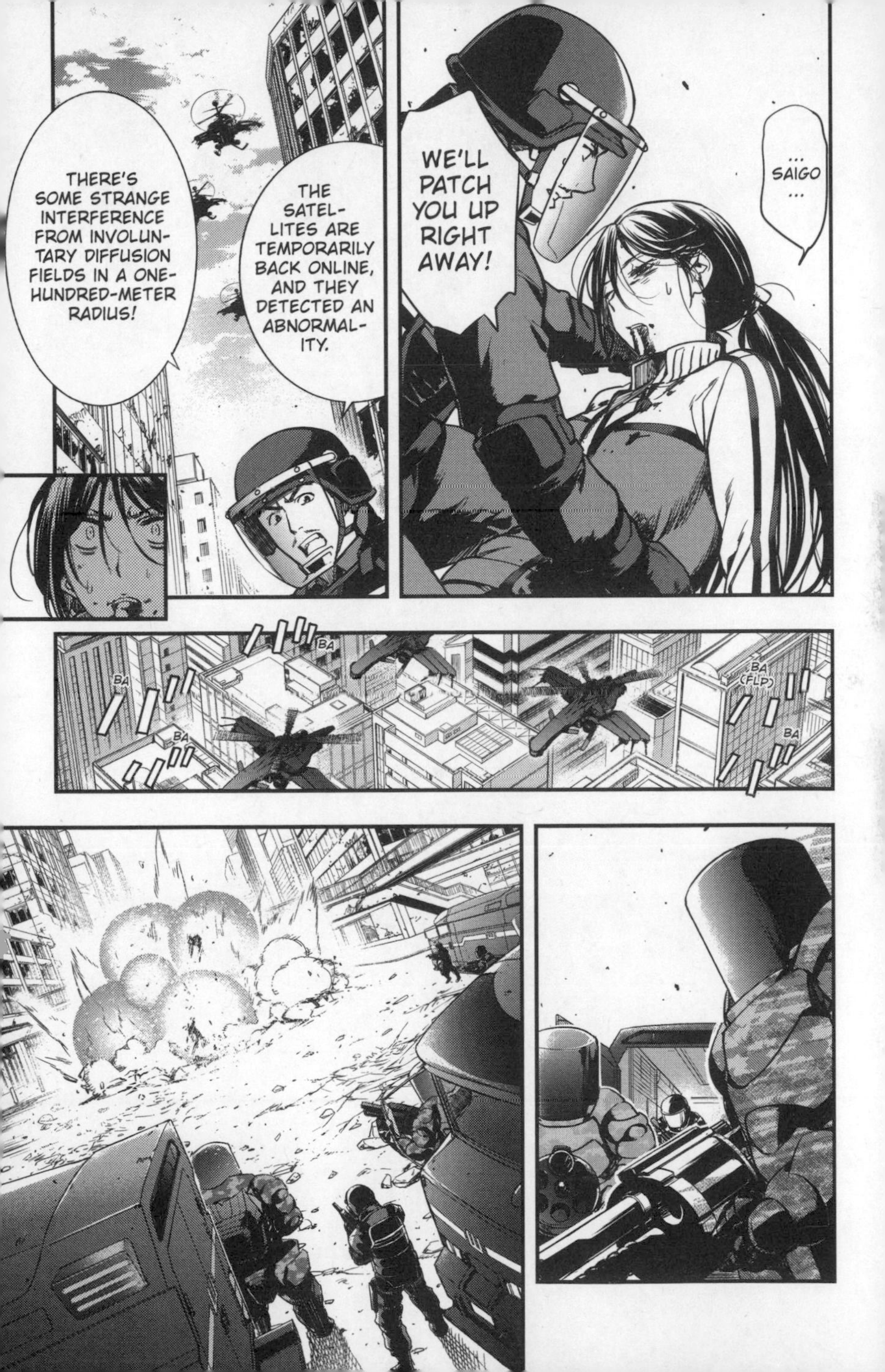
...SAIGO...
WE'LL PATCH YOU UP RIGHT AWAY!
THE SATEL-LITES ARE TEMPORARILY BACK ONLINE, AND THEY DETECTED AN ABNORMAL-ITY.
THERE'S SOME STRANGE INTERFERENCE FROM INVOLUN-TARY DIFFUSION FIELDS IN A ONE-HUNDRED-METER RADIUS!
BA (FLP)
BA
BA
BA
BA

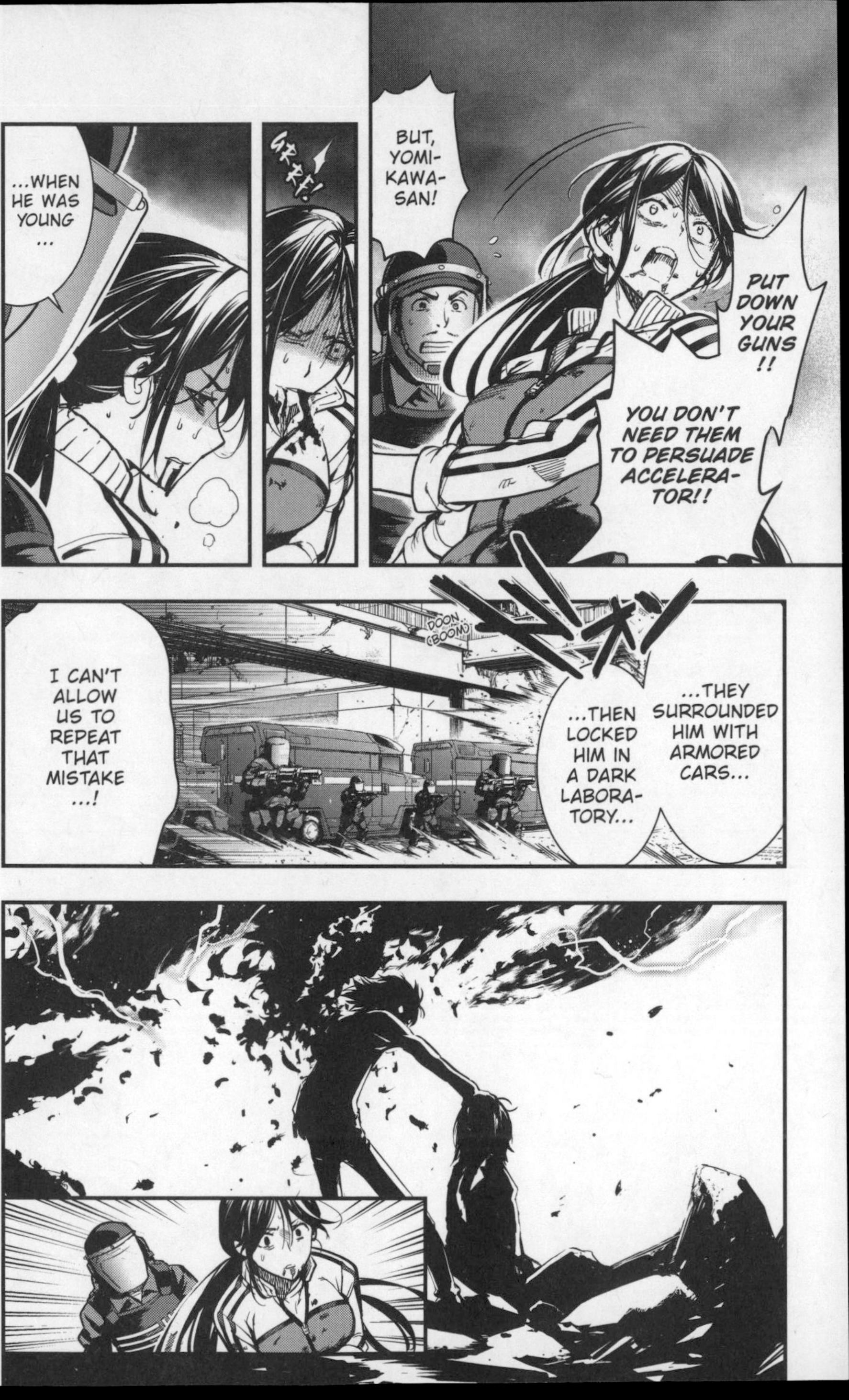
PUT DOWN YOUR GUNS!!
YOU DON'T NEED THEM TO PERSUADE ACCELERATOR!!
BUT, YOMIKAWA-SAN!
...WHEN HE WAS YOUNG...
...THEY SURROUNDED HIM WITH ARMORED CARS...
...THEN LOCKED HIM IN A DARK LABORATORY...
DOON (BOOM)
I CAN'T ALLOW US TO REPEAT THAT MISTAKE...!

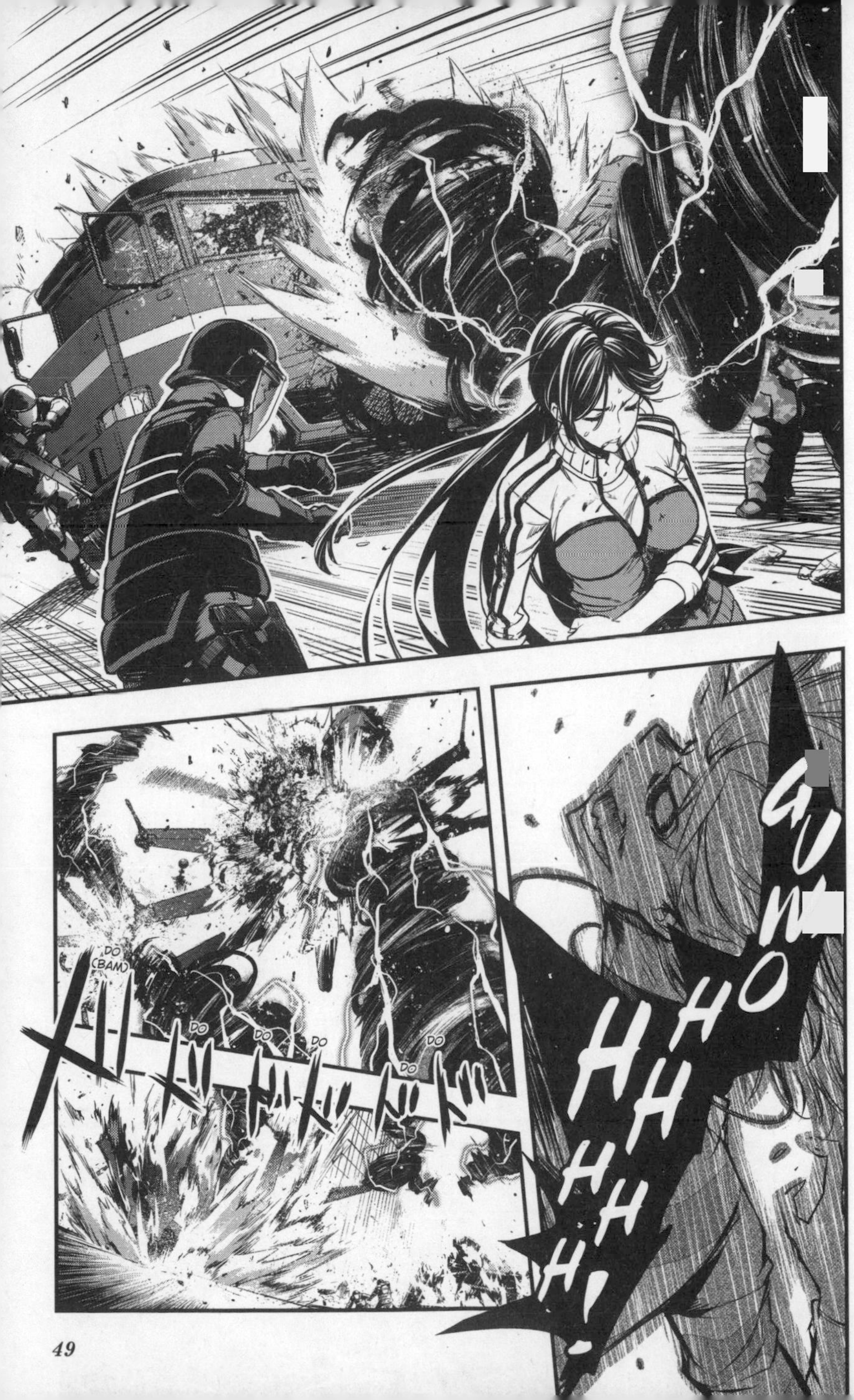
GUWOHHHHHHH!
DO
(BAM)
DO
DO
DO
DO
DO

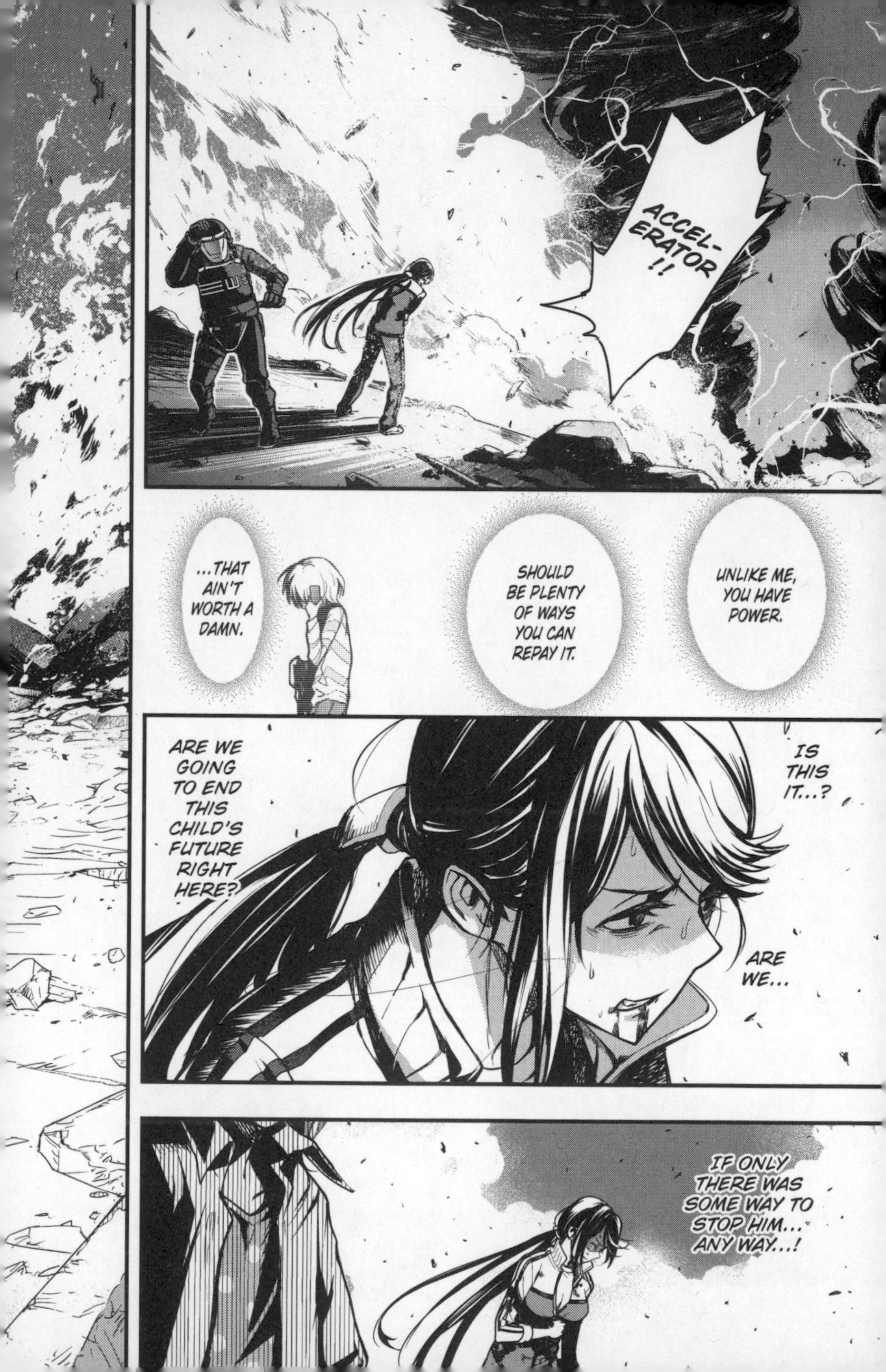
ACCEL-ERATOR!!
UNLIKE ME, YOU HAVE POWER.
SHOULD BE PLENTY OF WAYS YOU CAN REPAY IT.
...THAT AIN'T WORTH A DAMN.
IS THIS IT...?
ARE WE...
ARE WE GOING TO END THIS CHILD'S FUTURE RIGHT HERE?
IF ONLY THERE WAS SOME WAY TO STOP HIM... ANY WAY...!

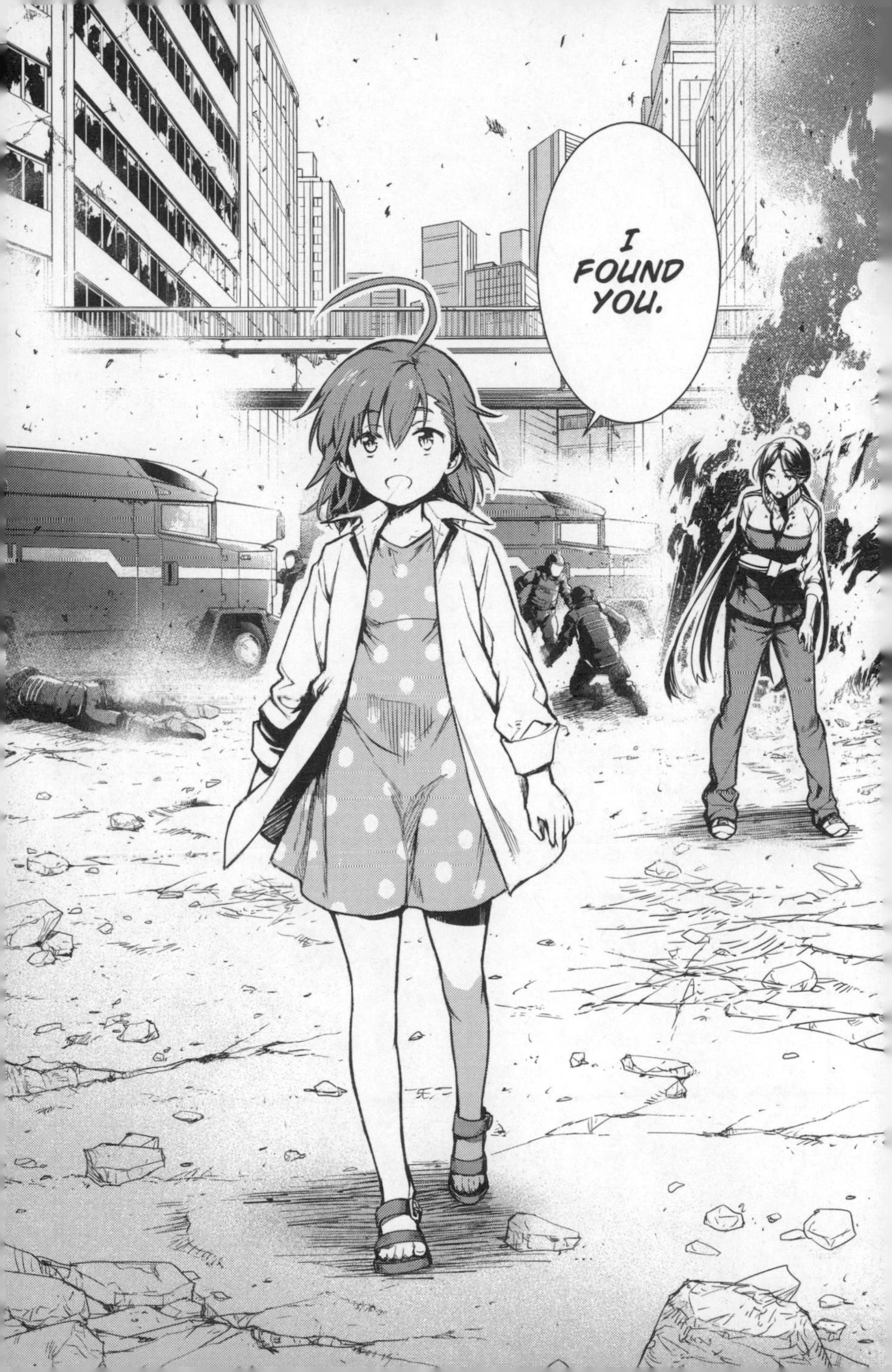
I FOUND YOU.

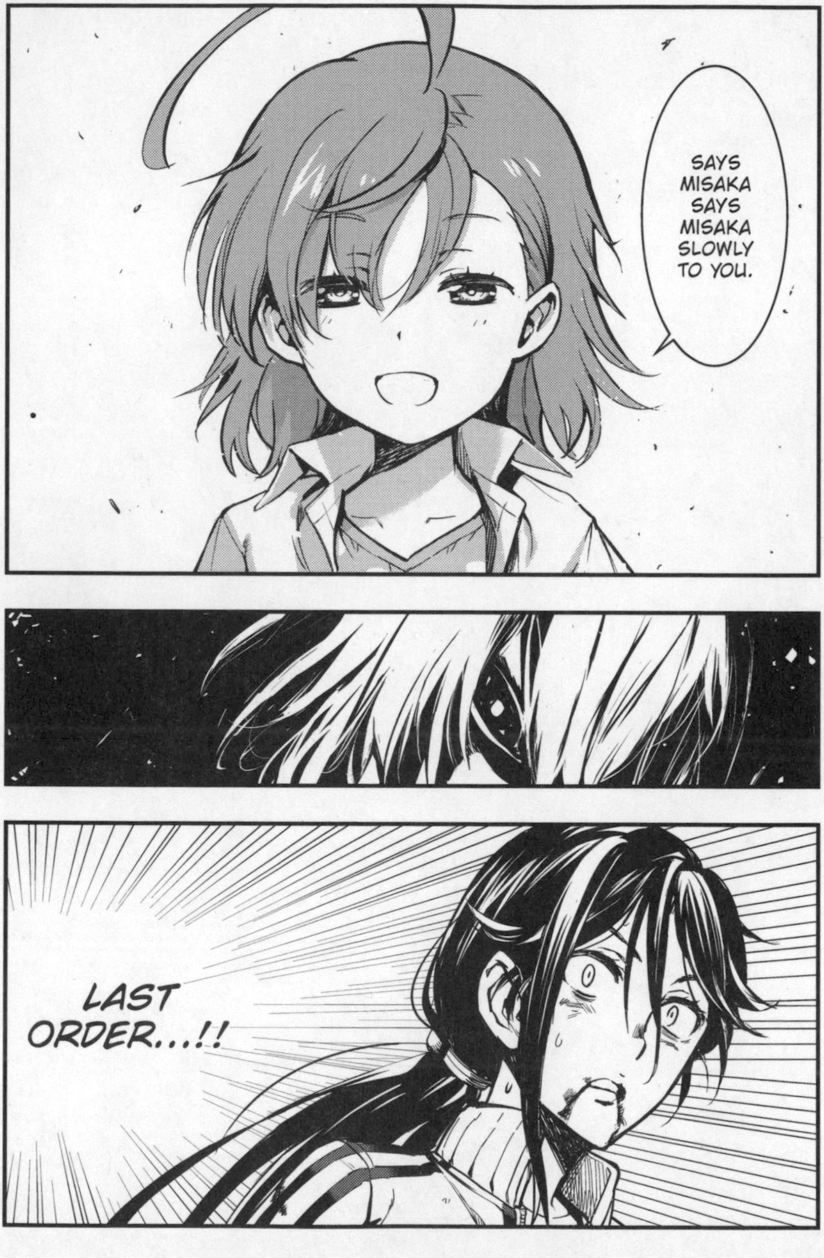
SAYS MISAKA SAYS MISAKA SLOWLY TO YOU.
LAST ORDER...!!

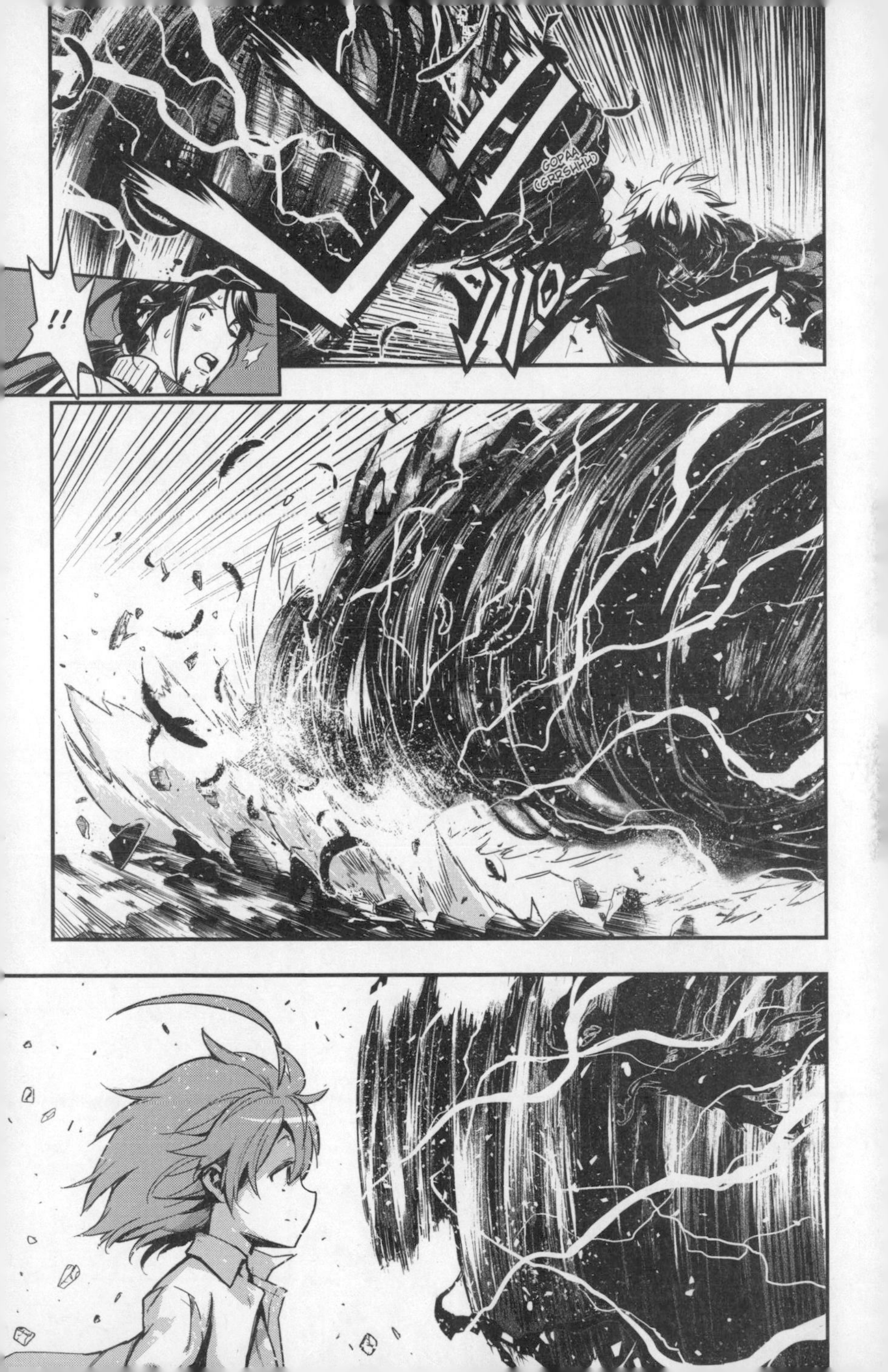
GOPAA
(GRRSHHH)
!!

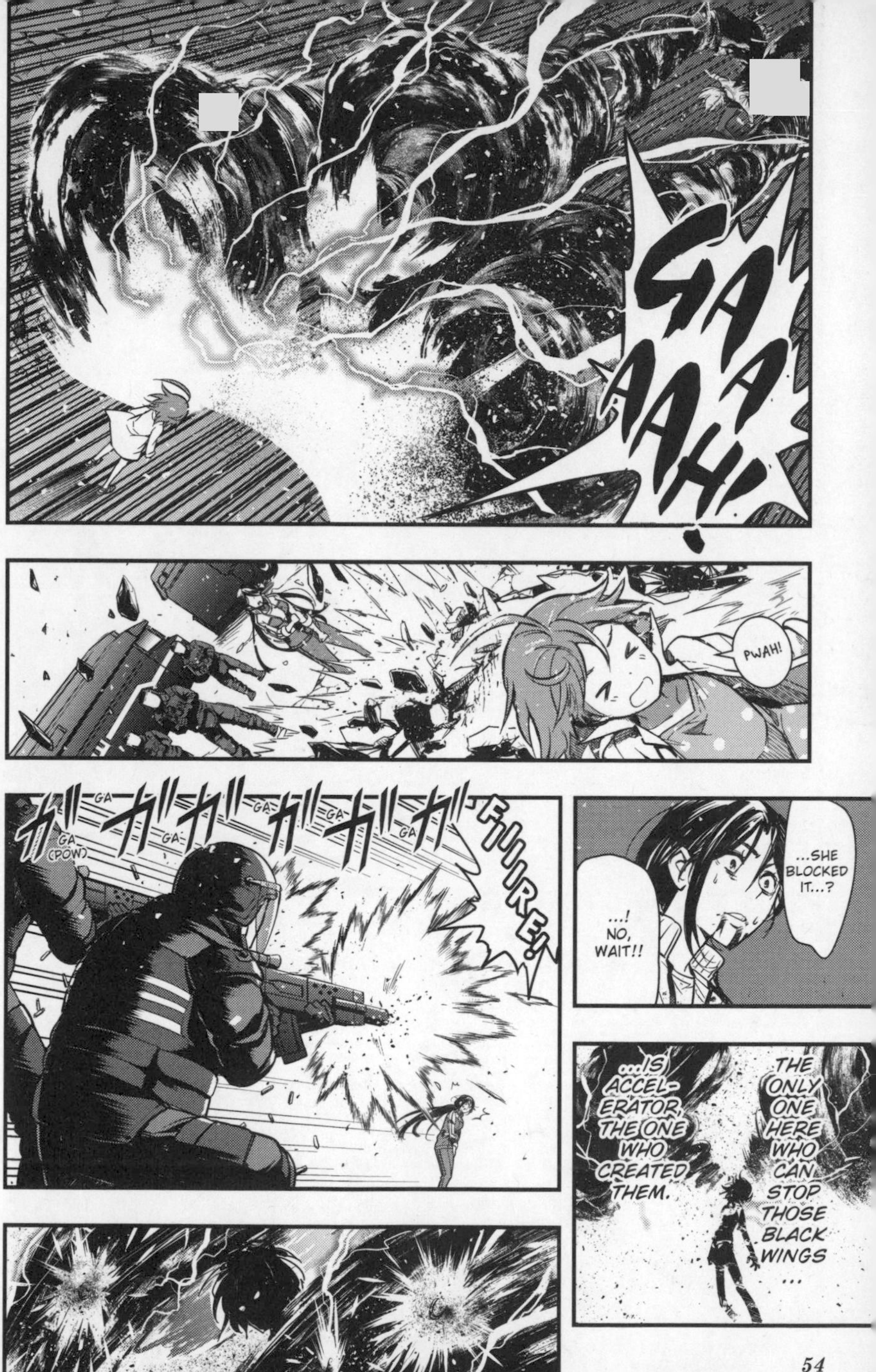
GAAAAAH!!
PWAH!
...SHE BLOCKED IT...?
...! NO, WAIT!!
THE ONLY ONE HERE WHO CAN STOP THOSE BLACK WINGS...
...IS ACCELERATOR, THE ONE WHO CREATED THEM.
FIIIRE!
GA GA GA GA GA GA GA (POW)

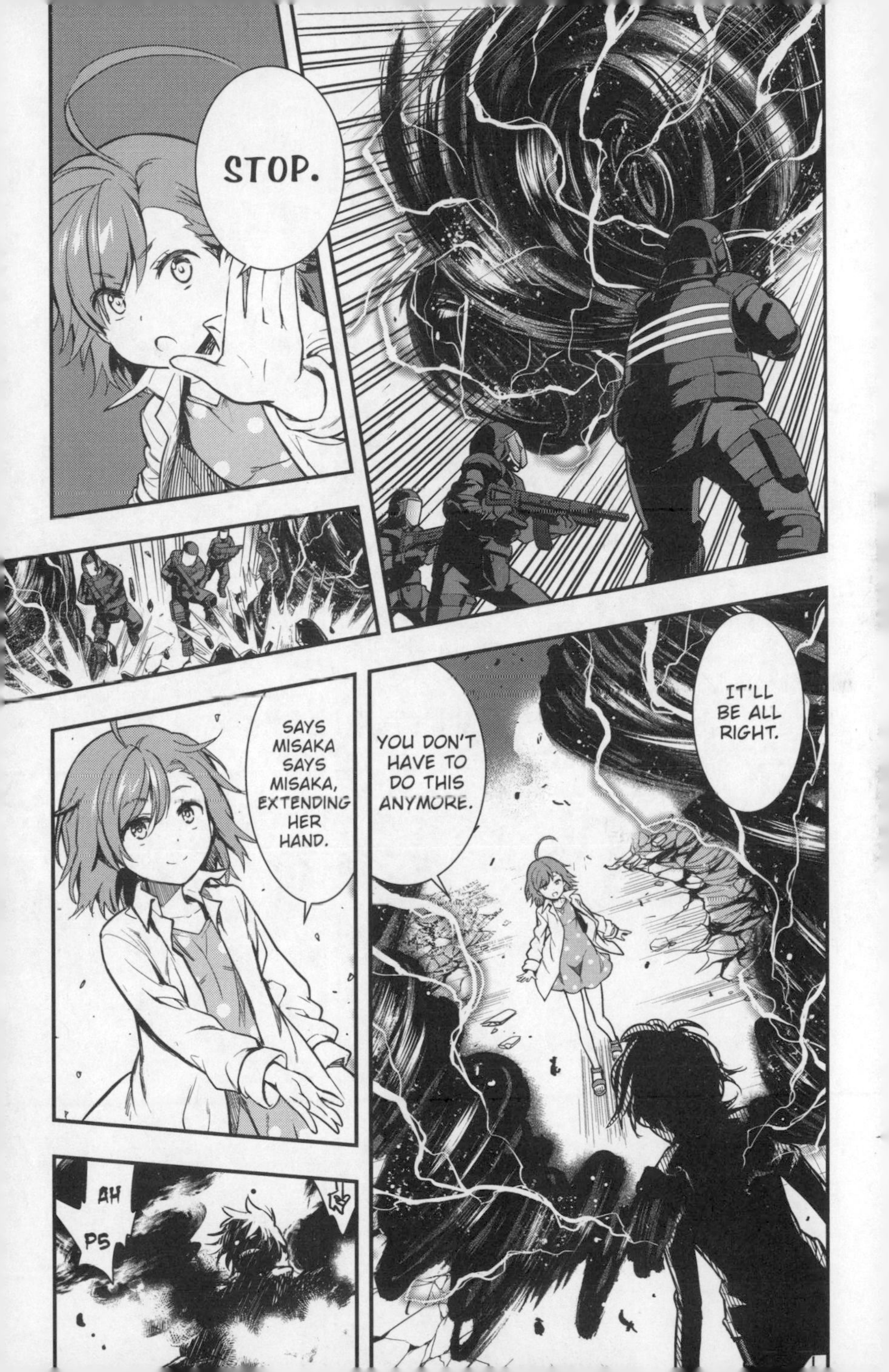
STOP.
IT'LL BE ALL RIGHT.
YOU DON'T HAVE TO DO THIS ANYMORE.
SAYS MISAKA SAYS MISAKA, EXTENDING HER HAND.
AH
PS

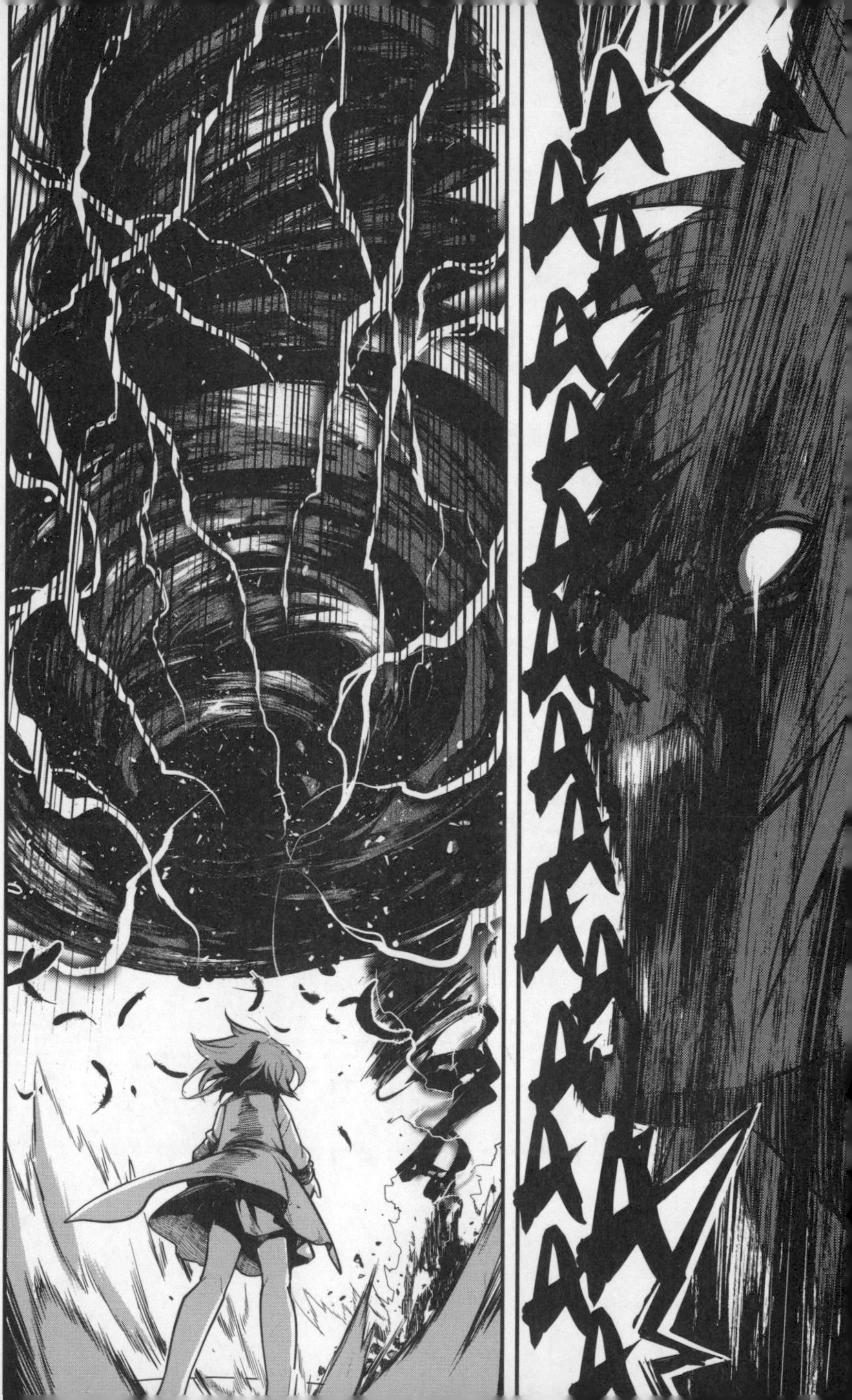
AAAAAAAAAAAAAAAAAAA

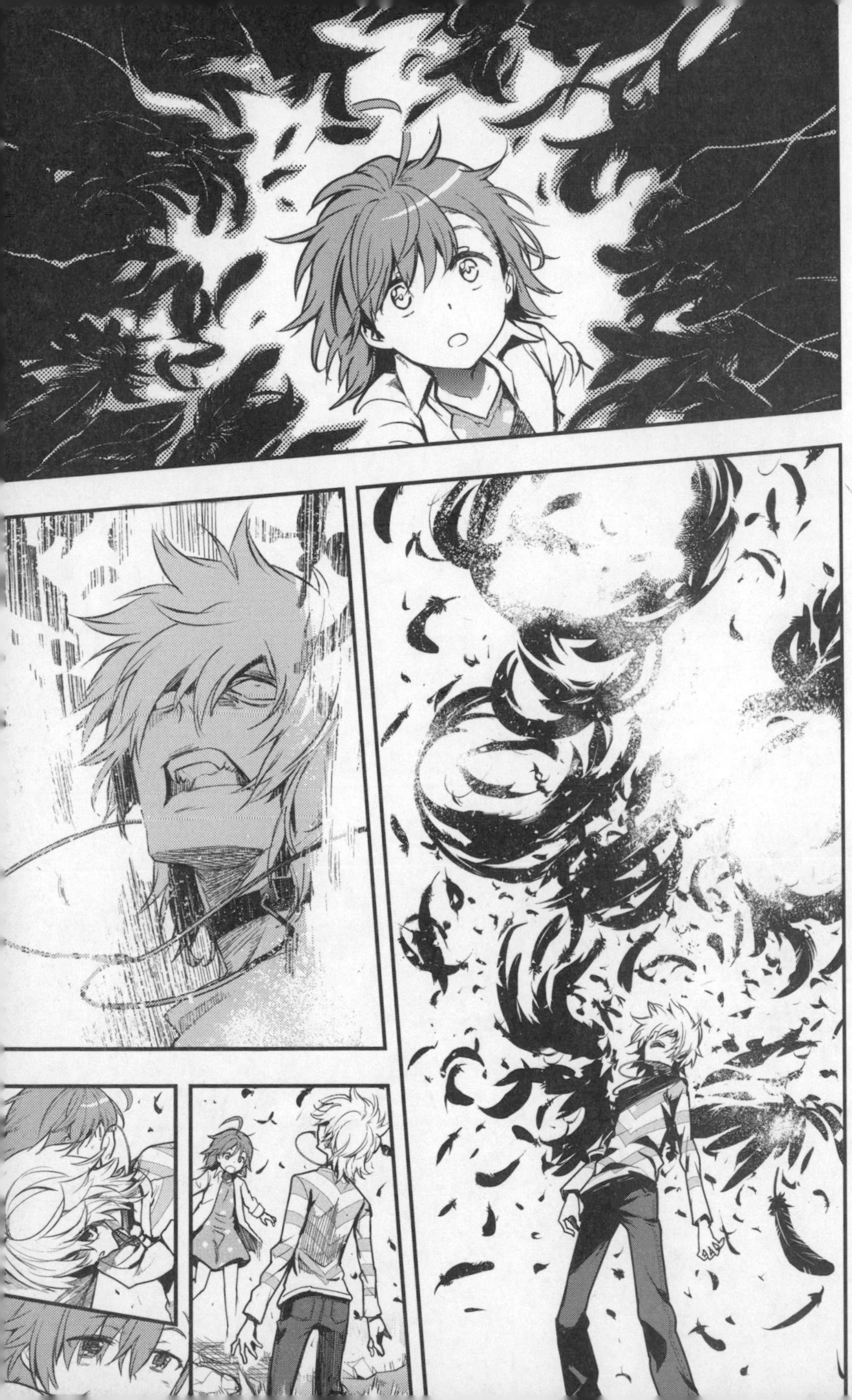

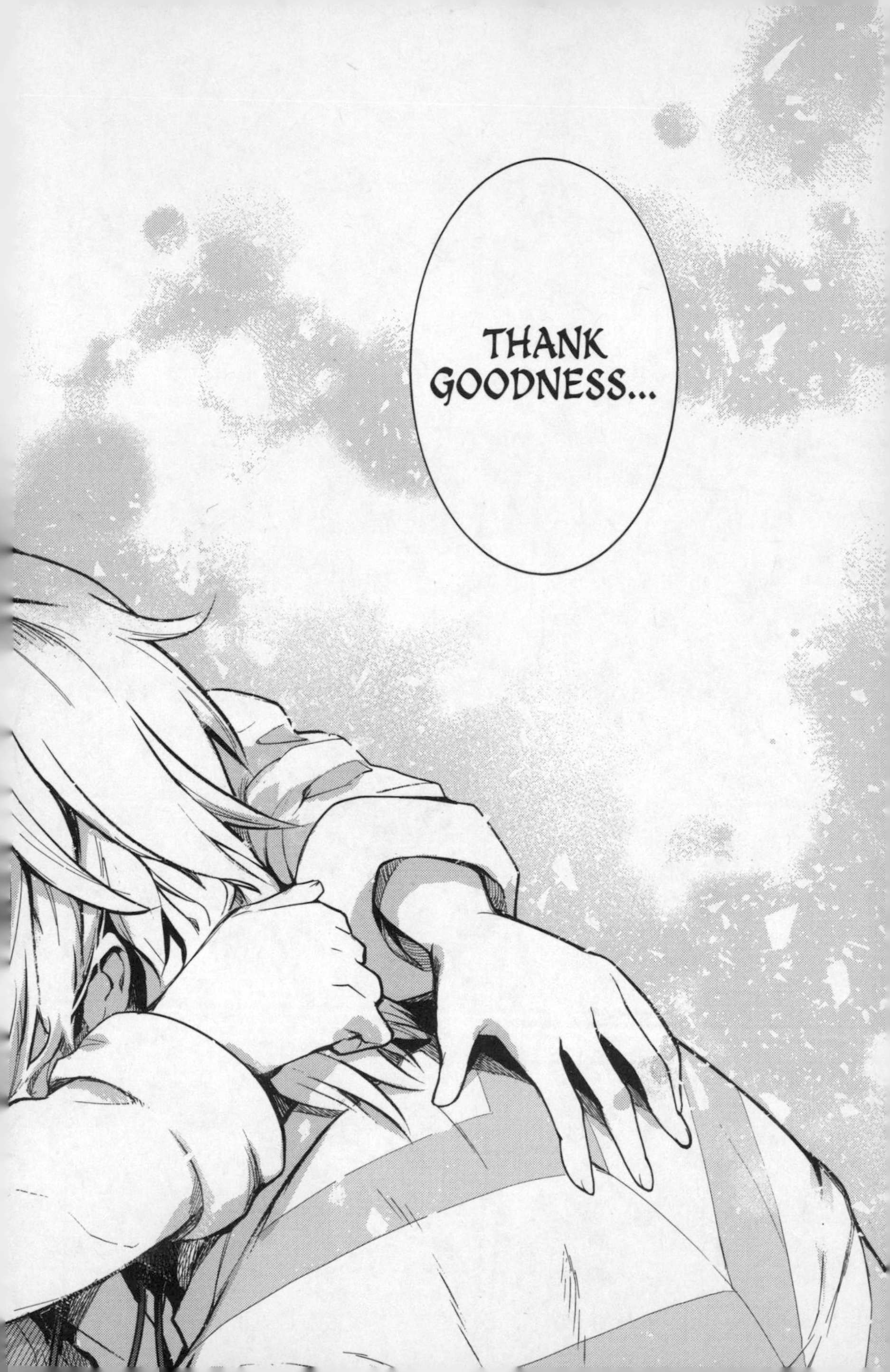
THANK GOODNESS...

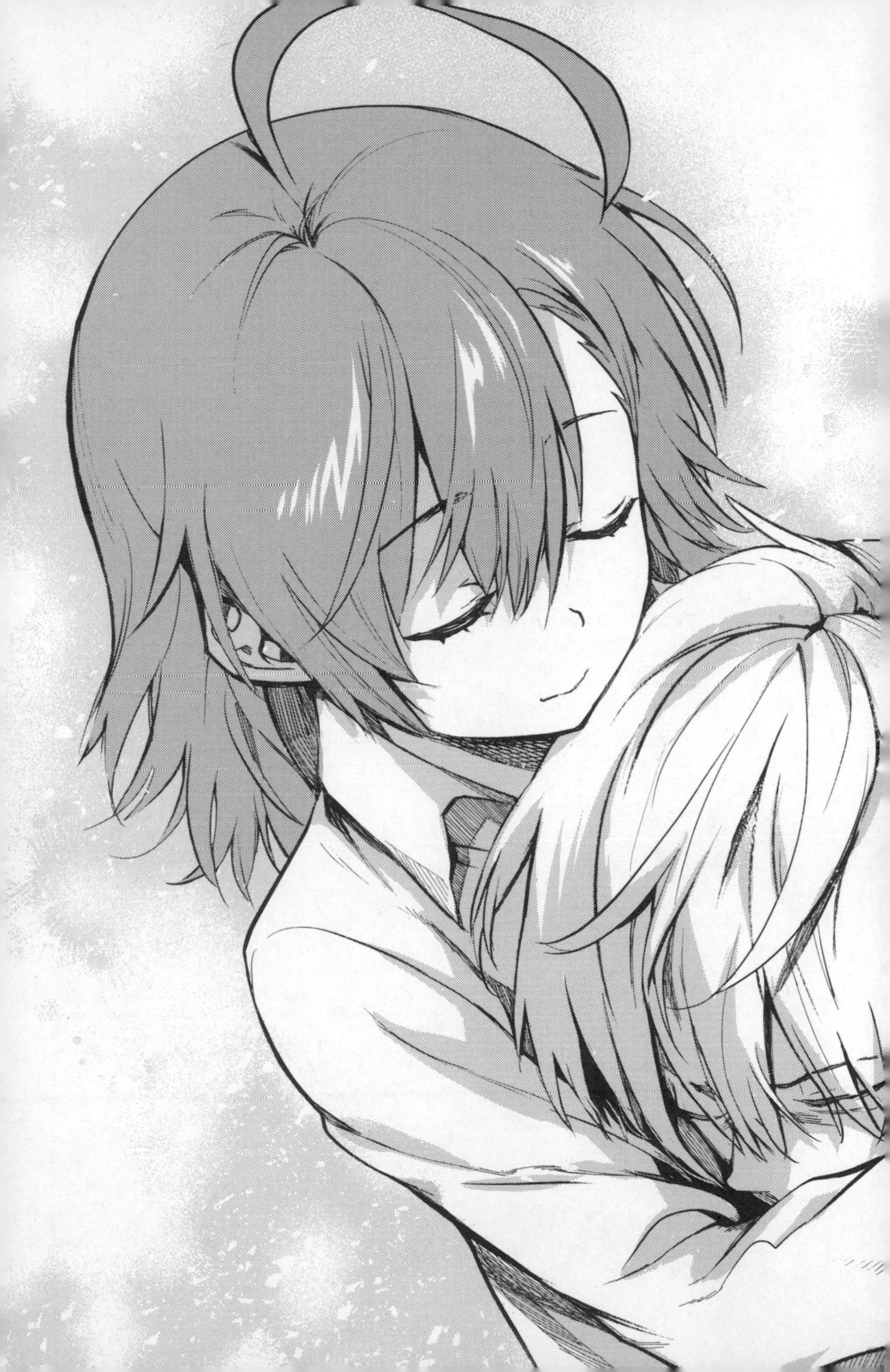

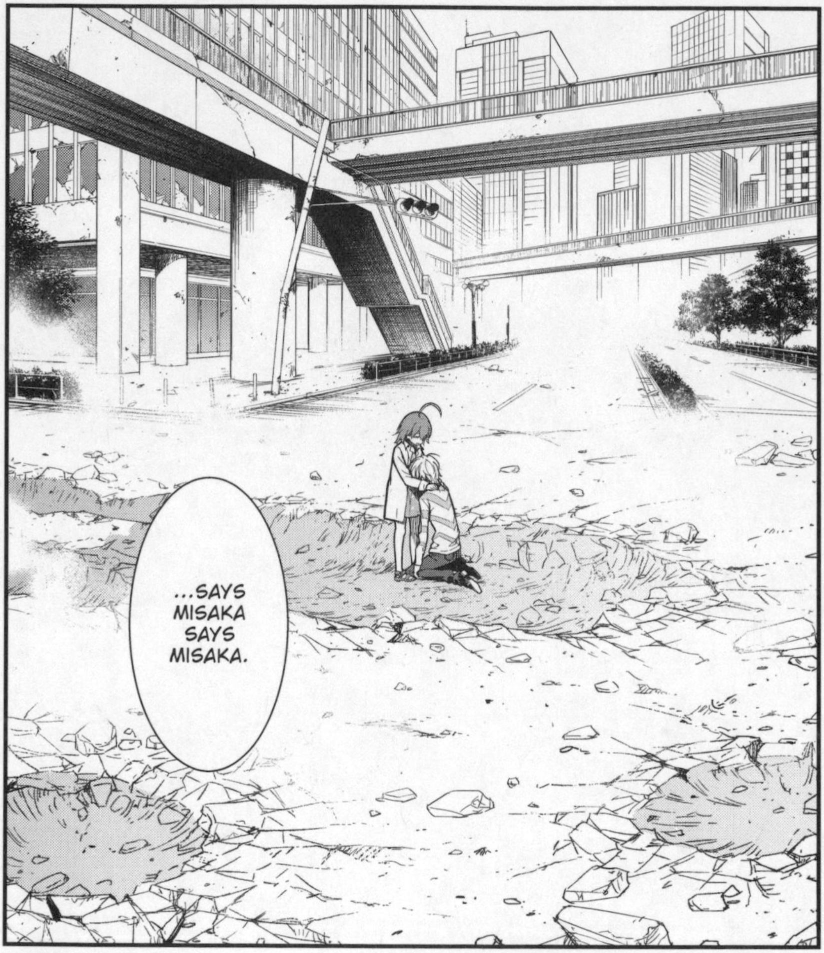
...SAYS MISAKA SAYS MISAKA.
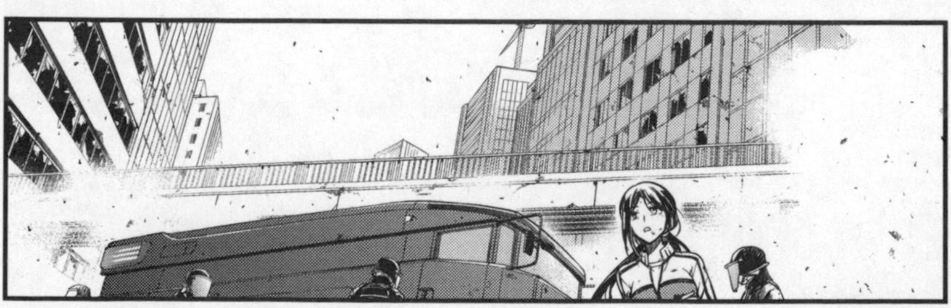

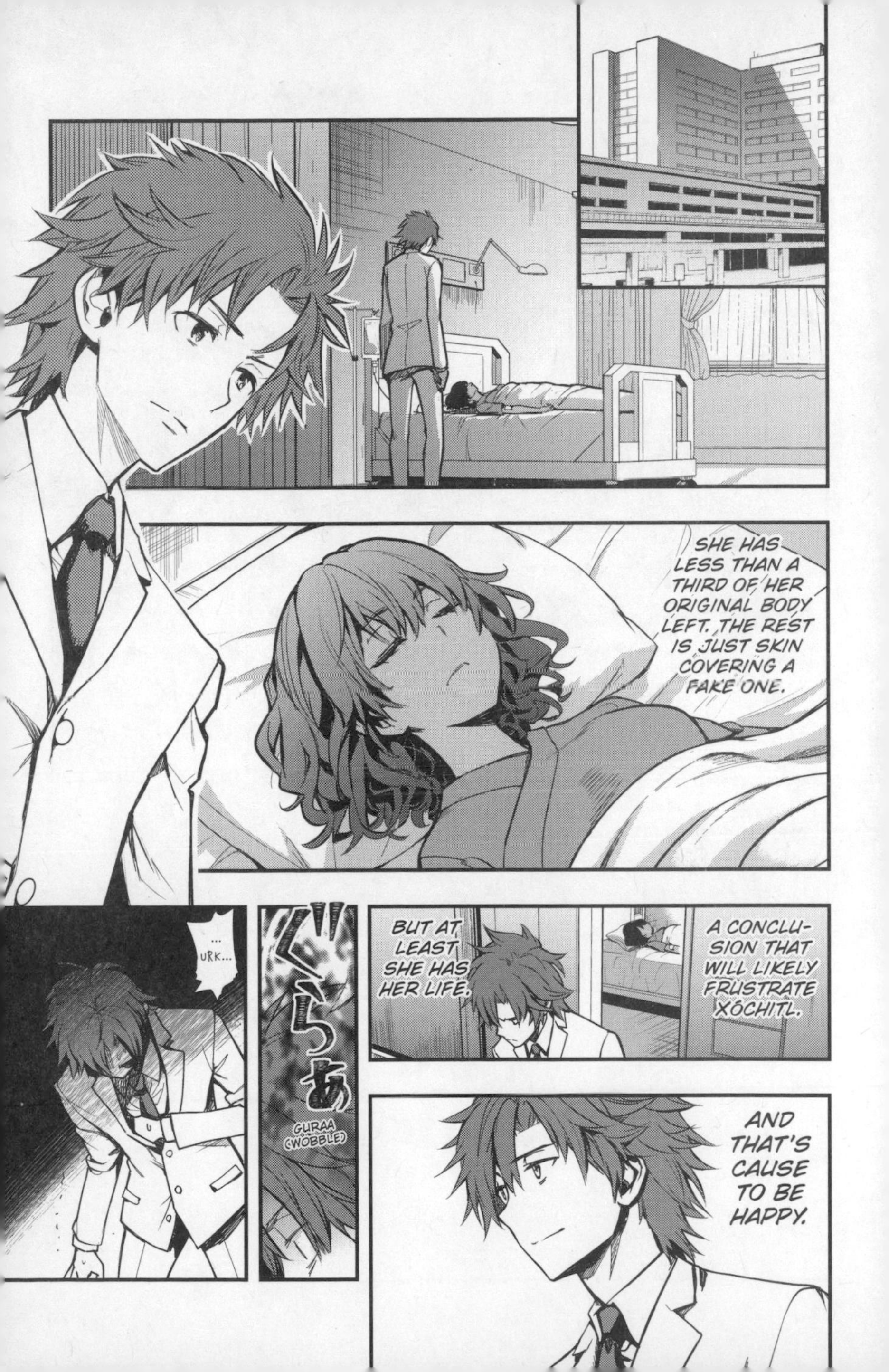

SHE HAS LESS THAN A THIRD OF HER ORIGINAL BODY LEFT. THE REST IS JUST SKIN COVERING A FAKE ONE.
A CONCLUSION THAT WILL LIKELY FRUSTRATE XOCHITL.
BUT AT LEAST SHE HAS HER LIFE.
AND THAT'S CAUSE TO BE HAPPY.
ぐらぁ
GURAA (WOBBLE)
...URK...

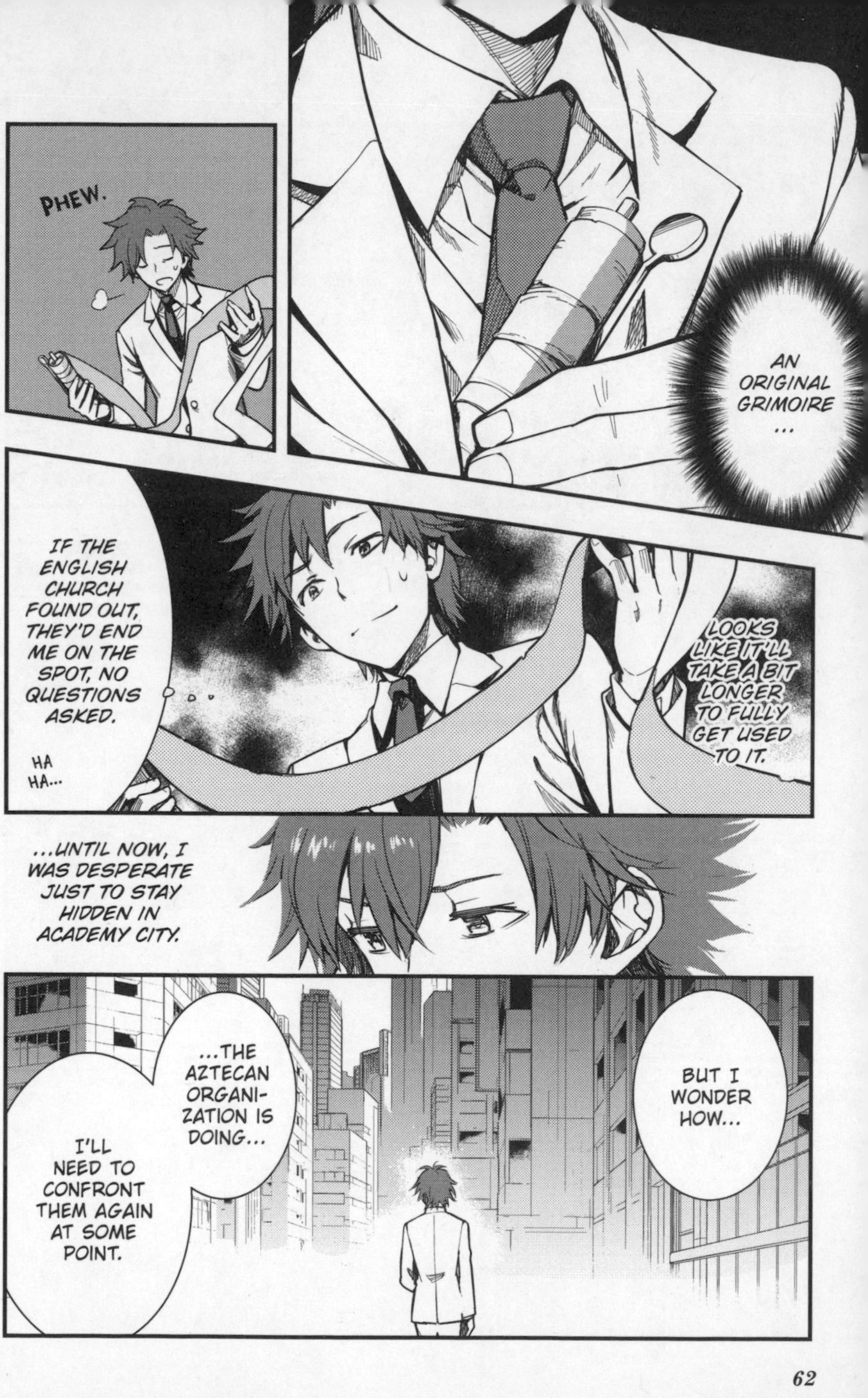
AN ORIGINAL GRIMOIRE...
PHEW.
LOOKS LIKE IT'LL TAKE A BIT LONGER TO FULLY GET USED TO IT.
IF THE ENGLISH CHURCH FOUND OUT, THEY'D END ME ON THE SPOT, NO QUESTIONS ASKED.
HA HA...
...UNTIL NOW, I WAS DESPERATE JUST TO STAY HIDDEN IN ACADEMY CITY.
BUT I WONDER HOW...
...THE AZTECAN ORGANIZATION IS DOING...
I'LL NEED TO CONFRONT THEM AGAIN AT SOME POINT.

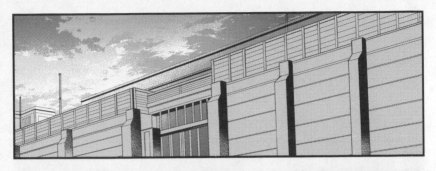

I WILL RESCUE YOU FROM THERE...

...SOME-DAY.

I PROMISE.

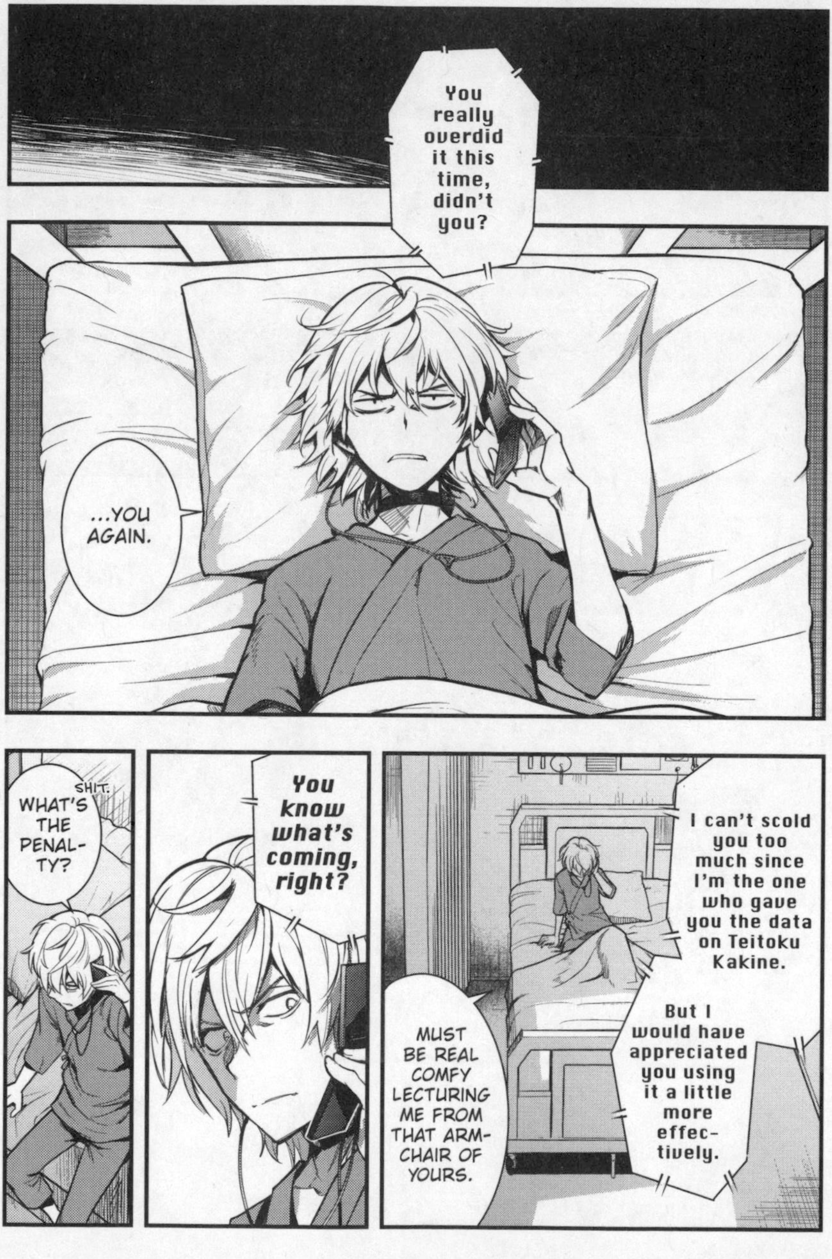
You really overdid it this time, didn't you?
...YOU AGAIN.
I can't scold you too much since I'm the one who gave you the data on Teitoku Kakine.
But I would have appreciated you using it a little more effec-tively.
MUST BE REAL COMFY LECTURING ME FROM THAT ARM-CHAIR OF YOURS.
You know what's coming, right?
SHIT.
WHAT'S THE PENAL-TY?

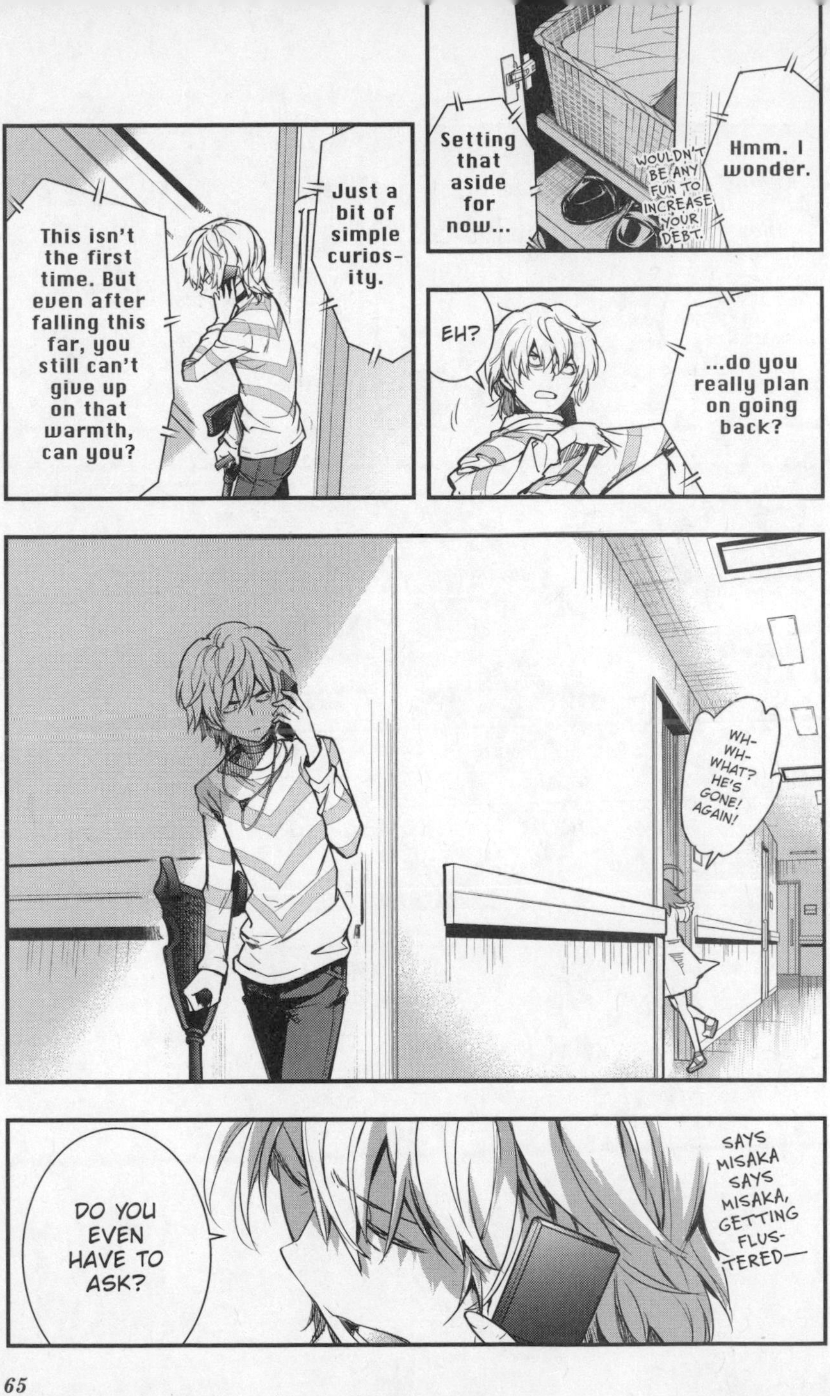

Hmm. I wonder.
WOULDN'T BE ANY FUN TO INCREASE YOUR DEBT.
Setting that aside for now...
...do you really plan on going back?
EH?
Just a bit of simple curiosity.
This isn't the first time. But even after falling this far, you still can't give up on that warmth, can you?
WH-WH-WHAT? HE'S GONE! AGAIN!
SAYS MISAKA SAYS MISAKA, GETTING FLUSTERED—
DO YOU EVEN HAVE TO ASK?

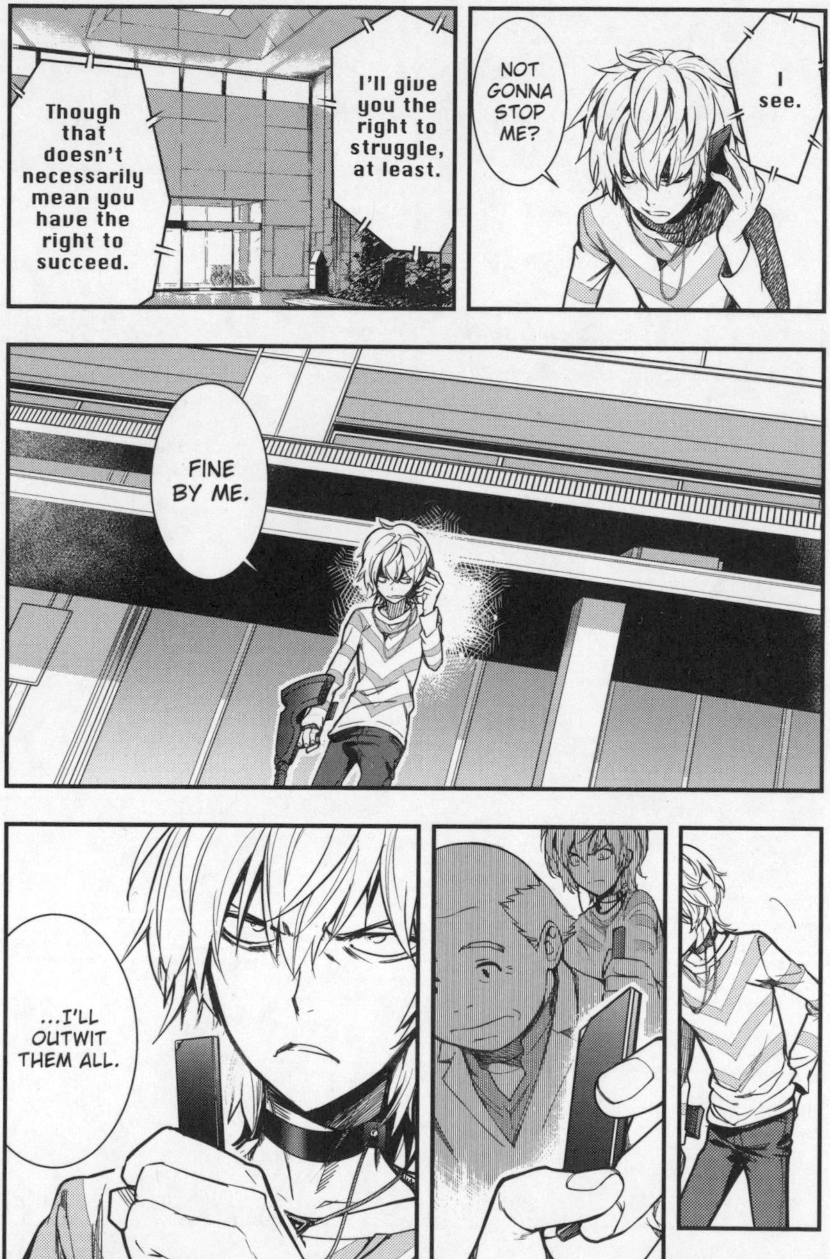
I see.
NOT GONNA STOP ME?
I'll give you the right to struggle, at least.
Though that doesn't necessarily mean you have the right to succeed.
FINE BY ME.
...I'LL OUTWIT THEM ALL.

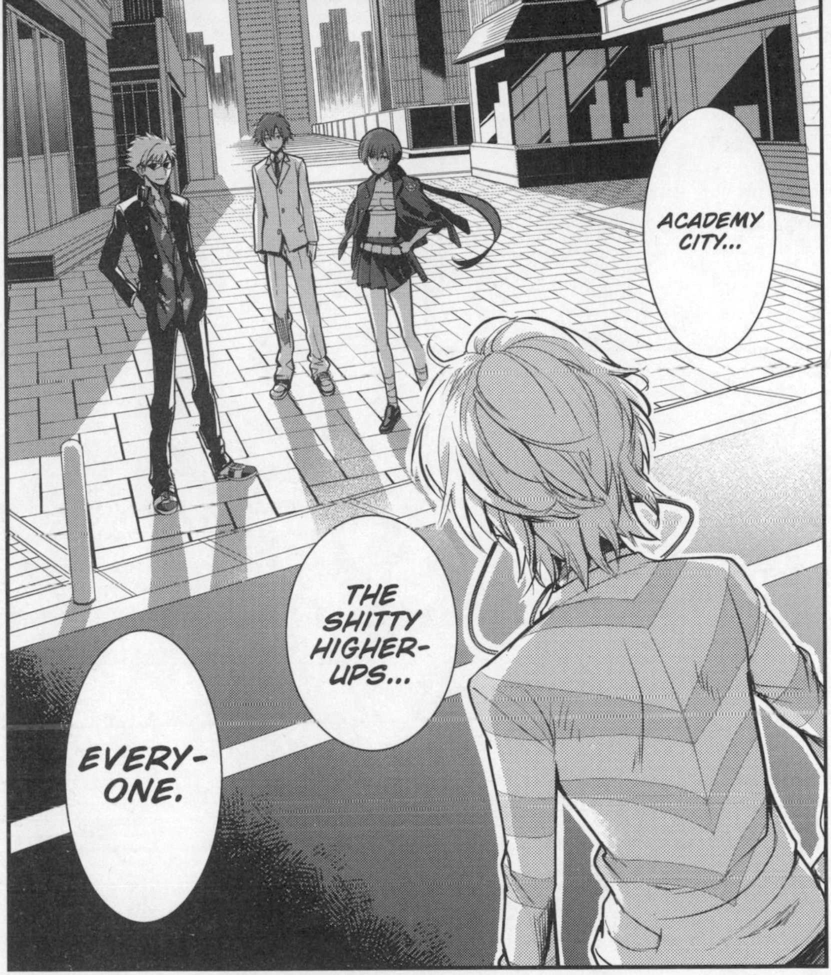
ACADEMY CITY...
THE SHITTY HIGHER-UPS...
EVERY-ONE.

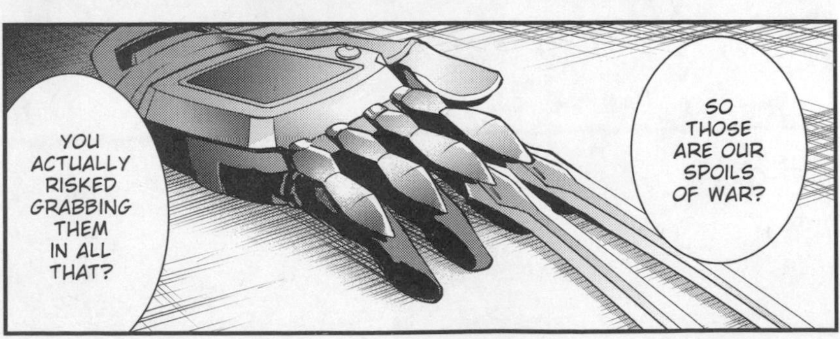
SO THOSE ARE OUR SPOILS OF WAR?
YOU ACTUALLY RISKED GRABBING THEM IN ALL THAT?

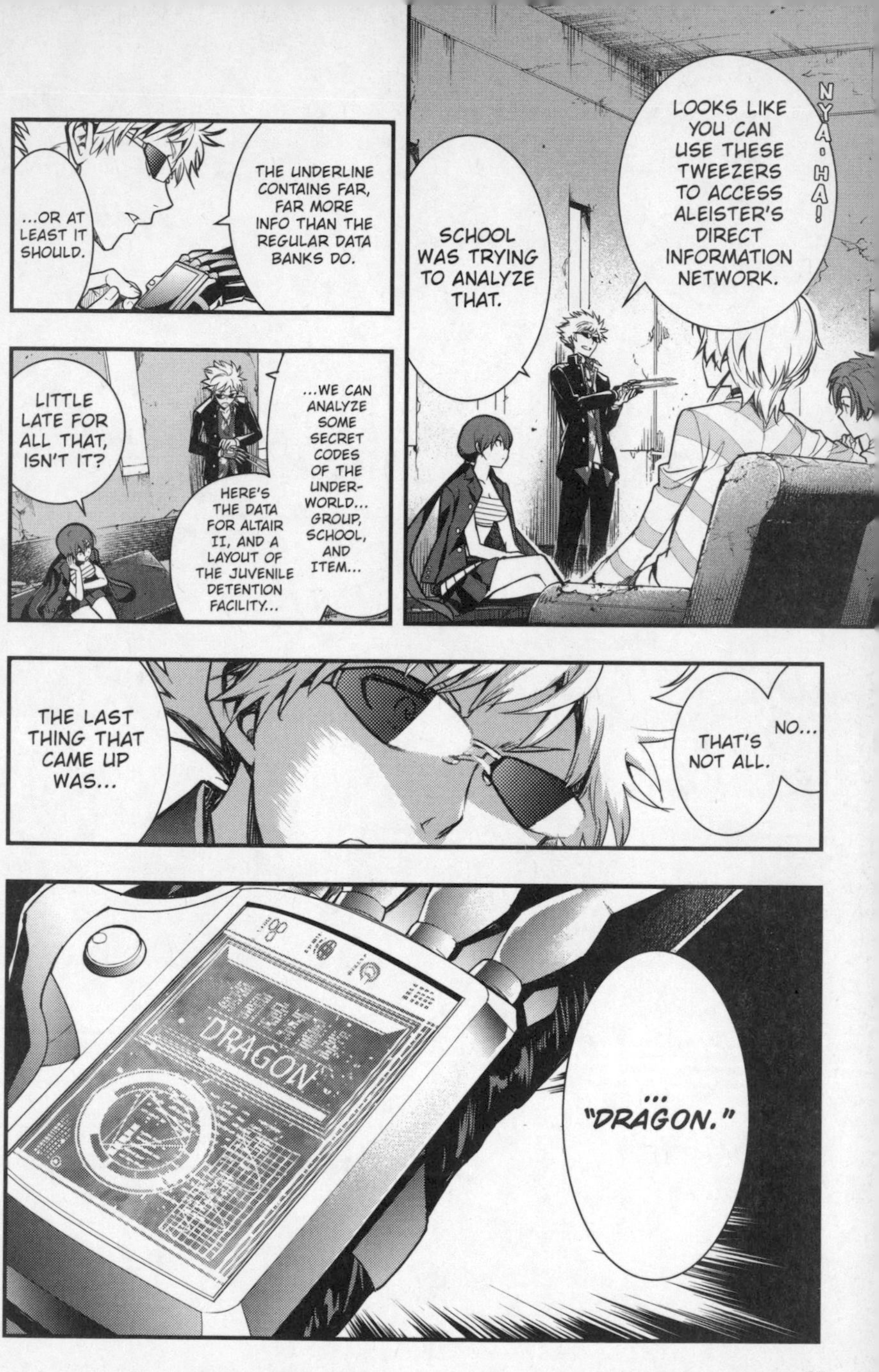
NYA-HA!
LOOKS LIKE YOU CAN USE THESE TWEEZERS TO ACCESS ALEISTER'S DIRECT INFORMATION NETWORK.
SCHOOL WAS TRYING TO ANALYZE THAT.
THE UNDERLINE CONTAINS FAR, FAR MORE INFO THAN THE REGULAR DATA BANKS DO.
...OR AT LEAST IT SHOULD.
...WE CAN ANALYZE SOME SECRET CODES OF THE UNDER-WORLD... GROUP, SCHOOL, AND ITEM...
HERE'S THE DATA FOR ALTAIR II, AND A LAYOUT OF THE JUVENILE DETENTION FACILITY...
LITTLE LATE FOR ALL THAT, ISN'T IT?
NO...
THAT'S NOT ALL.
THE LAST THING THAT CAME UP WAS...
DRAGON
..."DRAGON."

A Certain Magical Index

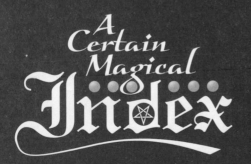

A Certain Magical Index

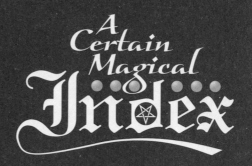

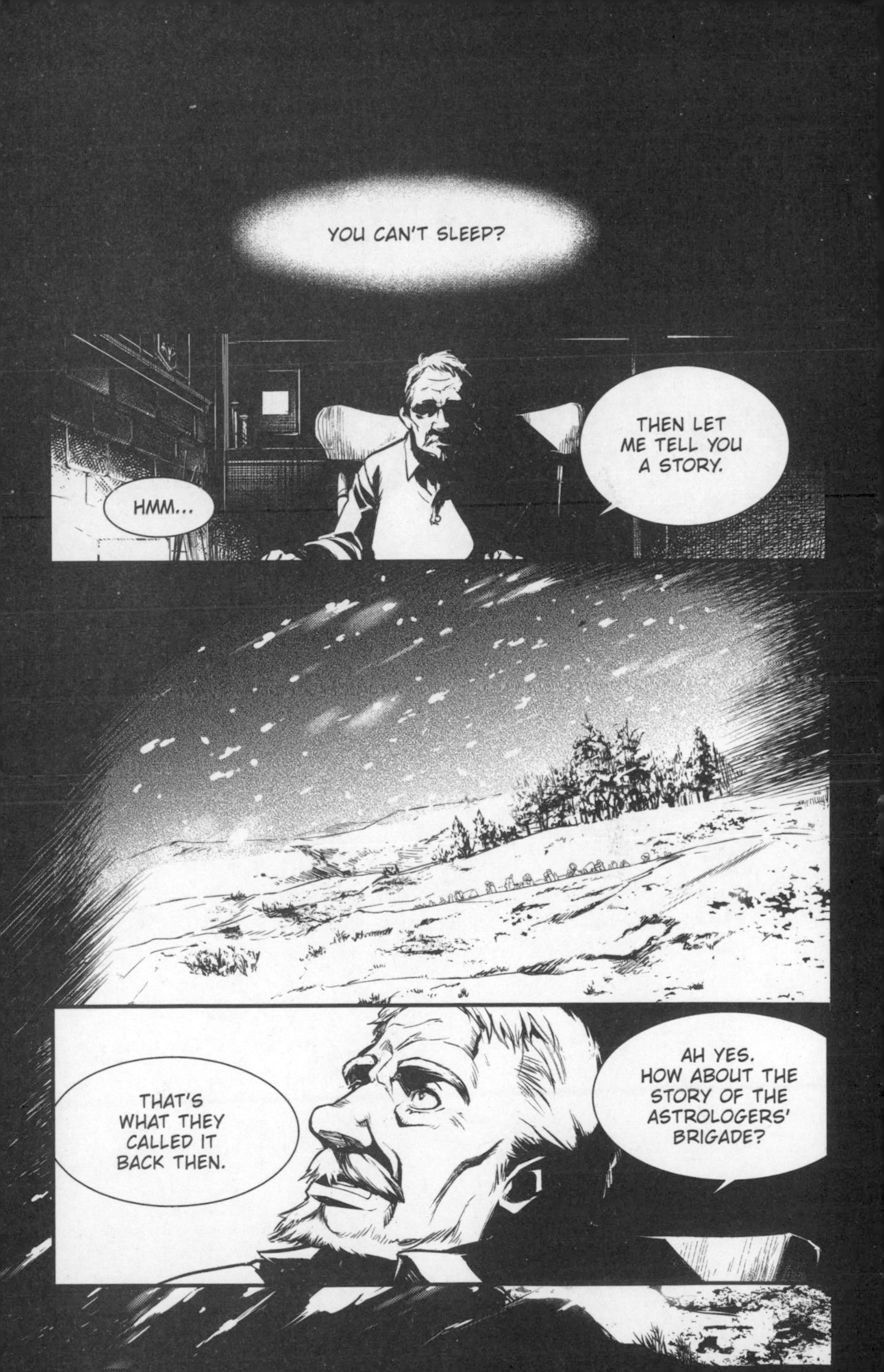
YOU CAN'T SLEEP?
HMM...
THEN LET ME TELL YOU A STORY.
AH YES. HOW ABOUT THE STORY OF THE ASTROLOGERS' BRIGADE?
THAT'S WHAT THEY CALLED IT BACK THEN.

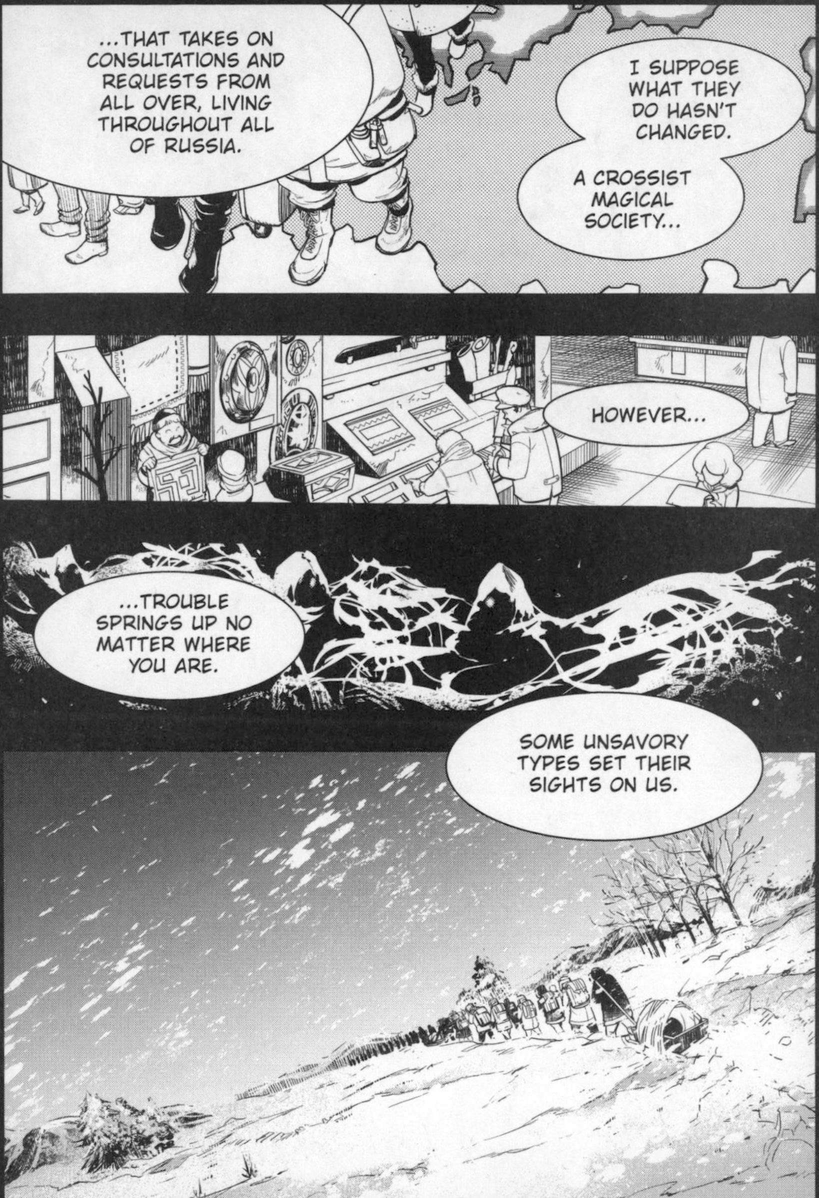
I SUPPOSE WHAT THEY DO HASN'T CHANGED.
A CROSSIST MAGICAL SOCIETY...
...THAT TAKES ON CONSULTATIONS AND REQUESTS FROM ALL OVER, LIVING THROUGHOUT ALL OF RUSSIA.
HOWEVER...
...TROUBLE SPRINGS UP NO MATTER WHERE YOU ARE.
SOME UNSAVORY TYPES SET THEIR SIGHTS ON US.

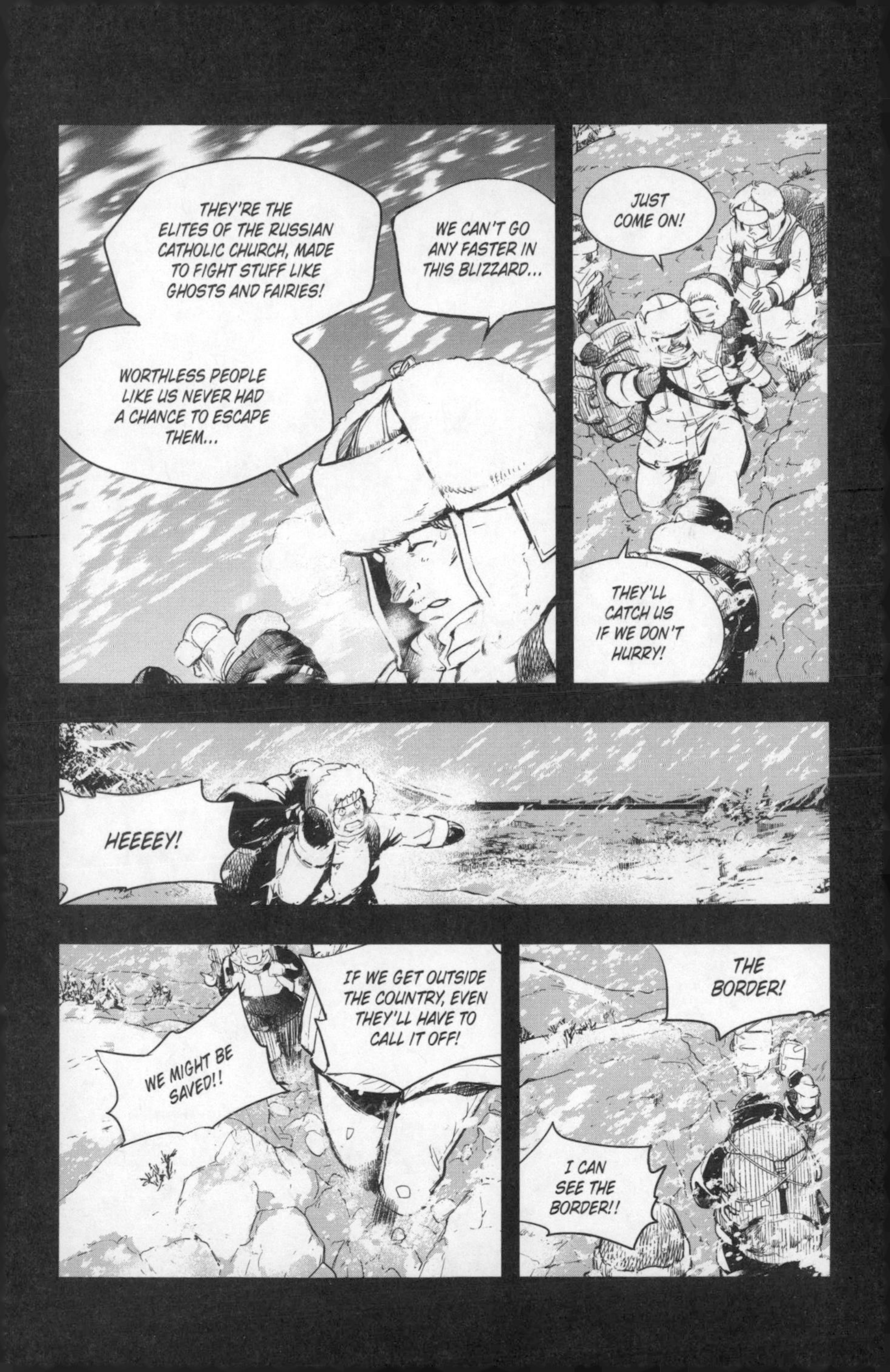
JUST COME ON!
THEY'LL CATCH US IF WE DON'T HURRY!
WE CAN'T GO ANY FASTER IN THIS BLIZZARD...
THEY'RE THE ELITES OF THE RUSSIAN CATHOLIC CHURCH, MADE TO FIGHT STUFF LIKE GHOSTS AND FAIRIES!
WORTHLESS PEOPLE LIKE US NEVER HAD A CHANCE TO ESCAPE THEM...
HEEEEY!
THE BORDER!
I CAN SEE THE BORDER!!
IF WE GET OUTSIDE THE COUNTRY, EVEN THEY'LL HAVE TO CALL IT OFF!
WE MIGHT BE SAVED!!

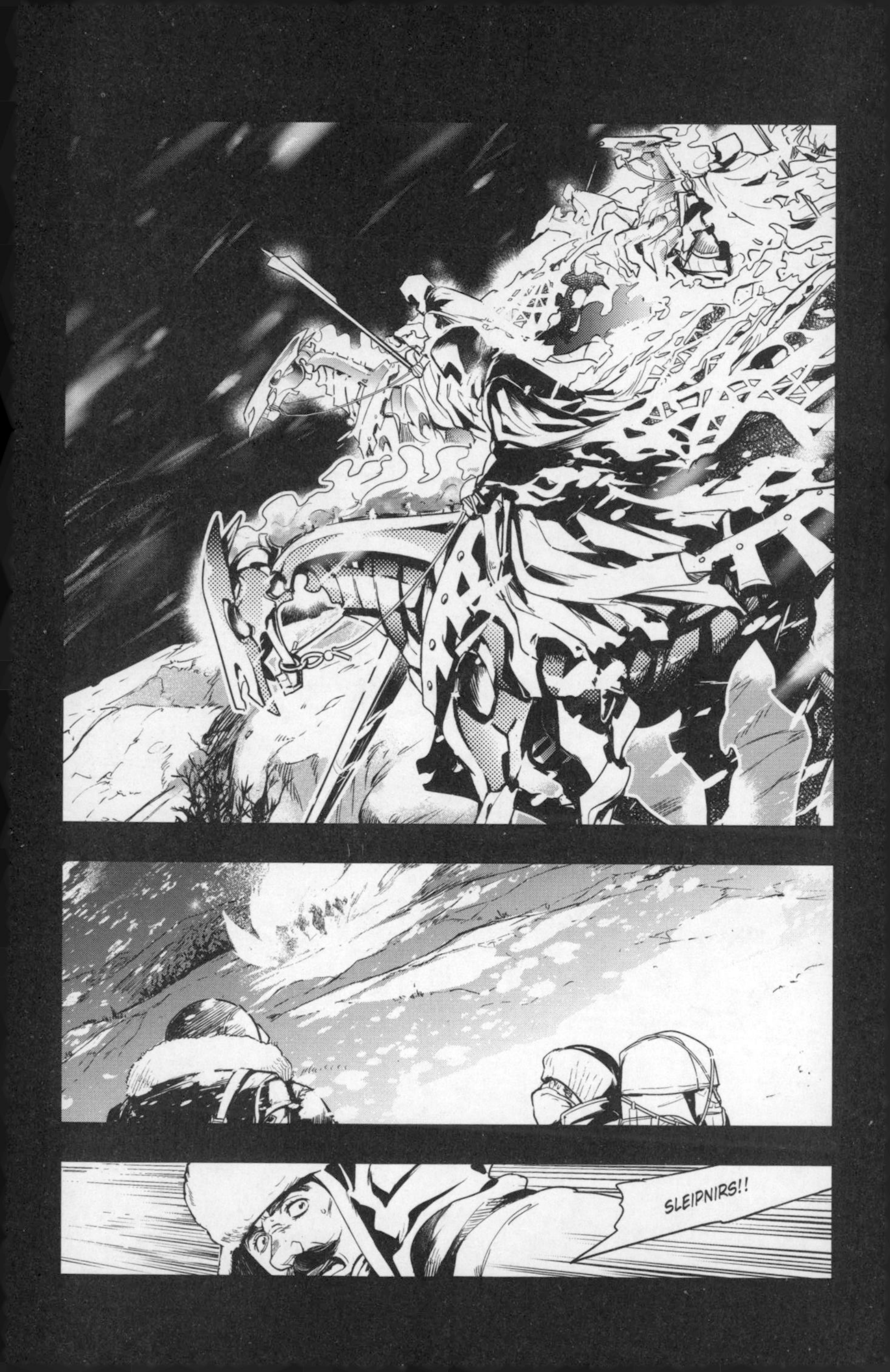
SLEIPNIRS!!

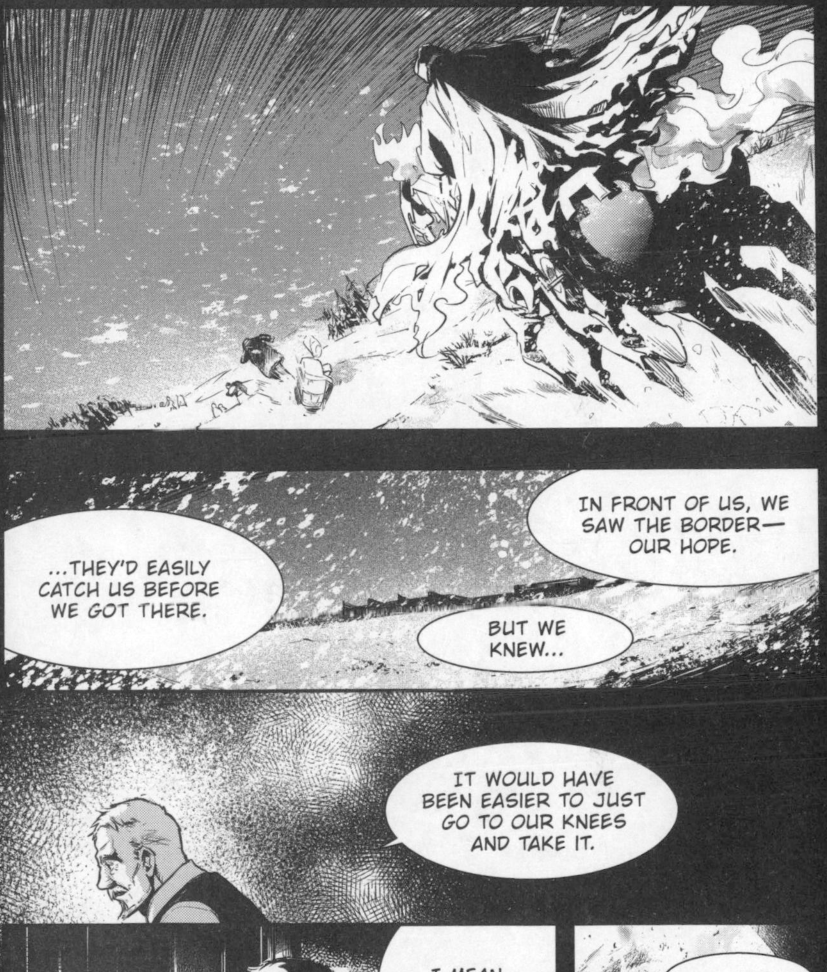
IN FRONT OF US, WE SAW THE BORDER—OUR HOPE.
BUT WE KNEW...
...THEY'D EASILY CATCH US BEFORE WE GOT THERE.
IT WOULD HAVE BEEN EASIER TO JUST GO TO OUR KNEES AND TAKE IT.
...HM?
WHAT HAPPENED AFTER THAT?
I MEAN, WE MANAGED TO FLEE!
IF NOT, YOUR OLD GRANDPA WOULDN'T BE HERE, WOULD HE?

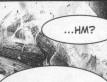

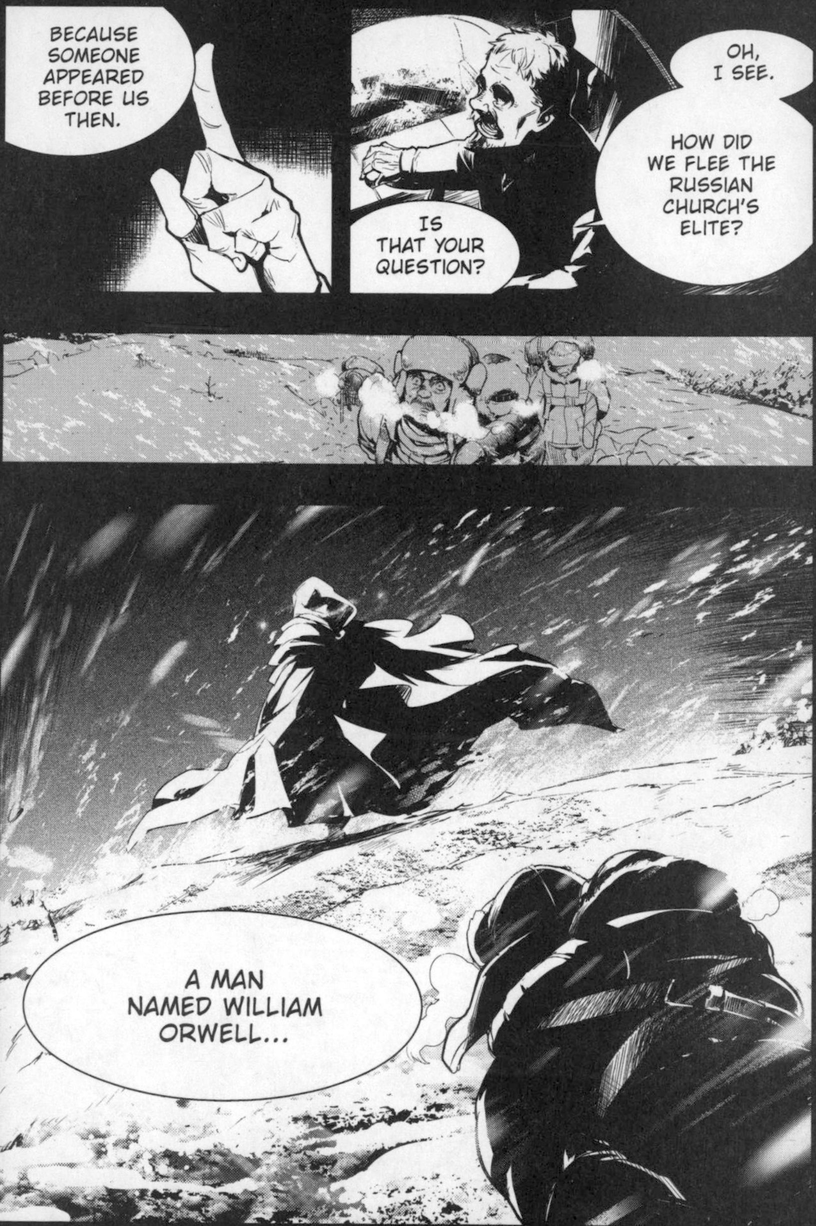
OH, I SEE.
HOW DID WE FLEE THE RUSSIAN CHURCH'S ELITE?
IS THAT YOUR QUESTION?
BECAUSE SOMEONE APPEARED BEFORE US THEN.
A MAN NAMED WILLIAM ORWELL...

#150 DECLARATION

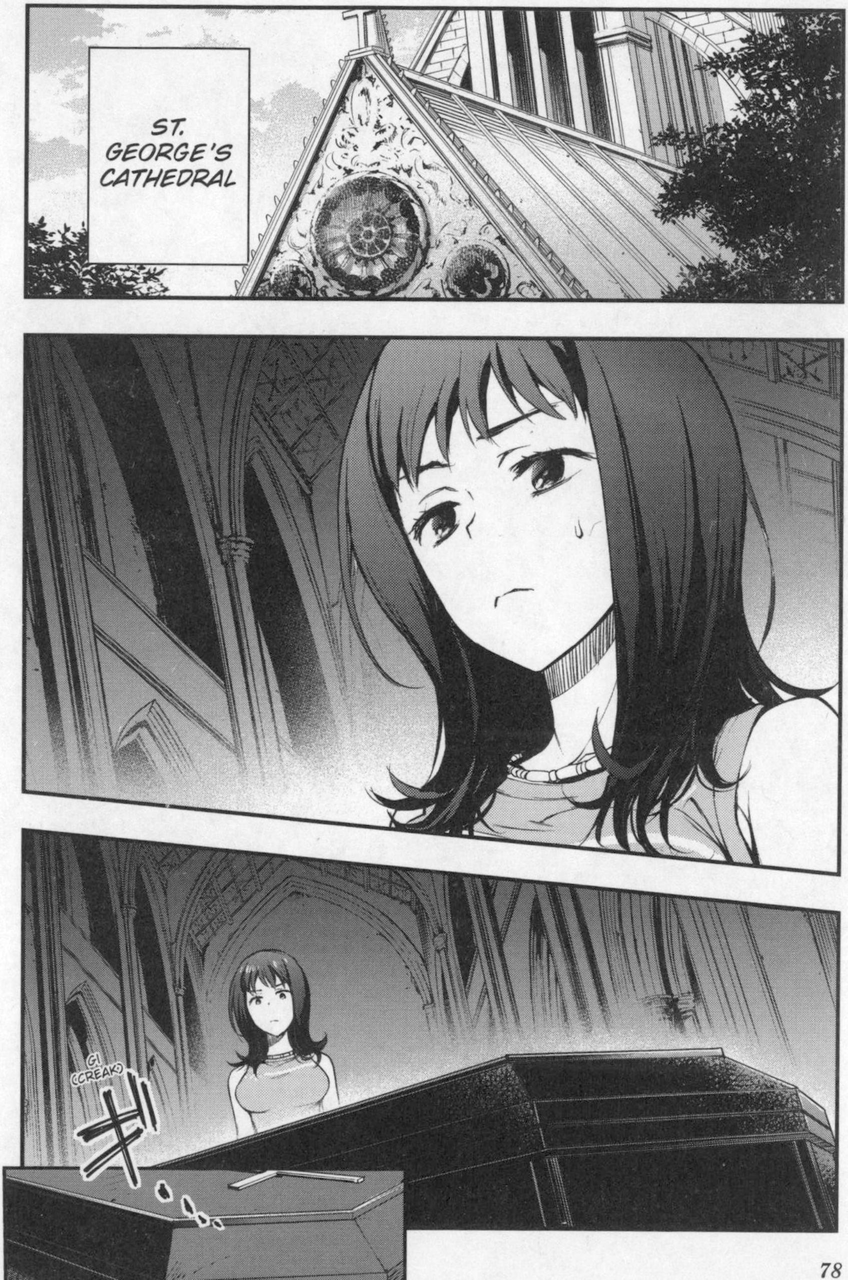
ST. GEORGE'S CATHEDRAL
GI (CREAK)

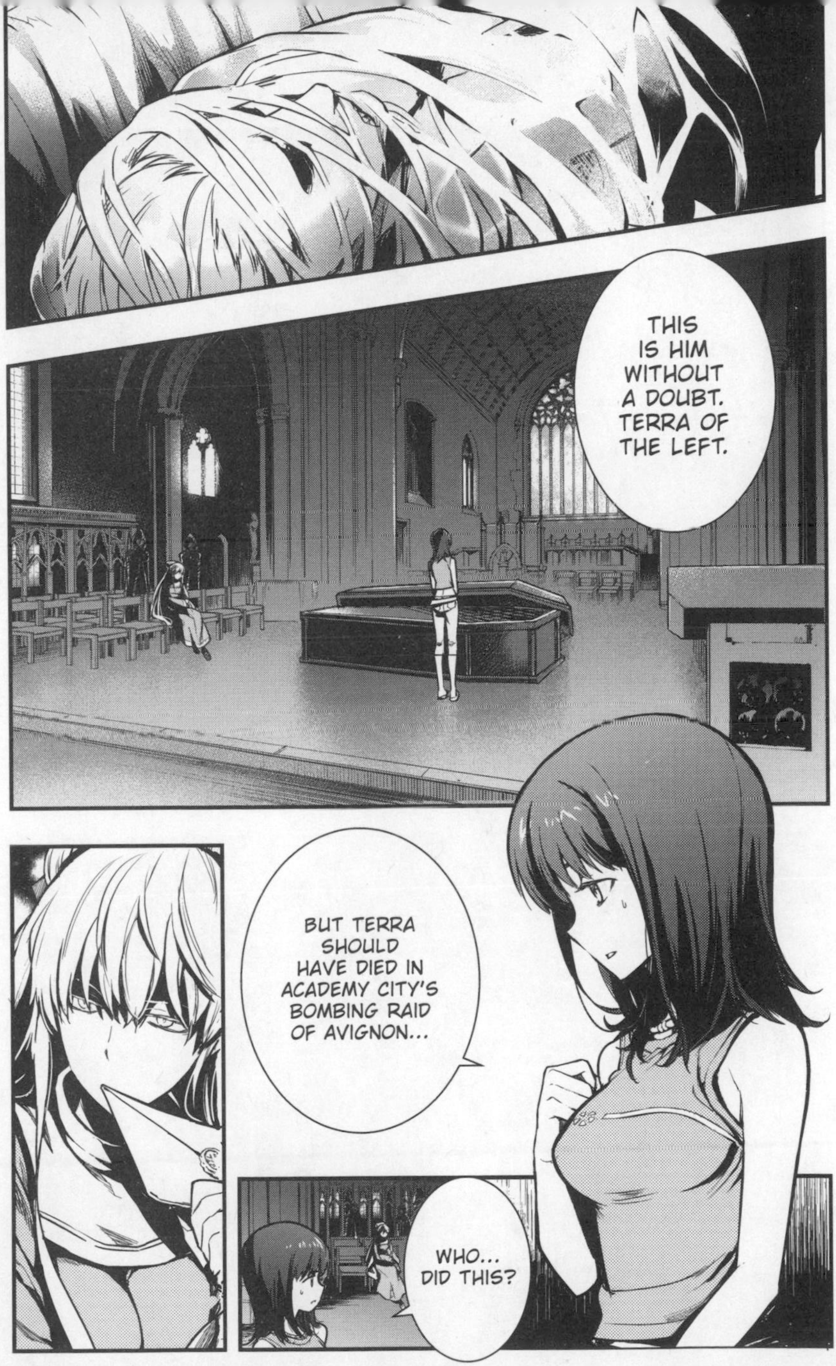
THIS IS HIM WITHOUT A DOUBT. TERRA OF THE LEFT.
BUT TERRA SHOULD HAVE DIED IN ACADEMY CITY'S BOMBING RAID OF AVIGNON...
WHO... DID THIS?

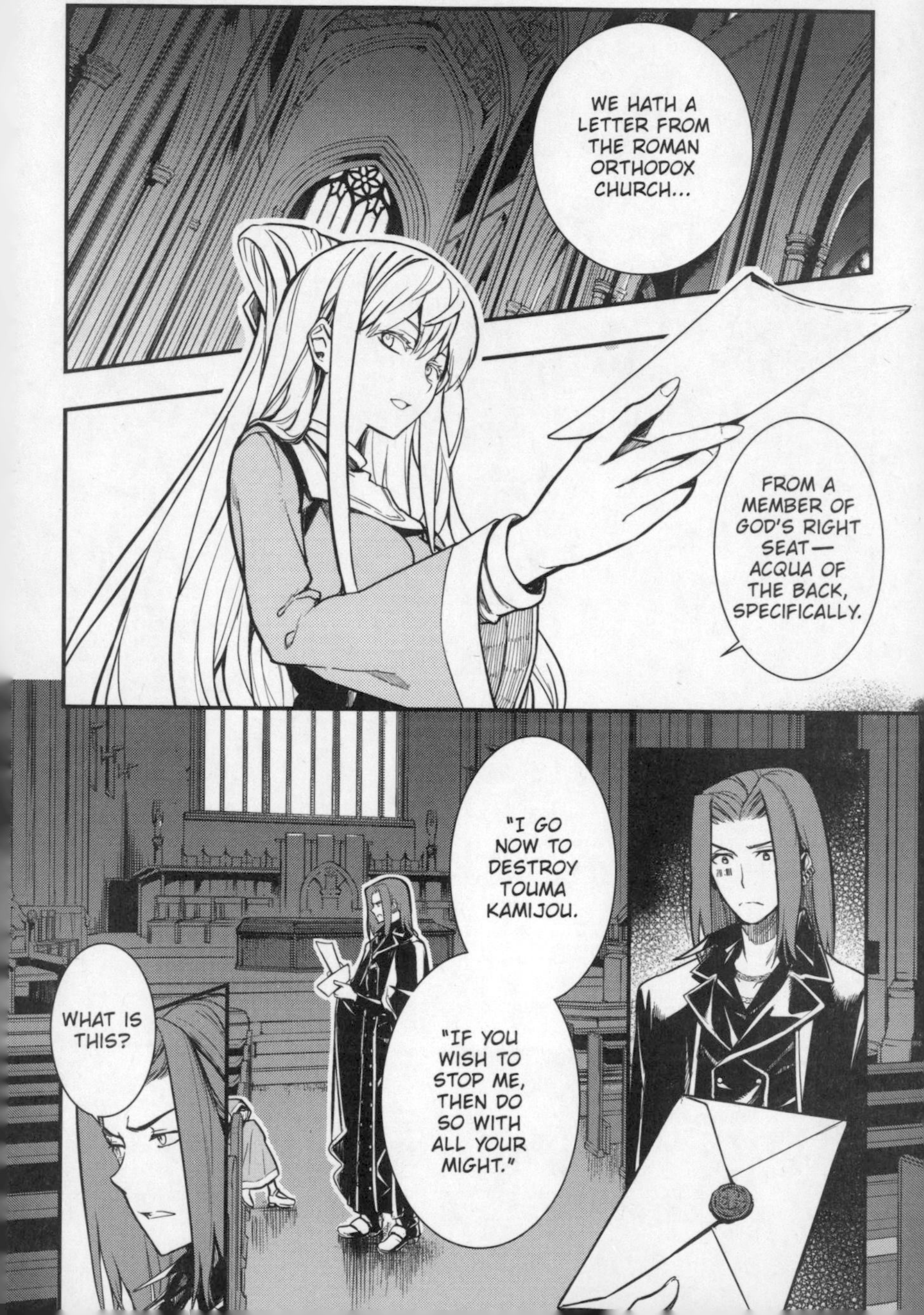
WE HATH A LETTER FROM THE ROMAN ORTHODOX CHURCH...
FROM A MEMBER OF GOD'S RIGHT SEAT—ACQUA OF THE BACK, SPECIFICALLY.
"I GO NOW TO DESTROY TOUMA KAMIJOU.
"IF YOU WISH TO STOP ME, THEN DO SO WITH ALL YOUR MIGHT."
WHAT IS THIS?

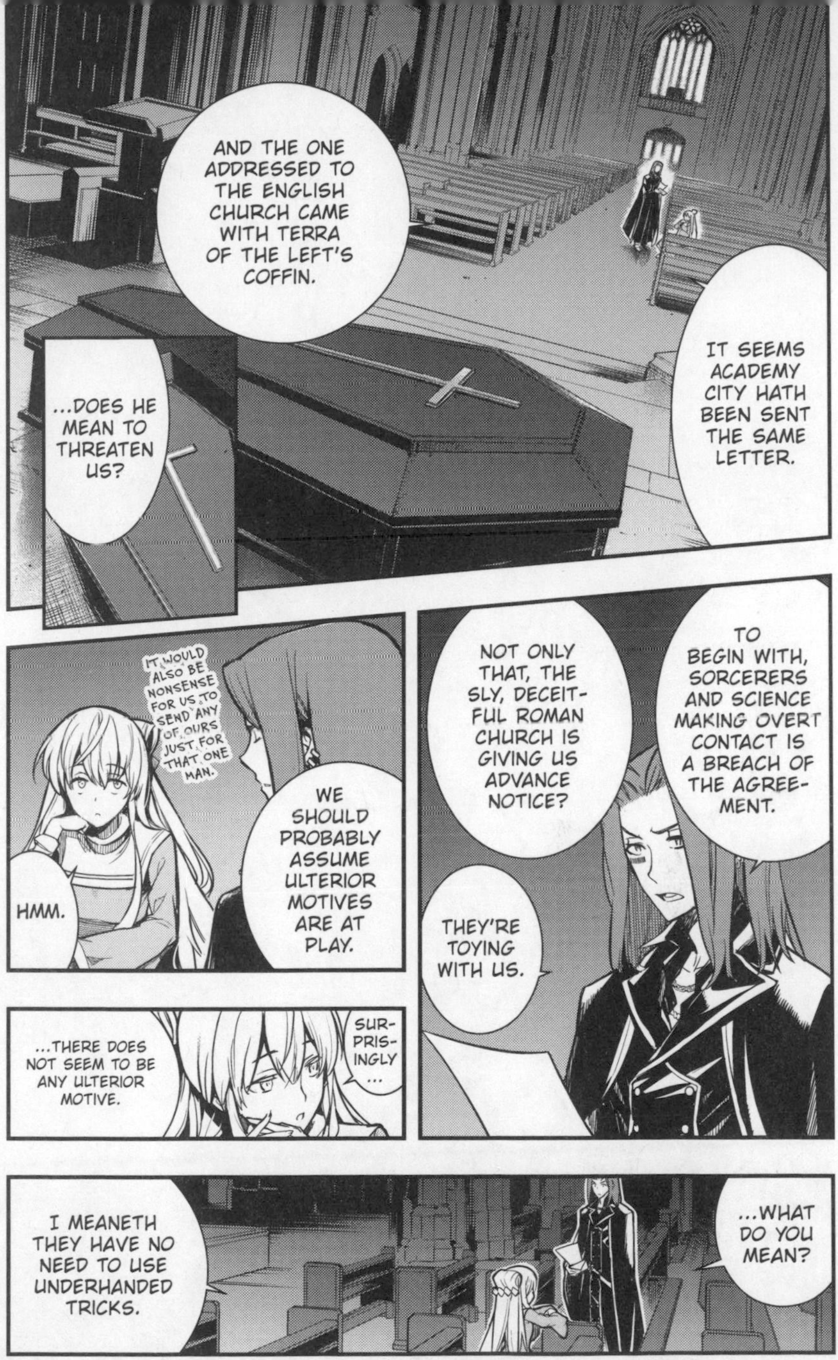
AND THE ONE ADDRESSED TO THE ENGLISH CHURCH CAME WITH TERRA OF THE LEFT'S COFFIN.
IT SEEMS ACADEMY CITY HATH BEEN SENT THE SAME LETTER.
...DOES HE MEAN TO THREATEN US?
TO BEGIN WITH, SORCERERS AND SCIENCE MAKING OVERT CONTACT IS A BREACH OF THE AGREEMENT.
NOT ONLY THAT, THE SLY, DECEITFUL ROMAN CHURCH IS GIVING US ADVANCE NOTICE?
THEY'RE TOYING WITH US.
IT WOULD ALSO BE NONSENSE FOR US TO SEND ANY OF OURS JUST FOR THAT ONE MAN.
WE SHOULD PROBABLY ASSUME ULTERIOR MOTIVES ARE AT PLAY.
HMM.
SURPRISINGLY...
...THERE DOES NOT SEEM TO BE ANY ULTERIOR MOTIVE.
...WHAT DO YOU MEAN?
I MEANETH THEY HAVE NO NEED TO USE UNDERHANDED TRICKS.

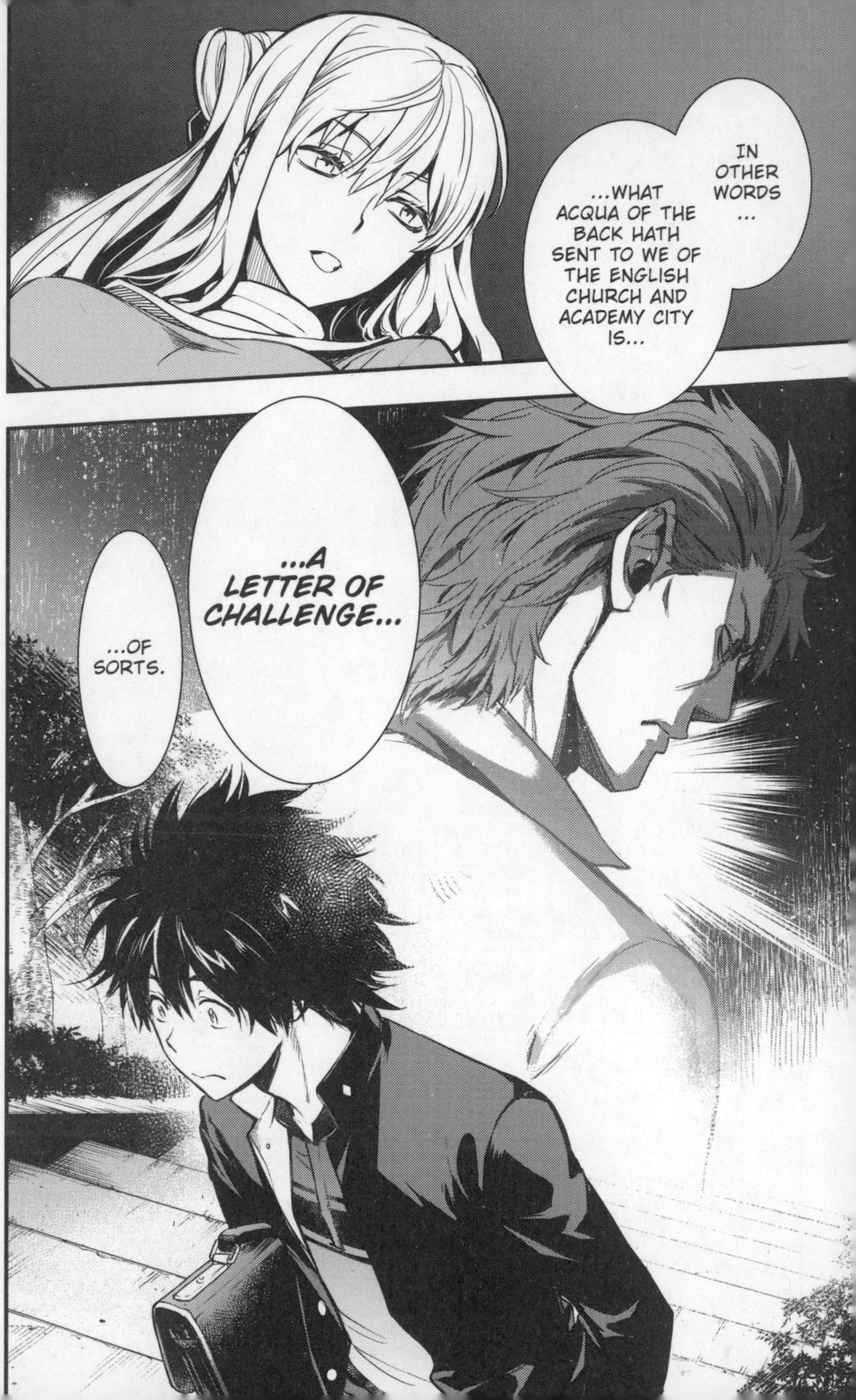
IN OTHER WORDS ...
...WHAT ACQUA OF THE BACK HATH SENT TO WE OF THE ENGLISH CHURCH AND ACADEMY CITY IS...
...A LETTER OF CHALLENGE...
...OF SORTS.

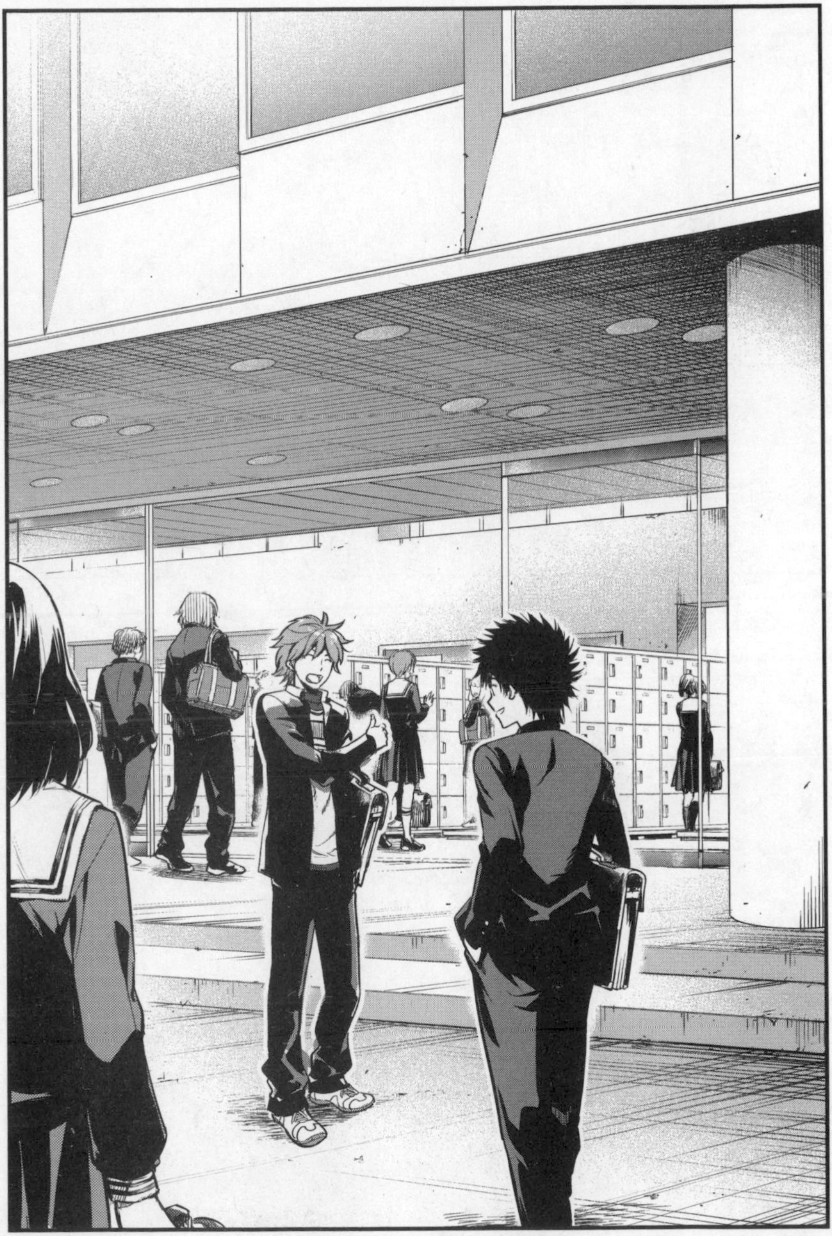

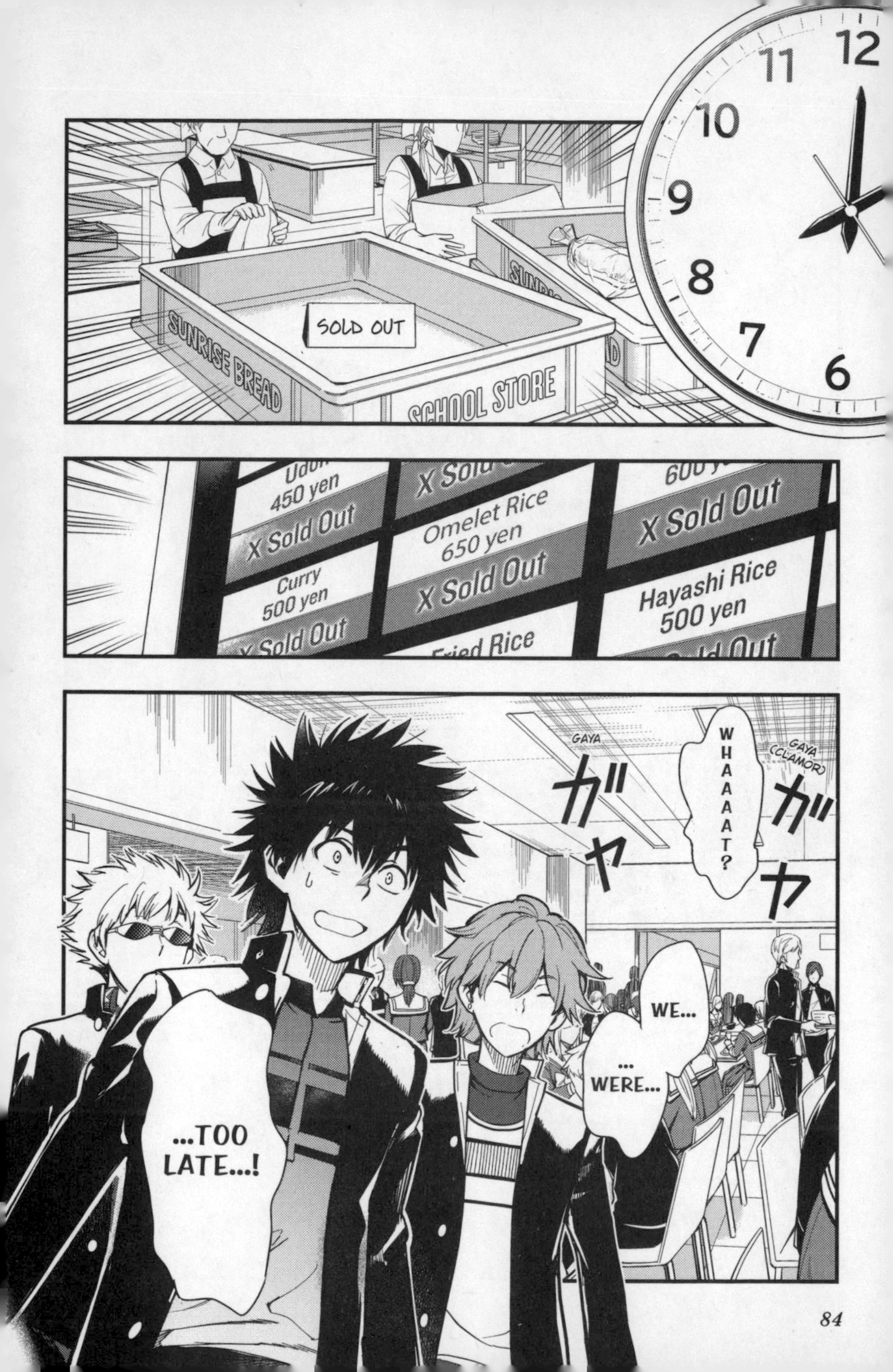
SOLD OUT
SUNRISE BREAD
SCHOOL STORE
Udon
450 yen
X Sold Out
Omelet Rice
650 yen
X Sold Out
Curry
500 yen
X Sold Out
Hayashi Rice
500 yen
Fried Rice
GAYA (CLAMOR)
ガヤ
WHAAAAAT?
GAYA
ガヤ
WE...
...WERE...
...TOO LATE...!

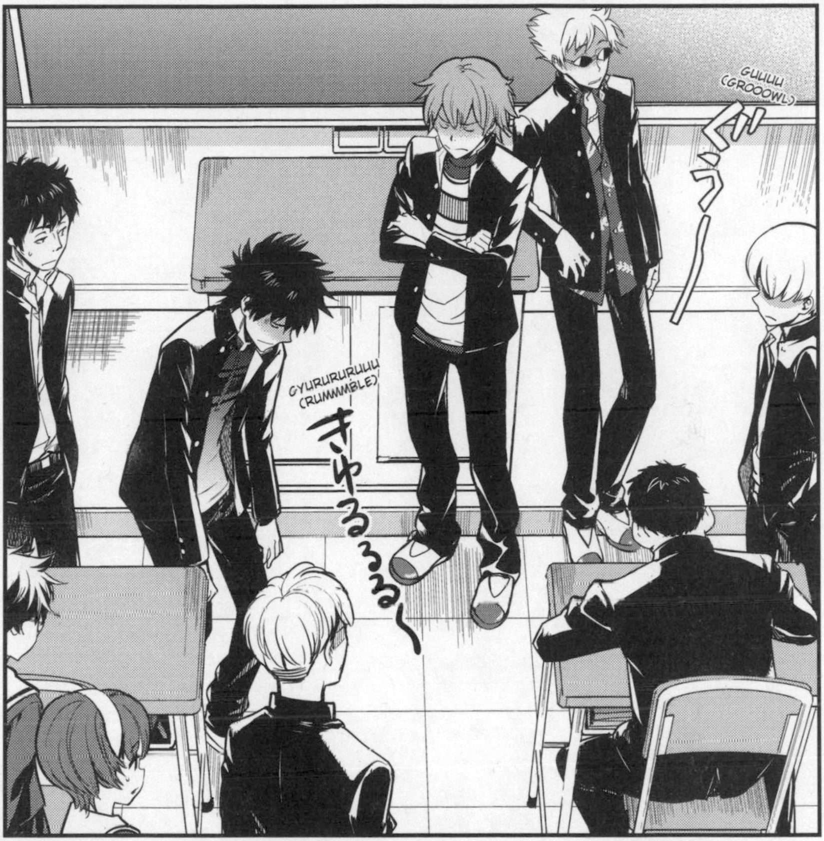
GUUUU (GROOOWL)
ぐう〜
GYURURURUUU (RUMMMBLE)
きゅるるる〜
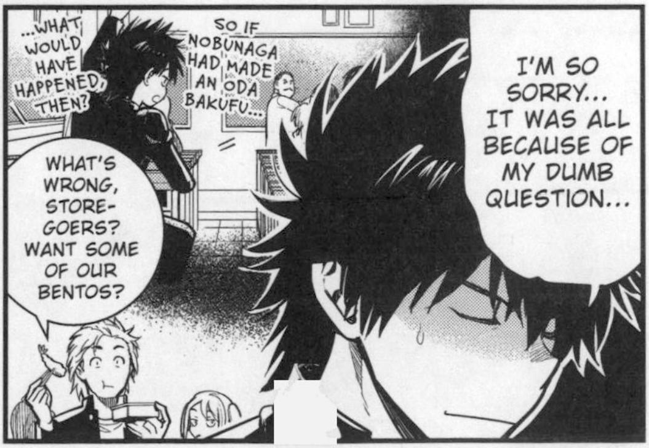
I'M SO SORRY... IT WAS ALL BECAUSE OF MY DUMB QUESTION...
SO IF NOBUNAGA HAD MADE AN ODA BAKUFU...
...WHAT WOULD HAVE HAPPENED, THEN?
WHAT'S WRONG, STORE-GOERS? WANT SOME OF OUR BENTOS?
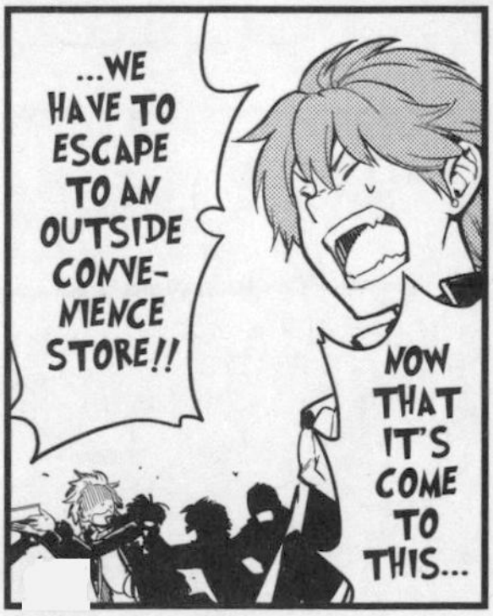
NOW THAT IT'S COME TO THIS...
...WE HAVE TO ESCAPE TO AN OUTSIDE CONVE-NIENCE STORE!!

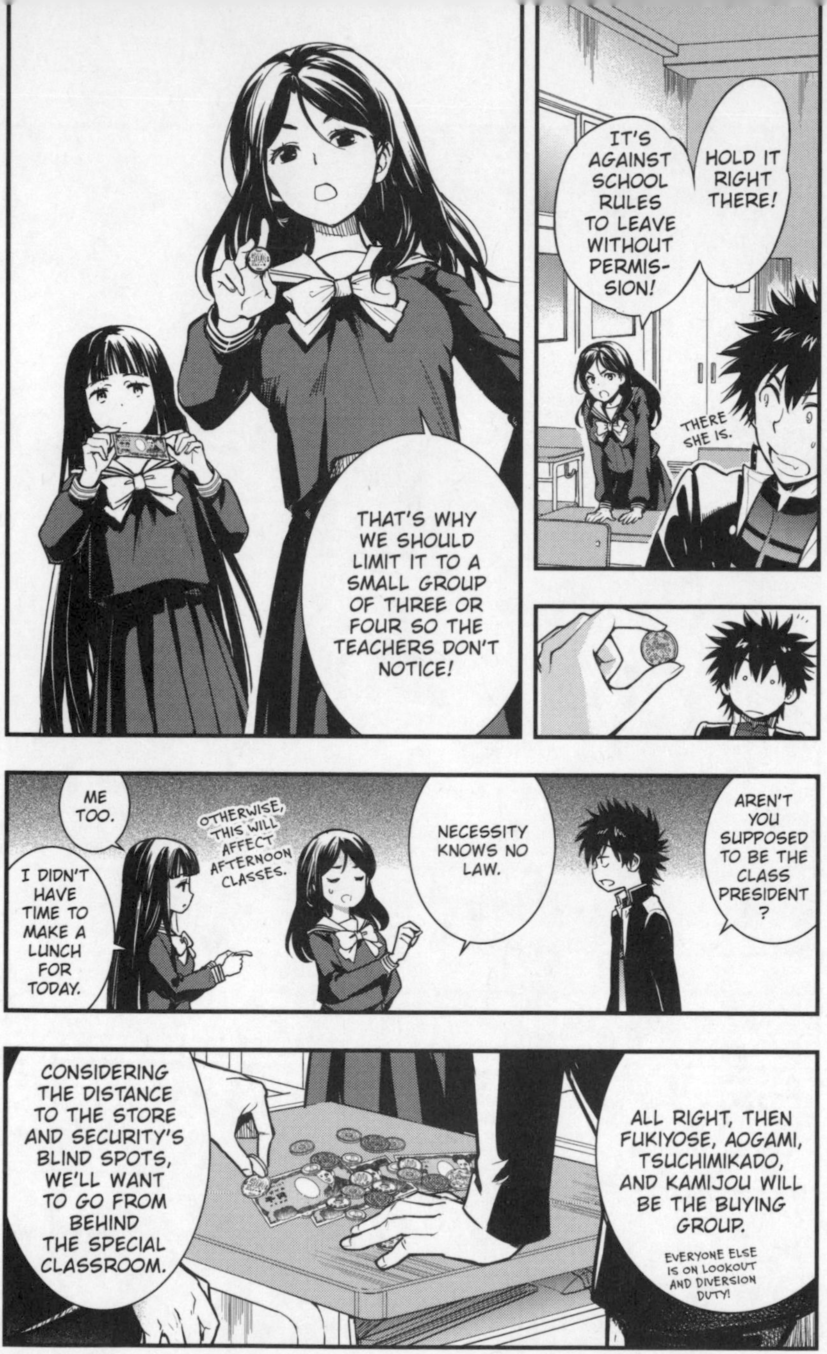
HOLD IT RIGHT THERE!
IT'S AGAINST SCHOOL RULES TO LEAVE WITHOUT PERMISSION!
THERE SHE IS.
THAT'S WHY WE SHOULD LIMIT IT TO A SMALL GROUP OF THREE OR FOUR SO THE TEACHERS DON'T NOTICE!
AREN'T YOU SUPPOSED TO BE THE CLASS PRESIDENT?
NECESSITY KNOWS NO LAW.
OTHERWISE, THIS WILL AFFECT AFTERNOON CLASSES.
ME TOO.
I DIDN'T HAVE TIME TO MAKE A LUNCH FOR TODAY.
ALL RIGHT, THEN FUKIYOSE, AOGAMI, TSUCHIMIKADO, AND KAMIJOU WILL BE THE BUYING GROUP.
EVERYONE ELSE IS ON LOOKOUT AND DIVERSION DUTY!
CONSIDERING THE DISTANCE TO THE STORE AND SECURITY'S BLIND SPOTS, WE'LL WANT TO GO FROM BEHIND THE SPECIAL CLASSROOM.

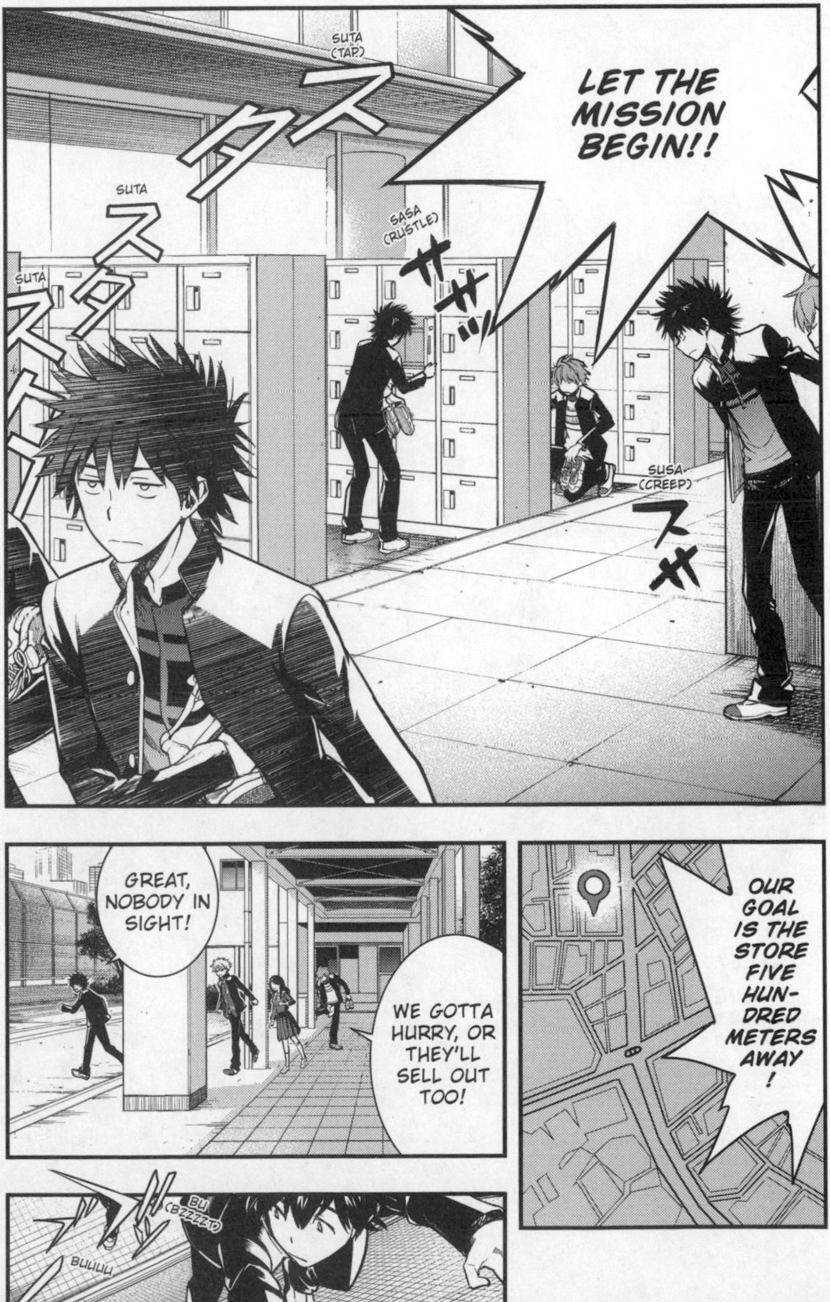
LET THE MISSION BEGIN!!
SUTA (TAP)
SASA (RUSTLE)
SUTA
SUTA
SUSA (CREEP)
OUR GOAL IS THE STORE FIVE HUN-DRED METERS AWAY!
GREAT, NOBODY IN SIGHT!
WE GOTTA HURRY, OR THEY'LL SELL OUT TOO!
BU (BZZZZT)
BUUUU

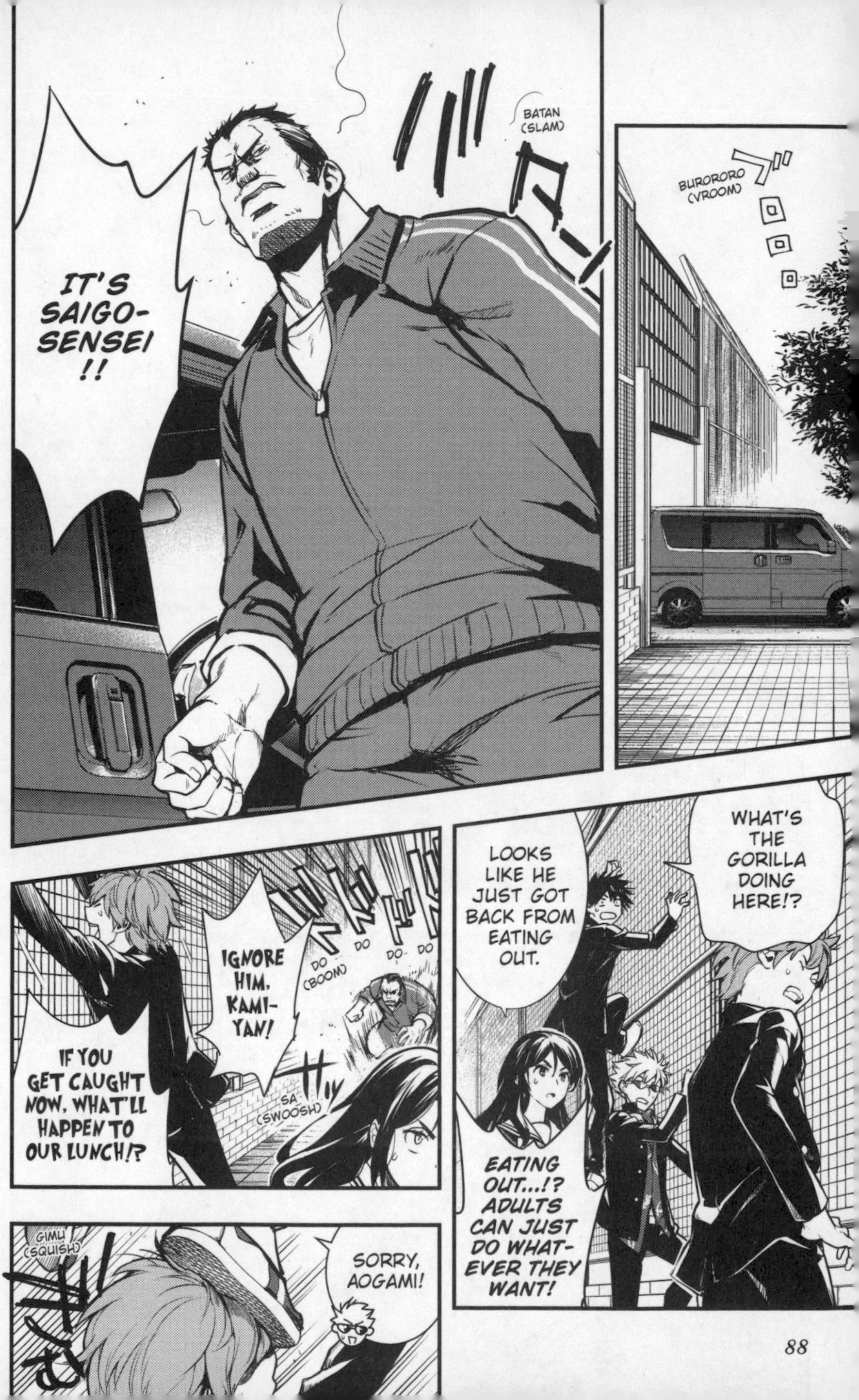
BURORORO (VROOM)
BATAN (SLAM)
IT'S SAIGO-SENSEI!!
WHAT'S THE GORILLA DOING HERE!?
LOOKS LIKE HE JUST GOT BACK FROM EATING OUT.
EATING OUT...!? ADULTS CAN JUST DO WHAT-EVER THEY WANT!
DO DO DO DO (BOOM)
IGNORE HIM, KAMI-YAN!
SA (SWOOSH)
IF YOU GET CAUGHT NOW, WHAT'LL HAPPEN TO OUR LUNCH!?
GIMU (SQUISH)
SORRY, AOGAMI!

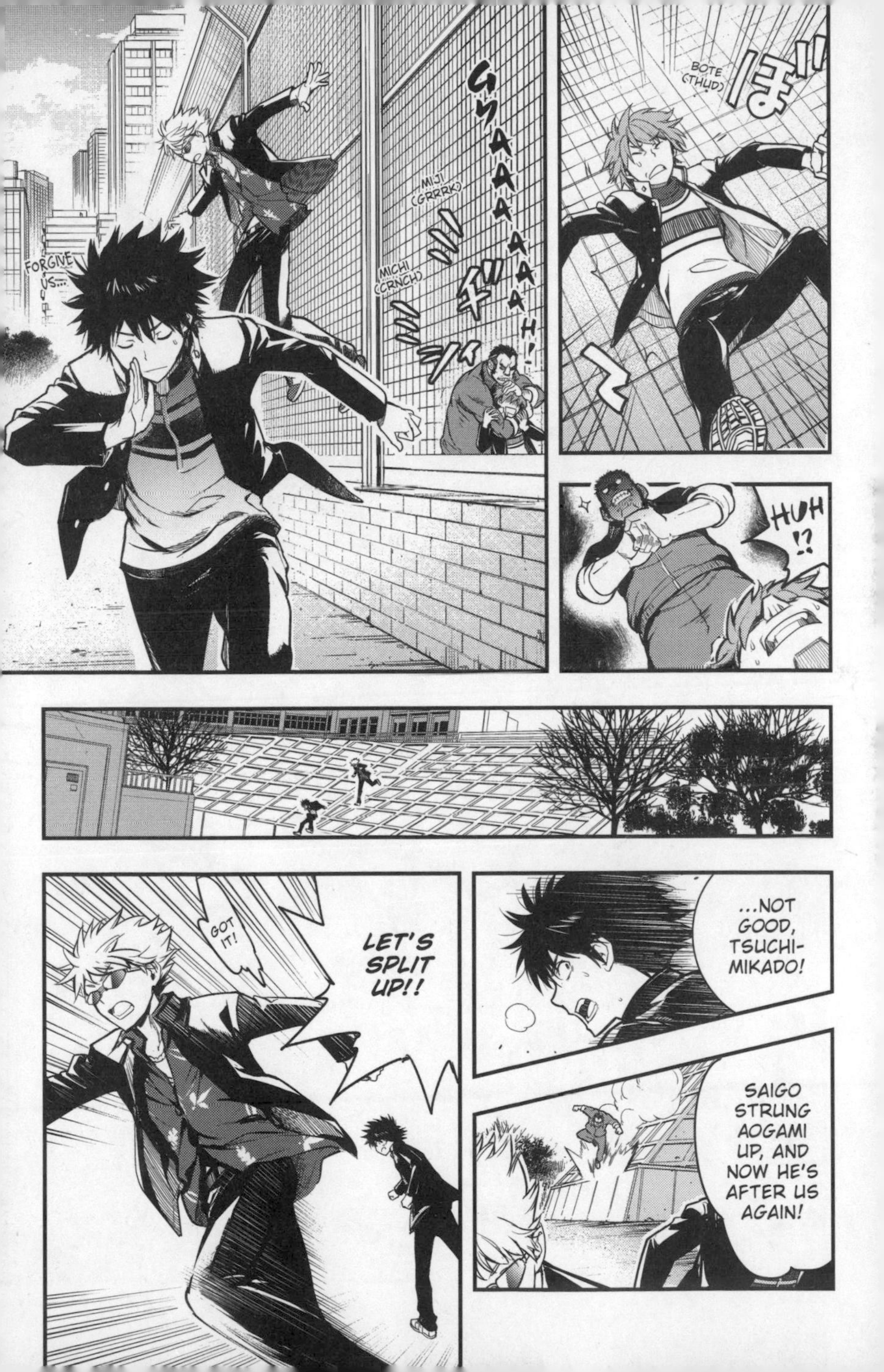
BOTE (THUD)
HUH!?
MIJI (GRRRK)
MICHI (CRNCH)
FORGIVE US...
...NOT GOOD, TSUCHIMIKADO!
SAIGO STRUNG AOGAMI UP, AND NOW HE'S AFTER US AGAIN!
LET'S SPLIT UP!!
GOT IT!

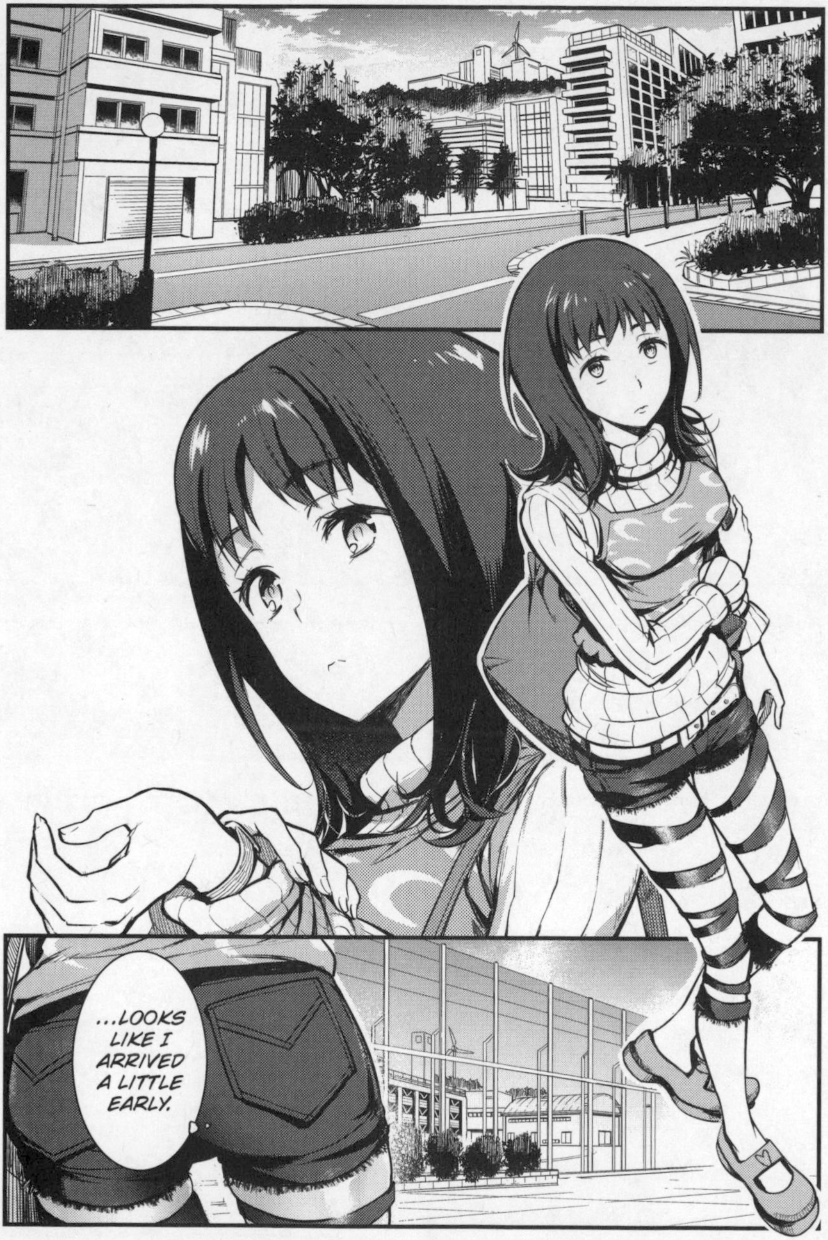
...LOOKS LIKE I ARRIVED A LITTLE EARLY.

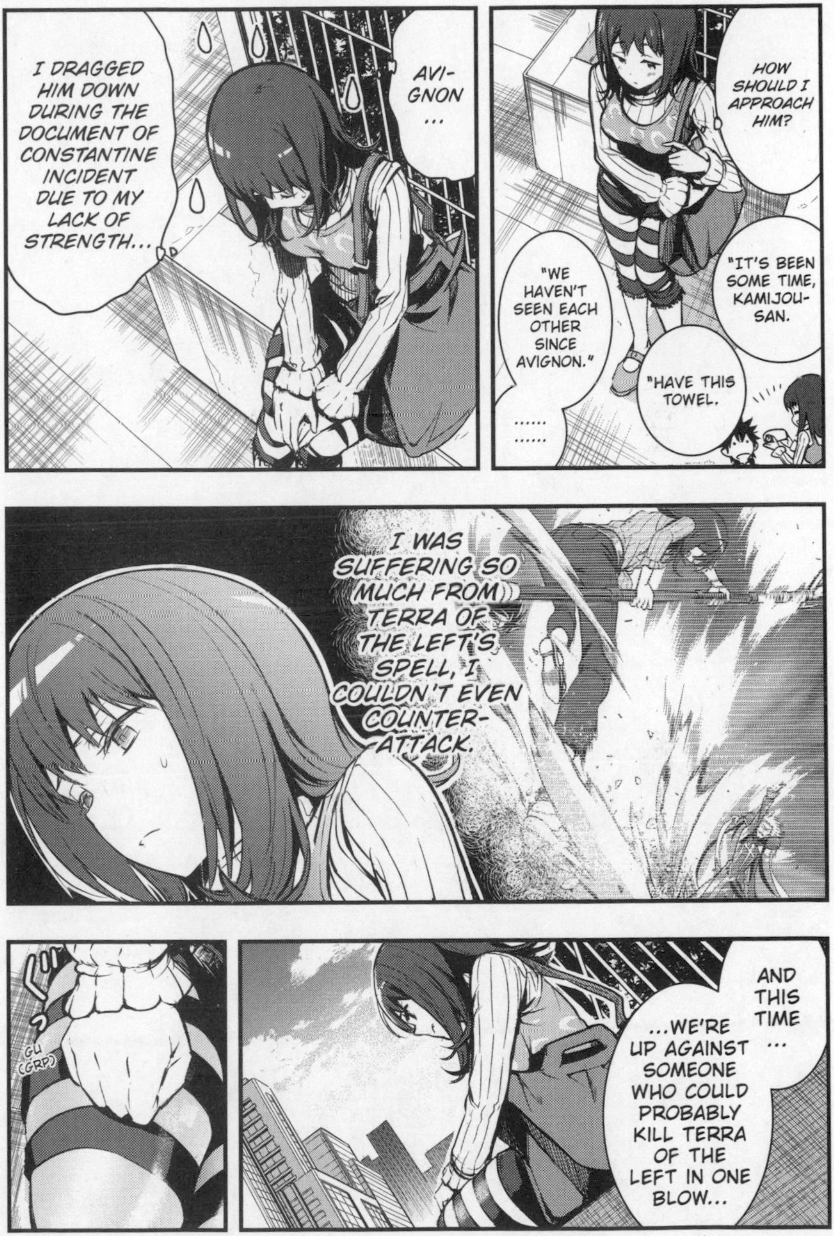
HOW SHOULD I APPROACH HIM?
"IT'S BEEN SOME TIME, KAMIJOU-SAN.
"HAVE THIS TOWEL.
"WE HAVEN'T SEEN EACH OTHER SINCE AVIGNON."
....
AVI-GNON ...
I DRAGGED HIM DOWN DURING THE DOCUMENT OF CONSTANTINE INCIDENT DUE TO MY LACK OF STRENGTH...
I WAS SUFFERING SO MUCH FROM TERRA OF THE LEFT'S SPELL, I COULDN'T EVEN COUNTER-ATTACK.
AND THIS TIME ...
...WE'RE UP AGAINST SOMEONE WHO COULD PROBABLY KILL TERRA OF THE LEFT IN ONE BLOW...
GU (GRP)

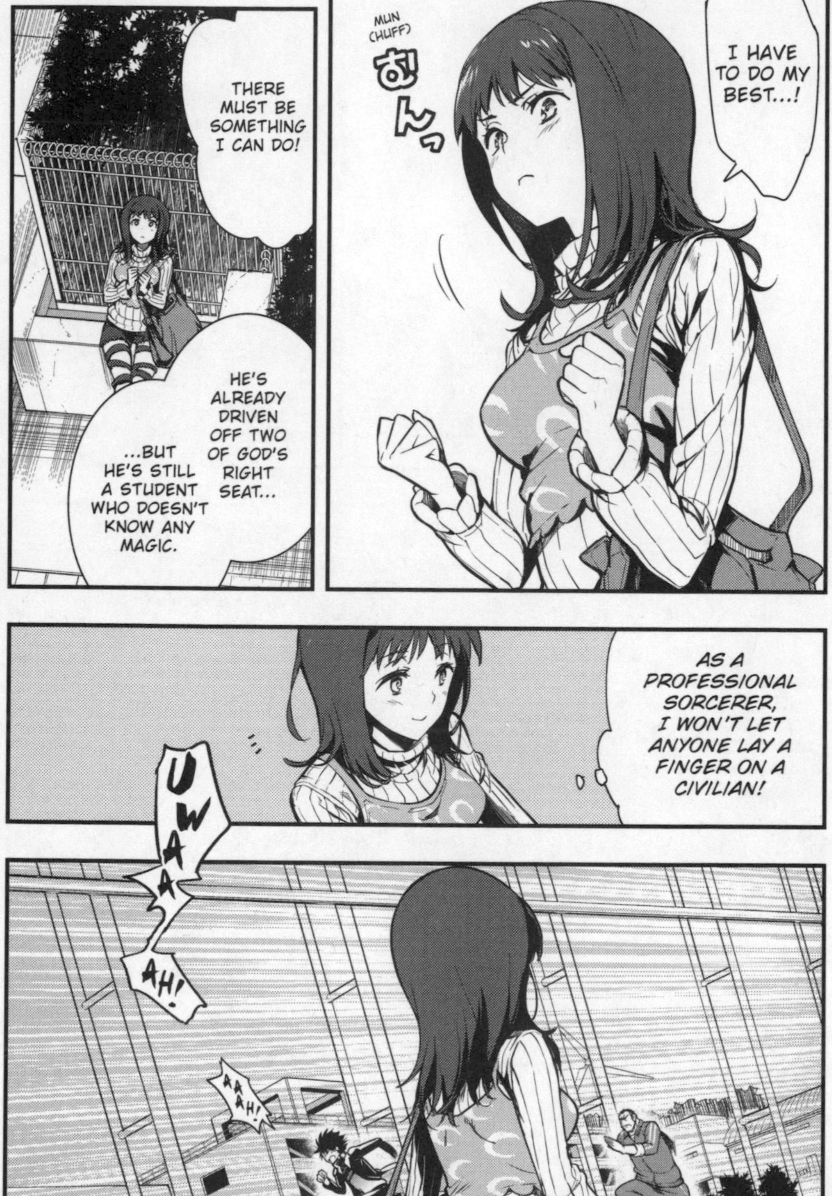
I HAVE TO DO MY BEST...!
MUN (HUFF)
むんっ
THERE MUST BE SOMETHING I CAN DO!
HE'S ALREADY DRIVEN OFF TWO OF GOD'S RIGHT SEAT...
...BUT HE'S STILL A STUDENT WHO DOESN'T KNOW ANY MAGIC.
AS A PROFESSIONAL SORCERER, I WON'T LET ANYONE LAY A FINGER ON A CIVILIAN!
UWAAAAH!
AAAH!

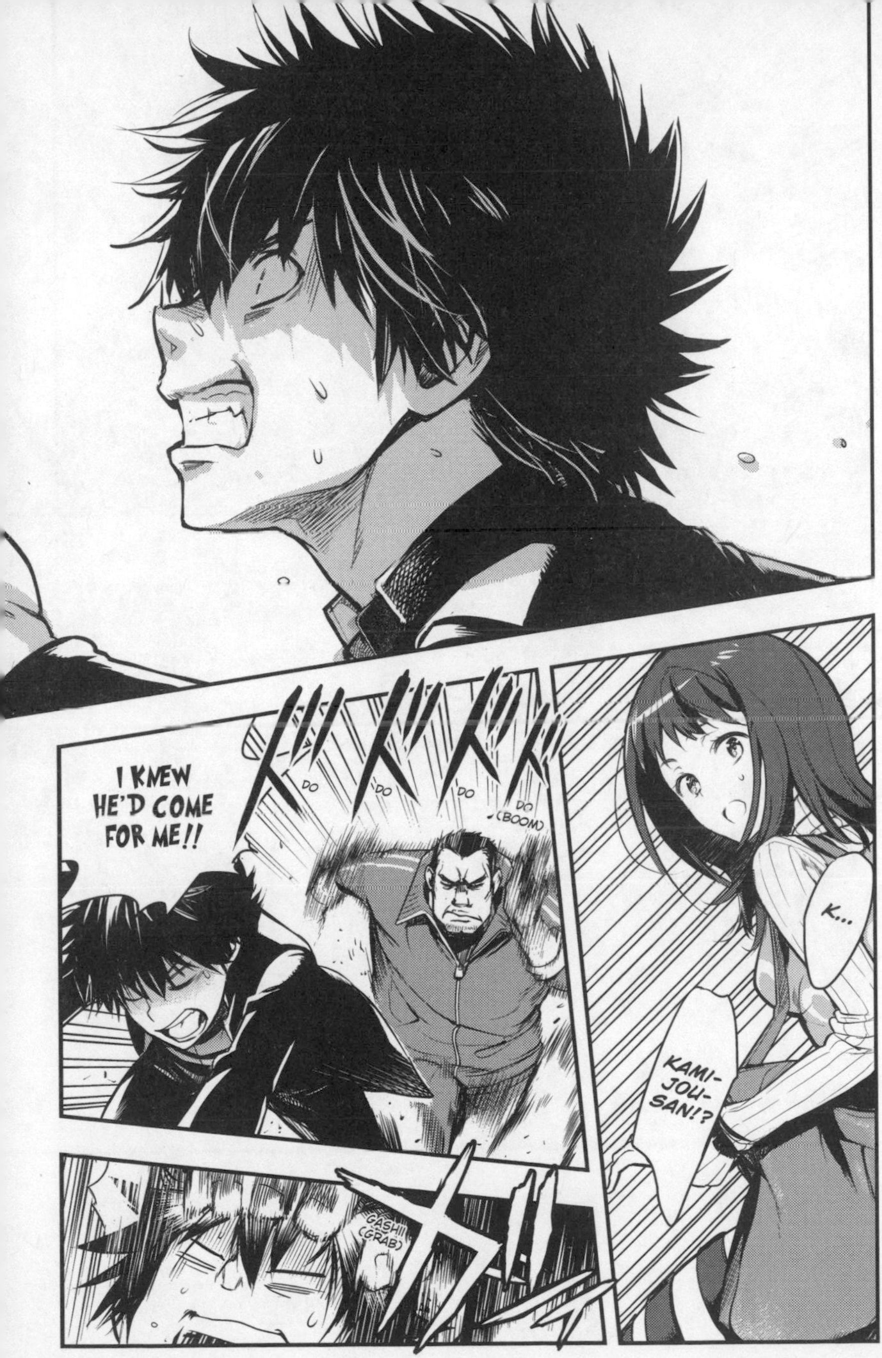
K...
KAMI-JOU-SAN!?
I KNEW HE'D COME FOR ME!!
DO DO DO DO (BOOM)
GASHI (GRAB)

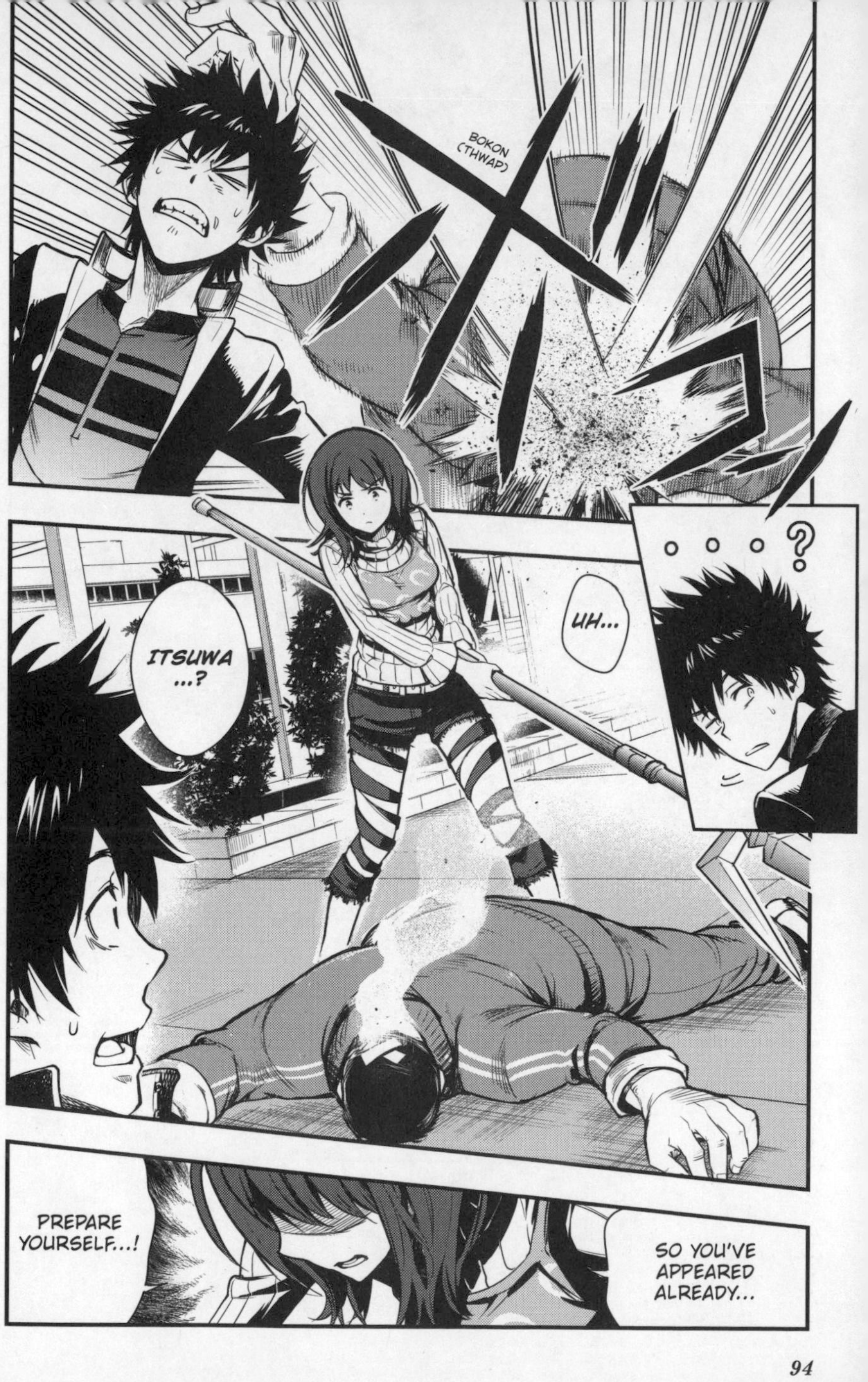
BOKON (THWAP)
...?
UH...
ITSUWA ...?
SO YOU'VE APPEARED ALREADY...
PREPARE YOURSELF...!

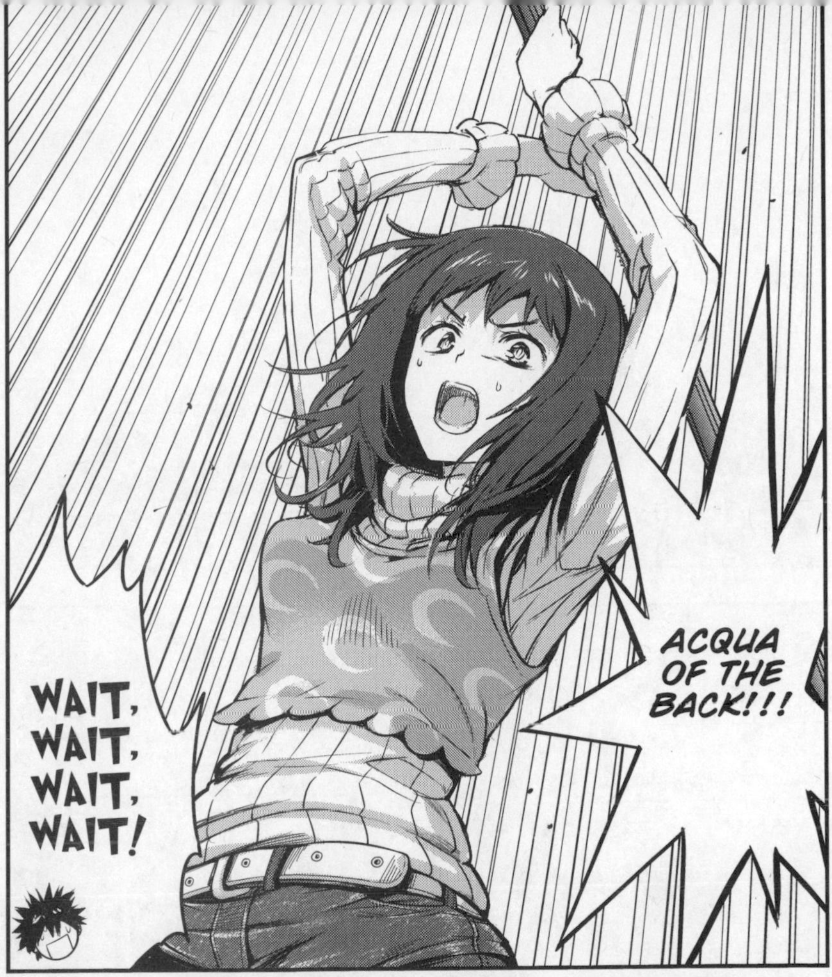
ACQUA OF THE BACK!!!
WAIT, WAIT, WAIT, WAIT!
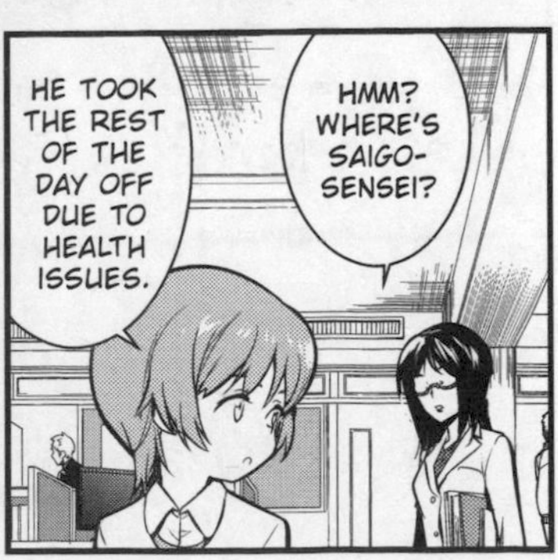
HMM? WHERE'S SAIGO-SENSEI?
HE TOOK THE REST OF THE DAY OFF DUE TO HEALTH ISSUES.
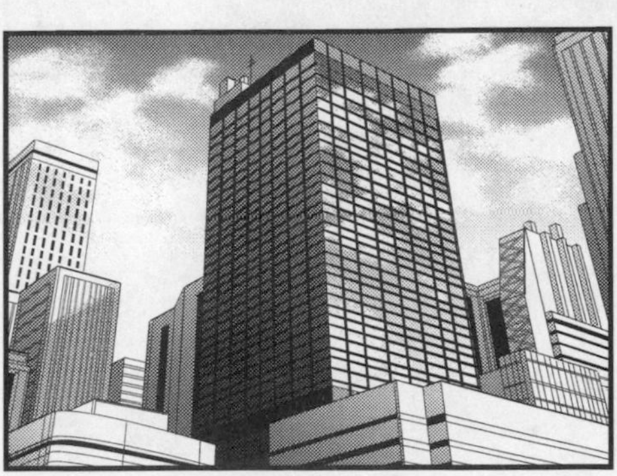

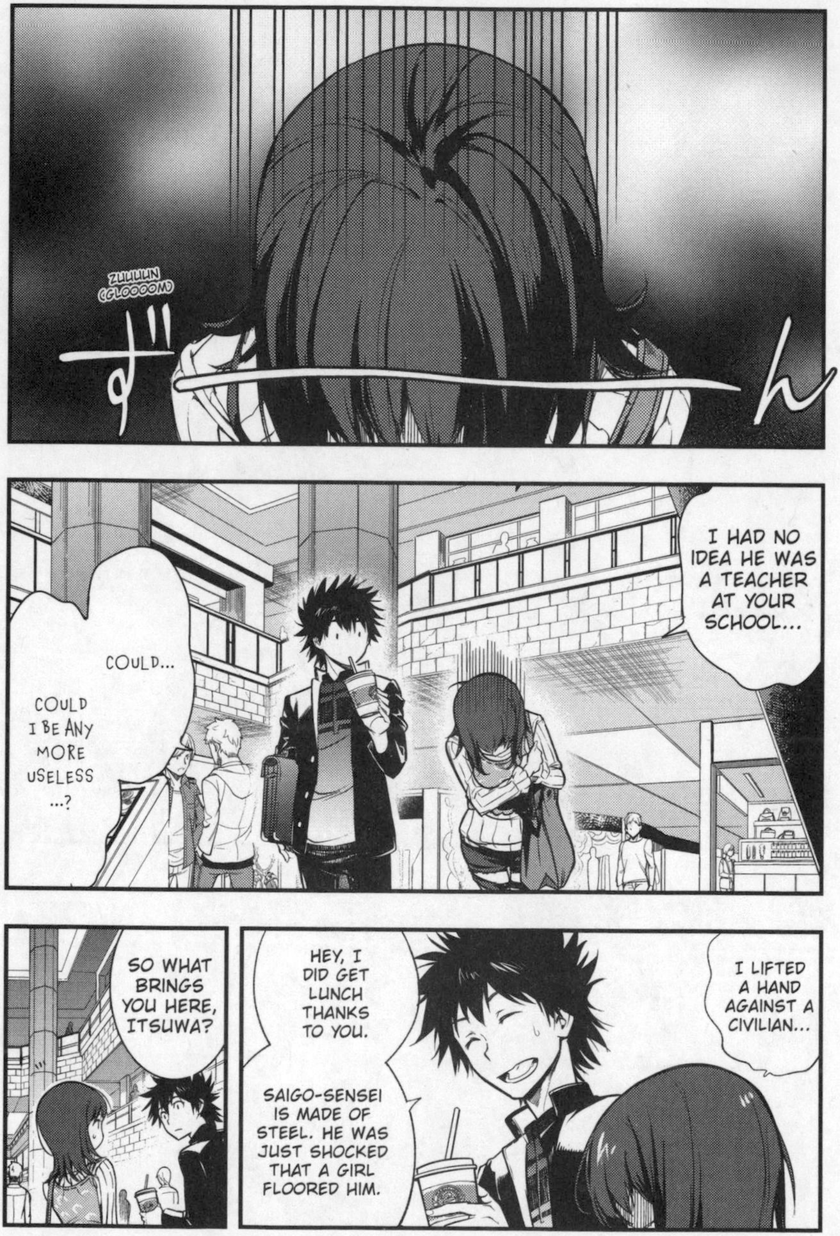
ZUUUUN (GLOOOOM)
ずーん
I HAD NO IDEA HE WAS A TEACHER AT YOUR SCHOOL...
COULD...
COULD I BE ANY MORE USELESS ...?
I LIFTED A HAND AGAINST A CIVILIAN...
HEY, I DID GET LUNCH THANKS TO YOU.
SAIGO-SENSEI IS MADE OF STEEL. HE WAS JUST SHOCKED THAT A GIRL FLOORED HIM.
SO WHAT BRINGS YOU HERE, ITSUWA?

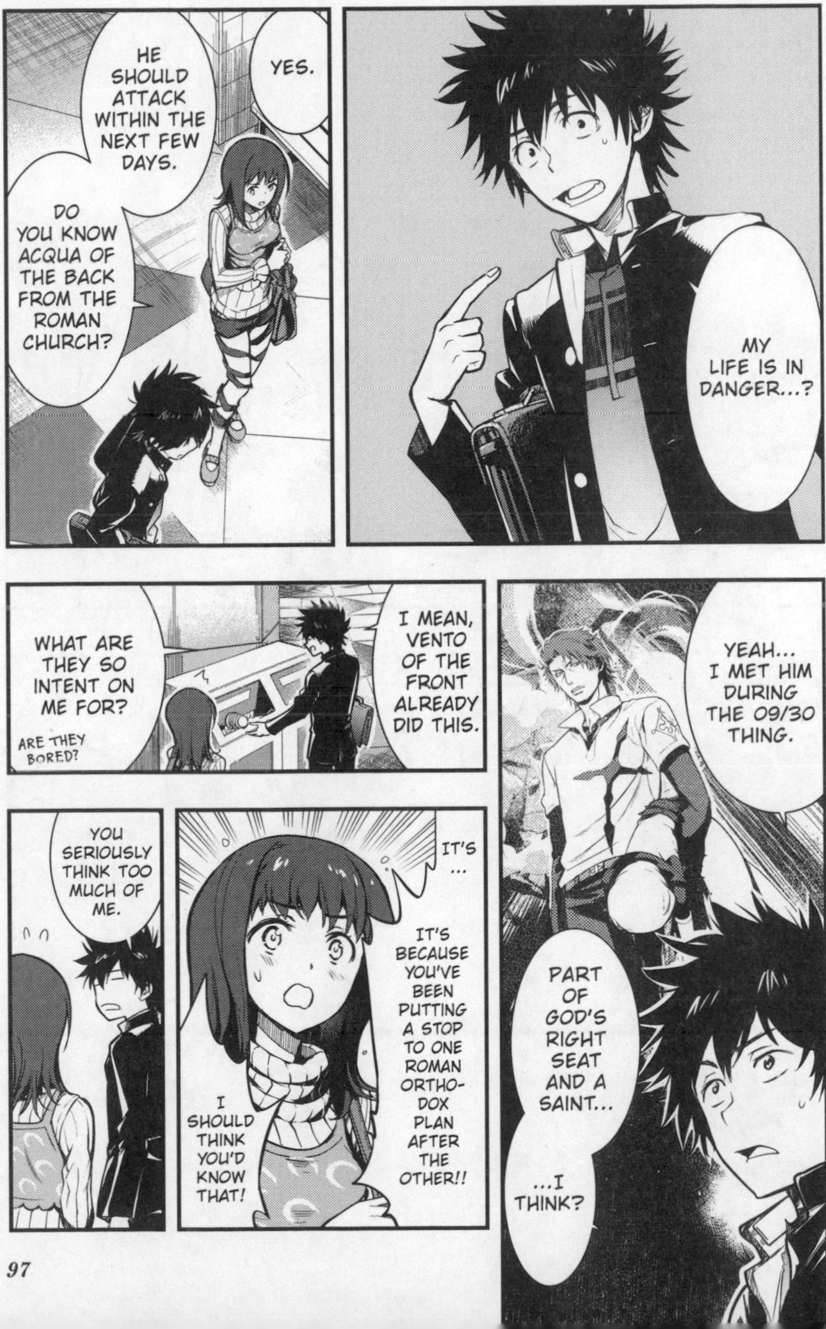

MY LIFE IS IN DANGER...?
YES.
HE SHOULD ATTACK WITHIN THE NEXT FEW DAYS.
DO YOU KNOW ACQUA OF THE BACK FROM THE ROMAN CHURCH?
YEAH... I MET HIM DURING THE 09/30 THING.
PART OF GOD'S RIGHT SEAT AND A SAINT...
...I THINK?
I MEAN, VENTO OF THE FRONT ALREADY DID THIS.
WHAT ARE THEY SO INTENT ON ME FOR?
ARE THEY BORED?
IT'S ...
IT'S BECAUSE YOU'VE BEEN PUTTING A STOP TO ONE ROMAN ORTHODOX PLAN AFTER THE OTHER!!
I SHOULD THINK YOU'D KNOW THAT!
YOU SERIOUSLY THINK TOO MUCH OF ME.

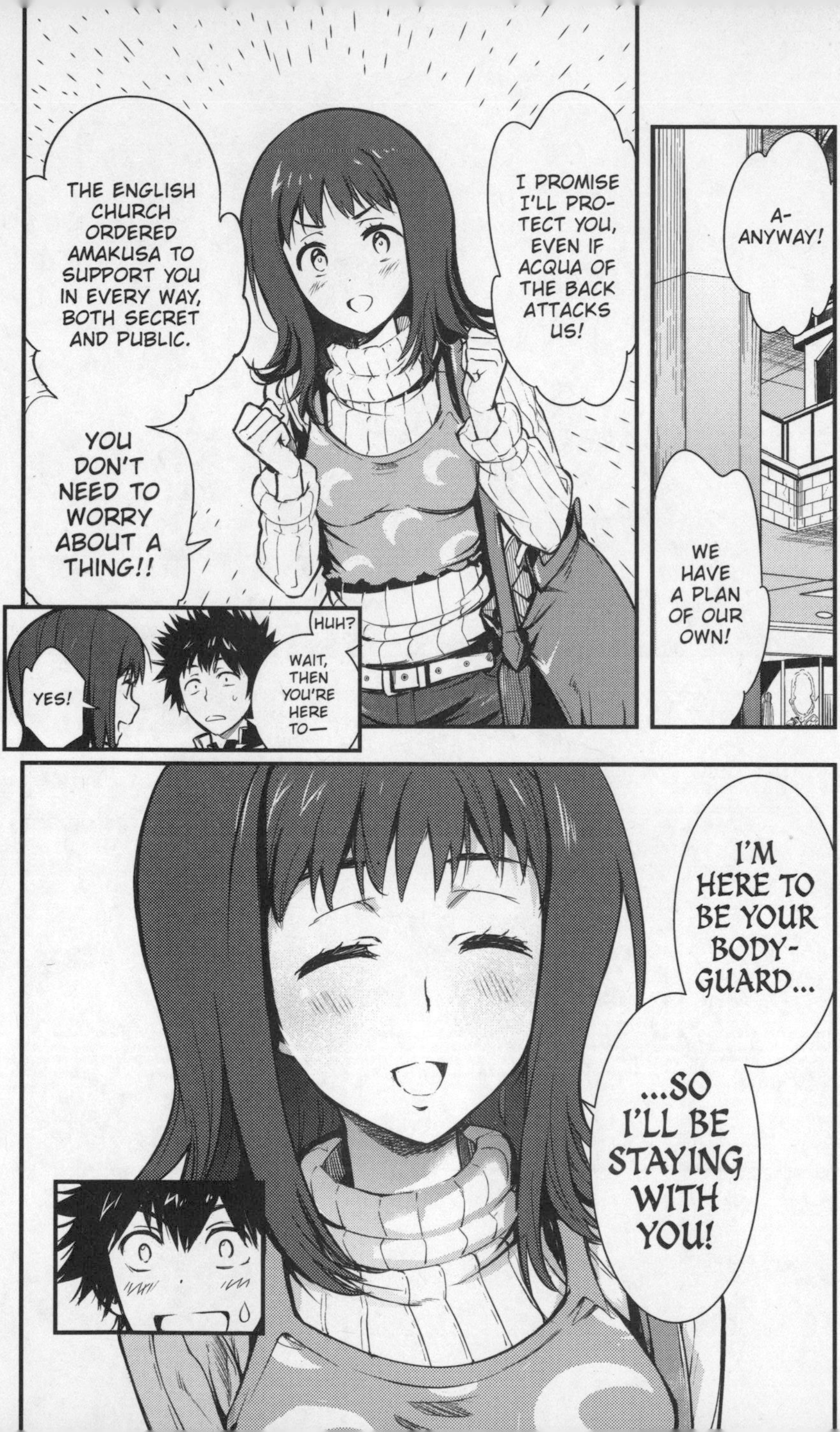
A- ANYWAY!
WE HAVE A PLAN OF OUR OWN!
I PROMISE I'LL PROTECT YOU, EVEN IF ACQUA OF THE BACK ATTACKS US!
THE ENGLISH CHURCH ORDERED AMAKUSA TO SUPPORT YOU IN EVERY WAY, BOTH SECRET AND PUBLIC.
YOU DON'T NEED TO WORRY ABOUT A THING!!
HUH?
WAIT, THEN YOU'RE HERE TO—
YES!
I'M HERE TO BE YOUR BODY-GUARD...
...SO I'LL BE STAYING WITH YOU!

#151 THE AMAKUSA LIVE-IN GUARDIAN

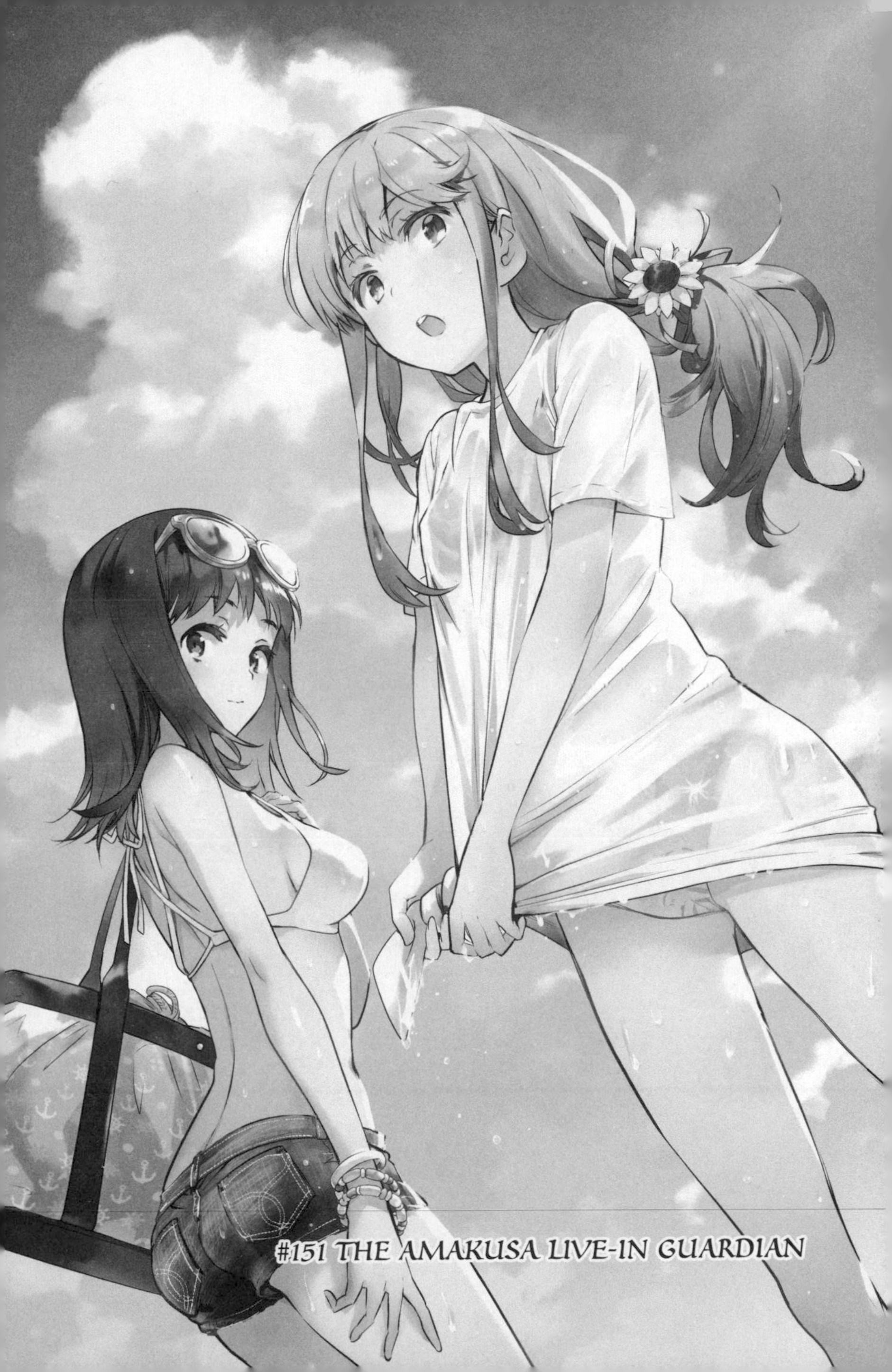

A Certain Magical Index

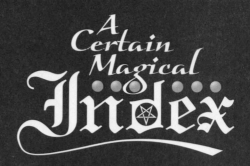

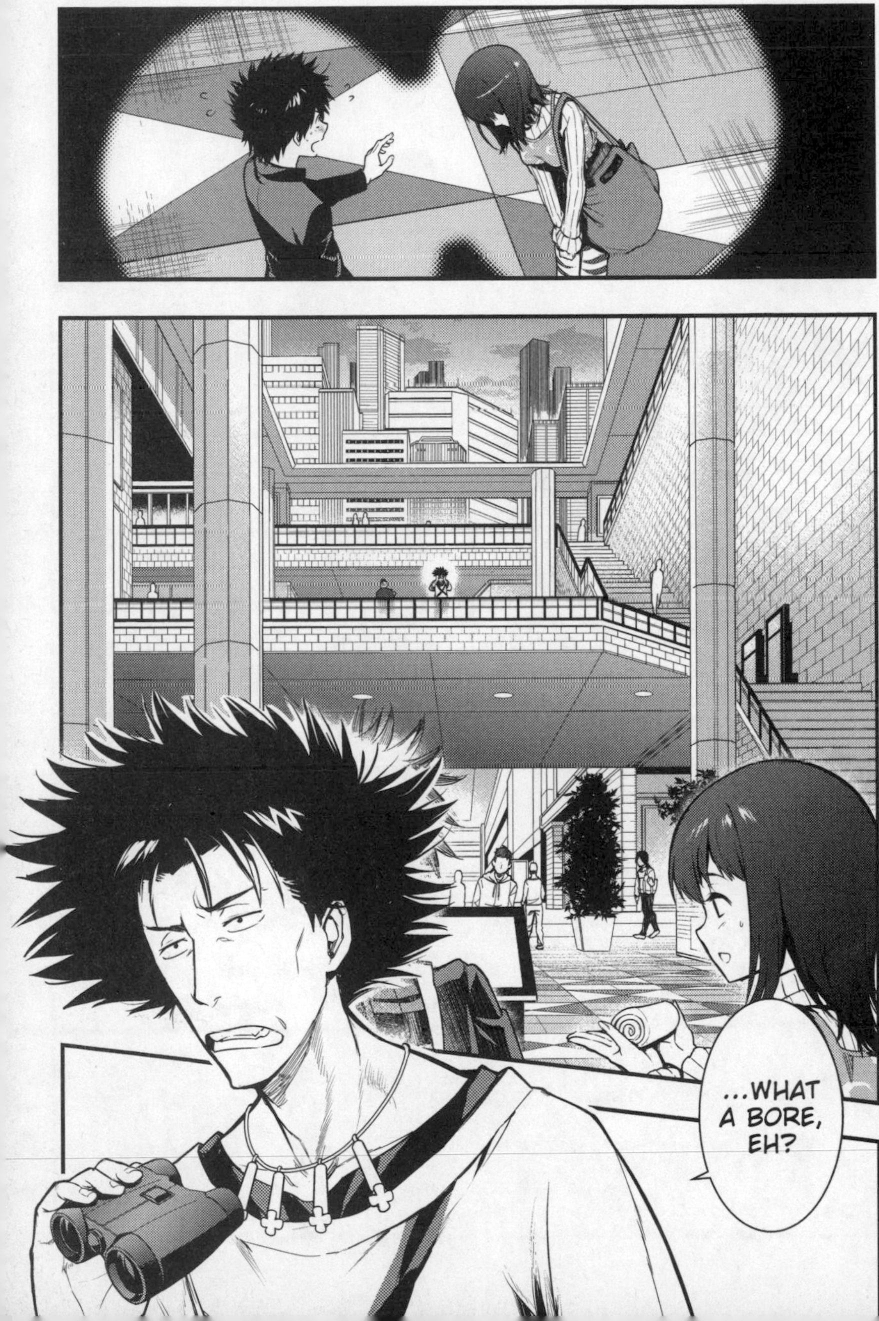
...WHAT A BORE, EH?

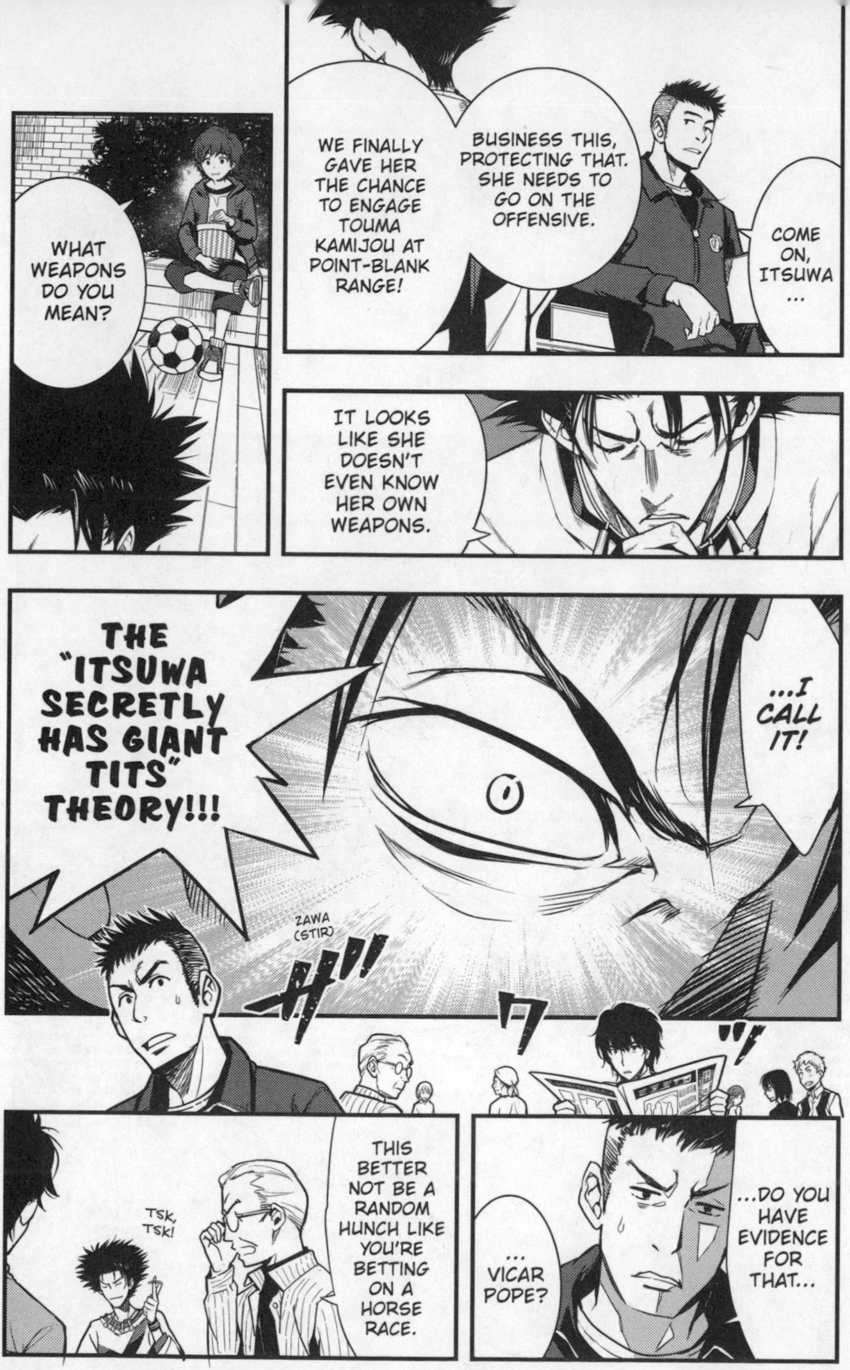
COME ON, ITSUWA ...
BUSINESS THIS, PROTECTING THAT. SHE NEEDS TO GO ON THE OFFENSIVE.
WE FINALLY GAVE HER THE CHANCE TO ENGAGE TOUMA KAMIJOU AT POINT-BLANK RANGE!
IT LOOKS LIKE SHE DOESN'T EVEN KNOW HER OWN WEAPONS.
WHAT WEAPONS DO YOU MEAN?
...I CALL IT!
THE "ITSUWA SECRETLY HAS GIANT TITS" THEORY!!!
ZAWA (STIR)
...DO YOU HAVE EVIDENCE FOR THAT...
... VICAR POPE?
THIS BETTER NOT BE A RANDOM HUNCH LIKE YOU'RE BETTING ON A HORSE RACE.
TSK, TSK!

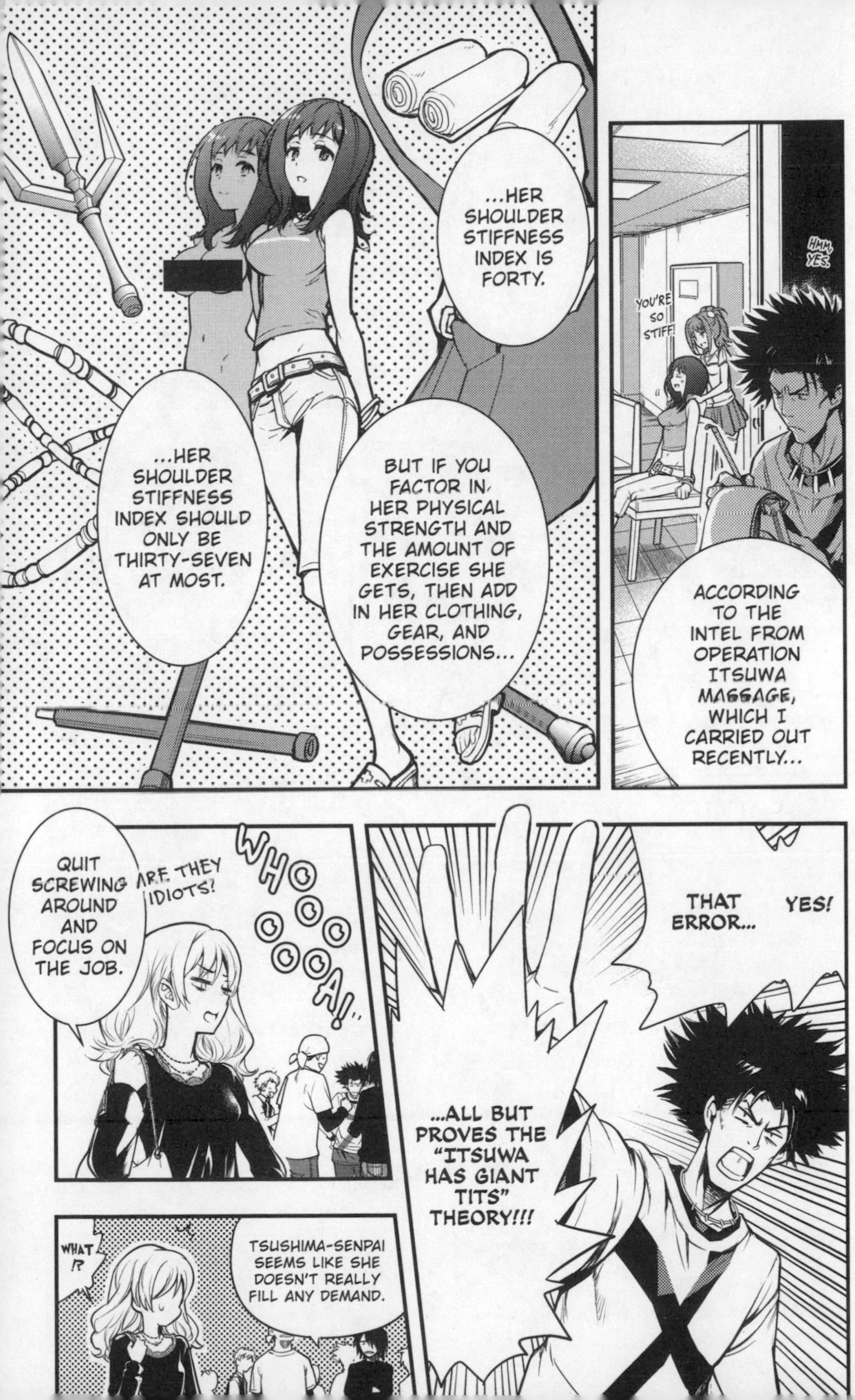
HMM, YES.
YOU'RE SO STIFF!
ACCORDING TO THE INTEL FROM OPERATION ITSUWA MASSAGE, WHICH I CARRIED OUT RECENTLY...
...HER SHOULDER STIFFNESS INDEX IS FORTY.
BUT IF YOU FACTOR IN HER PHYSICAL STRENGTH AND THE AMOUNT OF EXERCISE SHE GETS, THEN ADD IN HER CLOTHING, GEAR, AND POSSESSIONS...
...HER SHOULDER STIFFNESS INDEX SHOULD ONLY BE THIRTY-SEVEN AT MOST.
YES!
THAT ERROR...
...ALL BUT PROVES THE "ITSUWA HAS GIANT TITS" THEORY!!!
WHOOOOOOA!
ARE THEY IDIOTS?
QUIT SCREWING AROUND AND FOCUS ON THE JOB.
TSUSHIMA-SENPAI SEEMS LIKE SHE DOESN'T REALLY FILL ANY DEMAND.
WHAT!?

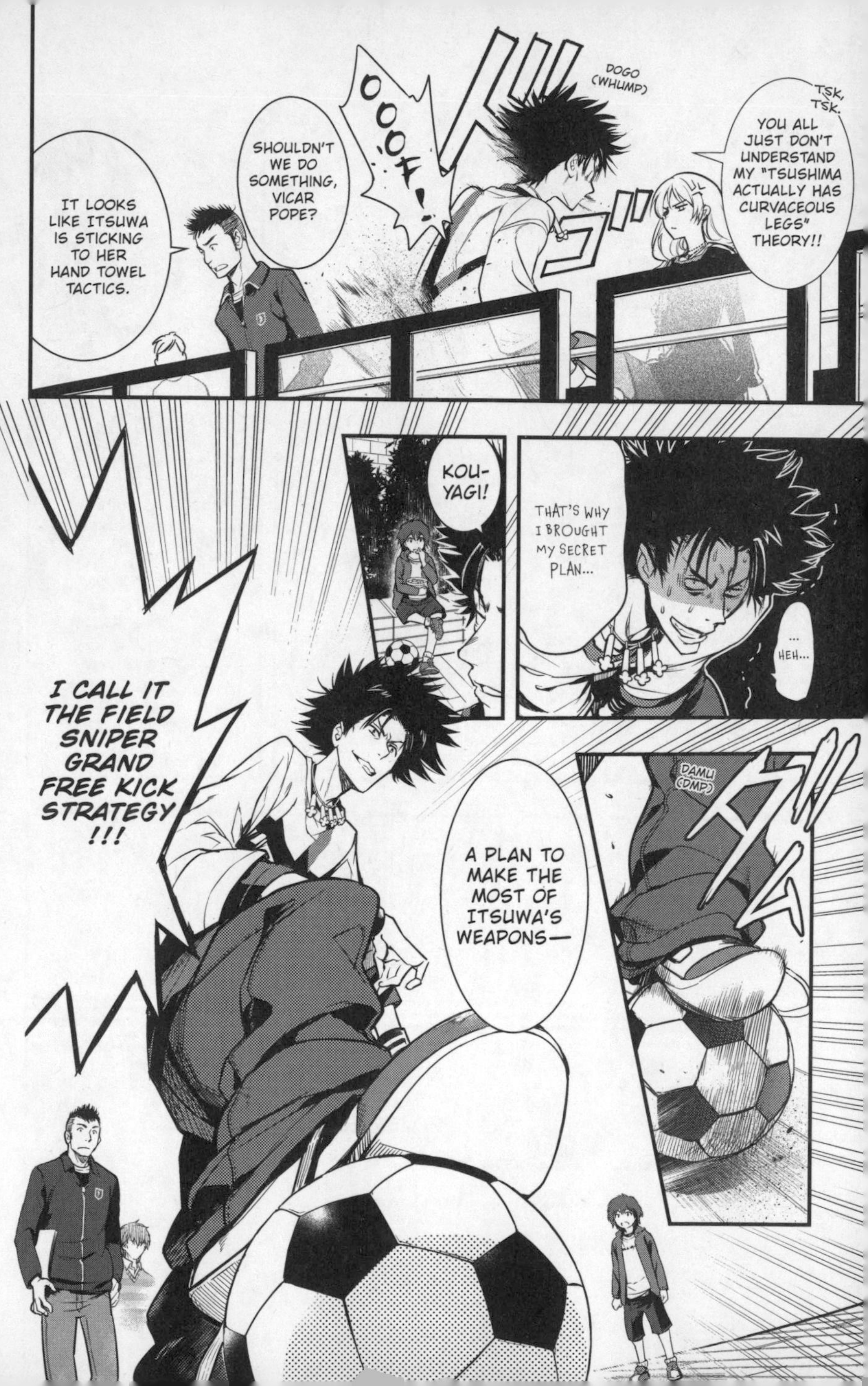
TSK, TSK.
YOU ALL JUST DON'T UNDERSTAND MY "TSUSHIMA ACTUALLY HAS CURVACEOUS LEGS" THEORY!!
DOGO (WHUMP)
OOOF!
SHOULDN'T WE DO SOMETHING, VICAR POPE?
IT LOOKS LIKE ITSUWA IS STICKING TO HER HAND TOWEL TACTICS.
THAT'S WHY I BROUGHT MY SECRET PLAN...
... HEH...
KOU-YAGI!
DAMU (DMP)
A PLAN TO MAKE THE MOST OF ITSUWA'S WEAPONS—
I CALL IT THE FIELD SNIPER GRAND FREE KICK STRATEGY!!!

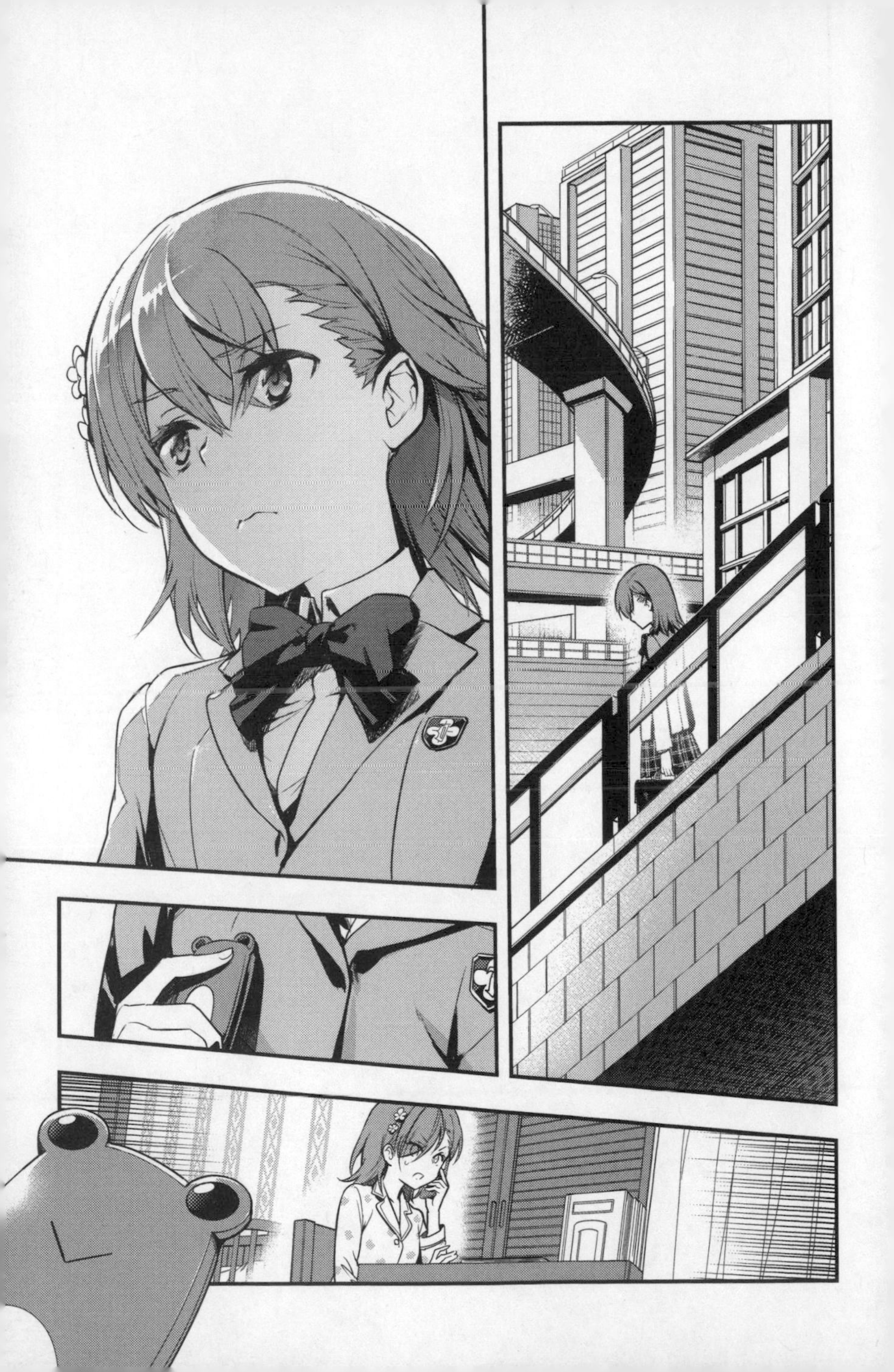

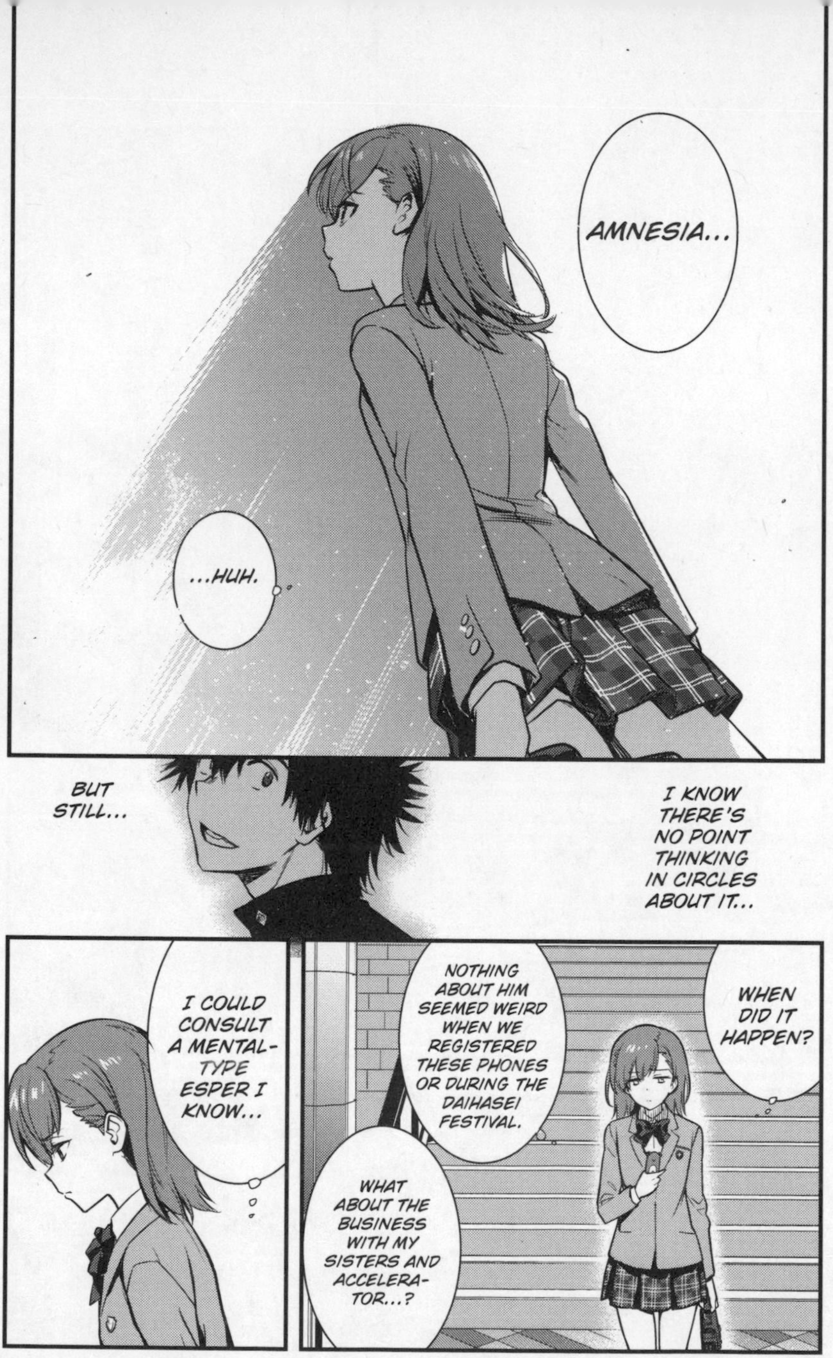
AMNESIA...
...HUH.
I KNOW THERE'S NO POINT THINKING IN CIRCLES ABOUT IT...
BUT STILL...
WHEN DID IT HAPPEN?
NOTHING ABOUT HIM SEEMED WEIRD WHEN WE REGISTERED THESE PHONES OR DURING THE DAIHASEI FESTIVAL.
WHAT ABOUT THE BUSINESS WITH MY SISTERS AND ACCELERA-TOR...?
I COULD CONSULT A MENTAL-TYPE ESPER I KNOW...

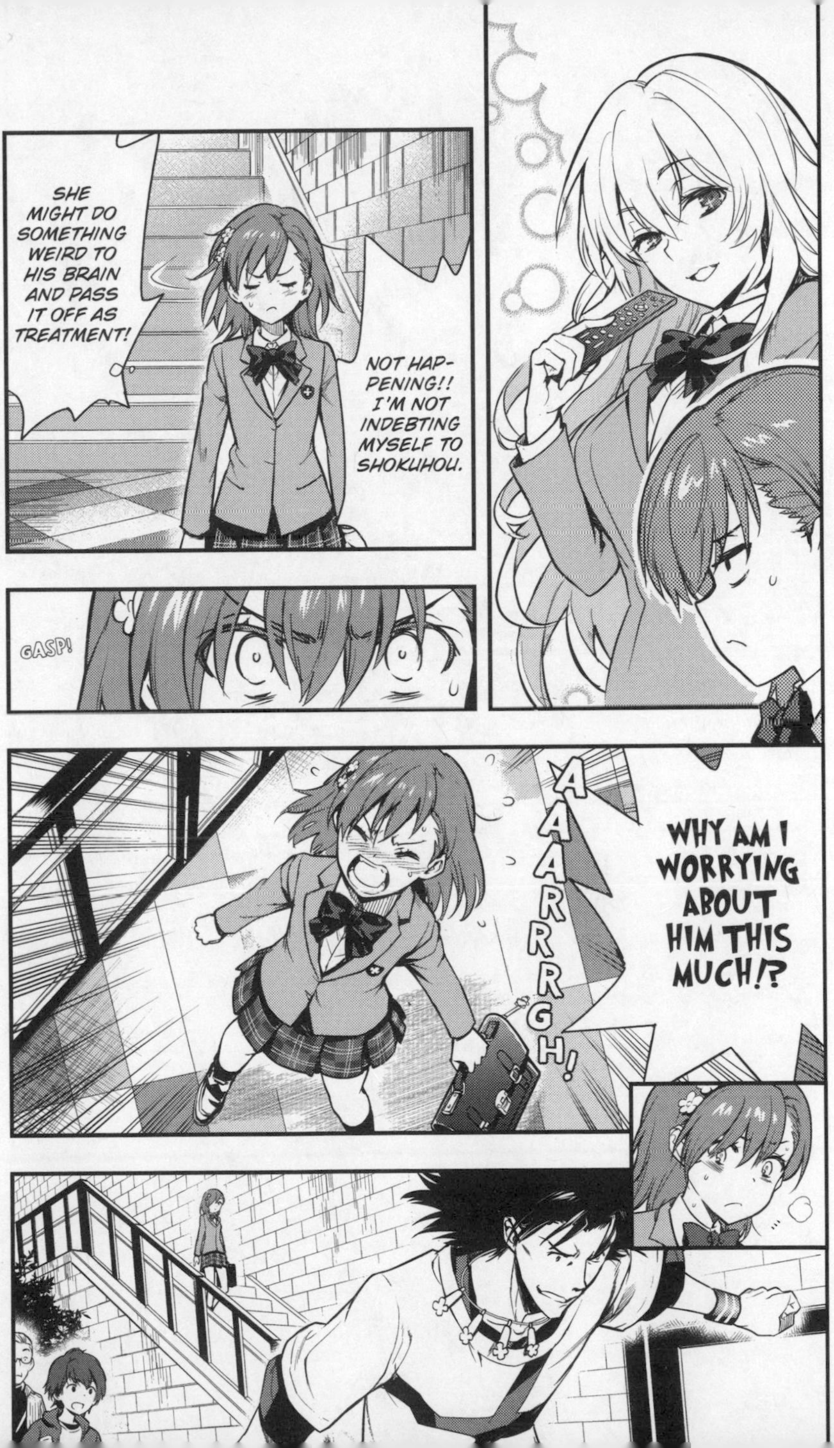
SHE MIGHT DO SOMETHING WEIRD TO HIS BRAIN AND PASS IT OFF AS TREATMENT!
NOT HAP-PENING!! I'M NOT INDEBTING MYSELF TO SHOKUHOU.
GASP!
WHY AM I WORRYING ABOUT HIM THIS MUCH!?
AAARRRGH!

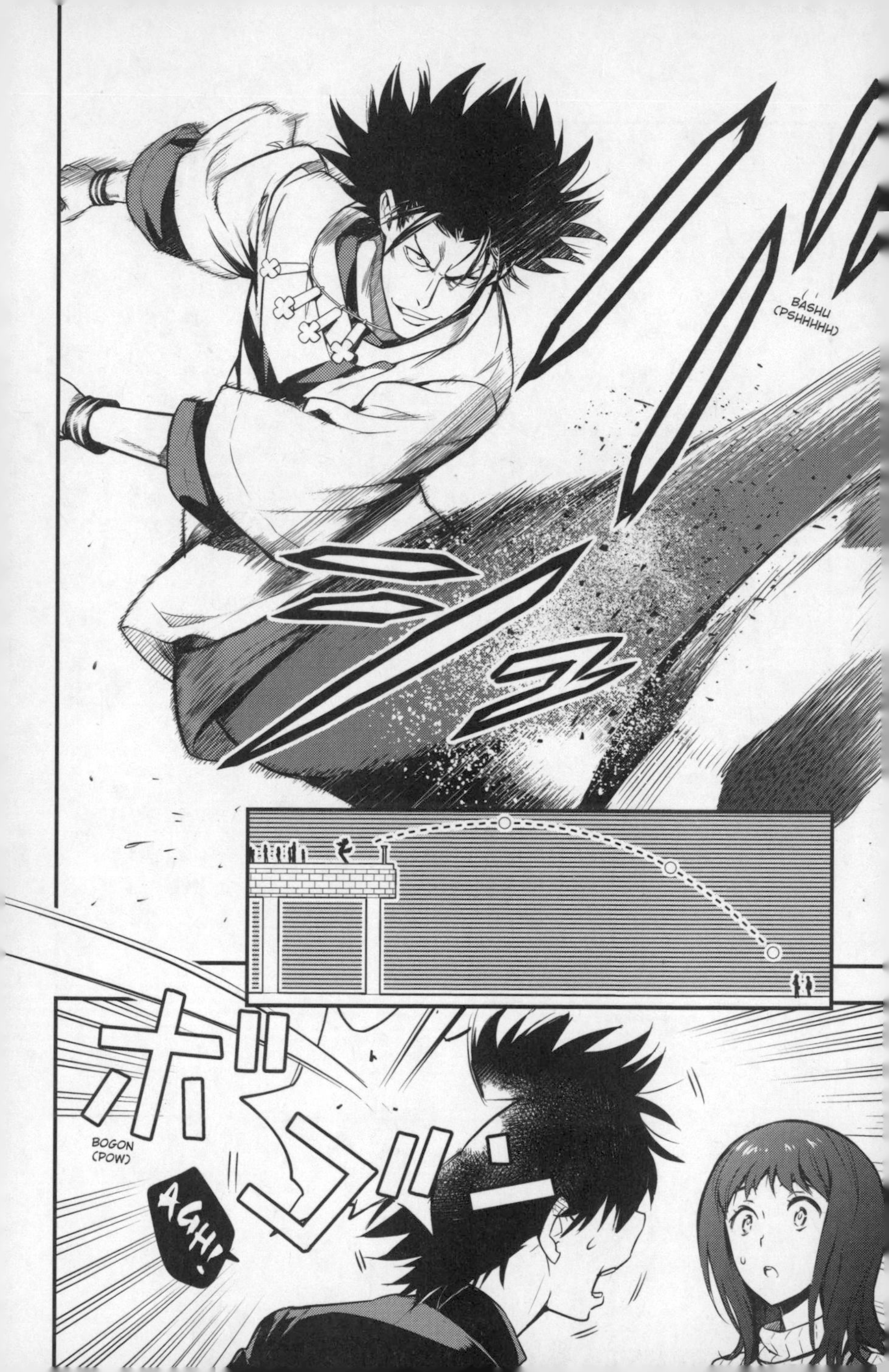
BASHU
(PSHHHHH)
BOGON
(POW)
AGH!

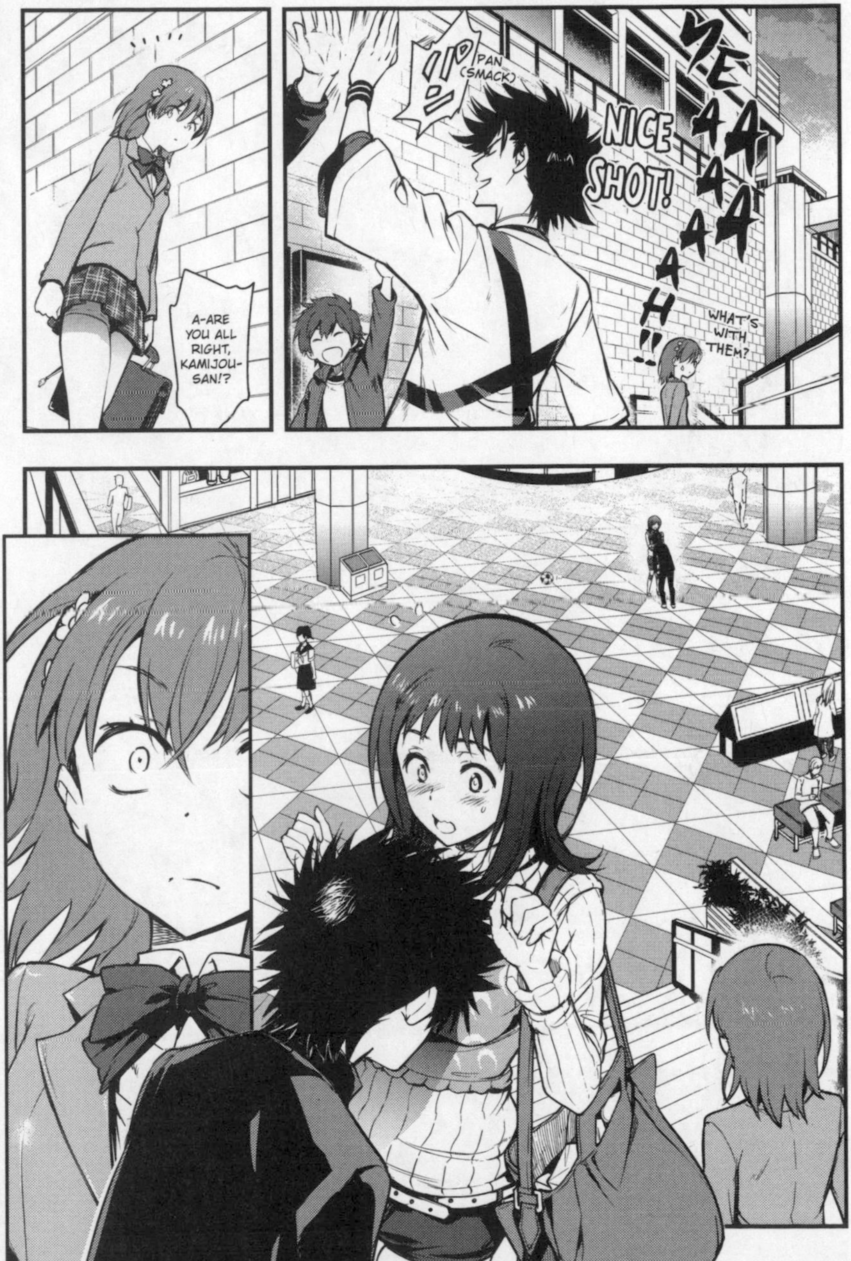
PAN (SMACK)
NICE SHOT!
YEAAAAAAH!!
WHAT'S WITH THEM?
A-ARE YOU ALL RIGHT, KAMIJOU-SAN!?

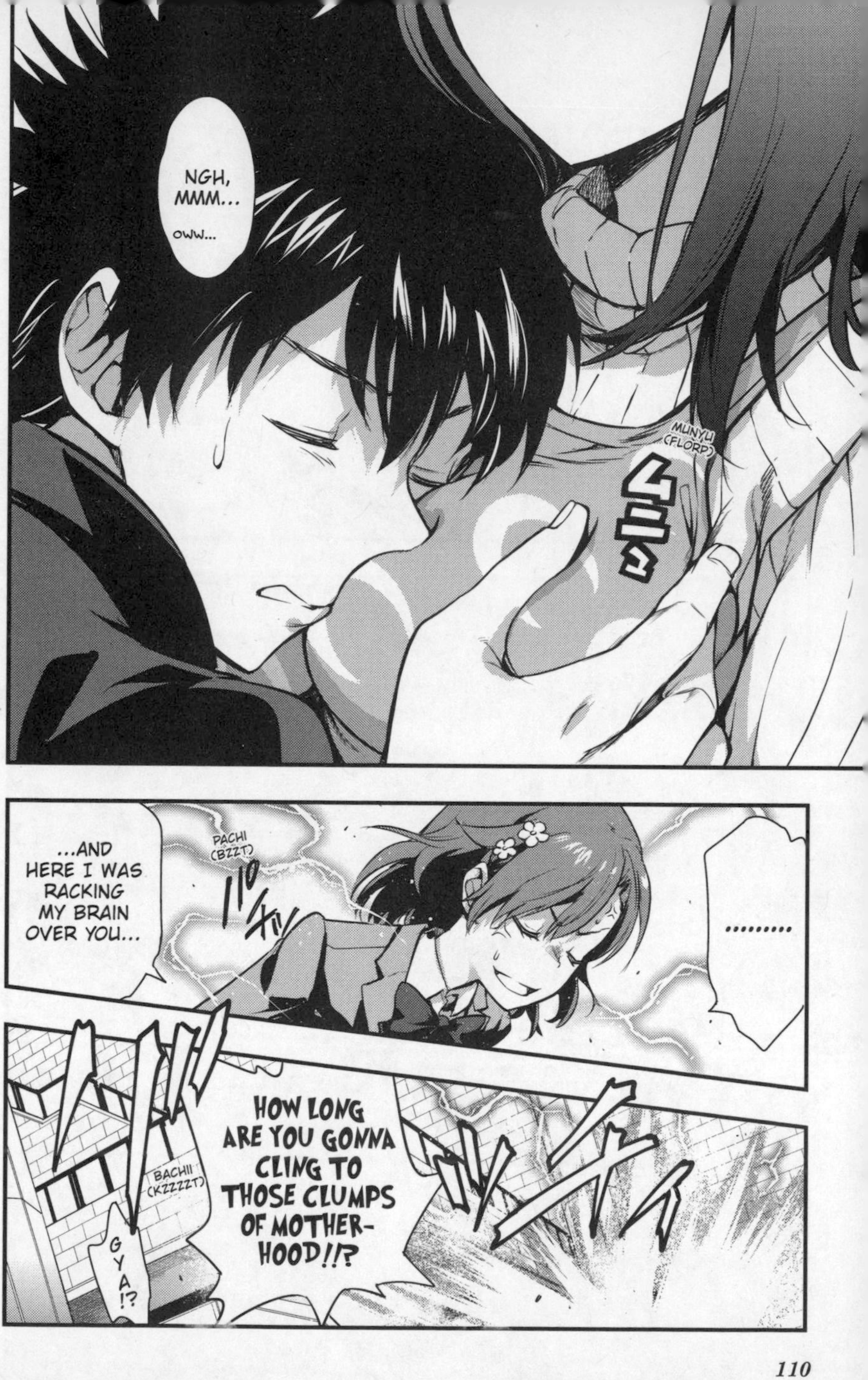
NGH, MMM...
OWW...
MUNYU (FLORP)
....
...AND HERE I WAS RACKING MY BRAIN OVER YOU...
PACHI (BZZT)
HOW LONG ARE YOU GONNA CLING TO THOSE CLUMPS OF MOTHER-HOOD!!?
BACHII (KZZZZT)
GYA!?

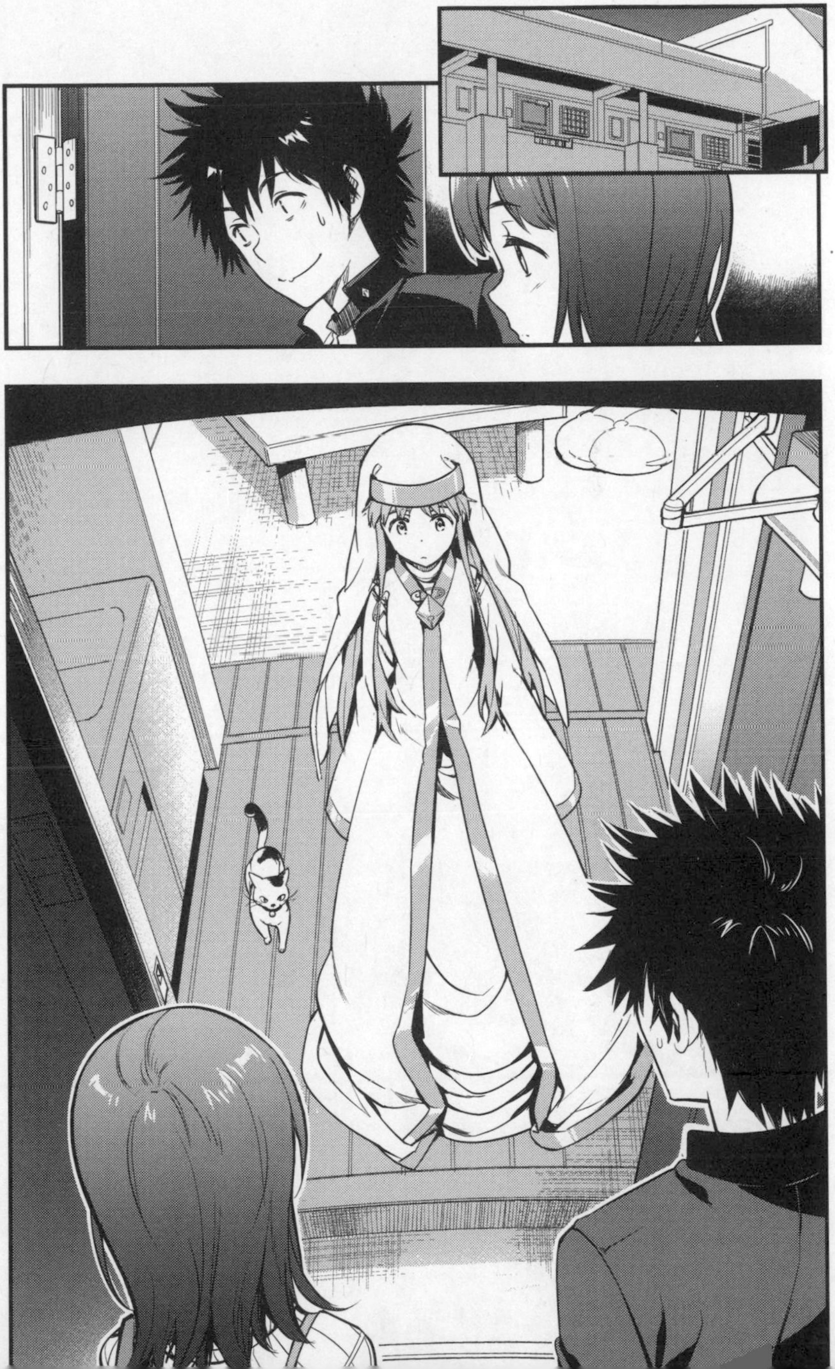

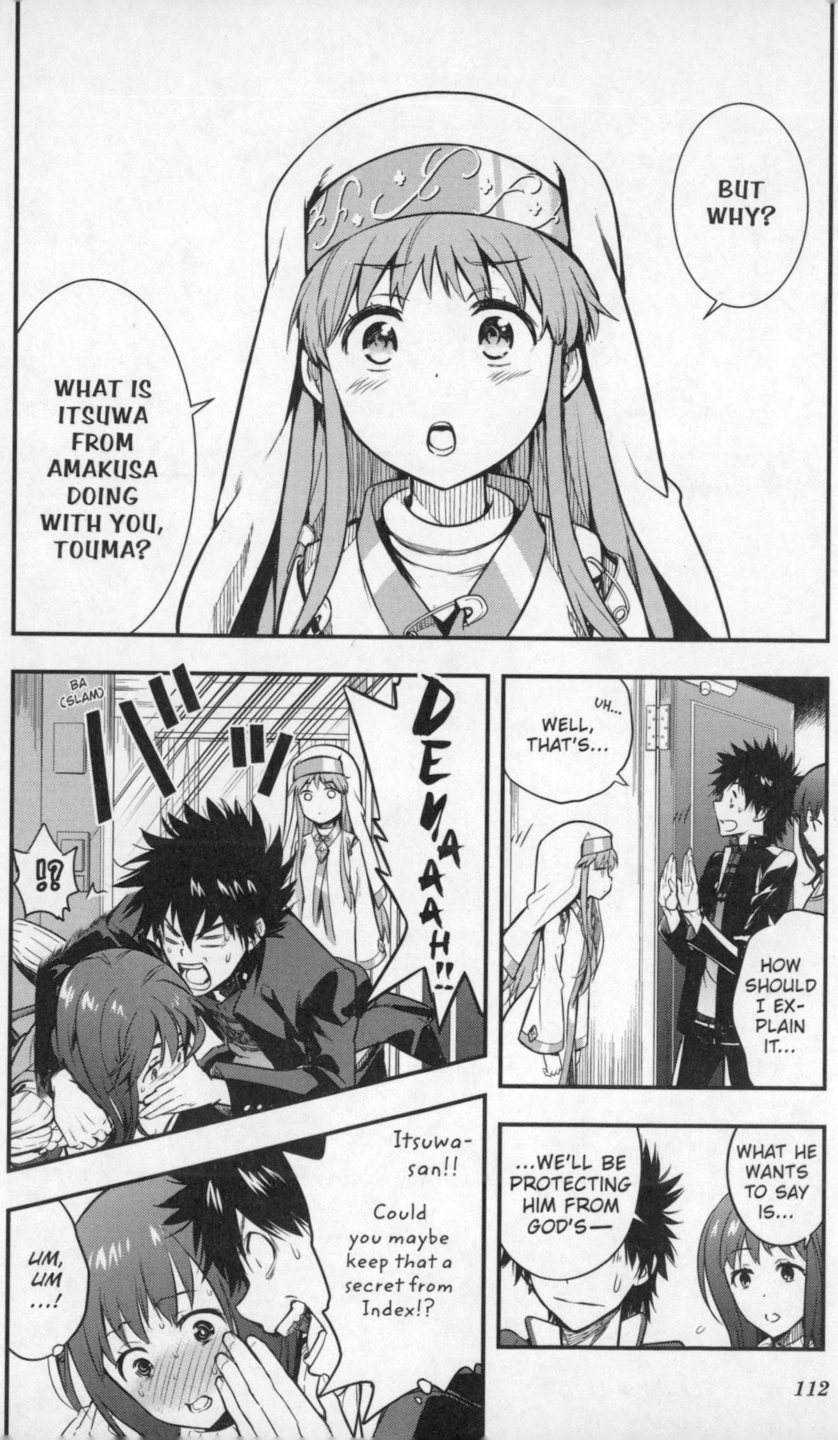
BUT WHY?
WHAT IS ITSUWA FROM AMAKUSA DOING WITH YOU, TOUMA?
UH... WELL, THAT'S...
HOW SHOULD I EX-PLAIN IT...
DEMAAAH!!
BA (SLAM)
!?
WHAT HE WANTS TO SAY IS...
...WE'LL BE PROTECTING HIM FROM GOD'S—
Itsuwa-san!!
Could you maybe keep that a secret from Index!?
UM, UM ...!

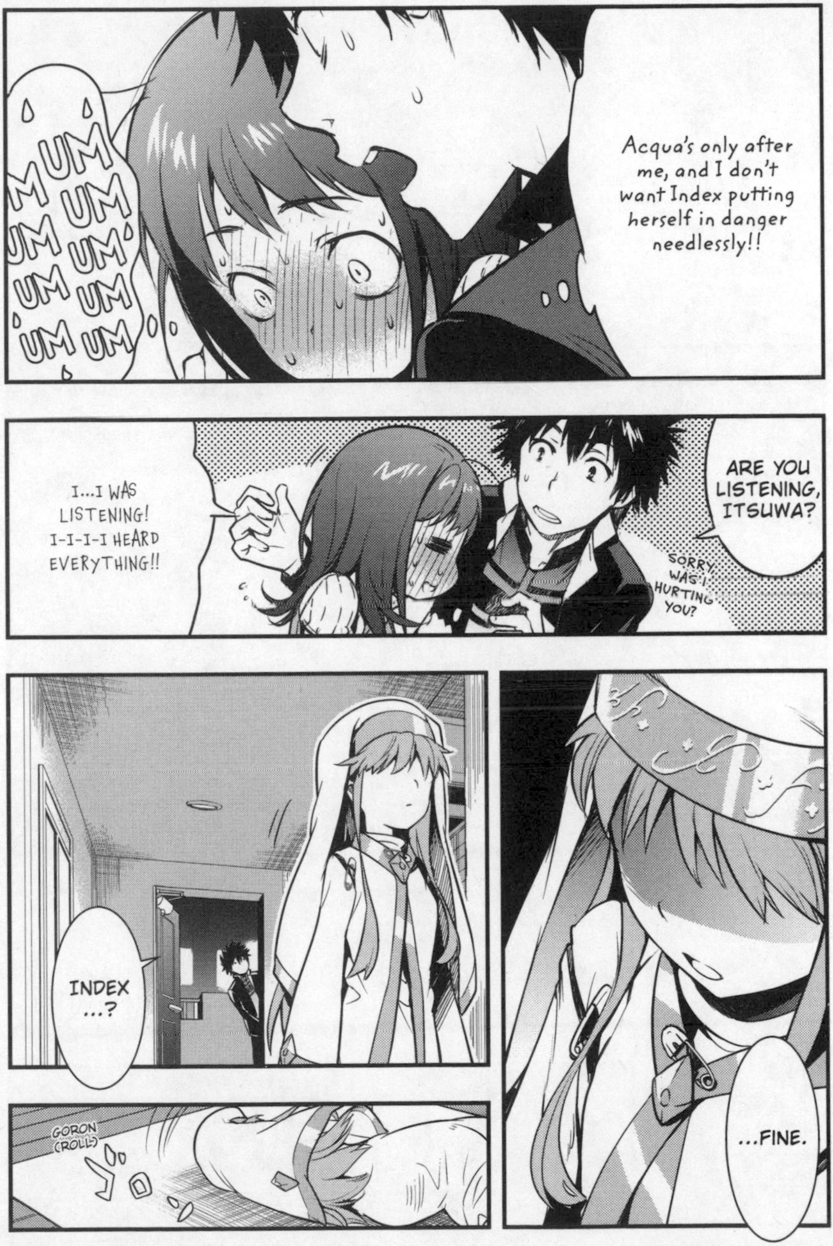
Acqua's only after me, and I don't want Index putting herself in danger needlessly!!
UM UM UM UM UM UM UM UM UM UM UM
ARE YOU LISTENING, ITSUWA?
SORRY, WAS I HURTING YOU?
I...I WAS LISTENING! I-I-I-I HEARD EVERYTHING!!
...FINE.
INDEX ...?
GORON (ROLL)

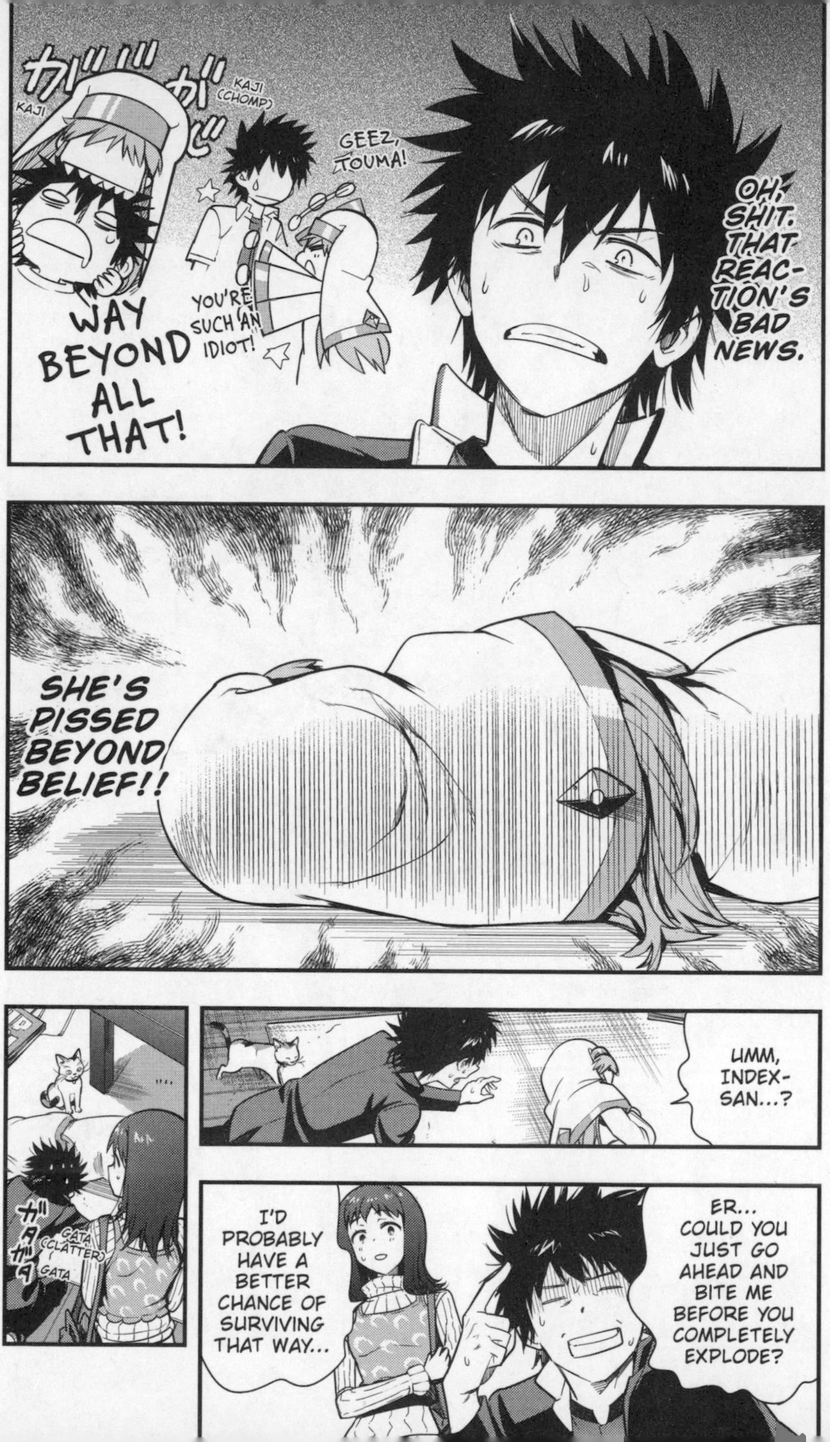
OH, SHIT. THAT REACTION'S BAD NEWS.
GEEZ, TOUMA!
KAJI (CHOMP)
KAJI
YOU'RE SUCH AN IDIOT!
WAY BEYOND ALL THAT!
SHE'S PISSED BEYOND BELIEF!!
UMM, INDEX-SAN...?
ER... COULD YOU JUST GO AHEAD AND BITE ME BEFORE YOU COMPLETELY EXPLODE?
I'D PROBABLY HAVE A BETTER CHANCE OF SURVIVING THAT WAY...
...
GATA (CLATTER)
GATA

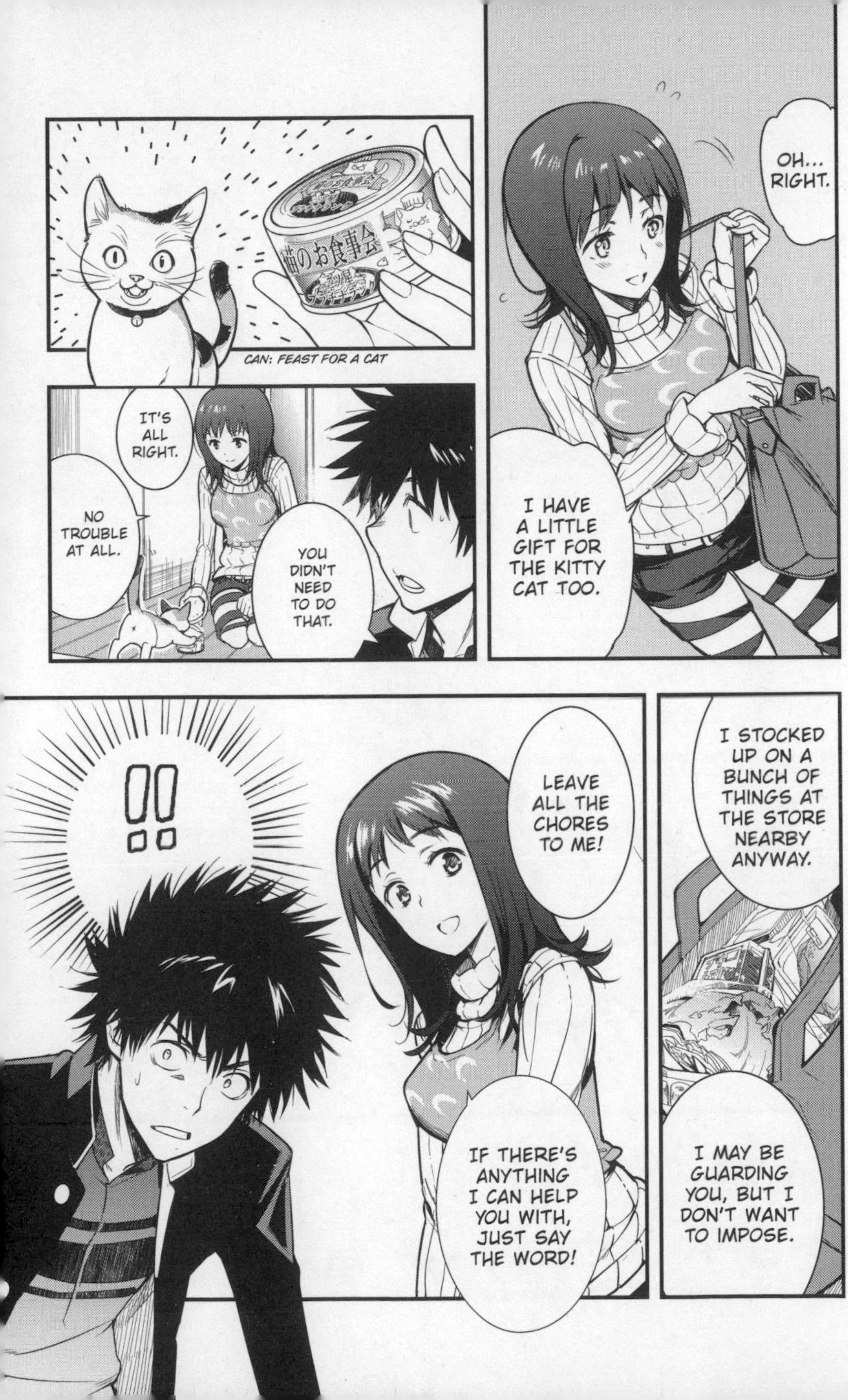
OH... RIGHT.
I HAVE A LITTLE GIFT FOR THE KITTY CAT TOO.
猫のお食事会
CAN: FEAST FOR A CAT
YOU DIDN'T NEED TO DO THAT.
IT'S ALL RIGHT.
NO TROUBLE AT ALL.
I STOCKED UP ON A BUNCH OF THINGS AT THE STORE NEARBY ANYWAY.
I MAY BE GUARDING YOU, BUT I DON'T WANT TO IMPOSE.
LEAVE ALL THE CHORES TO ME!
IF THERE'S ANYTHING I CAN HELP YOU WITH, JUST SAY THE WORD!
!!

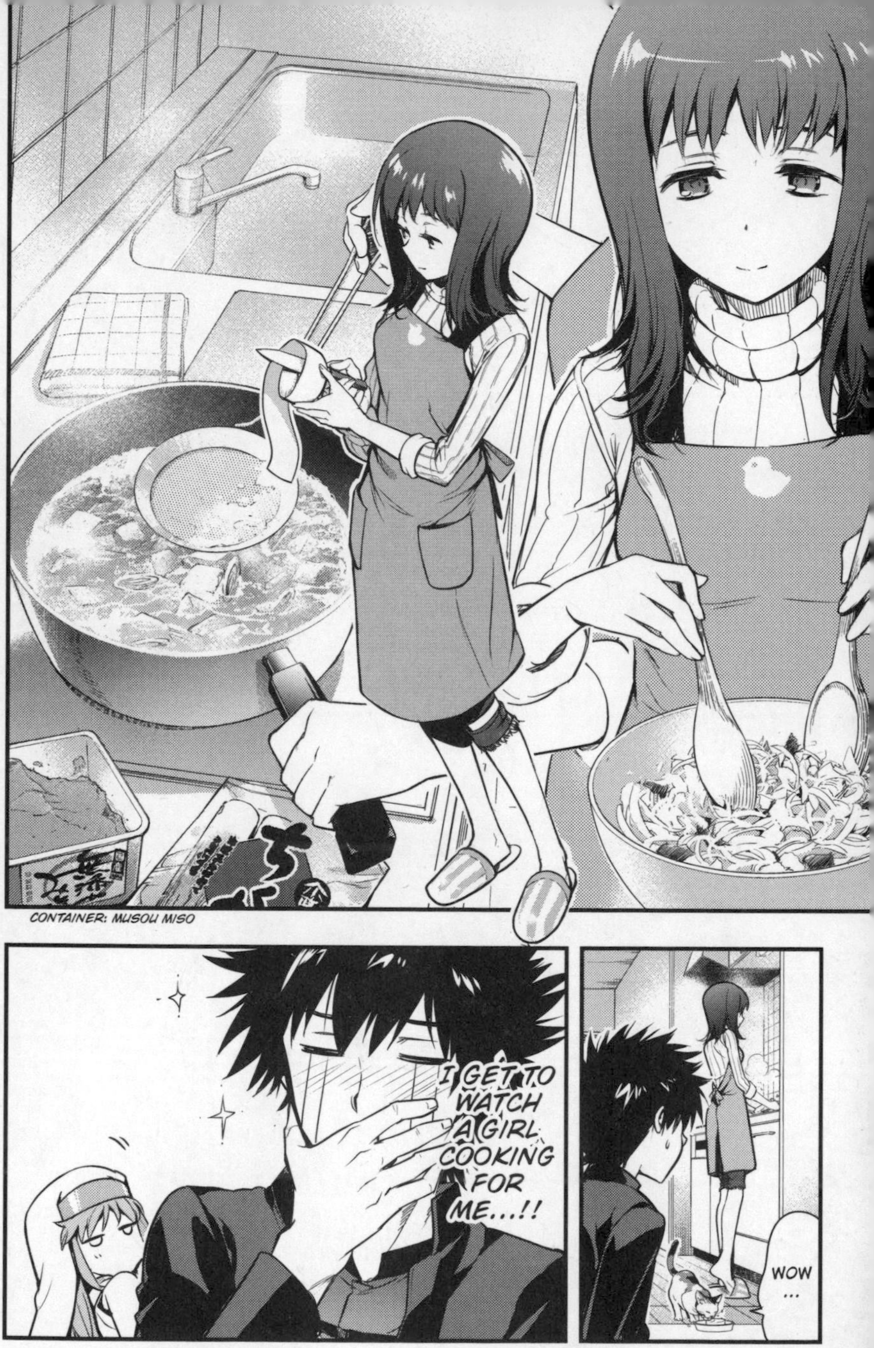
CONTAINER: MUSOU MISO
WOW ...
I GET TO WATCH A GIRL COOKING FOR ME...!!

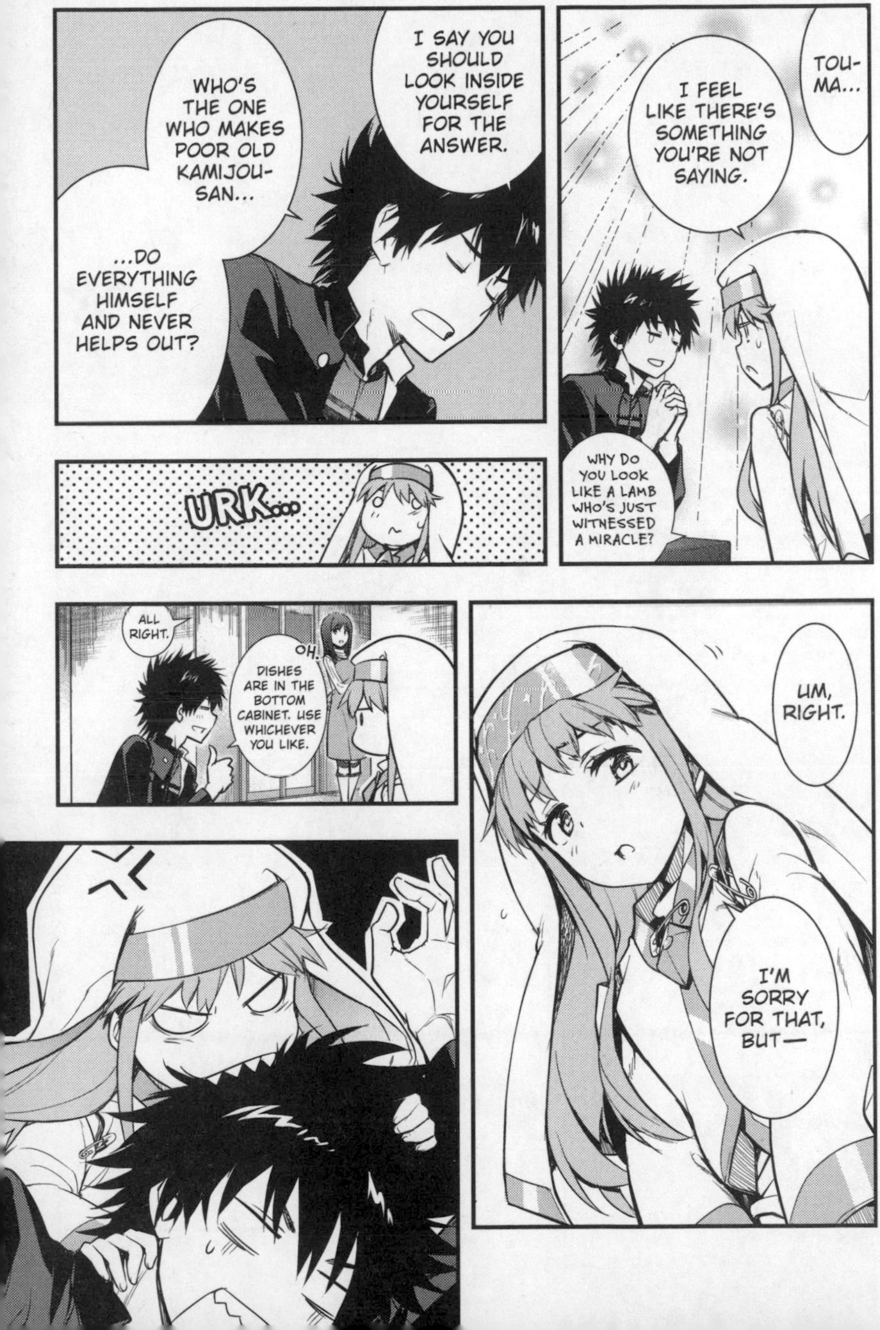
TOU-MA...
I FEEL LIKE THERE'S SOMETHING YOU'RE NOT SAYING.
WHY DO YOU LOOK LIKE A LAMB WHO'S JUST WITNESSED A MIRACLE?
I SAY YOU SHOULD LOOK INSIDE YOURSELF FOR THE ANSWER.
WHO'S THE ONE WHO MAKES POOR OLD KAMIJOU-SAN...
...DO EVERYTHING HIMSELF AND NEVER HELPS OUT?
URK...
UM, RIGHT.
I'M SORRY FOR THAT, BUT—
OH.
DISHES ARE IN THE BOTTOM CABINET. USE WHICHEVER YOU LIKE.
ALL RIGHT.

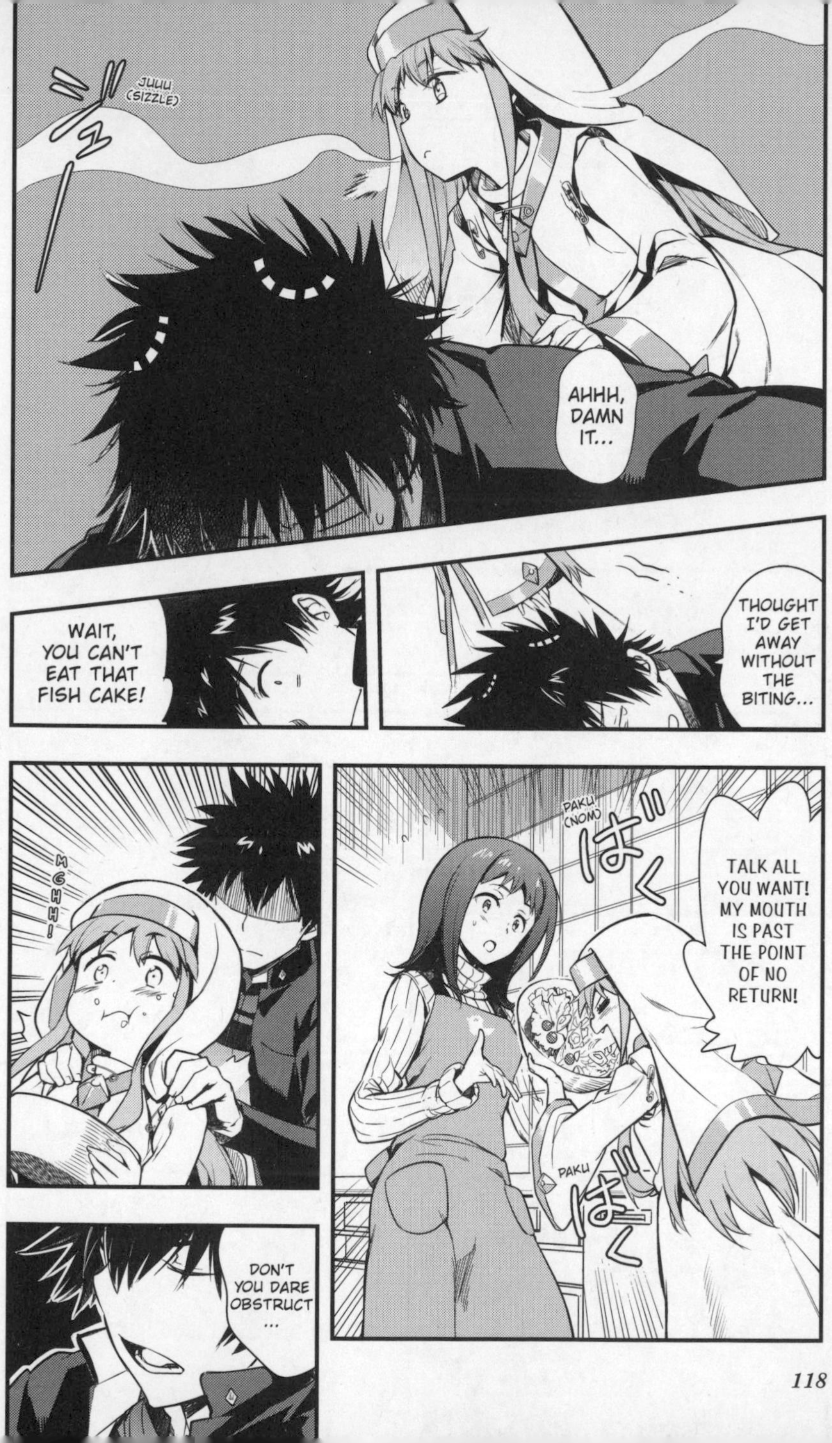
JUUU (SIZZLE)
AHHH, DAMN IT...
THOUGHT I'D GET AWAY WITHOUT THE BITING...
WAIT, YOU CAN'T EAT THAT FISH CAKE!
PAKU (NOM)
TALK ALL YOU WANT! MY MOUTH IS PAST THE POINT OF NO RETURN!
PAKU
MGHH!
DON'T YOU DARE OBSTRUCT ...

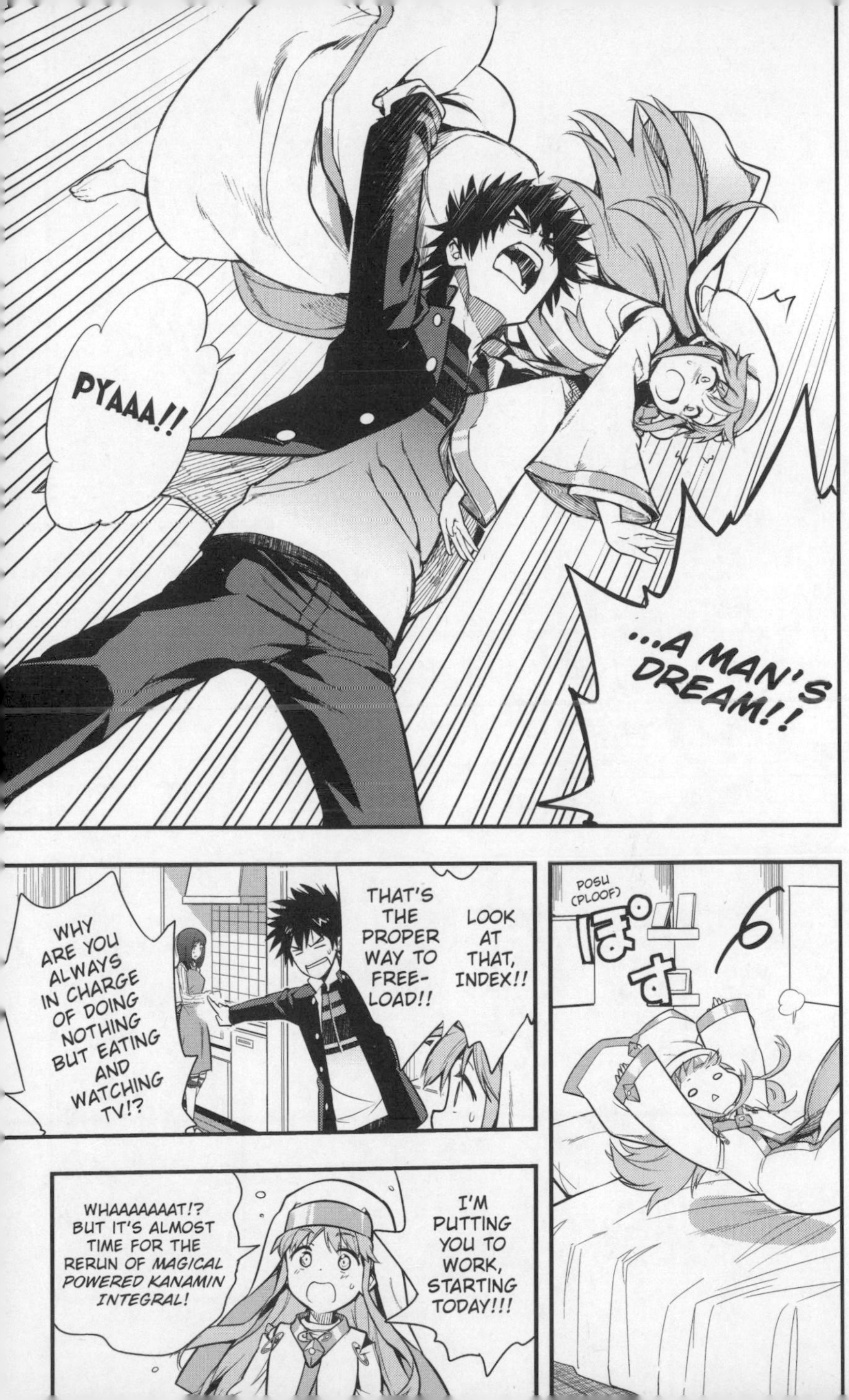

...A MAN'S DREAM!!
PYAAA!!
POSU (PLOOF)
ぽす
LOOK AT THAT, INDEX!!
THAT'S THE PROPER WAY TO FREE-LOAD!!
WHY ARE YOU ALWAYS IN CHARGE OF DOING NOTHING BUT EATING AND WATCHING TV!?
I'M PUTTING YOU TO WORK, STARTING TODAY!!!
WHAAAAAAAT!? BUT IT'S ALMOST TIME FOR THE RERUN OF *MAGICAL POWERED KANAMIN INTEGRAL*!

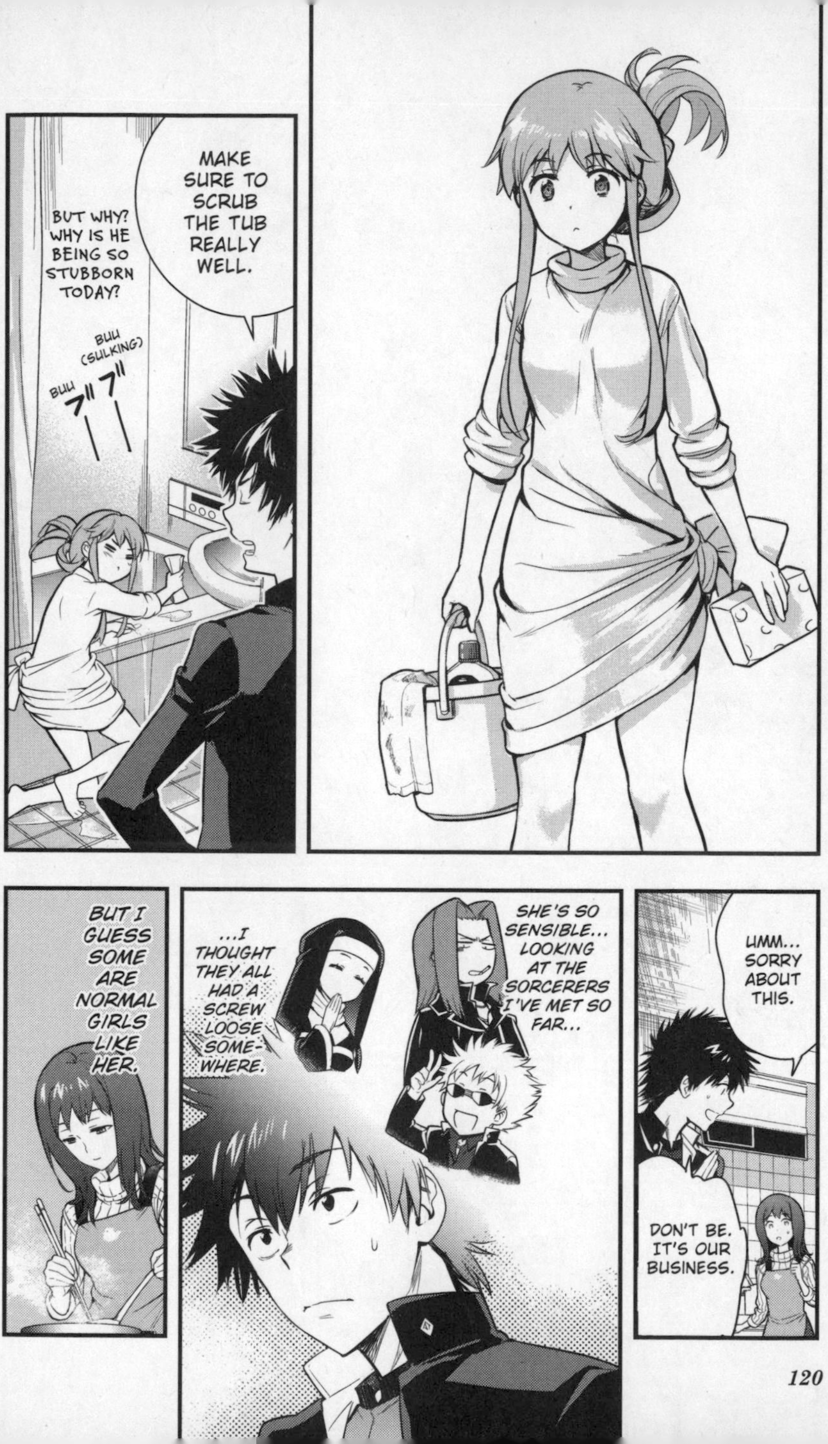
MAKE SURE TO SCRUB THE TUB REALLY WELL.
BUT WHY? WHY IS HE BEING SO STUBBORN TODAY?
BUU (SULKING)
BUU
UMM... SORRY ABOUT THIS.
DON'T BE. IT'S OUR BUSINESS.
SHE'S SO SENSIBLE... LOOKING AT THE SORCERERS I'VE MET SO FAR...
...I THOUGHT THEY ALL HAD A SCREW LOOSE SOME-WHERE.
BUT I GUESS SOME ARE NORMAL GIRLS LIKE HER.

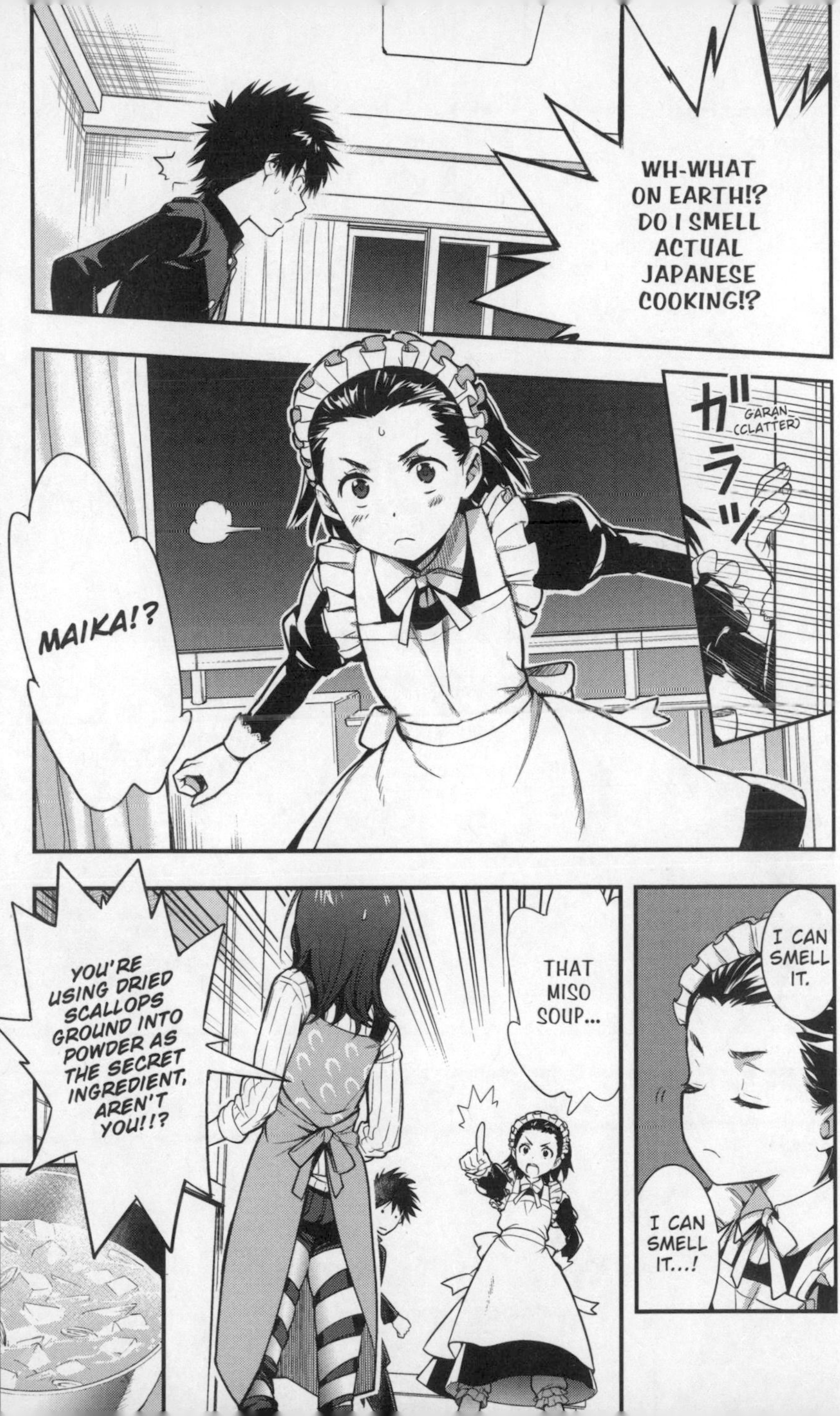
WH-WHAT ON EARTH!? DO I SMELL ACTUAL JAPANESE COOKING!?
ガラッ
GARAN (CLATTER)
MAIKA!?
I CAN SMELL IT.
I CAN SMELL IT...!
THAT MISO SOUP...
YOU'RE USING DRIED SCALLOPS GROUND INTO POWDER AS THE SECRET INGREDIENT, AREN'T YOU!!?

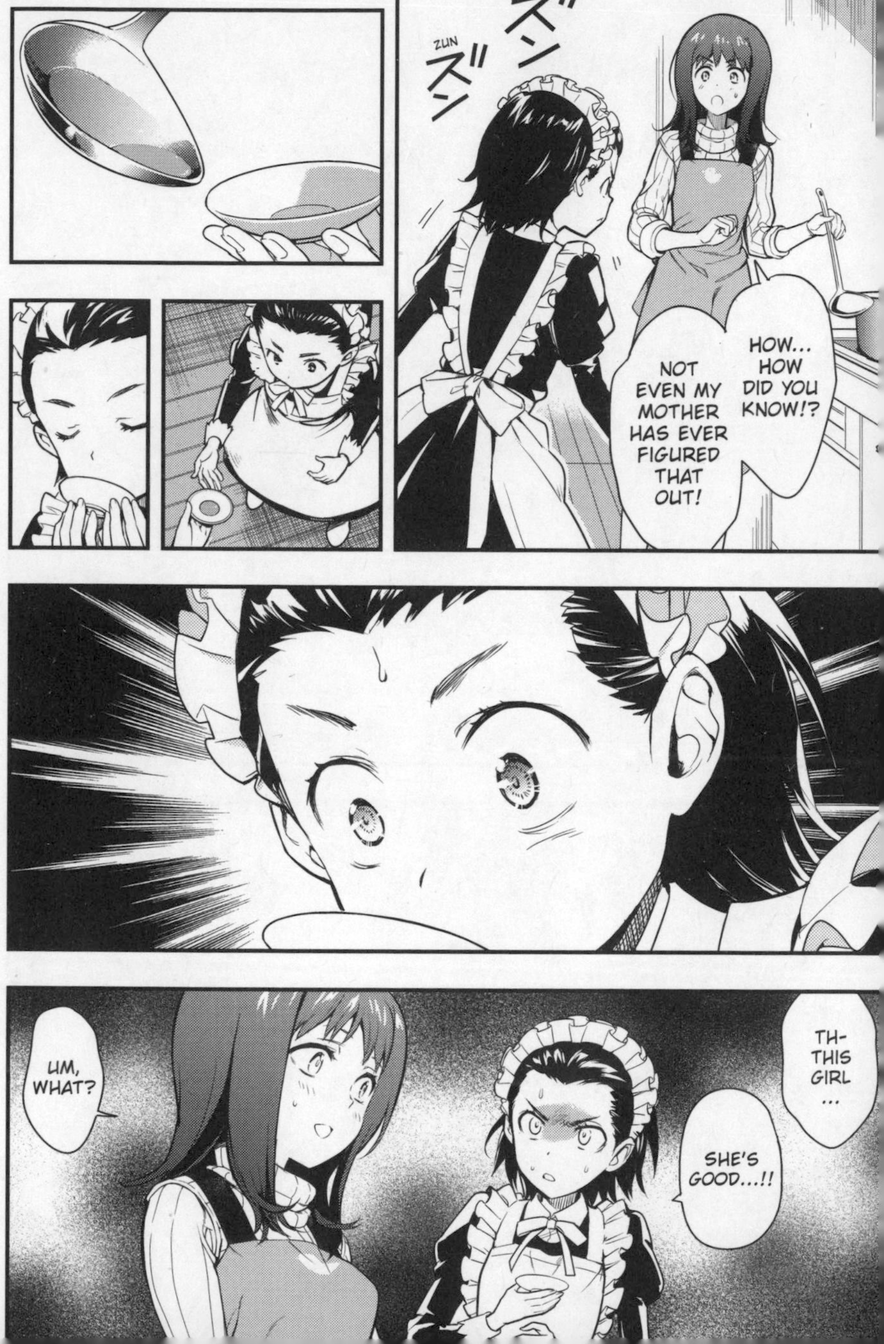
ZUN (STOMP)
ズン
ZUN
ズン
HOW... HOW DID YOU KNOW!?
NOT EVEN MY MOTHER HAS EVER FIGURED THAT OUT!
TH-THIS GIRL ...
SHE'S GOOD...!!
UM, WHAT?

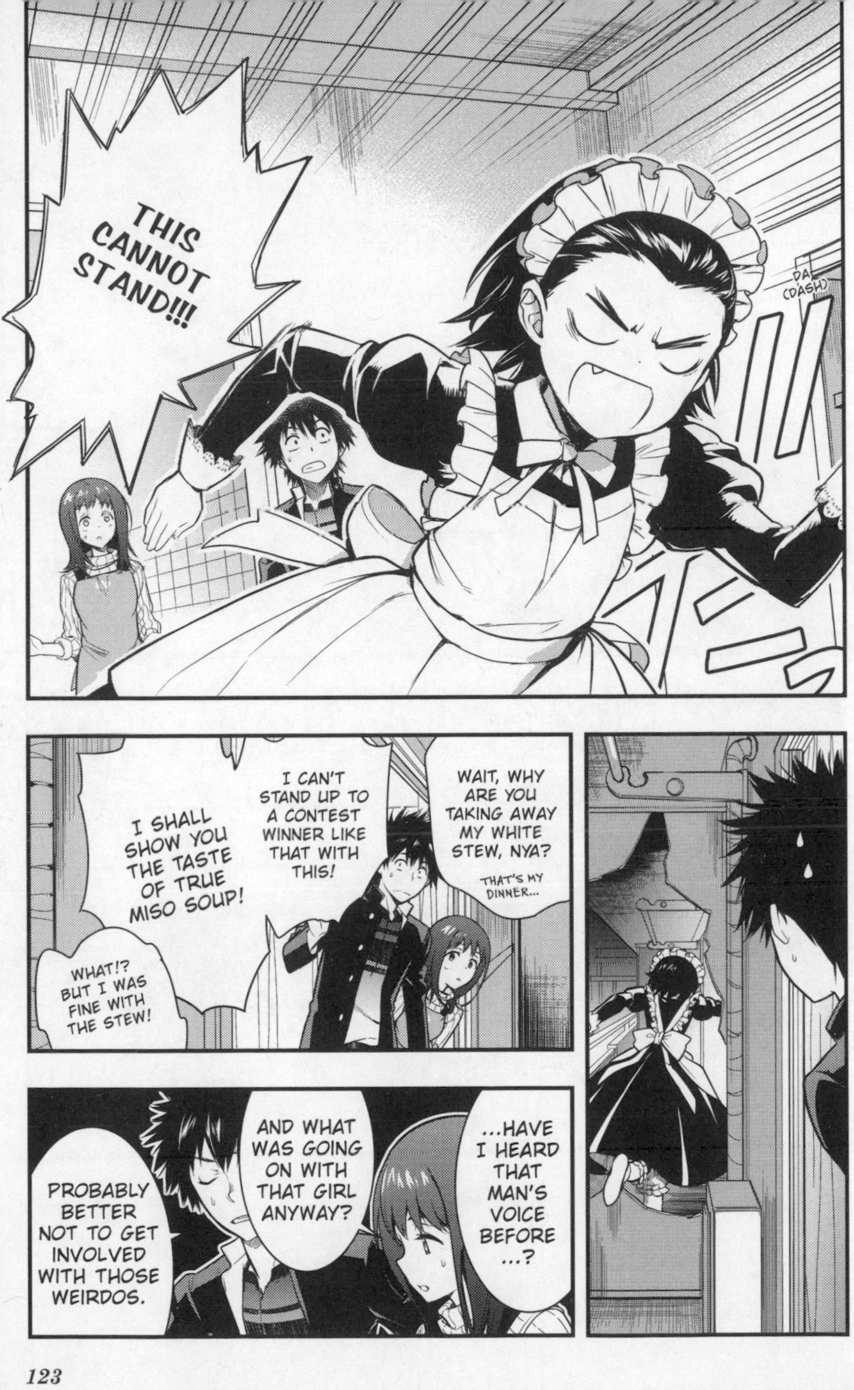
THIS CANNOT STAND!!!
DA (DASH)
WAIT, WHY ARE YOU TAKING AWAY MY WHITE STEW, NYA?
THAT'S MY DINNER...
I CAN'T STAND UP TO A CONTEST WINNER LIKE THAT WITH THIS!
I SHALL SHOW YOU THE TASTE OF TRUE MISO SOUP!
WHAT!? BUT I WAS FINE WITH THE STEW!
...HAVE I HEARD THAT MAN'S VOICE BEFORE ...?
AND WHAT WAS GOING ON WITH THAT GIRL ANYWAY?
PROBABLY BETTER NOT TO GET INVOLVED WITH THOSE WEIRDOS.

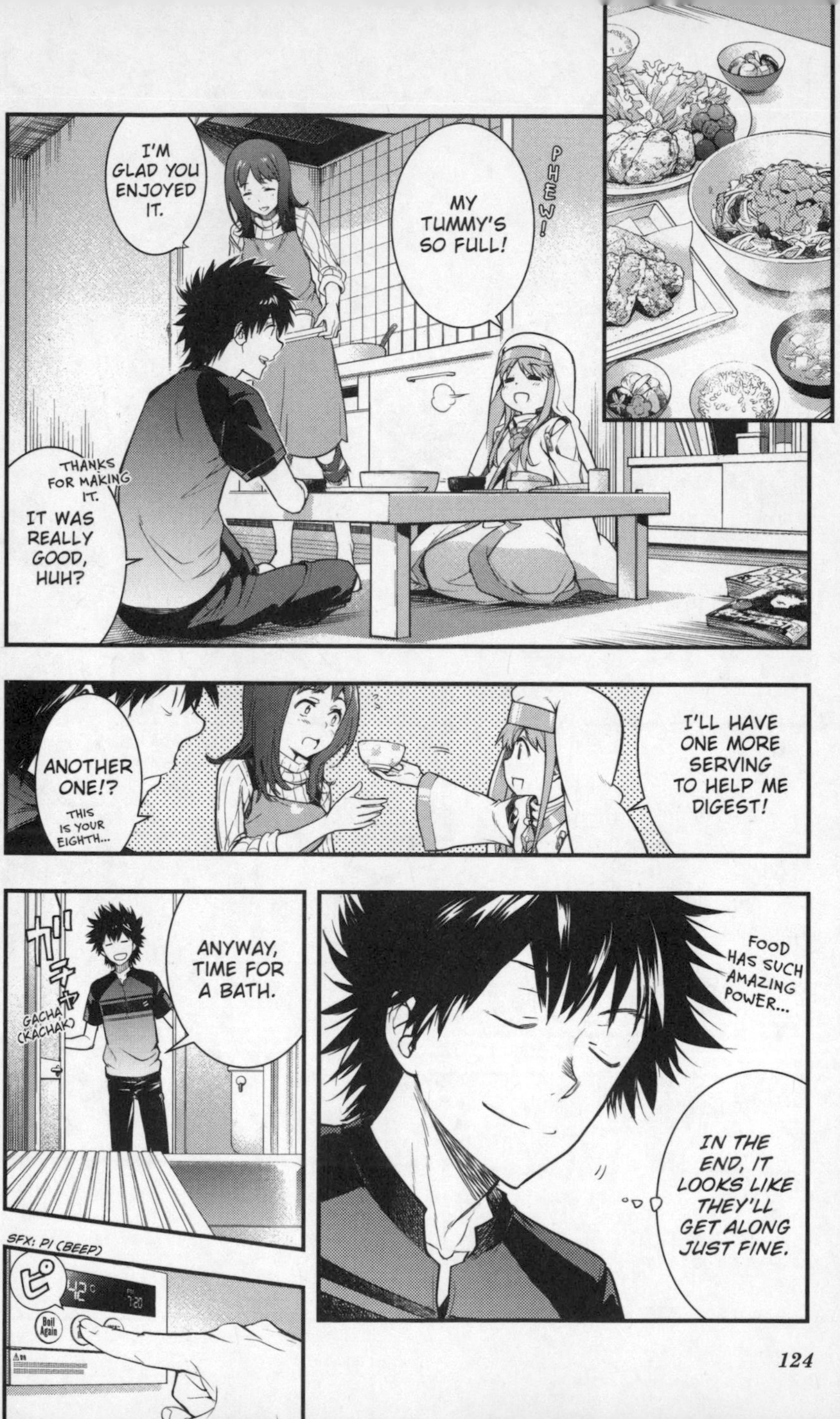
PHEW!
MY TUMMY'S SO FULL!
I'M GLAD YOU ENJOYED IT.
THANKS FOR MAKING IT.
IT WAS REALLY GOOD, HUH?
I'LL HAVE ONE MORE SERVING TO HELP ME DIGEST!
ANOTHER ONE!?
THIS IS YOUR EIGHTH...
FOOD HAS SUCH AMAZING POWER...
IN THE END, IT LOOKS LIKE THEY'LL GET ALONG JUST FINE.
ANYWAY, TIME FOR A BATH.
GACHA (KACHAK)
SFX: PI (BEEP)
42°C
7:20
Boil Again

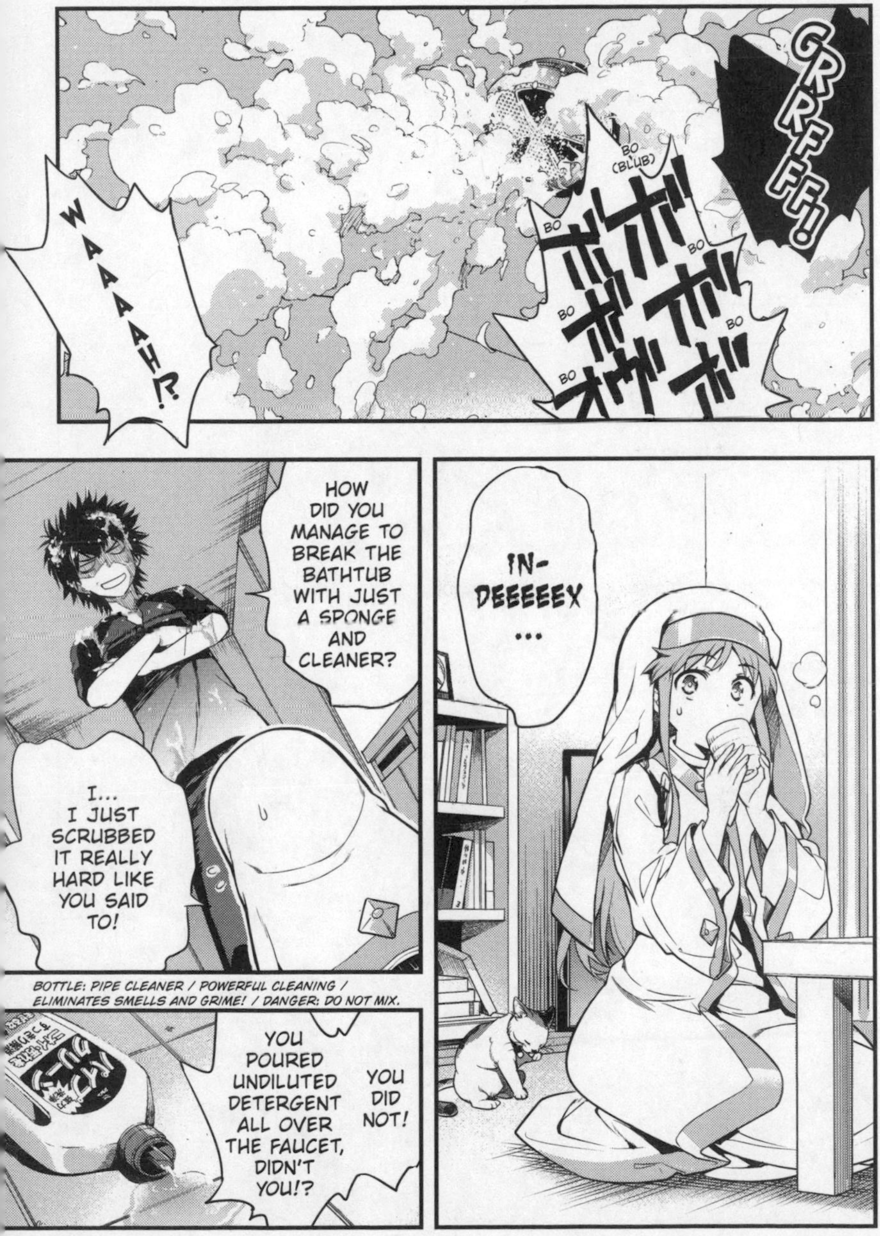
GRRFFF!
BO (BLUB)
BO BO BO BO BO
WAAAAAH!?
IN-DEEEEEX...
HOW DID YOU MANAGE TO BREAK THE BATHTUB WITH JUST A SPONGE AND CLEANER?
I... I JUST SCRUBBED IT REALLY HARD LIKE YOU SAID TO!
BOTTLE: PIPE CLEANER / POWERFUL CLEANING / ELIMINATES SMELLS AND GRIME! / DANGER: DO NOT MIX.
YOU POURED UNDILUTED DETERGENT ALL OVER THE FAUCET, DIDN'T YOU!?
YOU DID NOT!

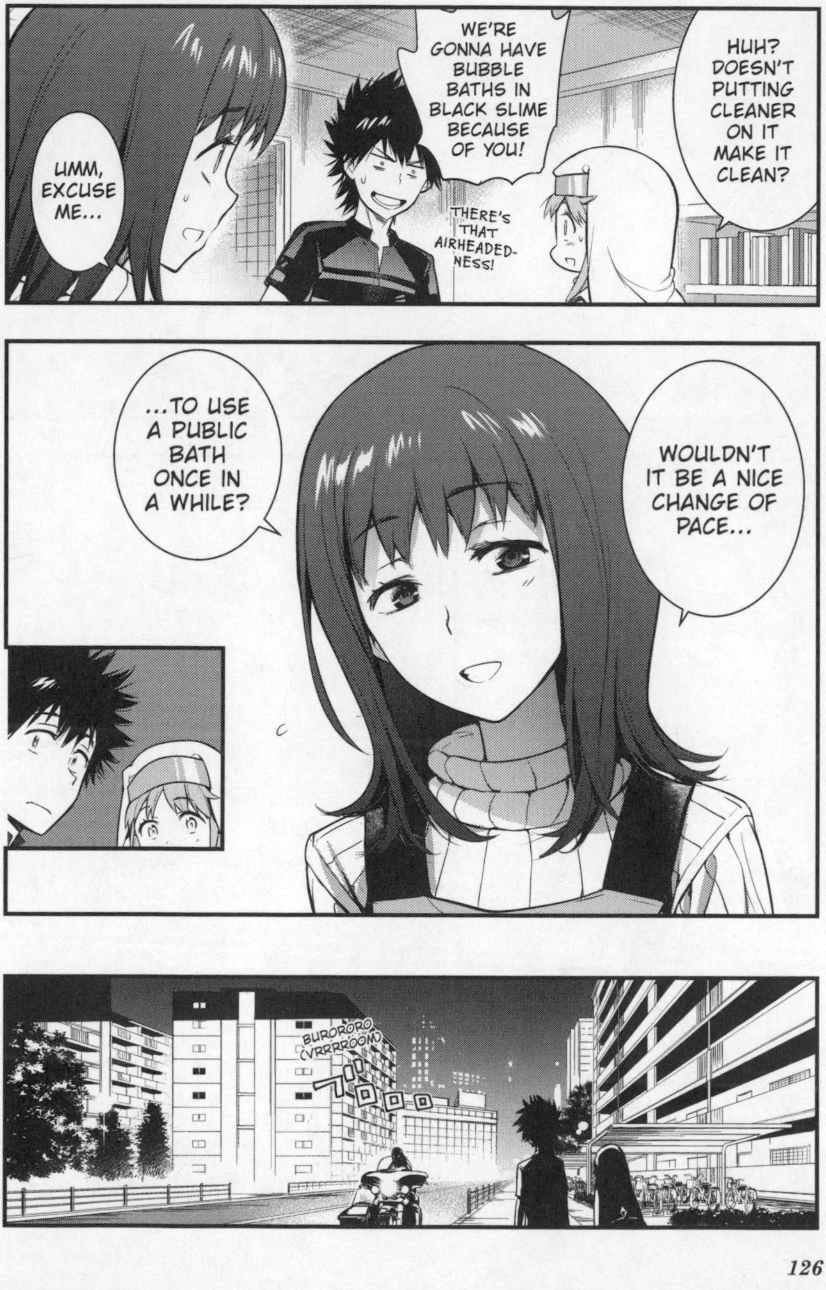
HUH? DOESN'T PUTTING CLEANER ON IT MAKE IT CLEAN?
WE'RE GONNA HAVE BUBBLE BATHS IN BLACK SLIME BECAUSE OF YOU!
THERE'S THAT AIRHEADED-NESS!
UMM, EXCUSE ME...
WOULDN'T IT BE A NICE CHANGE OF PACE...
...TO USE A PUBLIC BATH ONCE IN A WHILE?
BURORORO (VRRRROOM)

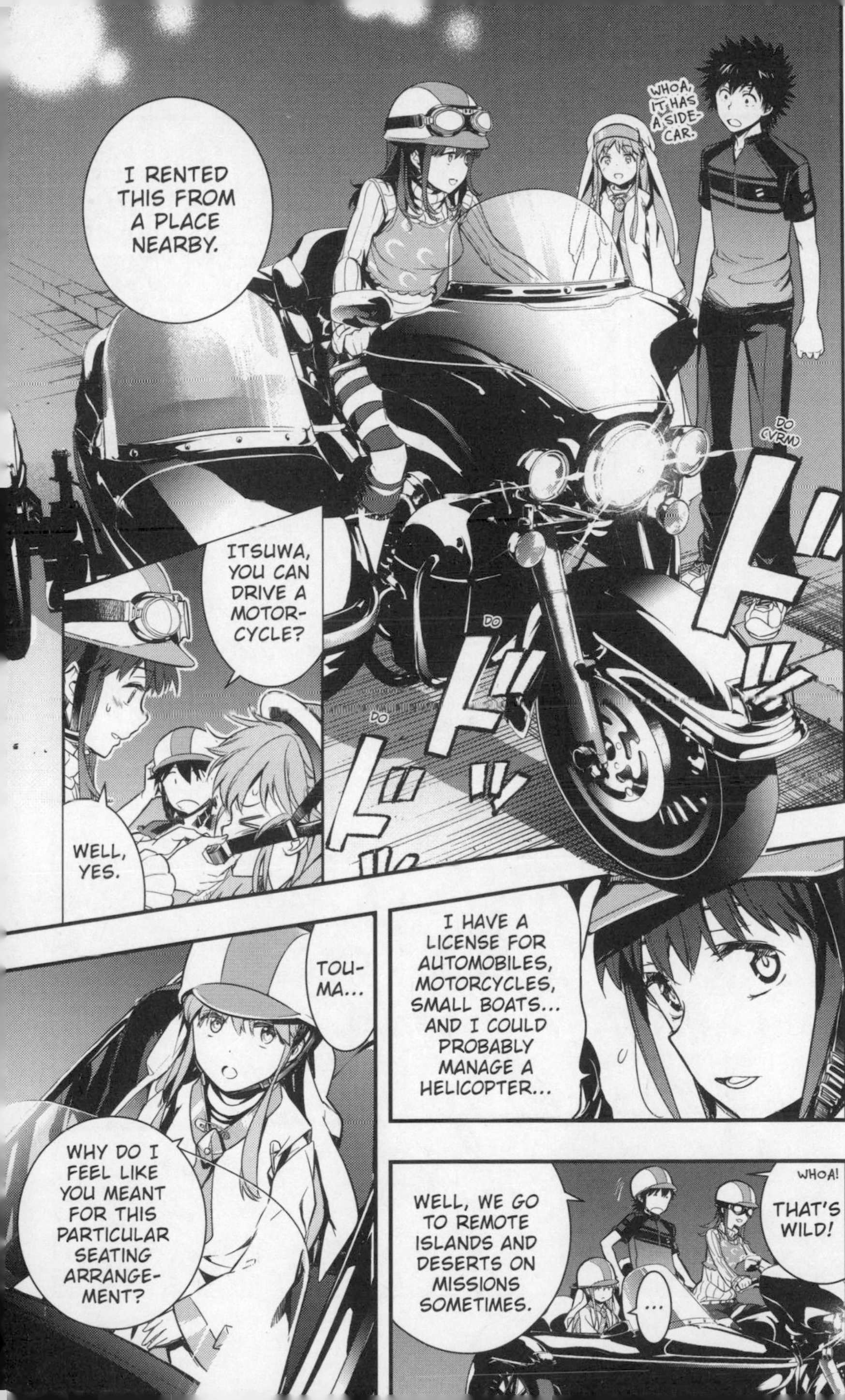

WHOA, IT HAS A SIDE-CAR.
I RENTED THIS FROM A PLACE NEARBY.
DO (VRM)
DO
DO
ITSUWA, YOU CAN DRIVE A MOTOR-CYCLE?
WELL, YES.
I HAVE A LICENSE FOR AUTOMOBILES, MOTORCYCLES, SMALL BOATS... AND I COULD PROBABLY MANAGE A HELICOPTER...
WHOA!
THAT'S WILD!
WELL, WE GO TO REMOTE ISLANDS AND DESERTS ON MISSIONS SOMETIMES.
...
TOU-MA...
WHY DO I FEEL LIKE YOU MEANT FOR THIS PARTICULAR SEATING ARRANGE-MENT?

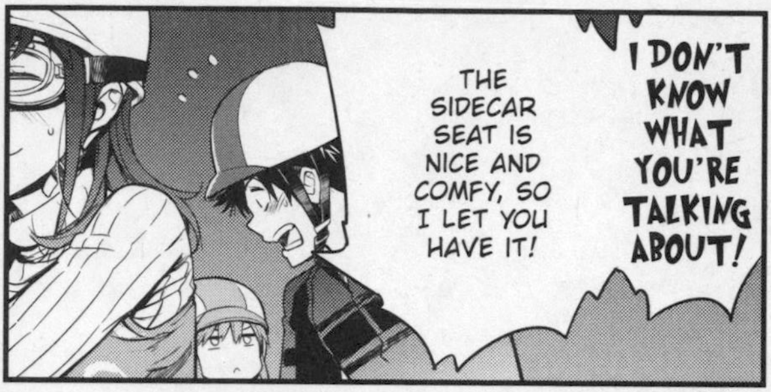
I DON'T KNOW WHAT YOU'RE TALKING ABOUT!
THE SIDECAR SEAT IS NICE AND COMFY, SO I LET YOU HAVE IT!

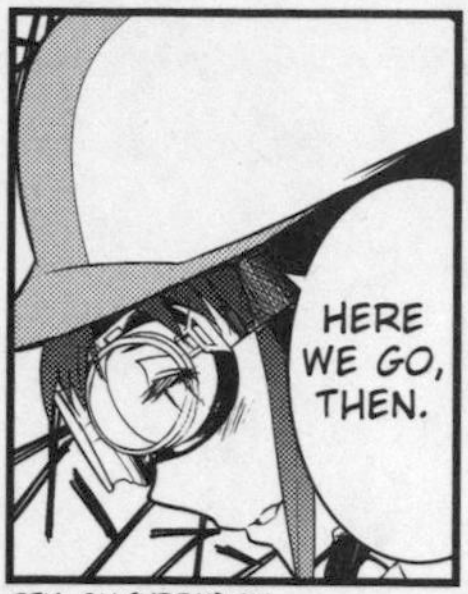
HERE WE GO, THEN.

SFX: ON (VRRM) ON

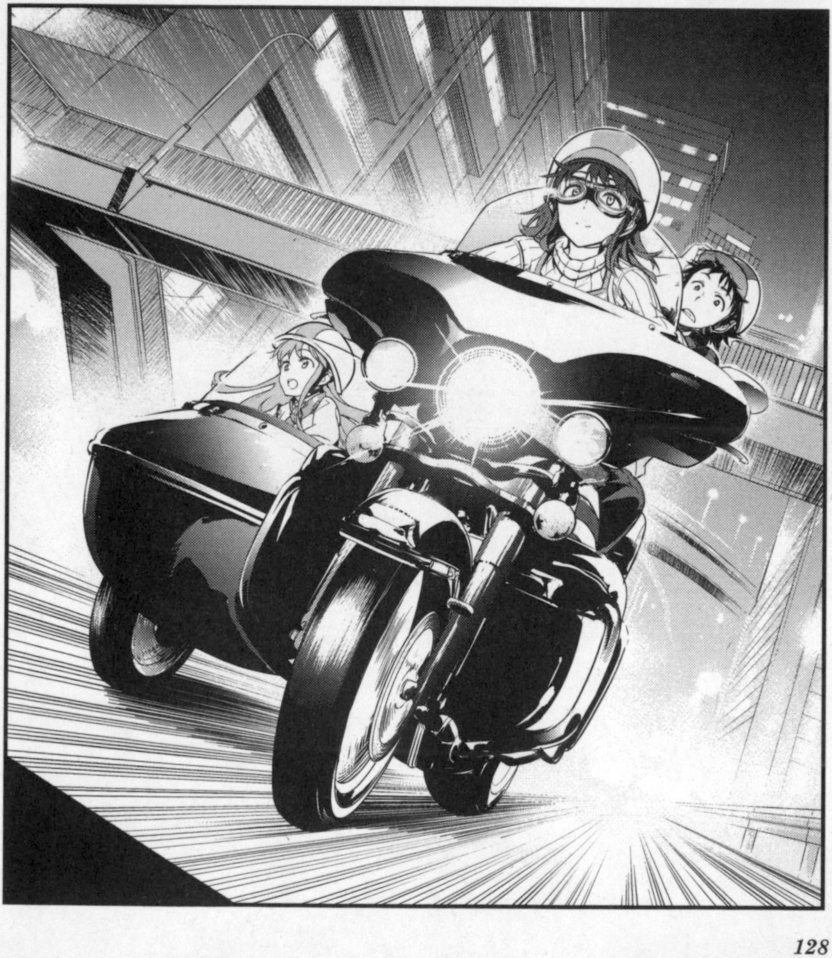

A
Certain
Magical
Index

A Certain Magical Index

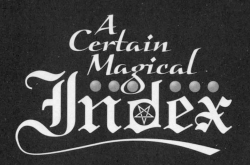

#152 DISTRICT 22

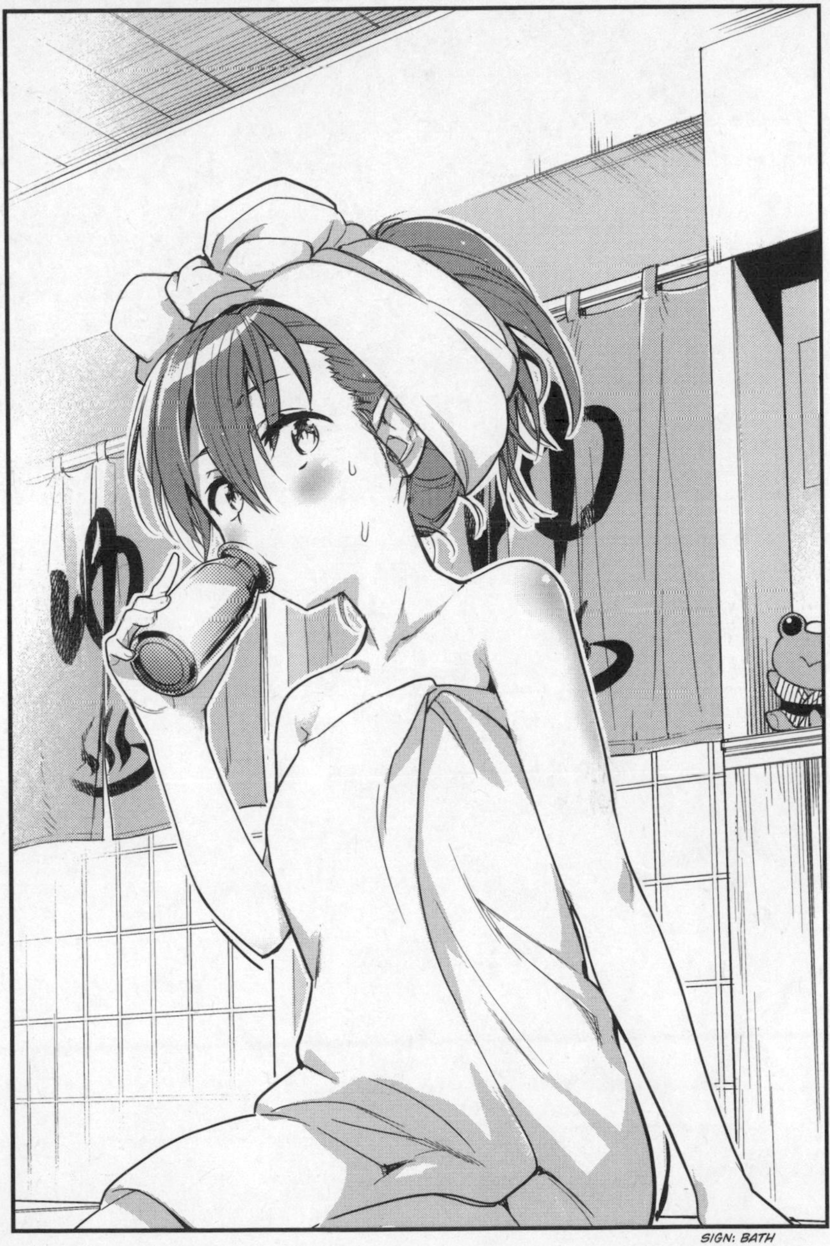

SIGN: BATH

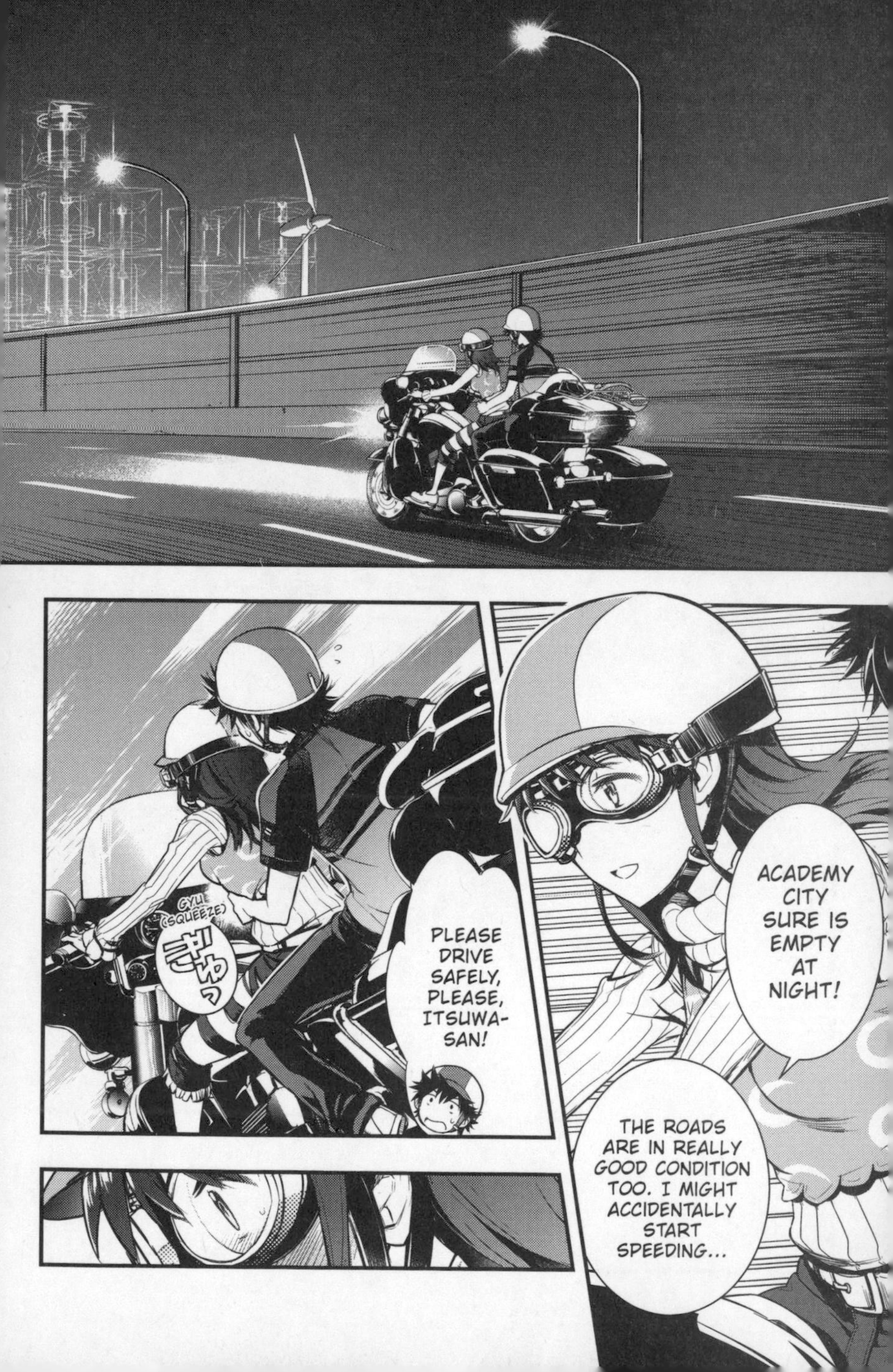
ACADEMY CITY SURE IS EMPTY AT NIGHT!
THE ROADS ARE IN REALLY GOOD CONDITION TOO. I MIGHT ACCIDENTALLY START SPEEDING...
PLEASE DRIVE SAFELY, PLEASE, ITSUWA-SAN!
GYU (SQUEEZE)
ぎゅっ

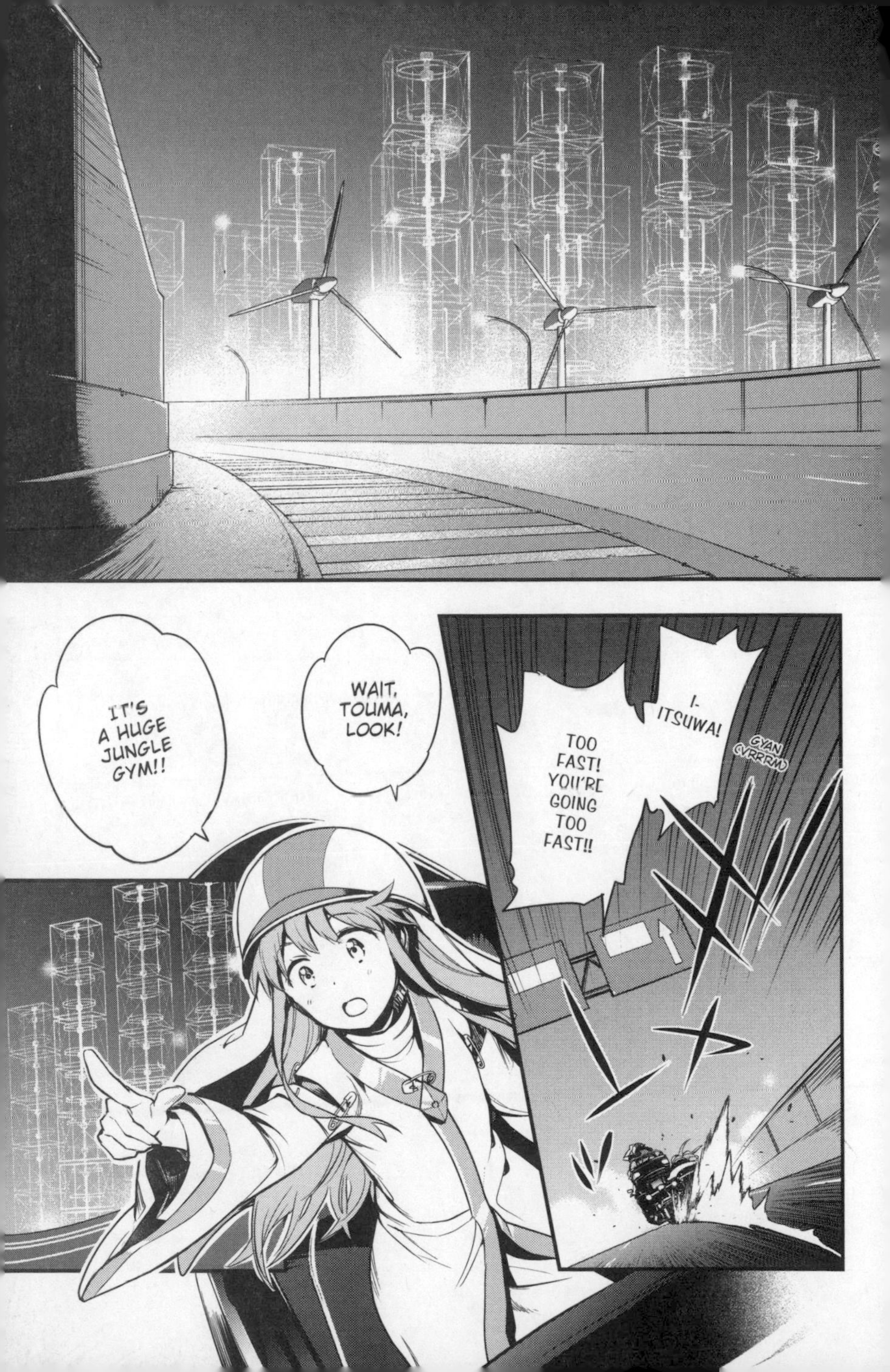
I-
ITSUWA!
GYAN
(VRRRM)
TOO FAST! YOU'RE GOING TOO FAST!!
WAIT, TOUMA, LOOK!
IT'S A HUGE JUNGLE GYM!!

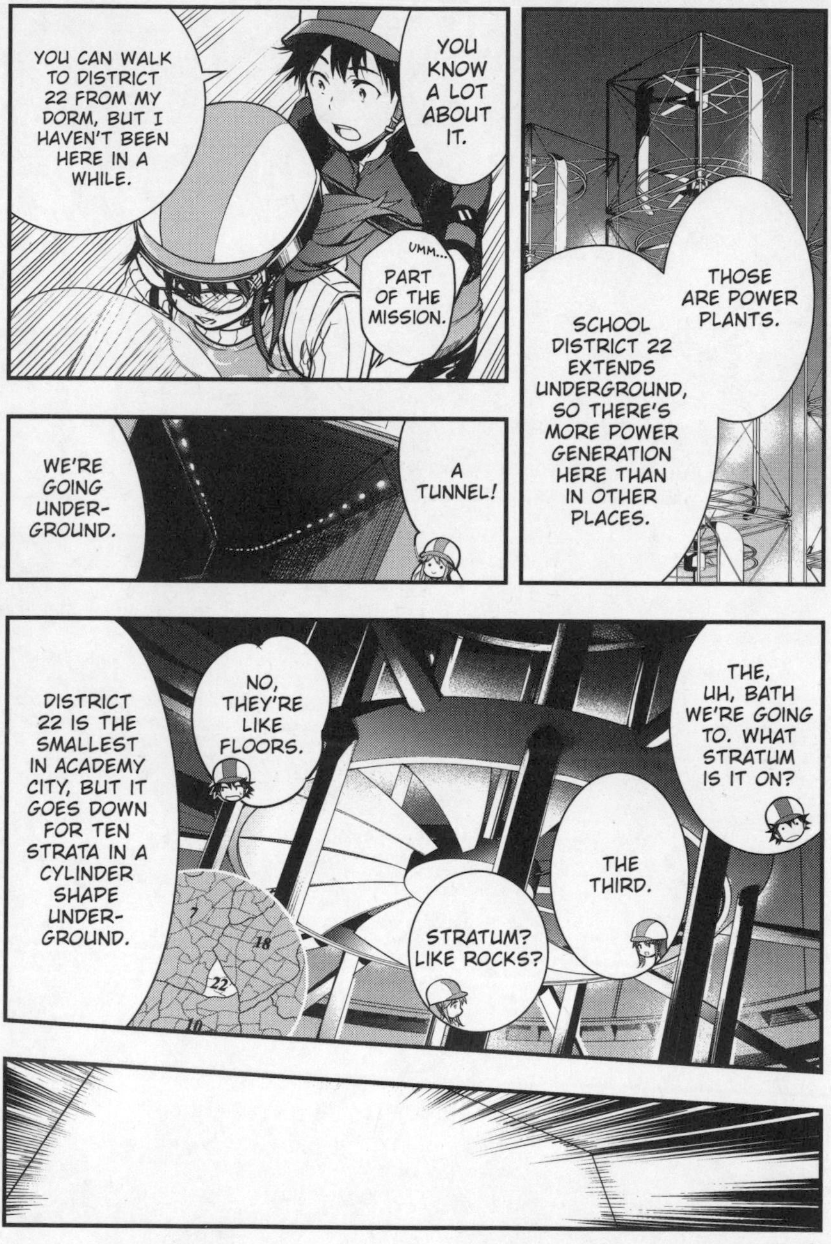
THOSE ARE POWER PLANTS.
SCHOOL DISTRICT 22 EXTENDS UNDERGROUND, SO THERE'S MORE POWER GENERATION HERE THAN IN OTHER PLACES.
YOU KNOW A LOT ABOUT IT.
UMM...
PART OF THE MISSION.
YOU CAN WALK TO DISTRICT 22 FROM MY DORM, BUT I HAVEN'T BEEN HERE IN A WHILE.
A TUNNEL!
WE'RE GOING UNDERGROUND.
THE, UH, BATH WE'RE GOING TO. WHAT STRATUM IS IT ON?
THE THIRD.
STRATUM? LIKE ROCKS?
NO, THEY'RE LIKE FLOORS.
DISTRICT 22 IS THE SMALLEST IN ACADEMY CITY, BUT IT GOES DOWN FOR TEN STRATA IN A CYLINDER SHAPE UNDERGROUND.
7
18
22
10

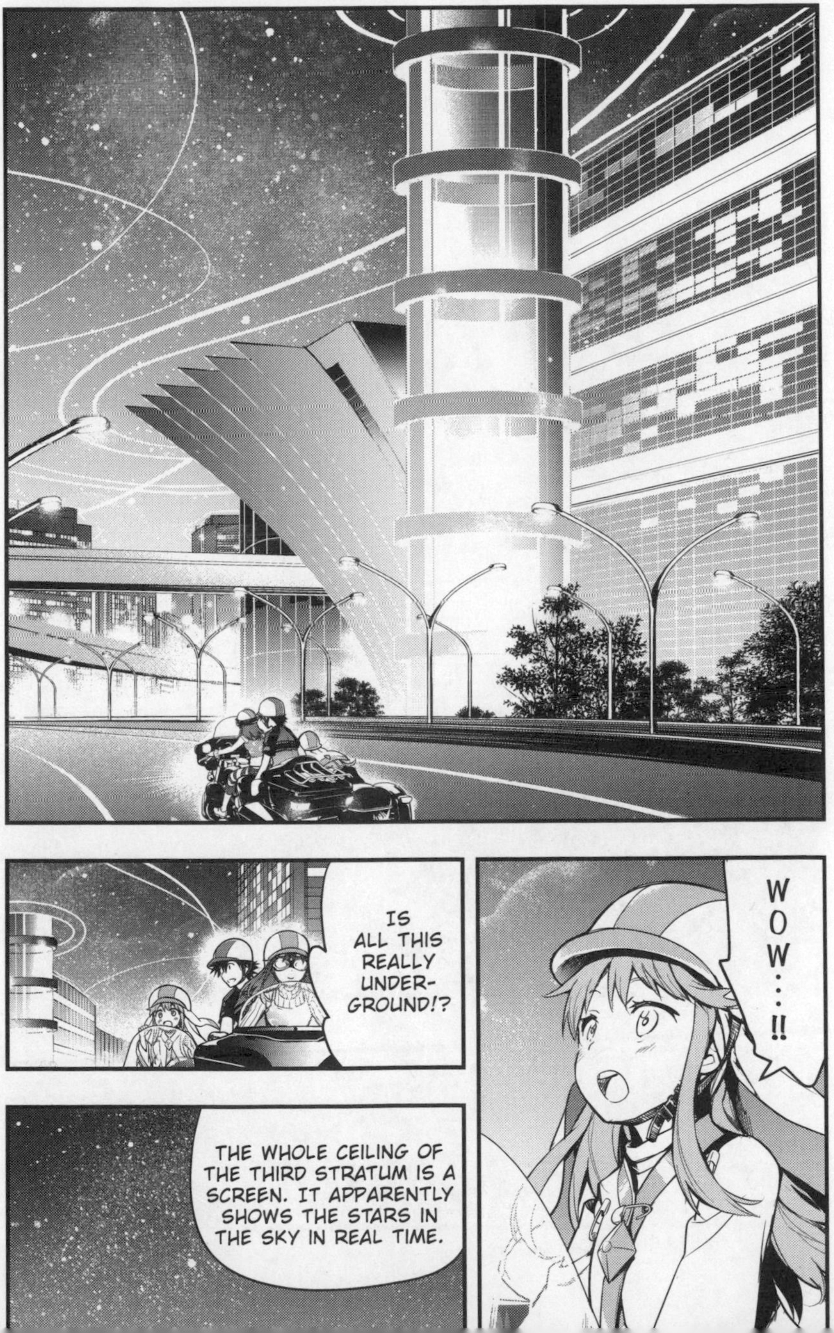
WOW...!!
IS ALL THIS REALLY UNDERGROUND!?
THE WHOLE CEILING OF THE THIRD STRATUM IS A SCREEN. IT APPARENTLY SHOWS THE STARS IN THE SKY IN REAL TIME.

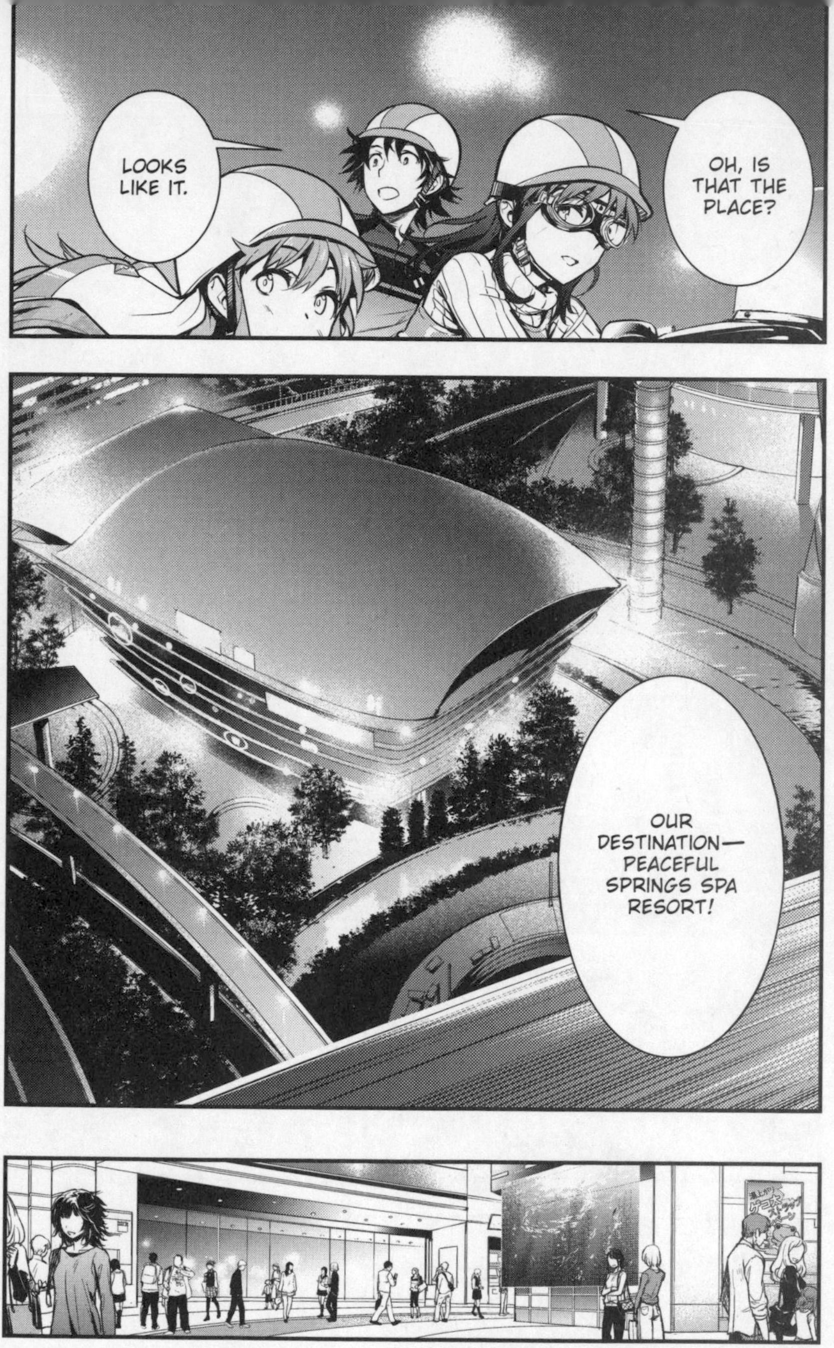
OH, IS THAT THE PLACE?
LOOKS LIKE IT.
OUR DESTINATION—PEACEFUL SPRINGS SPA RESORT!

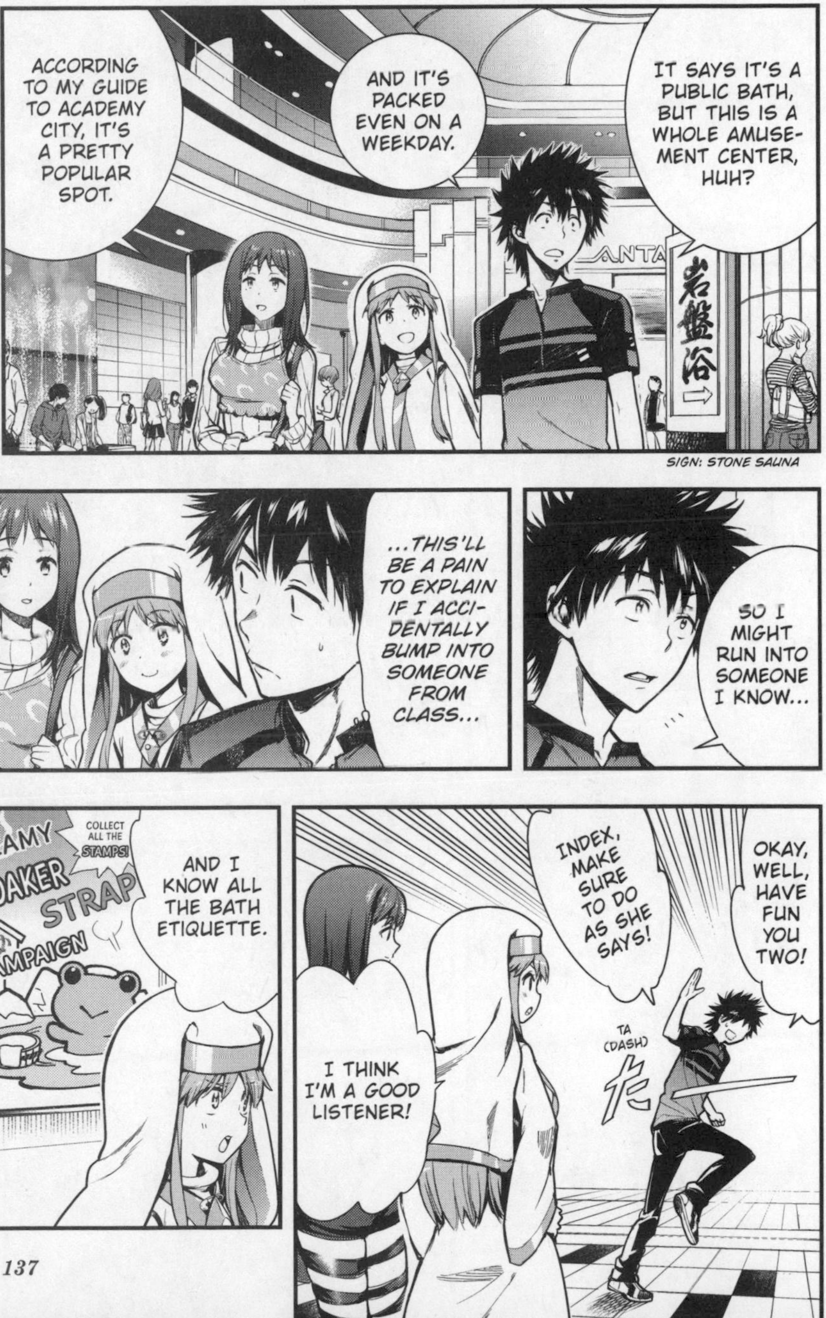
IT SAYS IT'S A PUBLIC BATH, BUT THIS IS A WHOLE AMUSEMENT CENTER, HUH?
AND IT'S PACKED EVEN ON A WEEKDAY.
ACCORDING TO MY GUIDE TO ACADEMY CITY, IT'S A PRETTY POPULAR SPOT.
岩盤浴
SIGN: STONE SAUNA
SO I MIGHT RUN INTO SOMEONE I KNOW...
...THIS'LL BE A PAIN TO EXPLAIN IF I ACCIDENTALLY BUMP INTO SOMEONE FROM CLASS...
OKAY, WELL, HAVE FUN YOU TWO!
INDEX, MAKE SURE TO DO AS SHE SAYS!
TA (DASH)
た
I THINK I'M A GOOD LISTENER!
AND I KNOW ALL THE BATH ETIQUETTE.
STEAMY CROAKER STRAP CAMPAIGN
COLLECT ALL THE STAMPS!

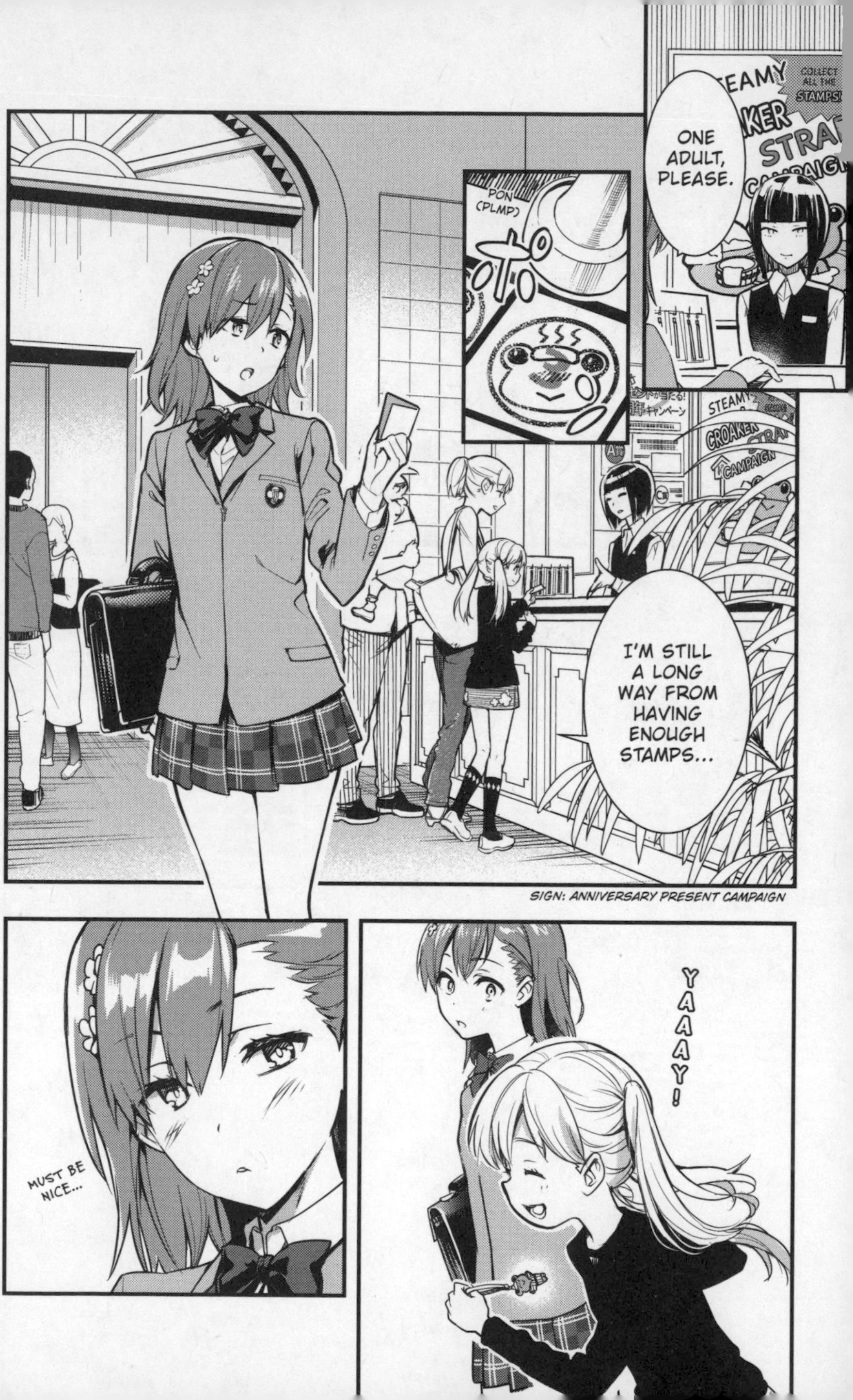
COLLECT ALL THE STAMPS!
ONE ADULT, PLEASE.
PON (PLMP)
I'M STILL A LONG WAY FROM HAVING ENOUGH STAMPS...
SIGN: ANNIVERSARY PRESENT CAMPAIGN
YAAAAY!
MUST BE NICE...

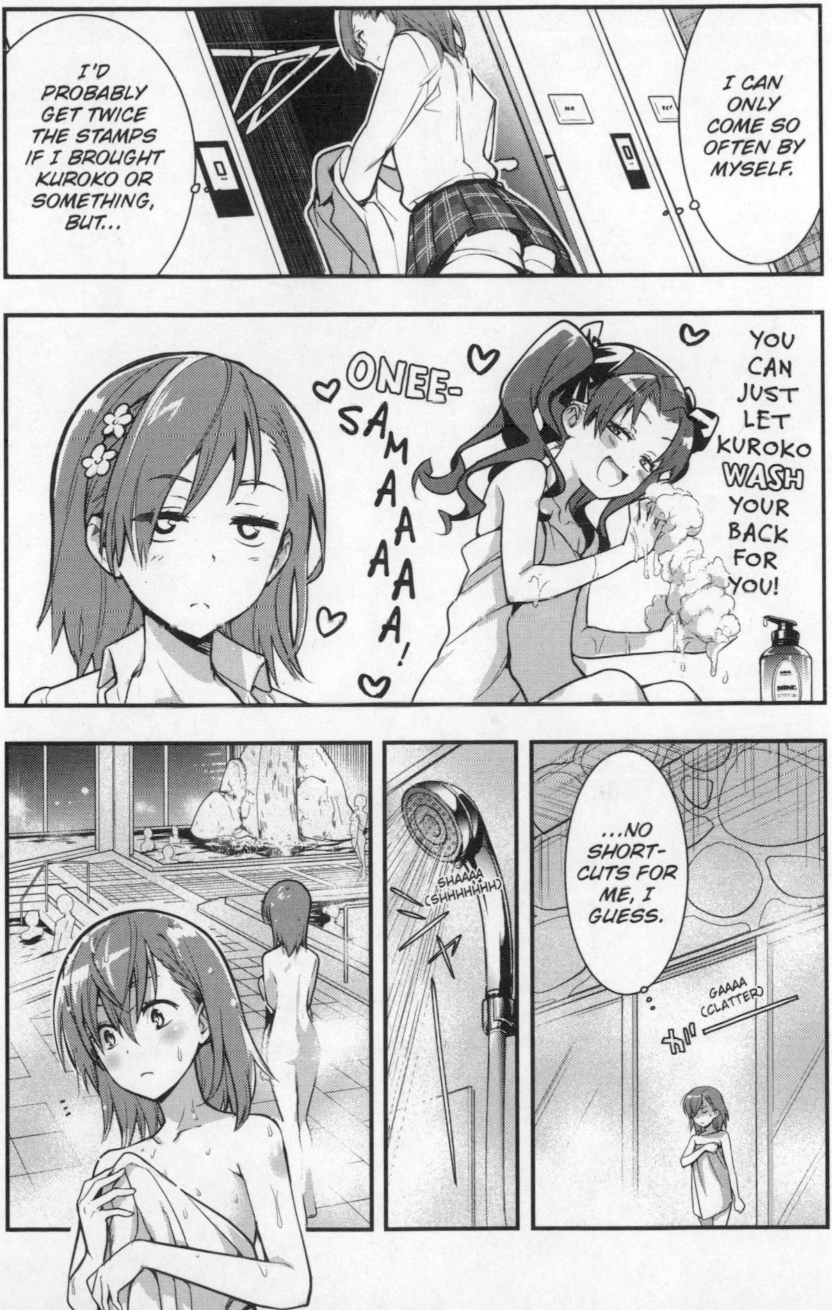
I CAN ONLY COME SO OFTEN BY MYSELF.
I'D PROBABLY GET TWICE THE STAMPS IF I BROUGHT KUROKO OR SOMETHING, BUT...
ONEE-SAMAAAAAAA!
YOU CAN JUST LET KUROKO WASH YOUR BACK FOR YOU!
...NO SHORT-CUTS FOR ME, I GUESS.
GAAAA (CLATTER)
SHAAAA (SHHHHHHH)
...

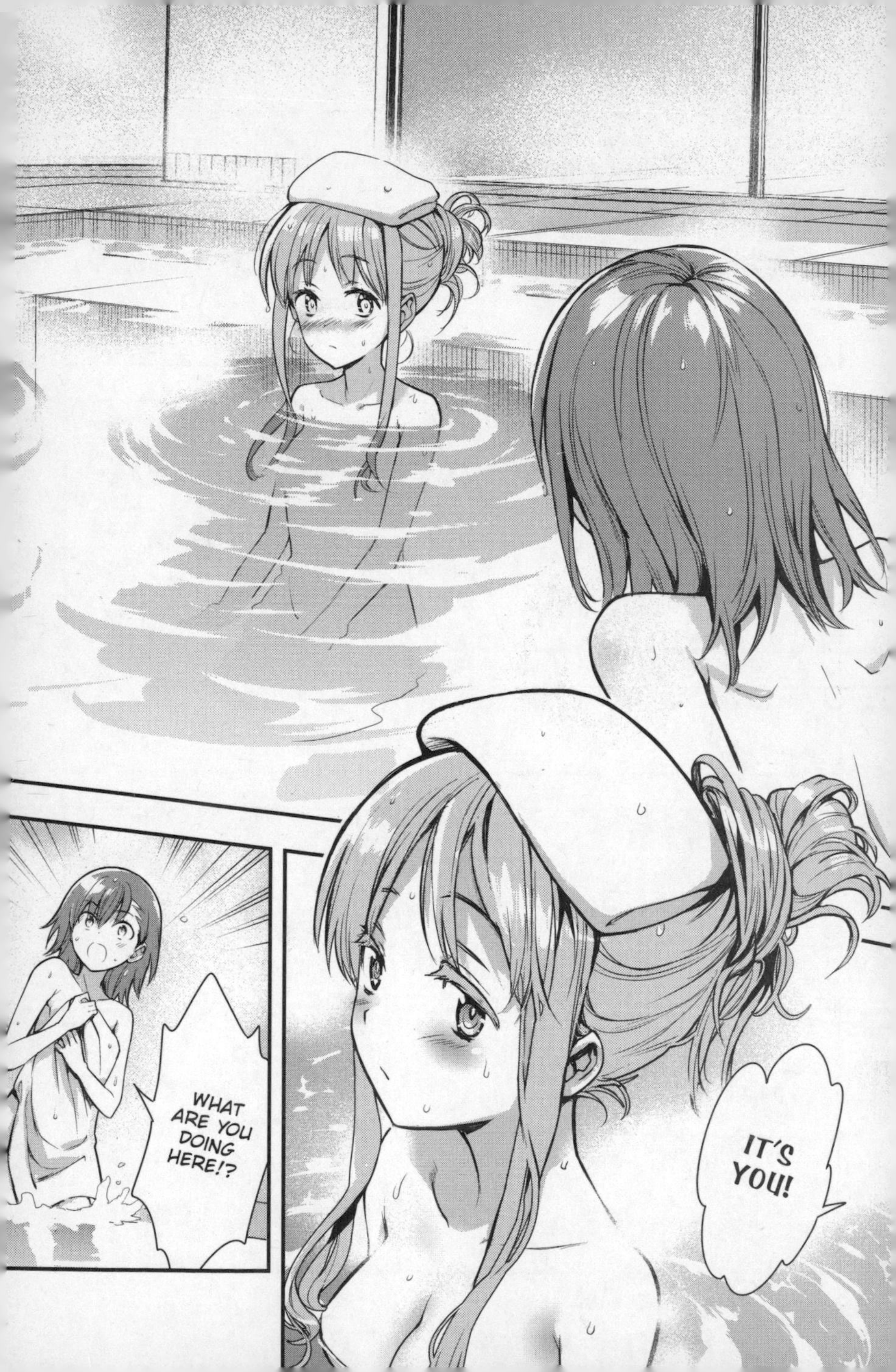
IT'S YOU!
WHAT ARE YOU DOING HERE!?

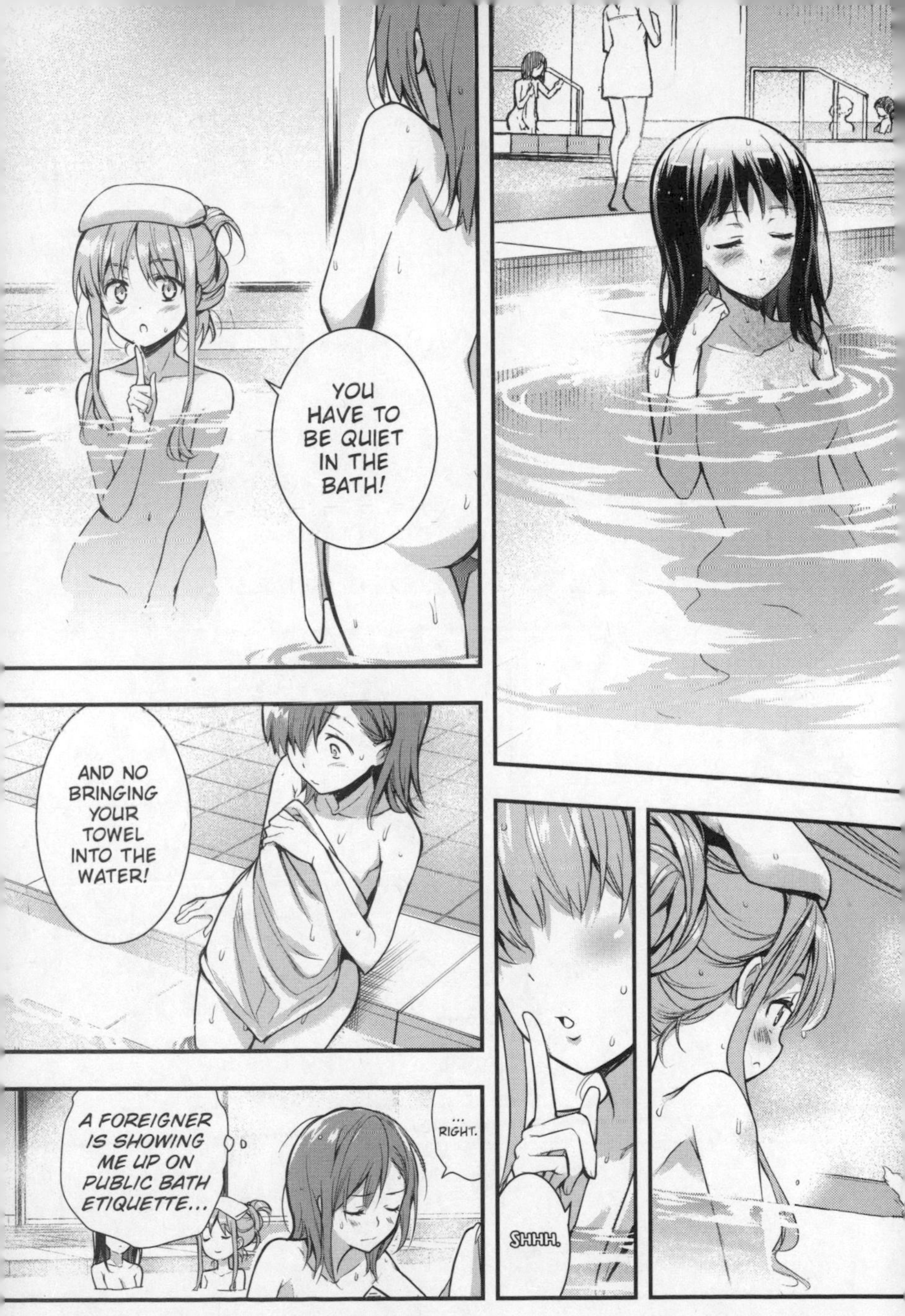
YOU HAVE TO BE QUIET IN THE BATH!
SHHH.
AND NO BRINGING YOUR TOWEL INTO THE WATER!
... RIGHT.
A FOREIGNER IS SHOWING ME UP ON PUBLIC BATH ETIQUETTE...

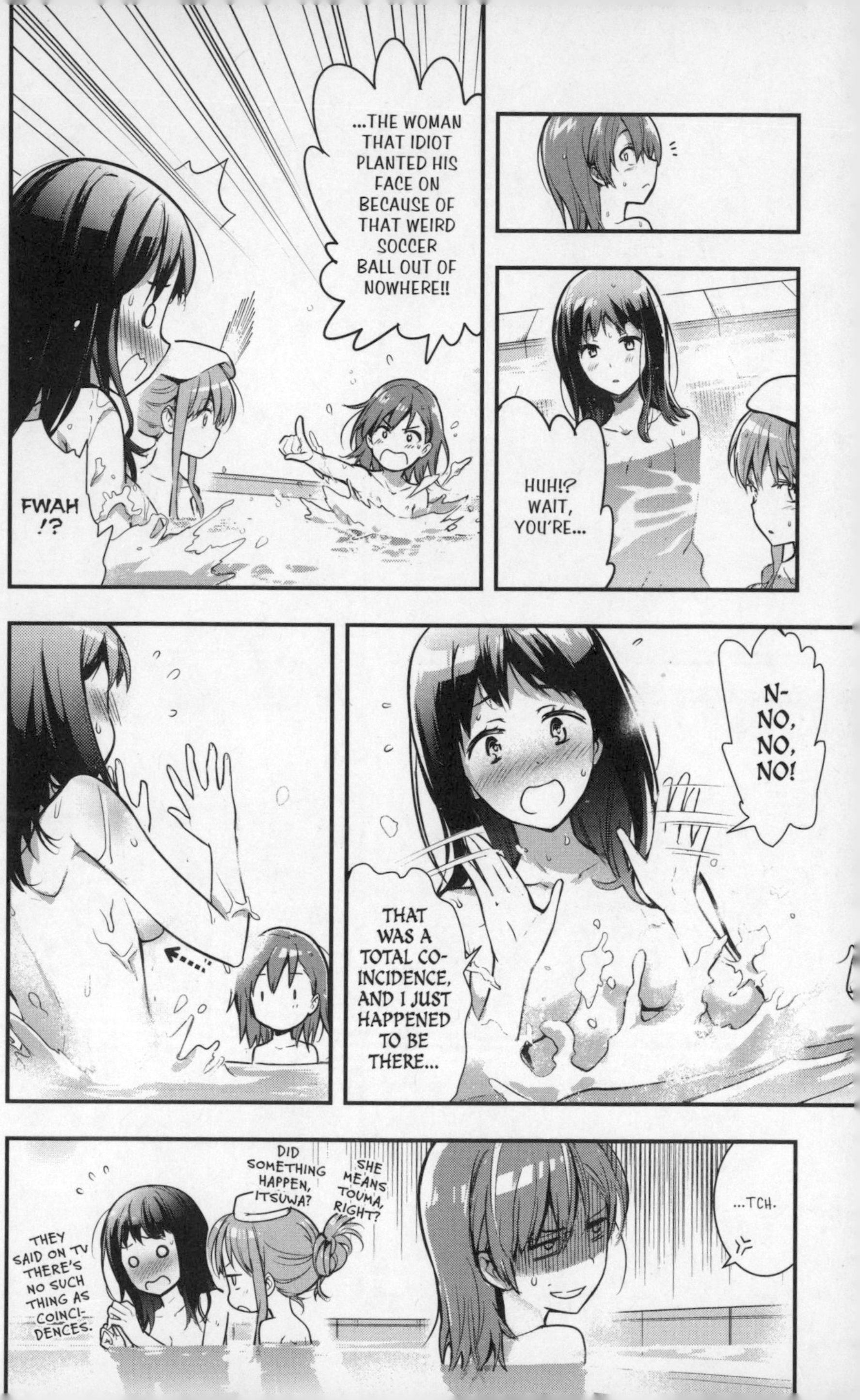
HUH!? WAIT, YOU'RE...
...THE WOMAN THAT IDIOT PLANTED HIS FACE ON BECAUSE OF THAT WEIRD SOCCER BALL OUT OF NOWHERE!!
FWAH !?
N-NO, NO, NO!
THAT WAS A TOTAL CO-INCIDENCE, AND I JUST HAPPENED TO BE THERE...
...TCH.
SHE MEANS TOUMA, RIGHT?
DID SOMETHING HAPPEN, ITSUWA?
THEY SAID ON TV THERE'S NO SUCH THING AS COINCI-DENCES.

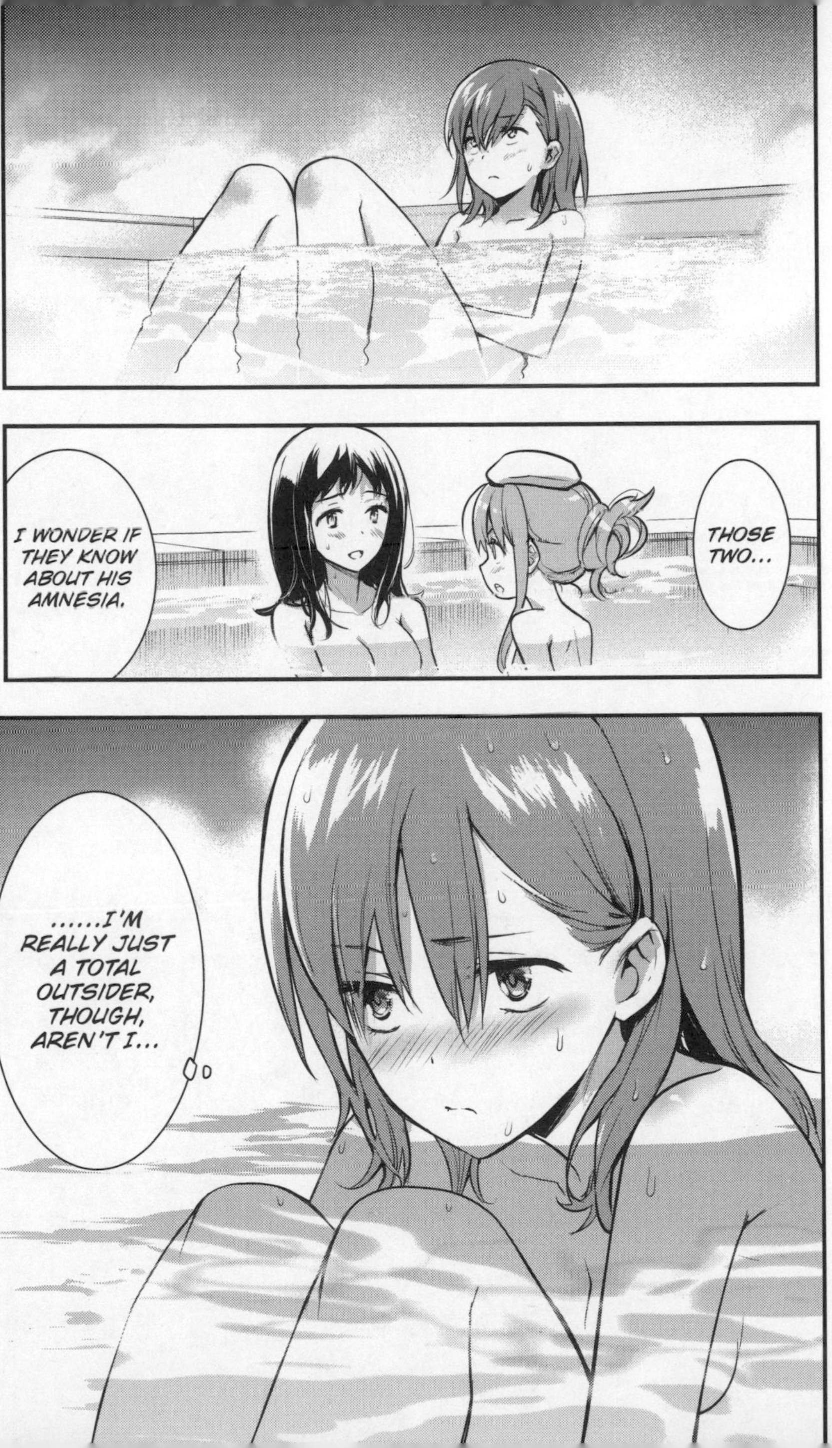
THOSE TWO...
I WONDER IF THEY KNOW ABOUT HIS AMNESIA.
......I'M REALLY JUST A TOTAL OUTSIDER, THOUGH, AREN'T I...

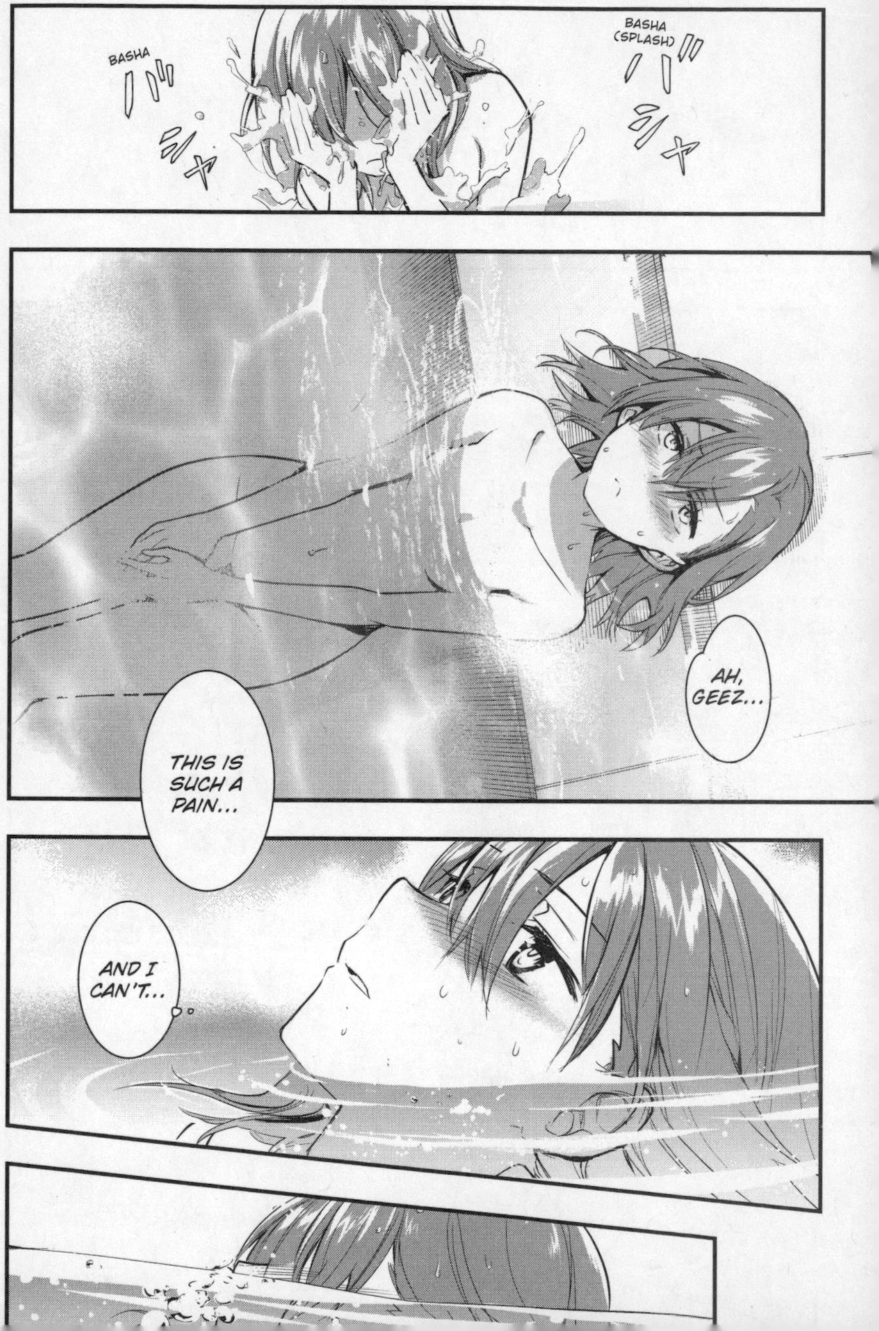
BASHA (SPLASH)
バシャ
BASHA
バシャ
AH, GEEZ...
THIS IS SUCH A PAIN...
AND I CAN'T...

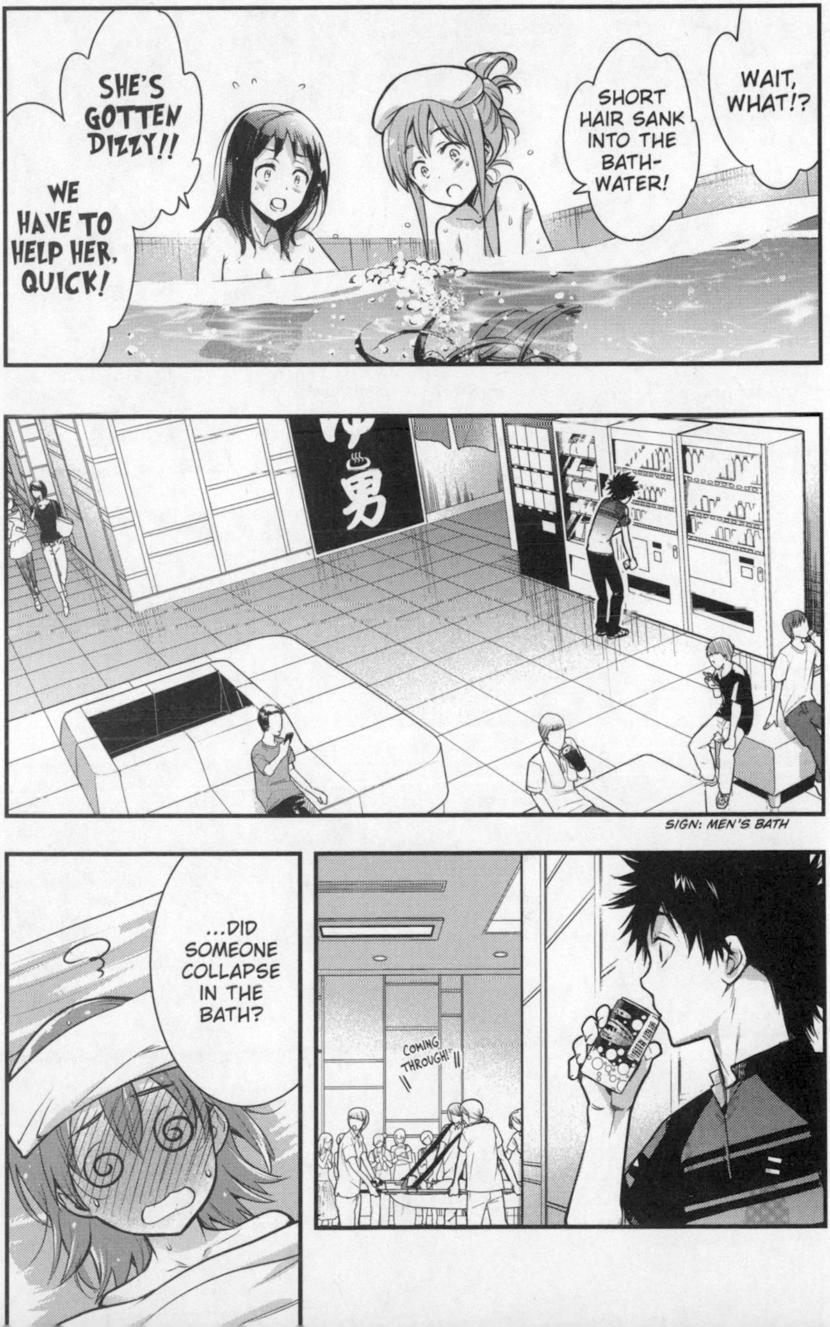
WAIT, WHAT!?
SHORT HAIR SANK INTO THE BATH-WATER!
SHE'S GOTTEN DIZZY!!
WE HAVE TO HELP HER, QUICK!
SIGN: MEN'S BATH
COMING THROUGH!
...DID SOMEONE COLLAPSE IN THE BATH?

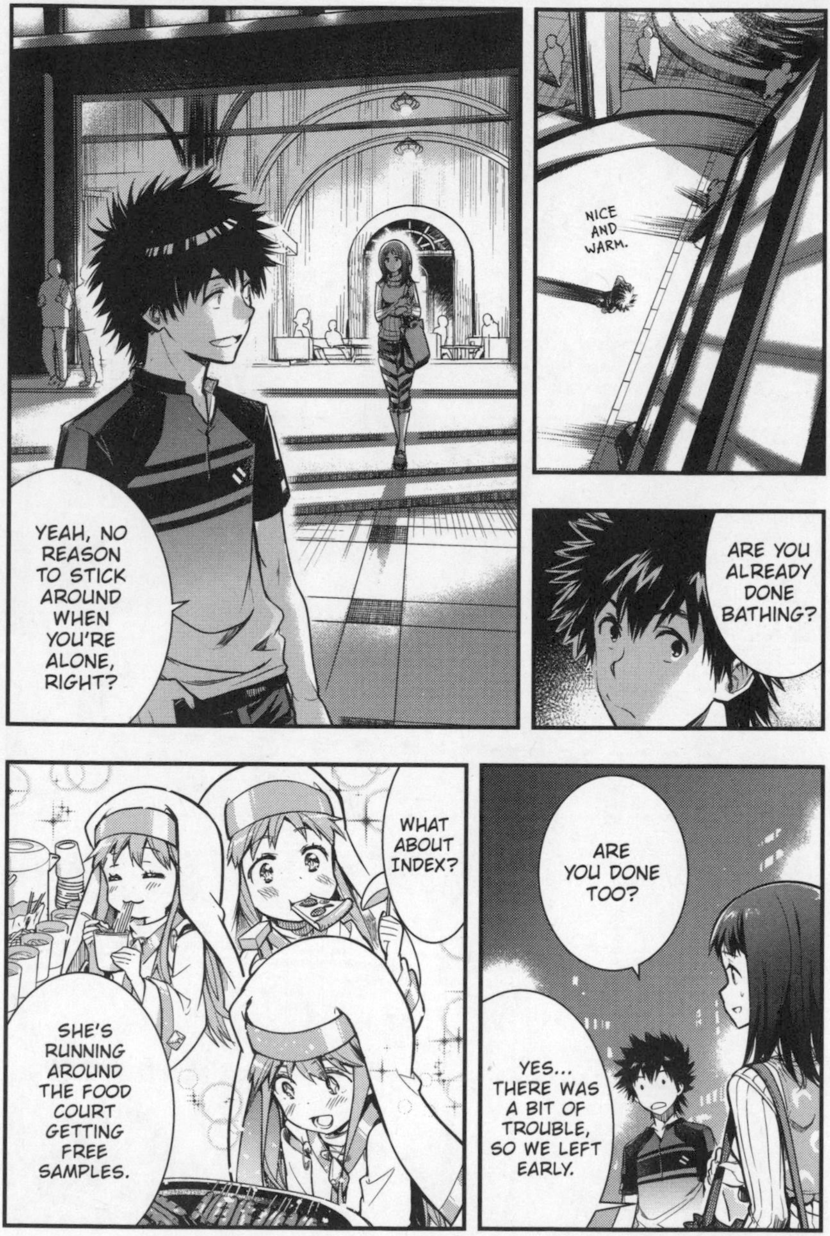
NICE AND WARM.
ARE YOU ALREADY DONE BATHING?
YEAH, NO REASON TO STICK AROUND WHEN YOU'RE ALONE, RIGHT?
ARE YOU DONE TOO?
YES... THERE WAS A BIT OF TROUBLE, SO WE LEFT EARLY.
WHAT ABOUT INDEX?
SHE'S RUNNING AROUND THE FOOD COURT GETTING FREE SAMPLES.

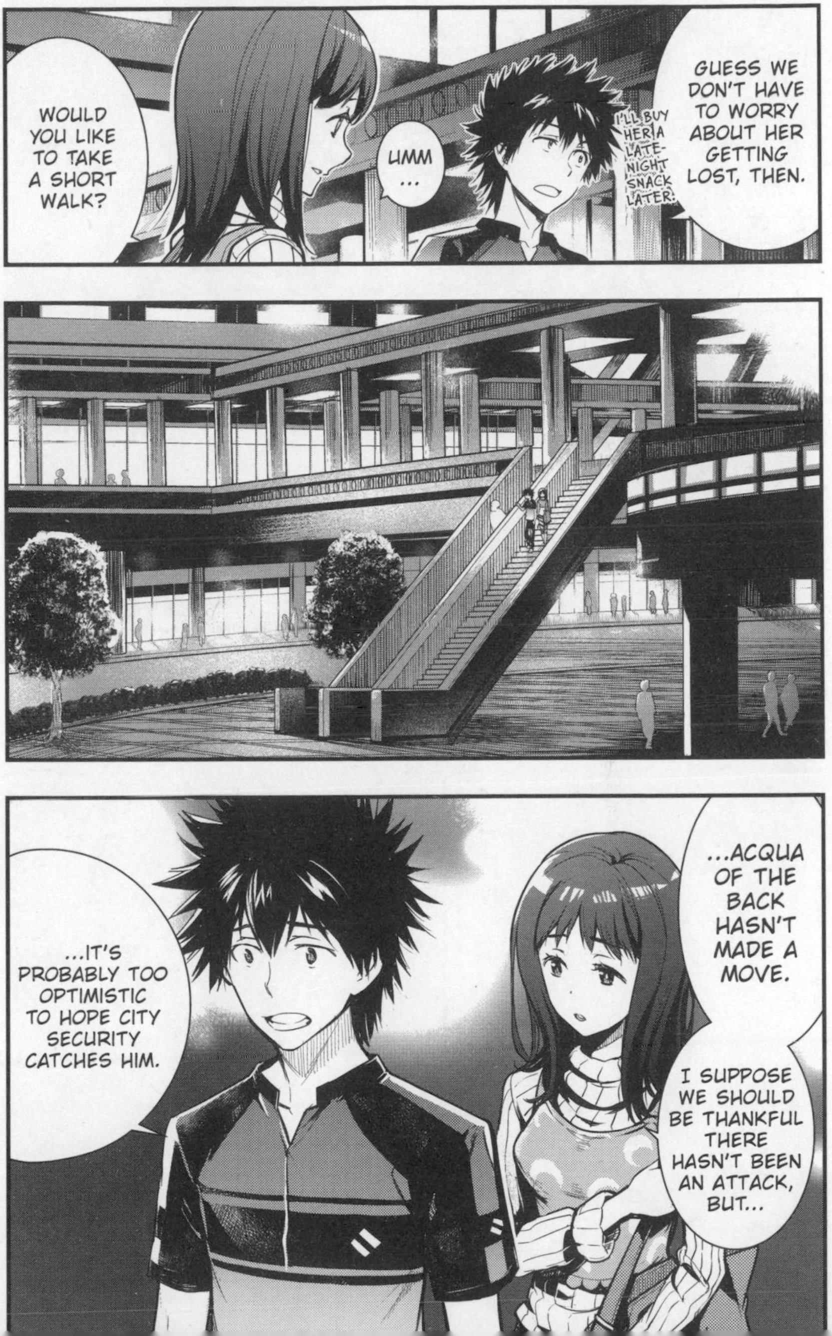
GUESS WE DON'T HAVE TO WORRY ABOUT HER GETTING LOST, THEN.
I'LL BUY HER A LATE-NIGHT SNACK LATER.
UMM ...
WOULD YOU LIKE TO TAKE A SHORT WALK?
...ACQUA OF THE BACK HASN'T MADE A MOVE.
I SUPPOSE WE SHOULD BE THANKFUL THERE HASN'T BEEN AN ATTACK, BUT...
...IT'S PROBABLY TOO OPTIMISTIC TO HOPE CITY SECURITY CATCHES HIM.

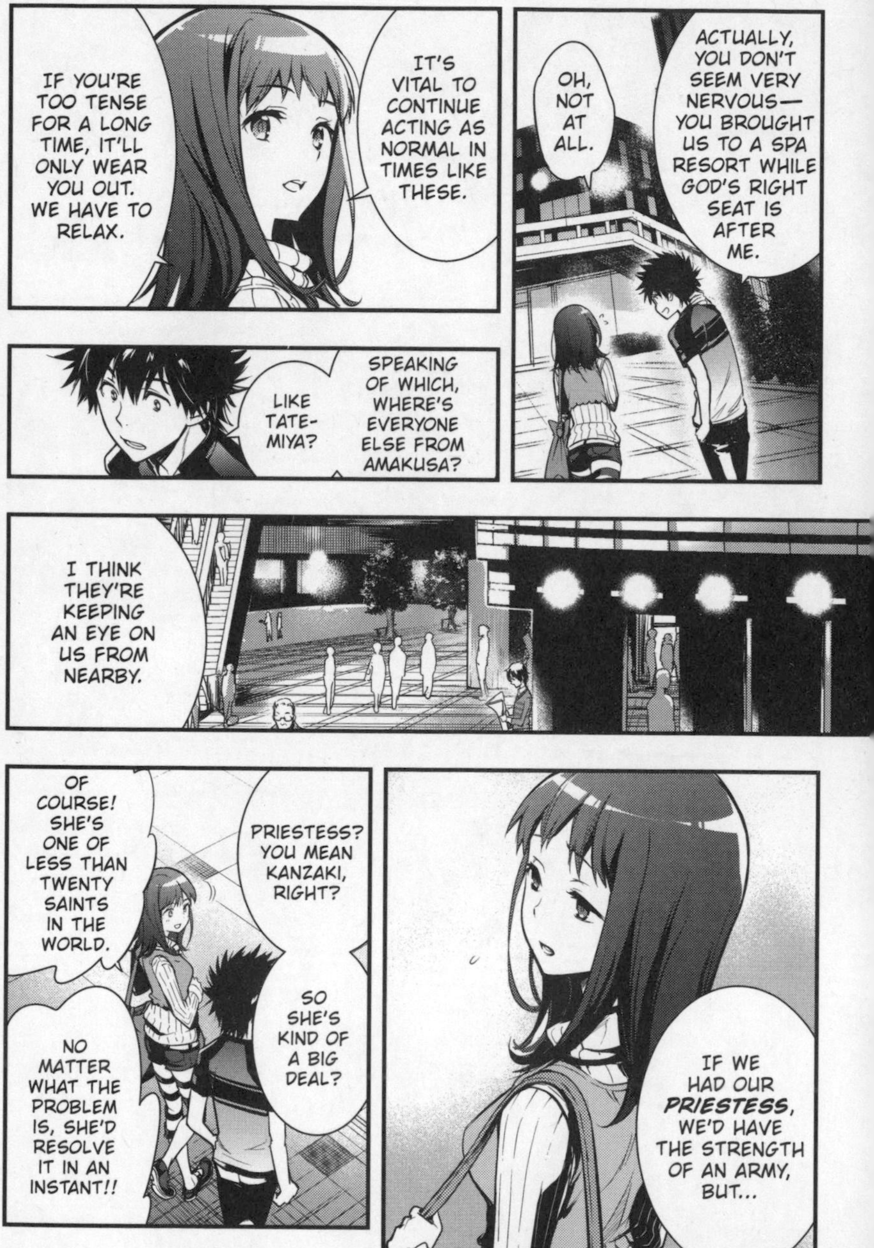
ACTUALLY, YOU DON'T SEEM VERY NERVOUS— YOU BROUGHT US TO A SPA RESORT WHILE GOD'S RIGHT SEAT IS AFTER ME.
OH, NOT AT ALL.
IT'S VITAL TO CONTINUE ACTING AS NORMAL IN TIMES LIKE THESE.
IF YOU'RE TOO TENSE FOR A LONG TIME, IT'LL ONLY WEAR YOU OUT. WE HAVE TO RELAX.
SPEAKING OF WHICH, WHERE'S EVERYONE ELSE FROM AMAKUSA?
LIKE TATE-MIYA?
I THINK THEY'RE KEEPING AN EYE ON US FROM NEARBY.
IF WE HAD OUR ***PRIESTESS***, WE'D HAVE THE STRENGTH OF AN ARMY, BUT...
PRIESTESS? YOU MEAN KANZAKI, RIGHT?
OF COURSE! SHE'S ONE OF LESS THAN TWENTY SAINTS IN THE WORLD.
SO SHE'S KIND OF A BIG DEAL?
NO MATTER WHAT THE PROBLEM IS, SHE'D RESOLVE IT IN AN INSTANT!!

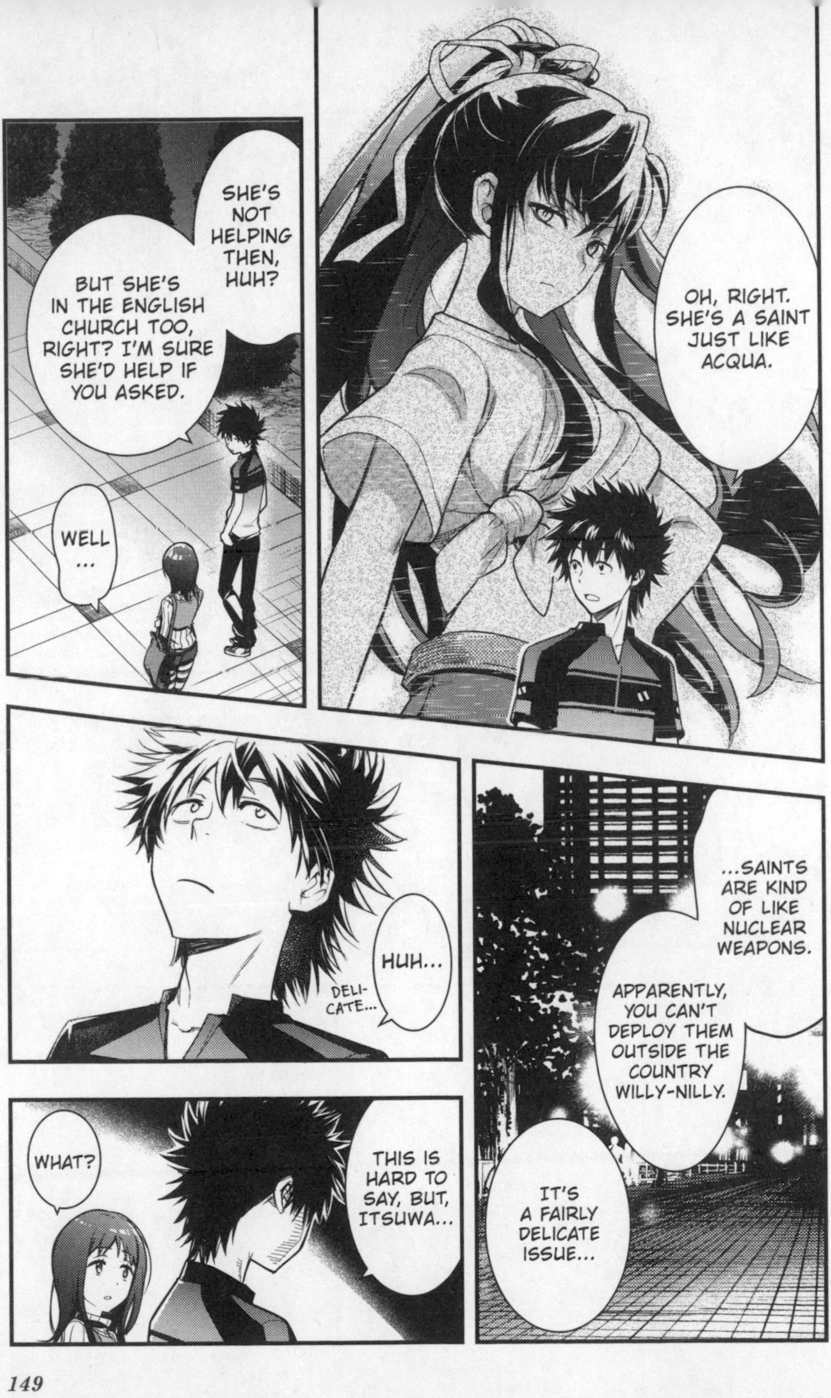
OH, RIGHT. SHE'S A SAINT JUST LIKE ACQUA.
SHE'S NOT HELPING THEN, HUH?
BUT SHE'S IN THE ENGLISH CHURCH TOO, RIGHT? I'M SURE SHE'D HELP IF YOU ASKED.
WELL...
...SAINTS ARE KIND OF LIKE NUCLEAR WEAPONS.
APPARENTLY, YOU CAN'T DEPLOY THEM OUTSIDE THE COUNTRY WILLY-NILLY.
IT'S A FAIRLY DELICATE ISSUE...
HUH...
DELICATE...
THIS IS HARD TO SAY, BUT, ITSUWA...
WHAT?

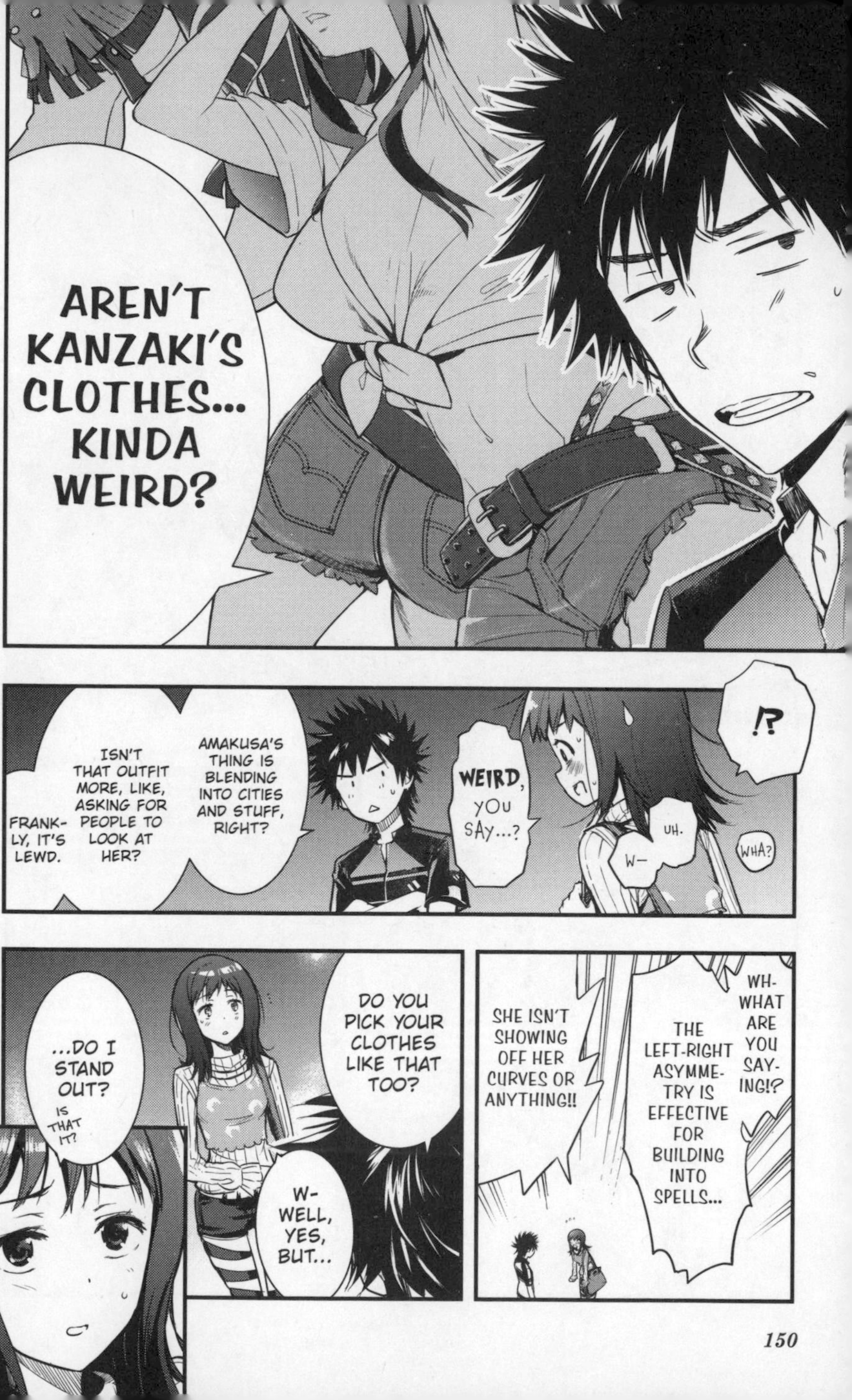
AREN'T KANZAKI'S CLOTHES... KINDA WEIRD?
!?
WHA?
UH.
W—
WEIRD, YOU SAY...?
AMAKUSA'S THING IS BLENDING INTO CITIES AND STUFF, RIGHT?
ISN'T THAT OUTFIT MORE, LIKE, ASKING FOR PEOPLE TO LOOK AT HER?
FRANKLY, IT'S LEWD.
WH-WHAT ARE YOU SAYING!?
THE LEFT-RIGHT ASYMMETRY IS EFFECTIVE FOR BUILDING INTO SPELLS...
SHE ISN'T SHOWING OFF HER CURVES OR ANYTHING!!
DO YOU PICK YOUR CLOTHES LIKE THAT TOO?
W-WELL, YES, BUT...
...DO I STAND OUT?
IS THAT IT?

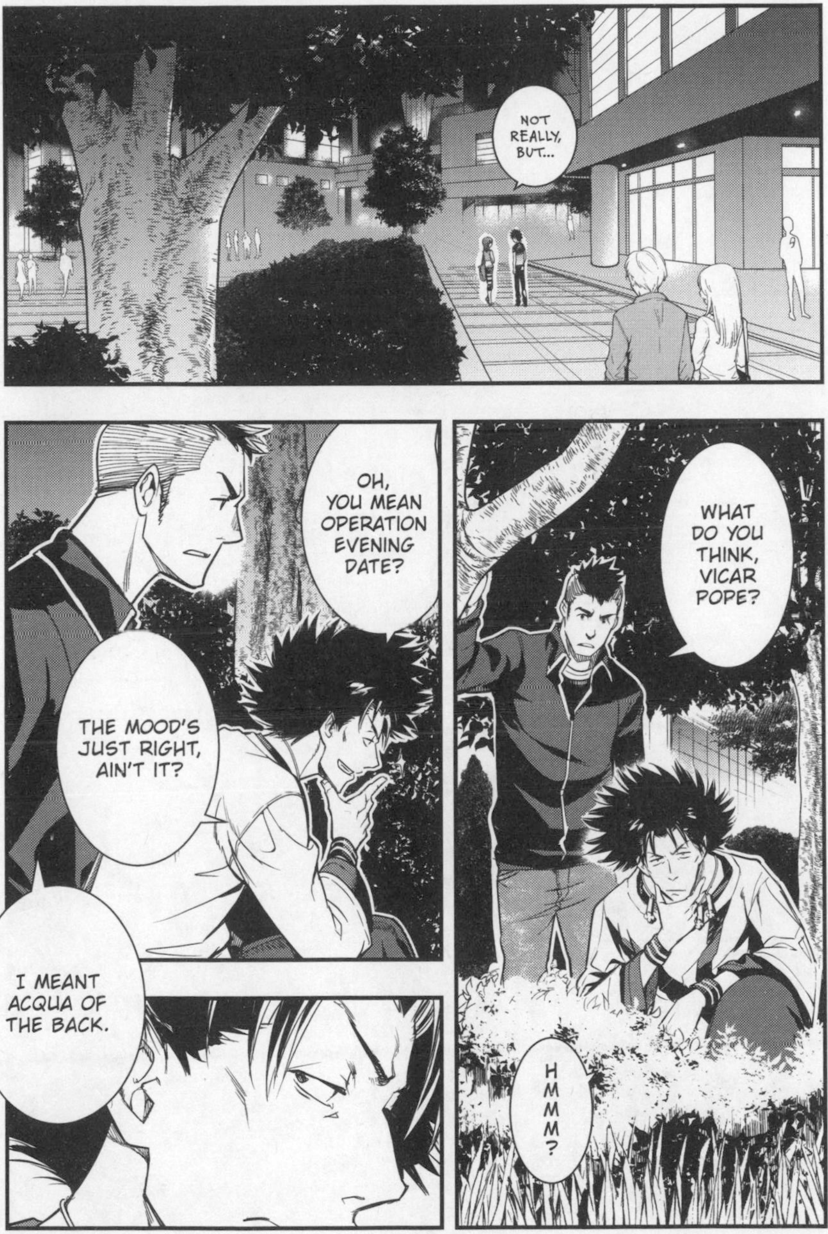
NOT REALLY, BUT...
WHAT DO YOU THINK, VICAR POPE?
HMMM?
OH, YOU MEAN OPERATION EVENING DATE?
THE MOOD'S JUST RIGHT, AIN'T IT?
I MEANT ACQUA OF THE BACK.

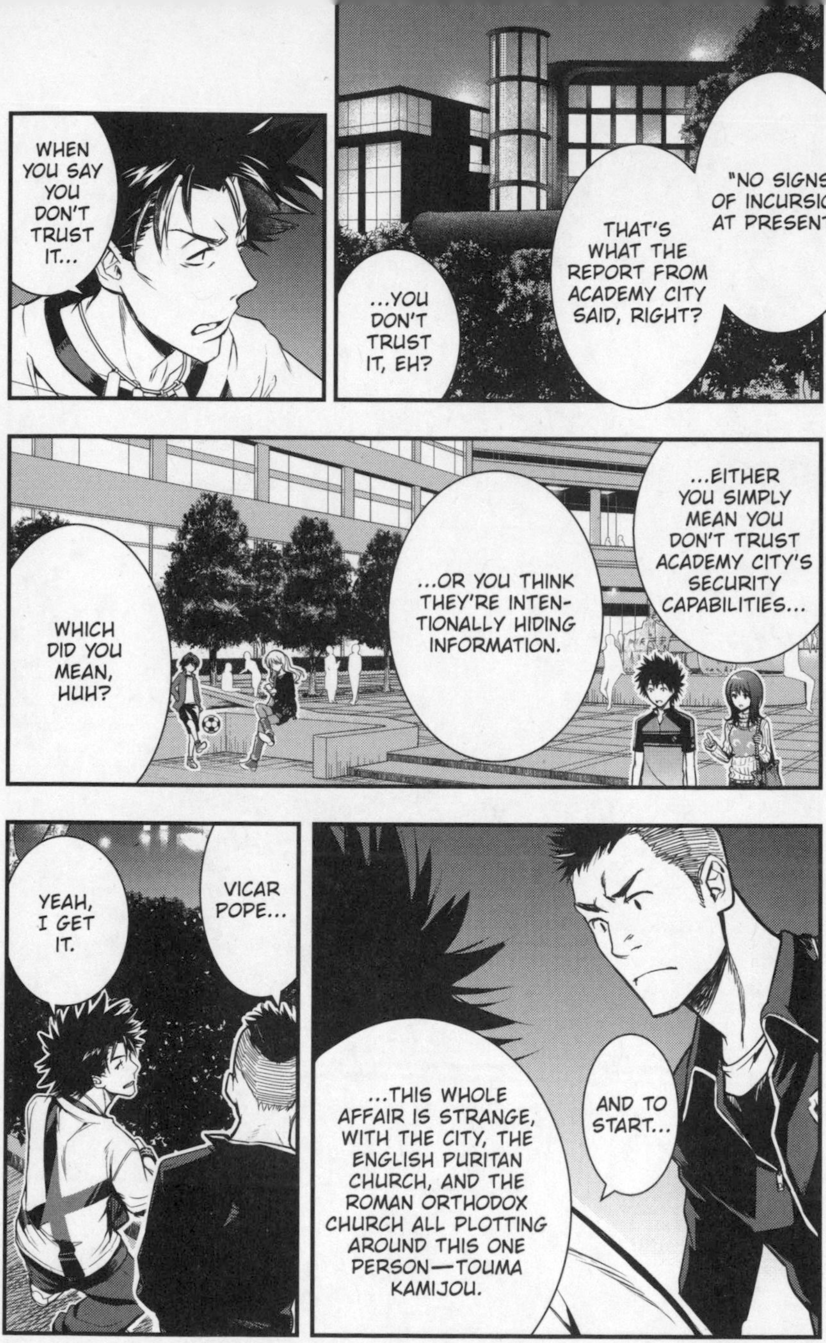
"NO SIGNS OF INCURSION AT PRESENT."
THAT'S WHAT THE REPORT FROM ACADEMY CITY SAID, RIGHT?
...YOU DON'T TRUST IT, EH?
WHEN YOU SAY YOU DON'T TRUST IT...
...EITHER YOU SIMPLY MEAN YOU DON'T TRUST ACADEMY CITY'S SECURITY CAPABILITIES...
...OR YOU THINK THEY'RE INTEN-TIONALLY HIDING INFORMATION.
WHICH DID YOU MEAN, HUH?
AND TO START...
...THIS WHOLE AFFAIR IS STRANGE, WITH THE CITY, THE ENGLISH PURITAN CHURCH, AND THE ROMAN ORTHODOX CHURCH ALL PLOTTING AROUND THIS ONE PERSON—TOUMA KAMIJOU.
VICAR POPE...
YEAH, I GET IT.

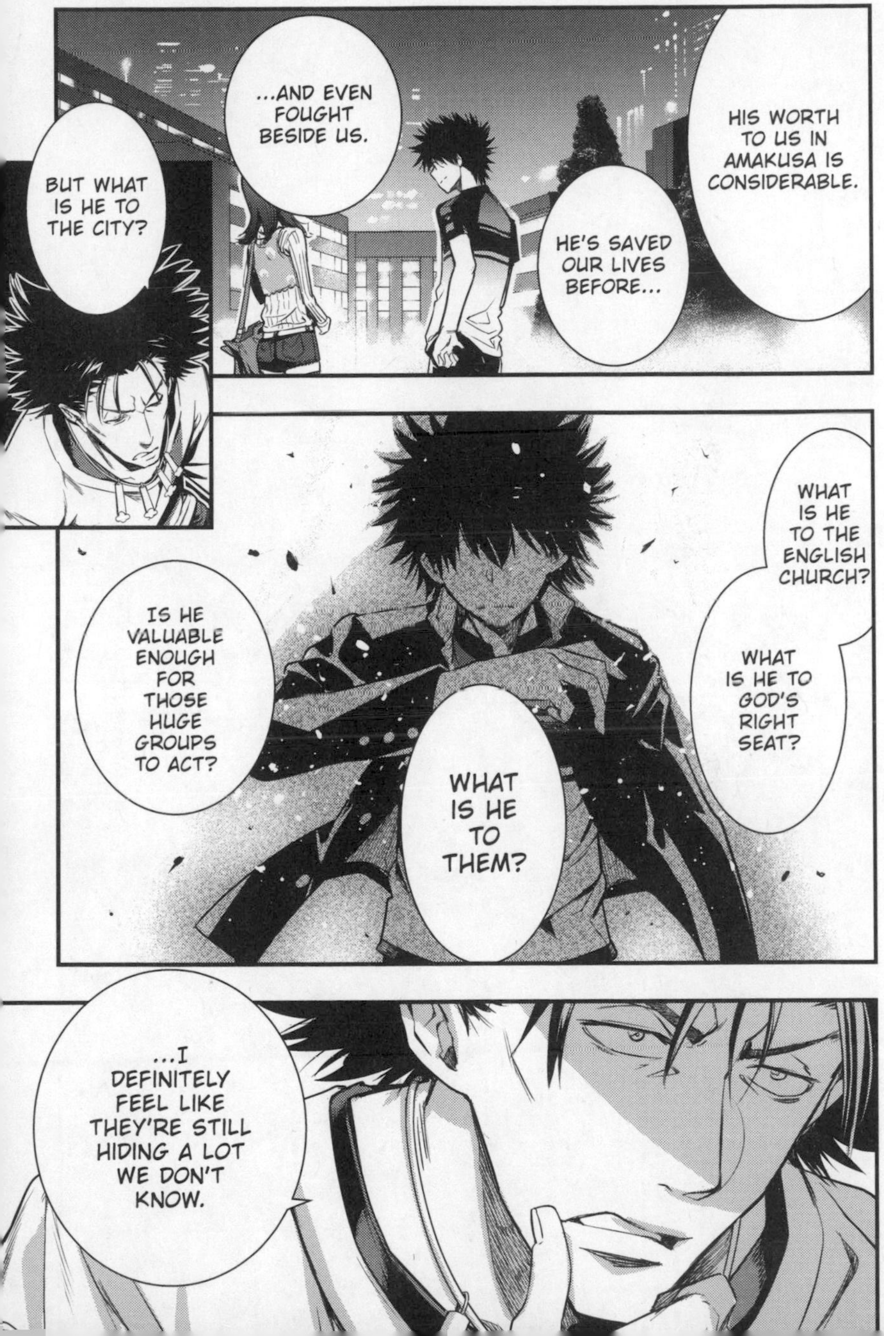
HIS WORTH TO US IN AMAKUSA IS CONSIDERABLE.
HE'S SAVED OUR LIVES BEFORE...
...AND EVEN FOUGHT BESIDE US.
BUT WHAT IS HE TO THE CITY?
WHAT IS HE TO THE ENGLISH CHURCH?
WHAT IS HE TO GOD'S RIGHT SEAT?
IS HE VALUABLE ENOUGH FOR THOSE HUGE GROUPS TO ACT?
WHAT IS HE TO THEM?
...I DEFINITELY FEEL LIKE THEY'RE STILL HIDING A LOT WE DON'T KNOW.

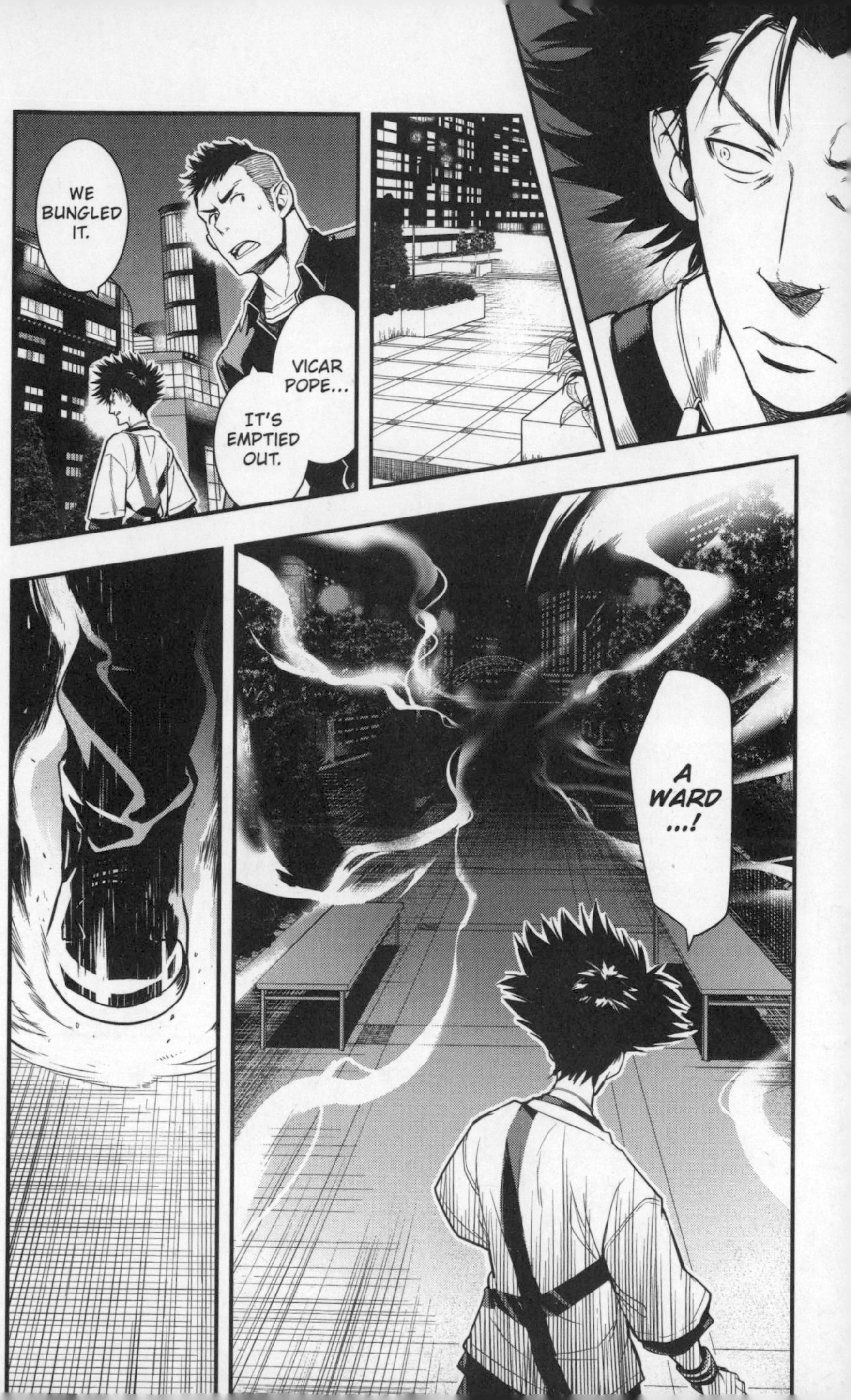
VICAR POPE...
IT'S EMPTIED OUT.
WE BUNGLED IT.
A WARD ...!

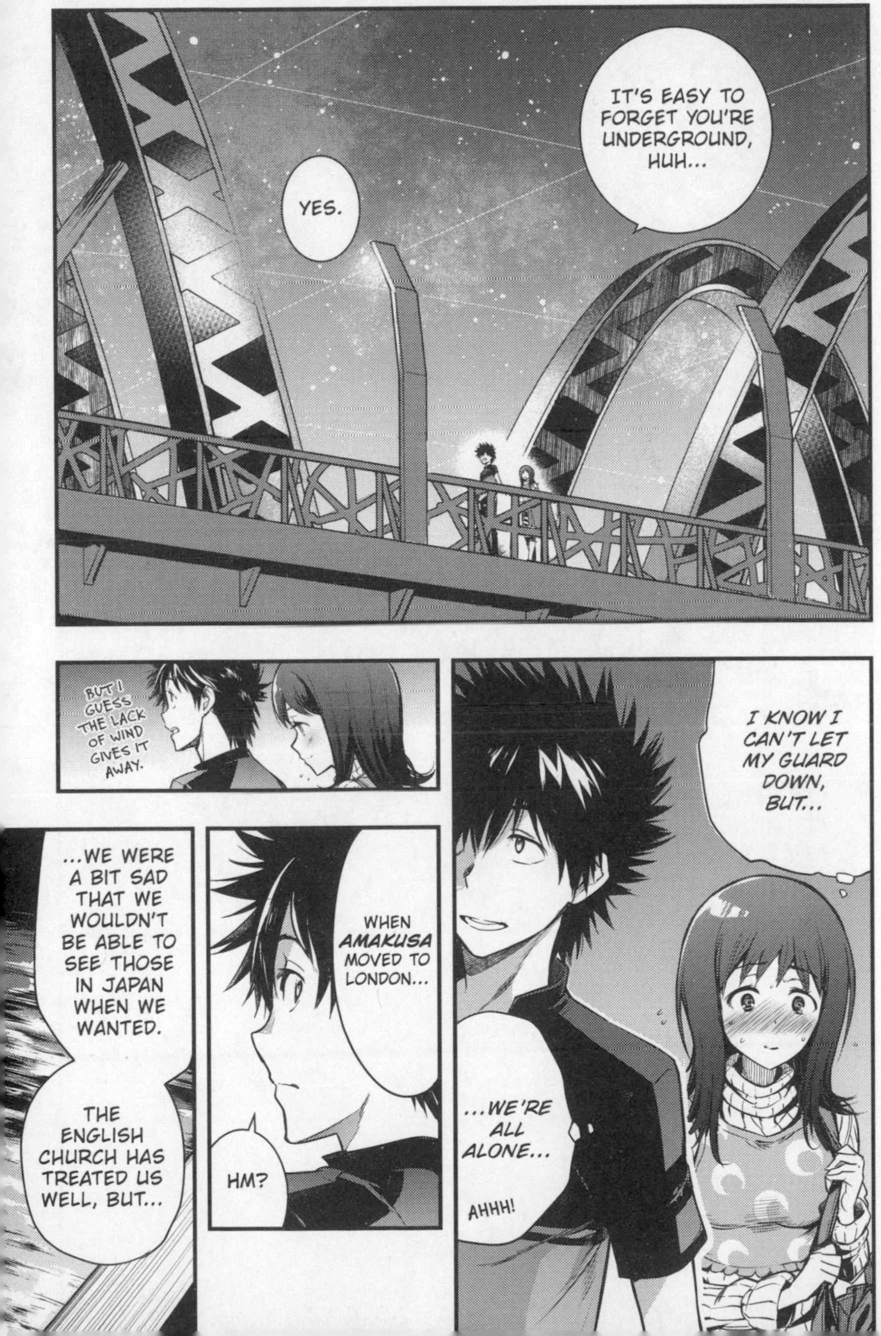
IT'S EASY TO FORGET YOU'RE UNDERGROUND, HUH...
YES.
I KNOW I CAN'T LET MY GUARD DOWN, BUT...
...WE'RE ALL ALONE...
AHHH!
BUT I GUESS THE LACK OF WIND GIVES IT AWAY.
WHEN *AMAKUSA* MOVED TO LONDON...
HM?
...WE WERE A BIT SAD THAT WE WOULDN'T BE ABLE TO SEE THOSE IN JAPAN WHEN WE WANTED.
THE ENGLISH CHURCH HAS TREATED US WELL, BUT...

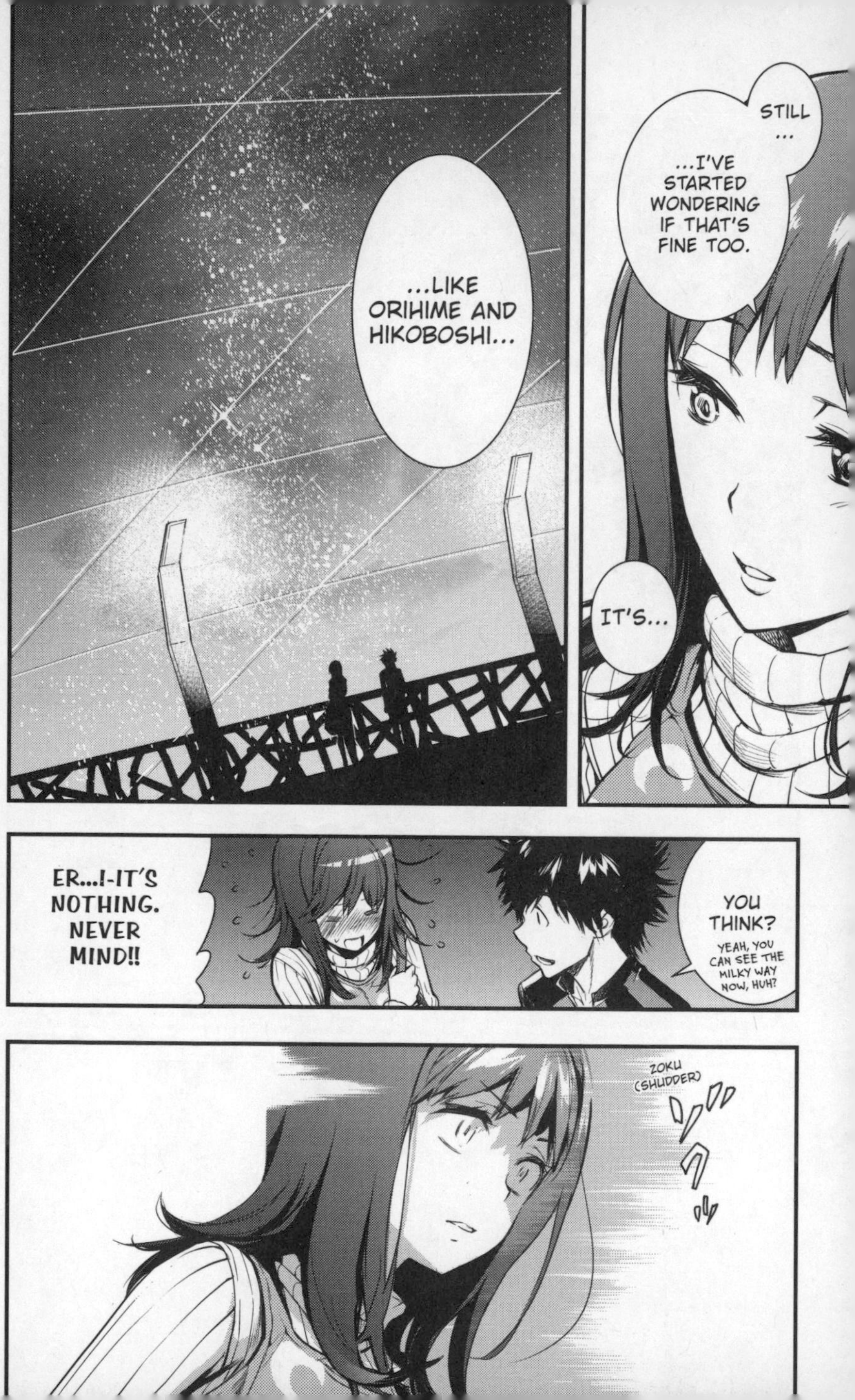
STILL ...
...I'VE STARTED WONDERING IF THAT'S FINE TOO.
IT'S...
...LIKE ORIHIME AND HIKOBOSHI...
YOU THINK?
YEAH, YOU CAN SEE THE MILKY WAY NOW, HUH?
ER...I-IT'S NOTHING. NEVER MIND!!
ZOKU (SHUDDER)

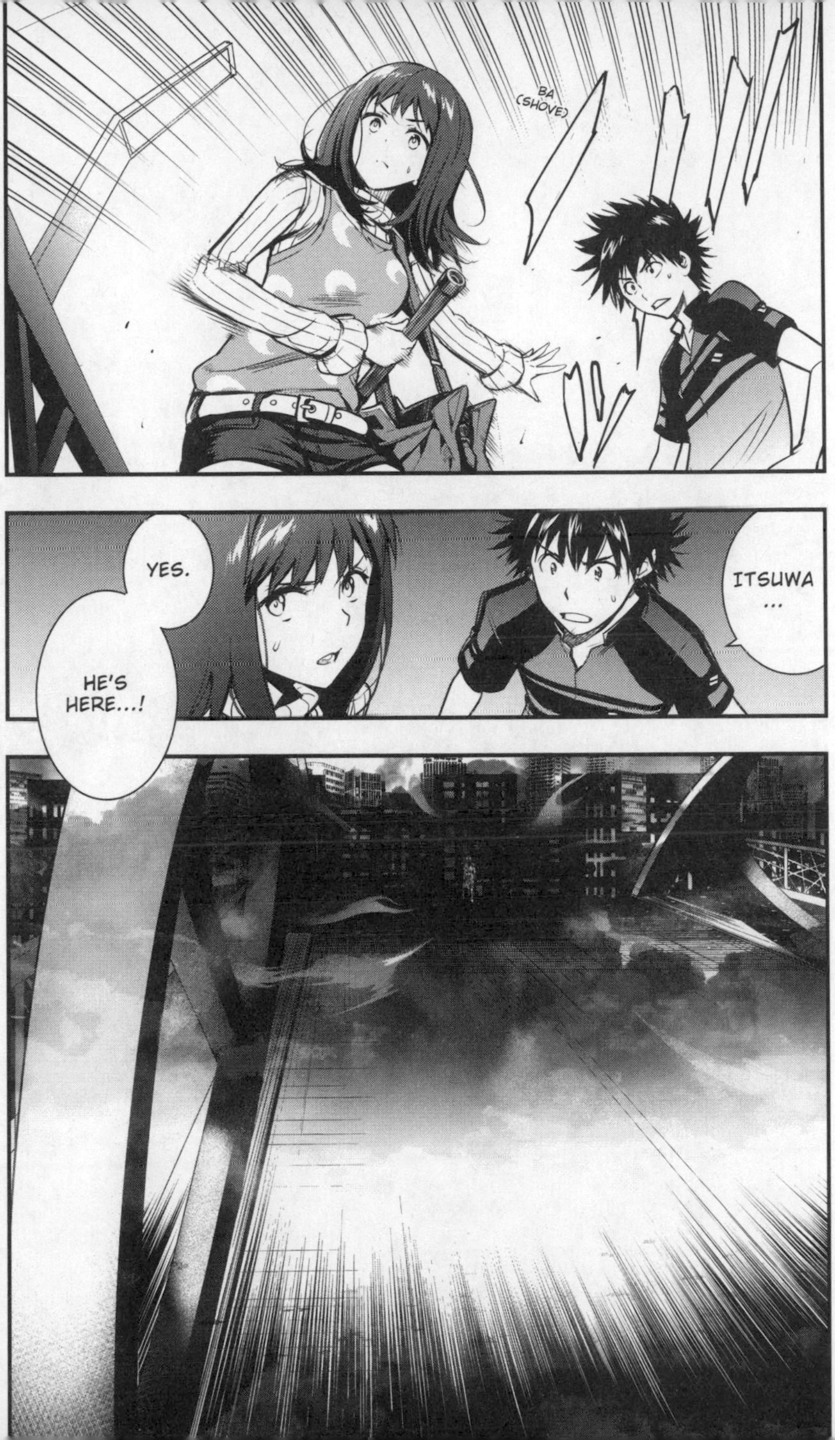
BA
(SHOVE)
ITSUWA ...
YES.
HE'S HERE...!

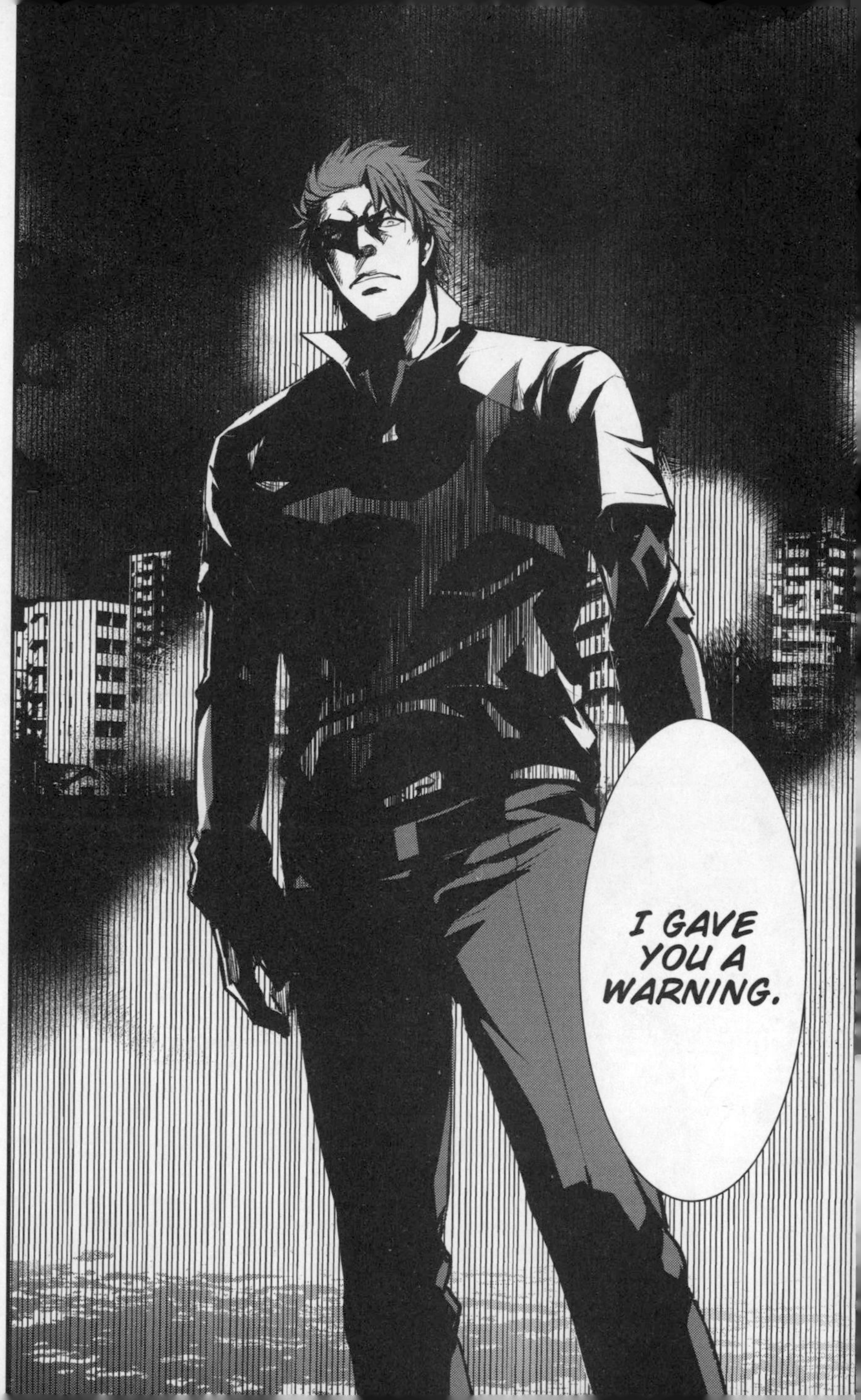
I GAVE YOU A WARNING.

A Certain Magical Index

A Certain Magical Index

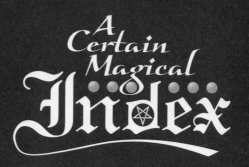

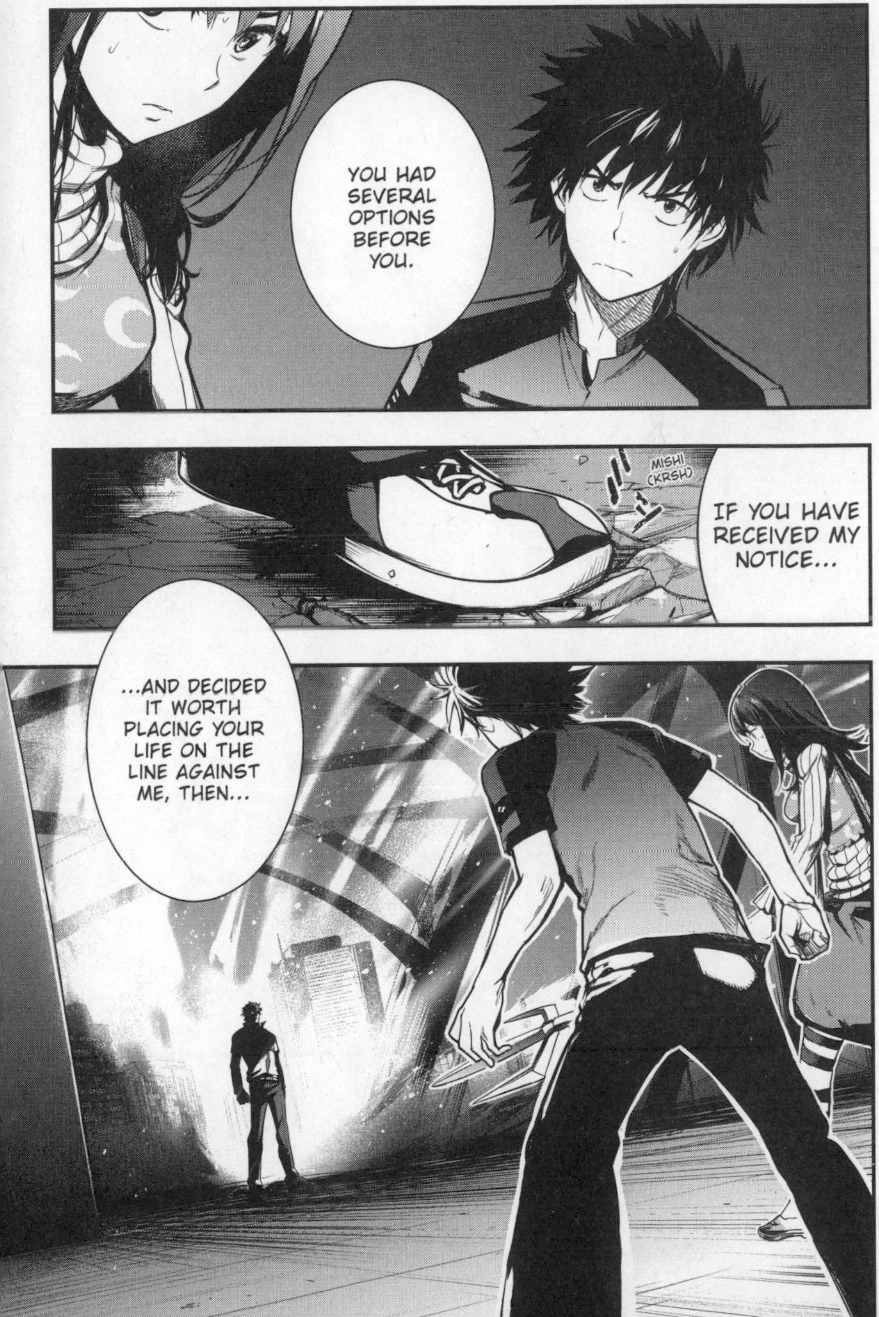
YOU HAD SEVERAL OPTIONS BEFORE YOU.
IF YOU HAVE RECEIVED MY NOTICE...
MISHI (KRSH)
...AND DECIDED IT WORTH PLACING YOUR LIFE ON THE LINE AGAINST ME, THEN...

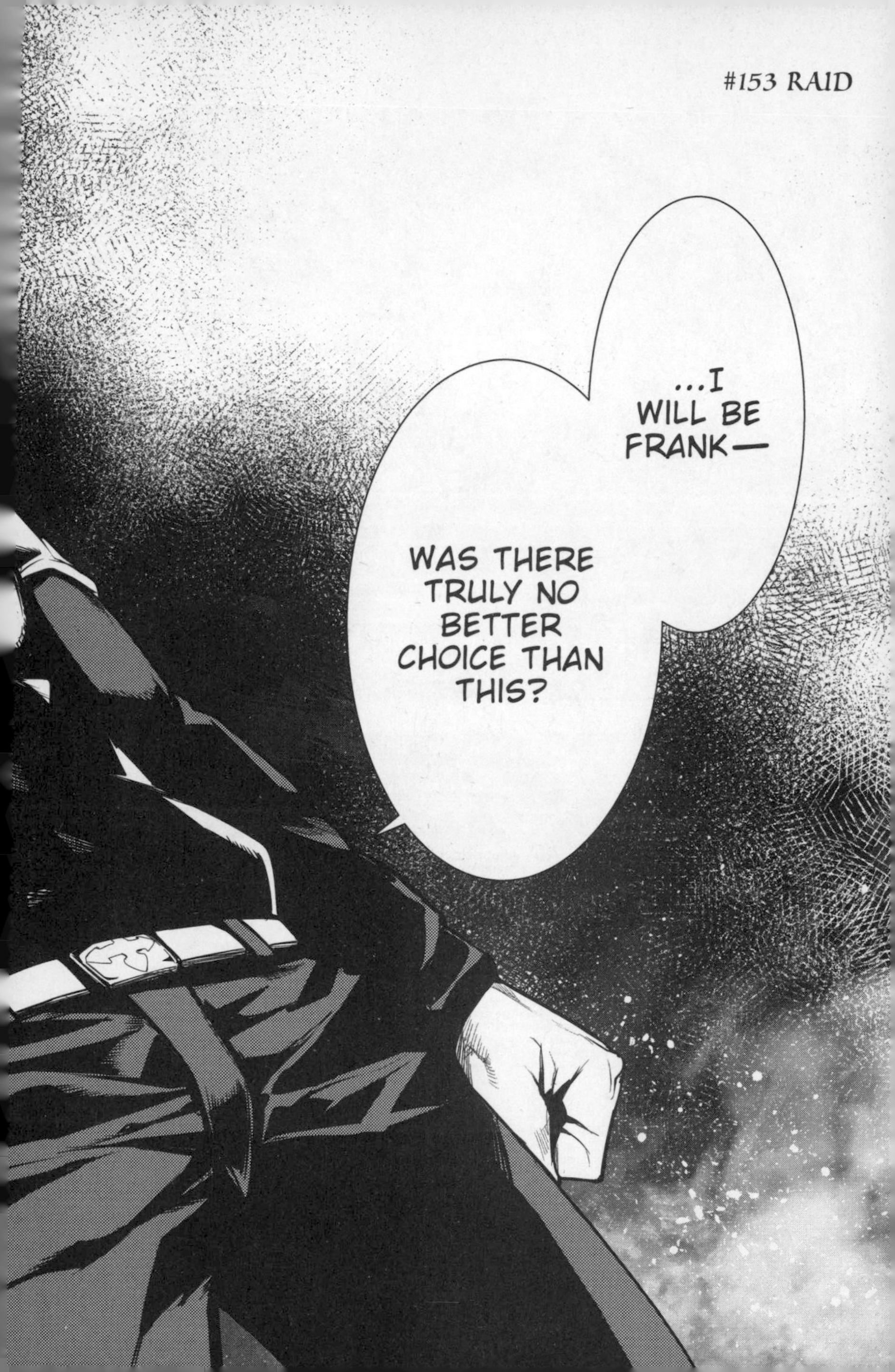
...I WILL BE FRANK—
WAS THERE TRULY NO BETTER CHOICE THAN THIS?

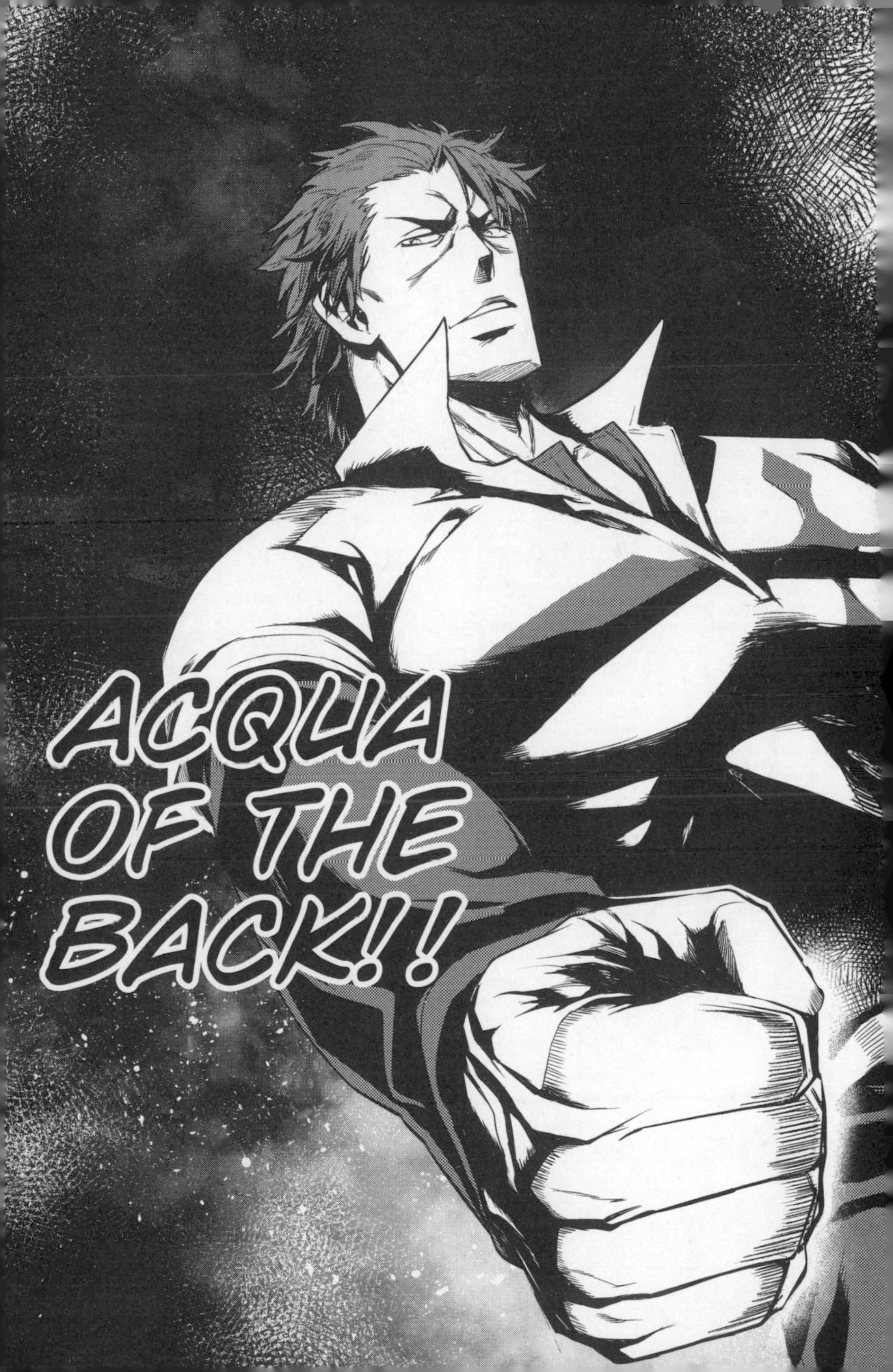
ACQUA OF THE BACK!!

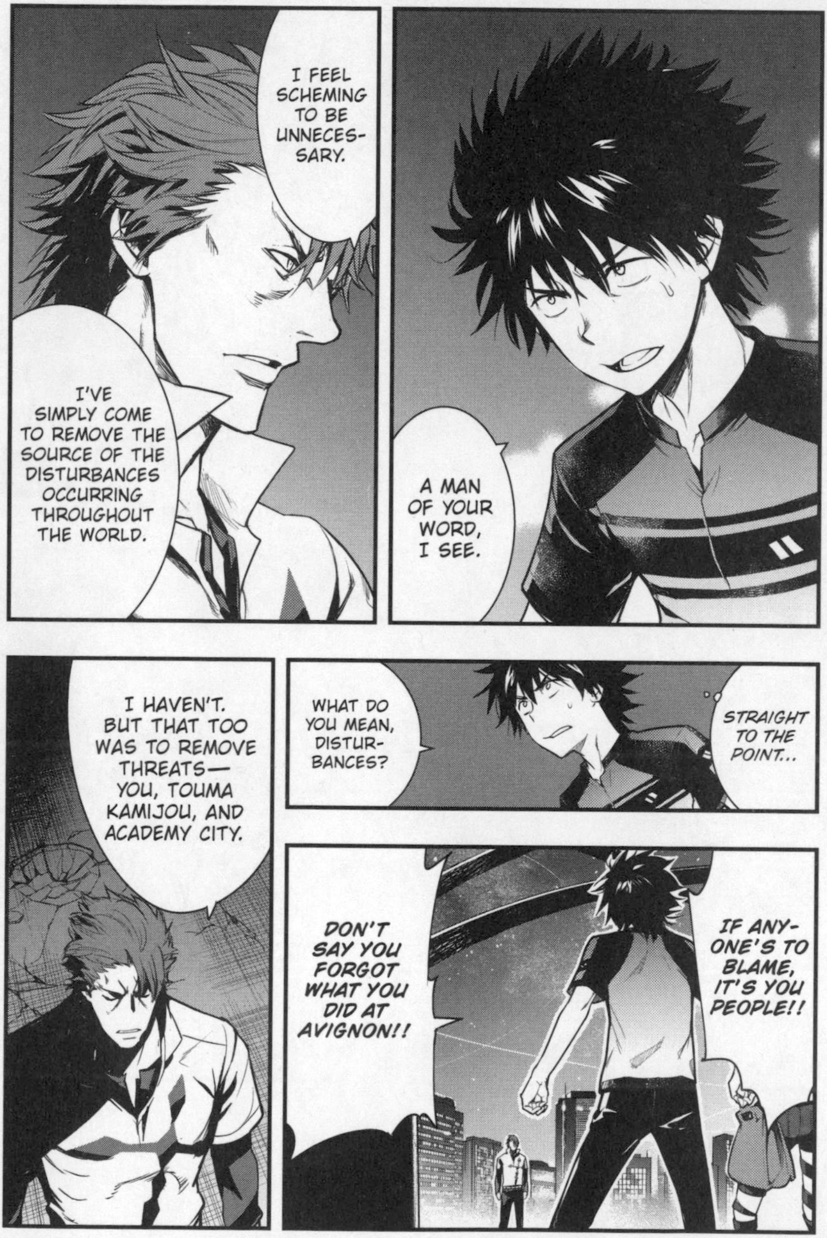
A MAN OF YOUR WORD, I SEE.
I FEEL SCHEMING TO BE UNNECES-SARY.
I'VE SIMPLY COME TO REMOVE THE SOURCE OF THE DISTURBANCES OCCURRING THROUGHOUT THE WORLD.
STRAIGHT TO THE POINT...
WHAT DO YOU MEAN, DISTUR-BANCES?
IF ANY-ONE'S TO BLAME, IT'S YOU PEOPLE!!
DON'T SAY YOU FORGOT WHAT YOU DID AT AVIGNON!!
I HAVEN'T. BUT THAT TOO WAS TO REMOVE THREATS— YOU, TOUMA KAMIJOU, AND ACADEMY CITY.

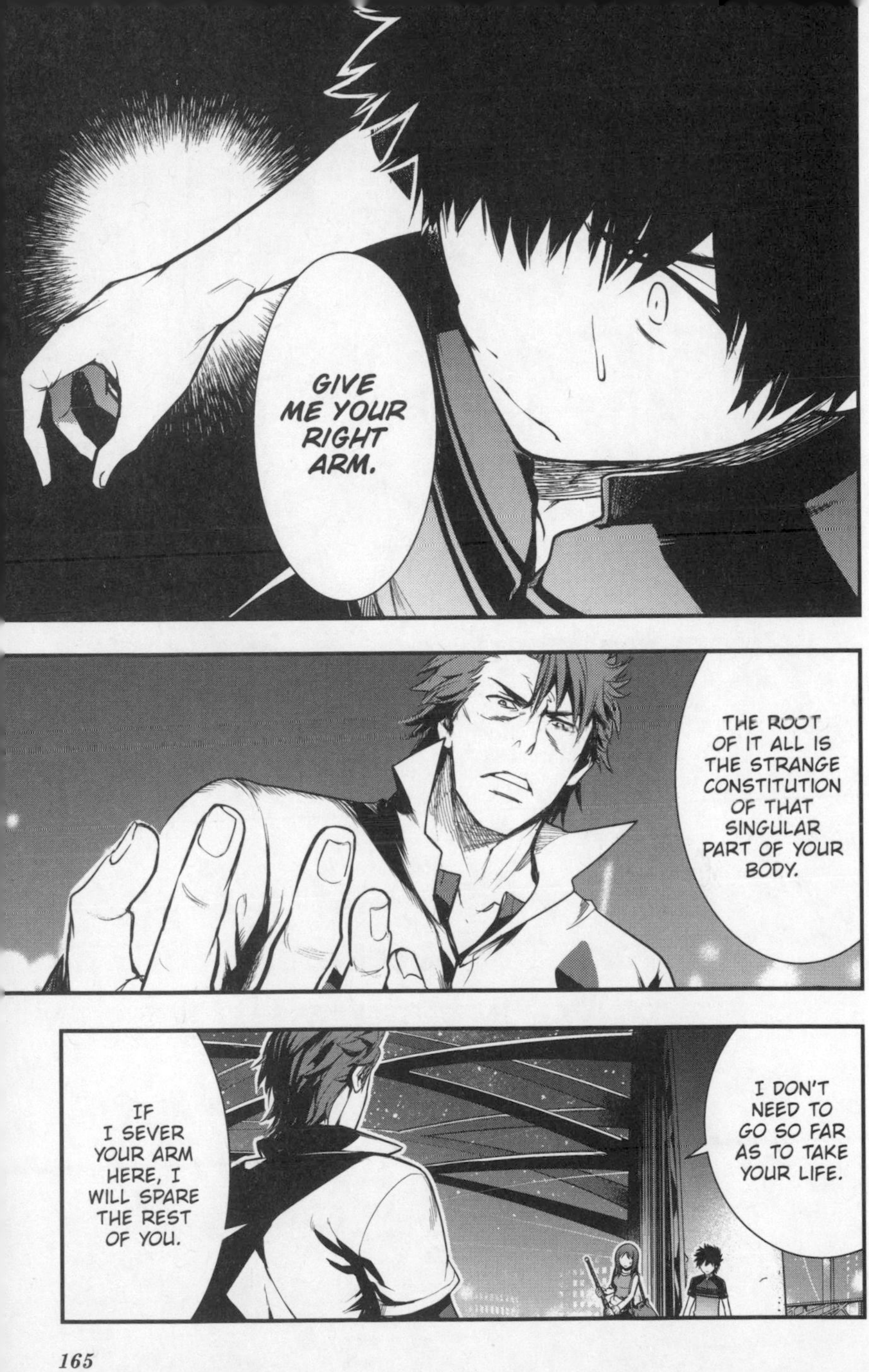
GIVE ME YOUR RIGHT ARM.
THE ROOT OF IT ALL IS THE STRANGE CONSTITUTION OF THAT SINGULAR PART OF YOUR BODY.
I DON'T NEED TO GO SO FAR AS TO TAKE YOUR LIFE.
IF I SEVER YOUR ARM HERE, I WILL SPARE THE REST OF YOU.

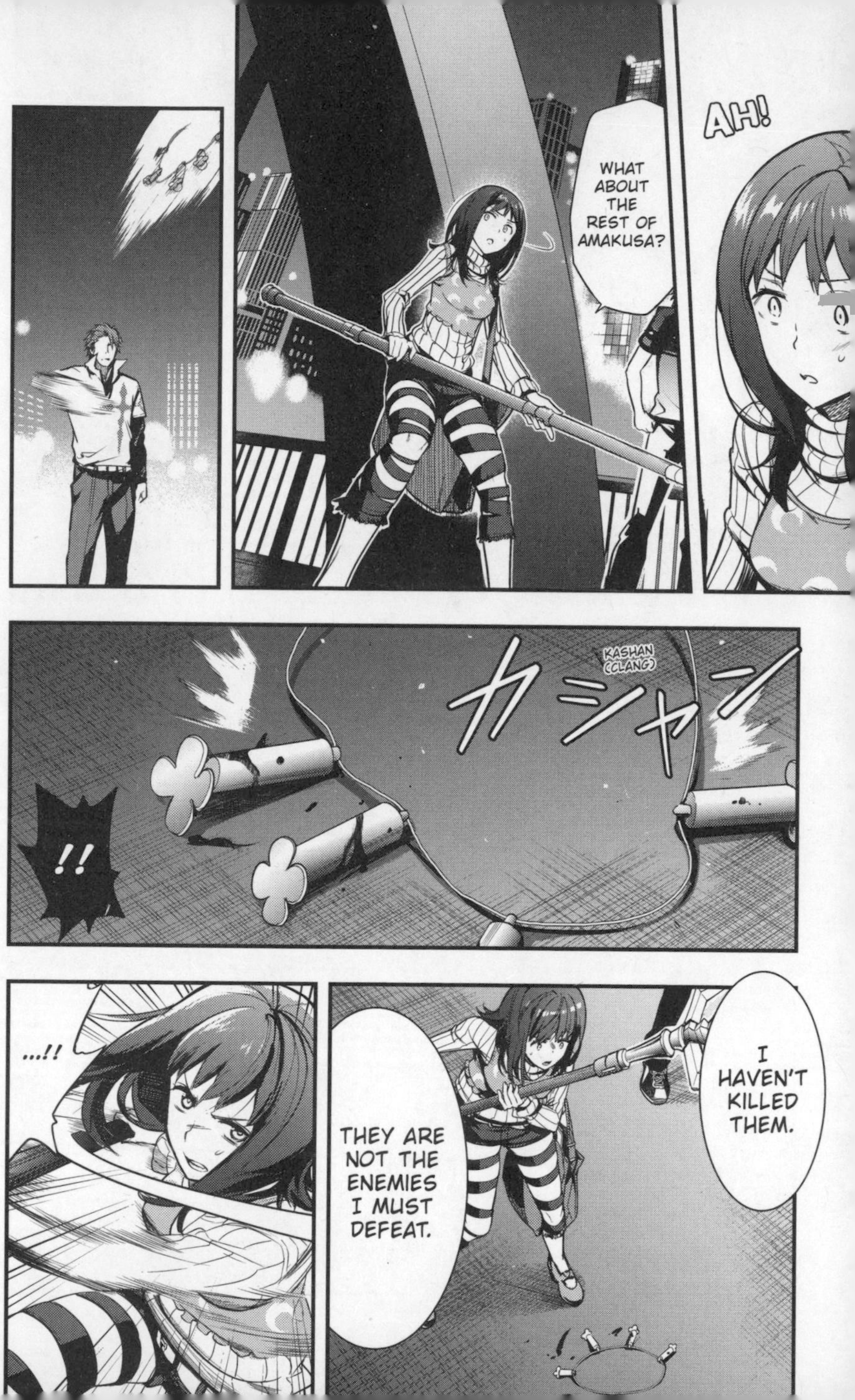
AH!
WHAT ABOUT THE REST OF AMAKUSA?
KASHAN (CLANG)
カシャン
!!
I HAVEN'T KILLED THEM.
THEY ARE NOT THE ENEMIES I MUST DEFEAT.
...!!

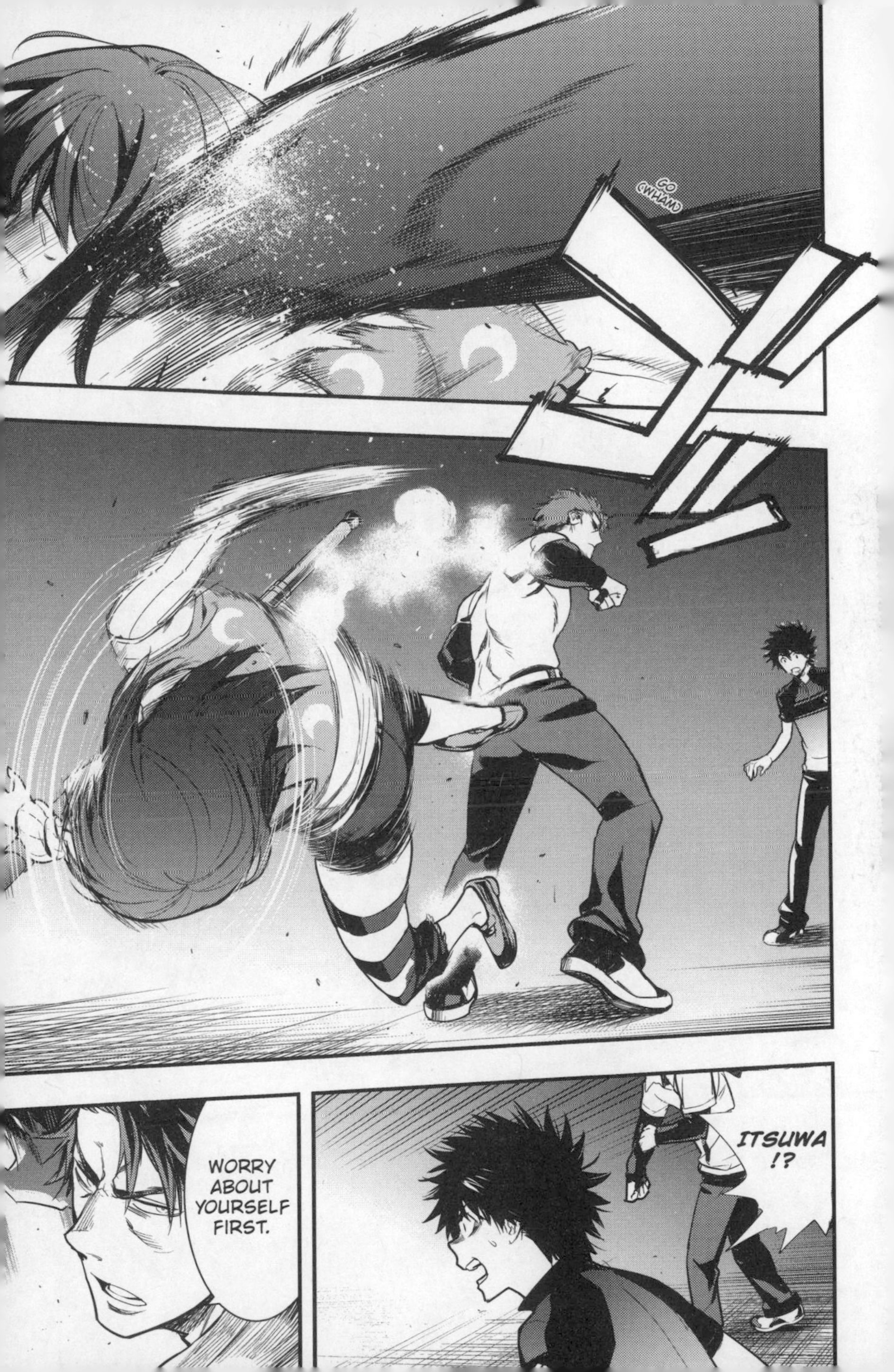
GO
(WHAM)
ITSUWA
!?
WORRY ABOUT YOURSELF FIRST.

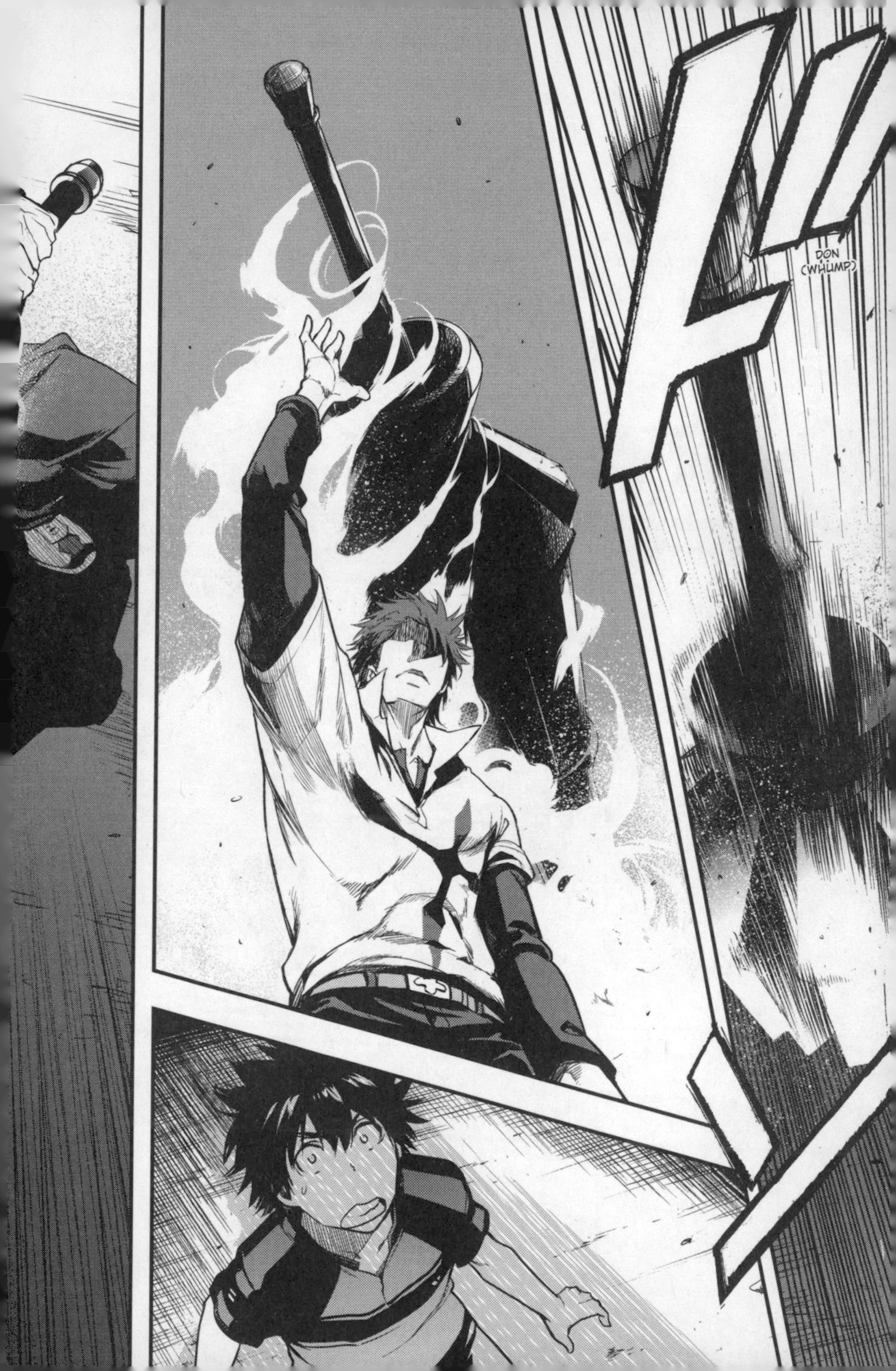
DON
(WHUMP)

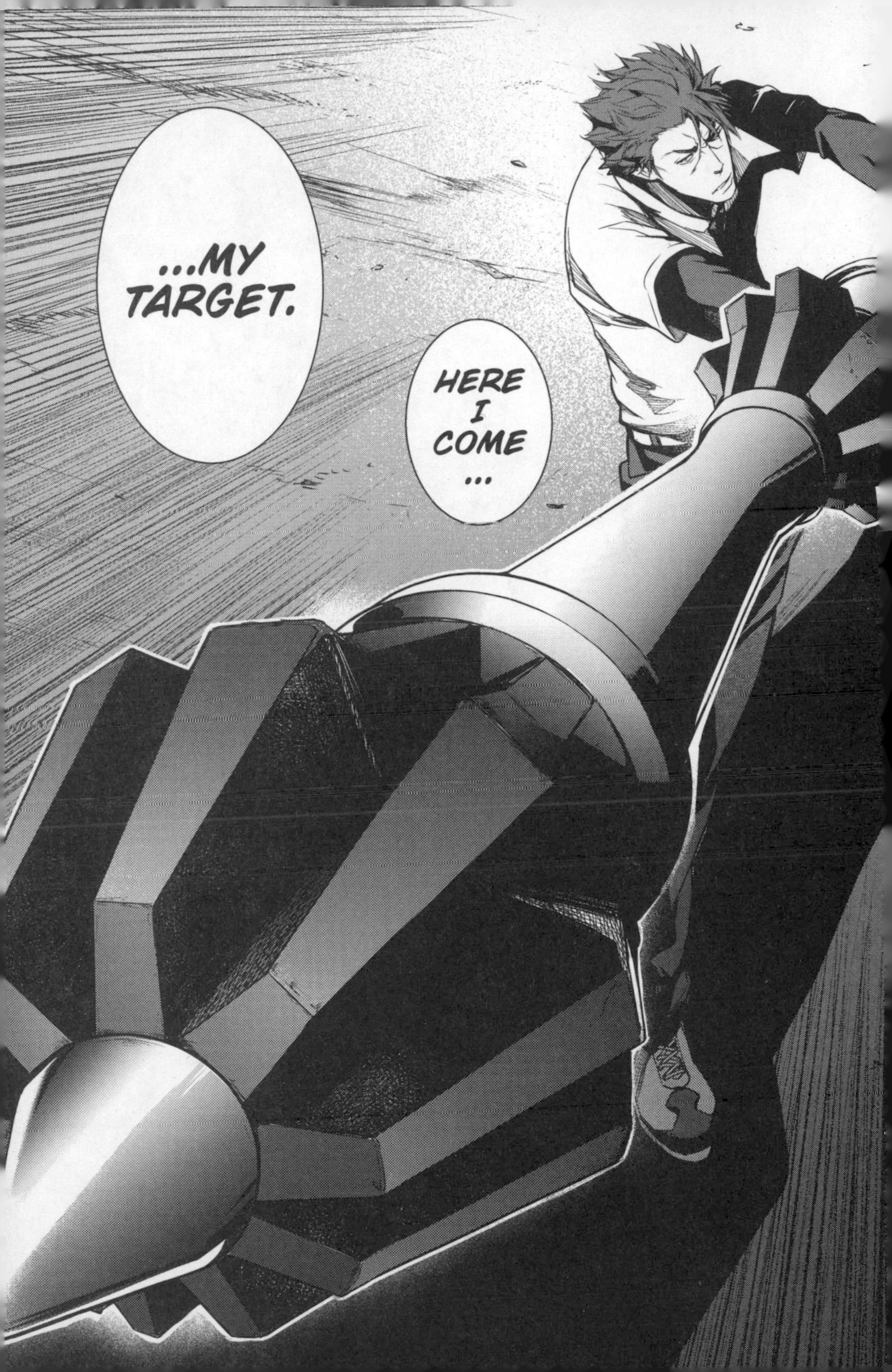
HERE I COME ...
...MY TARGET.

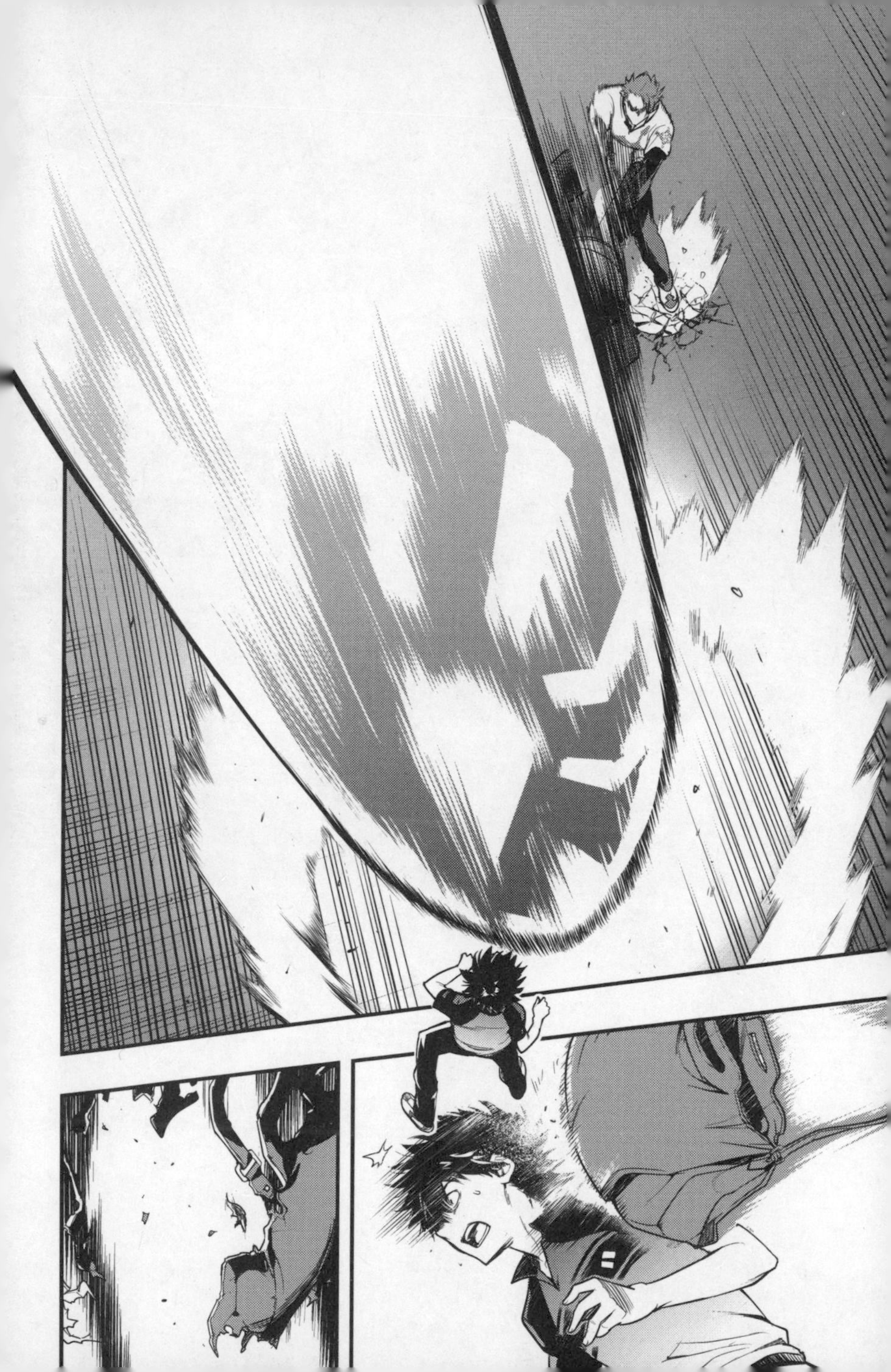

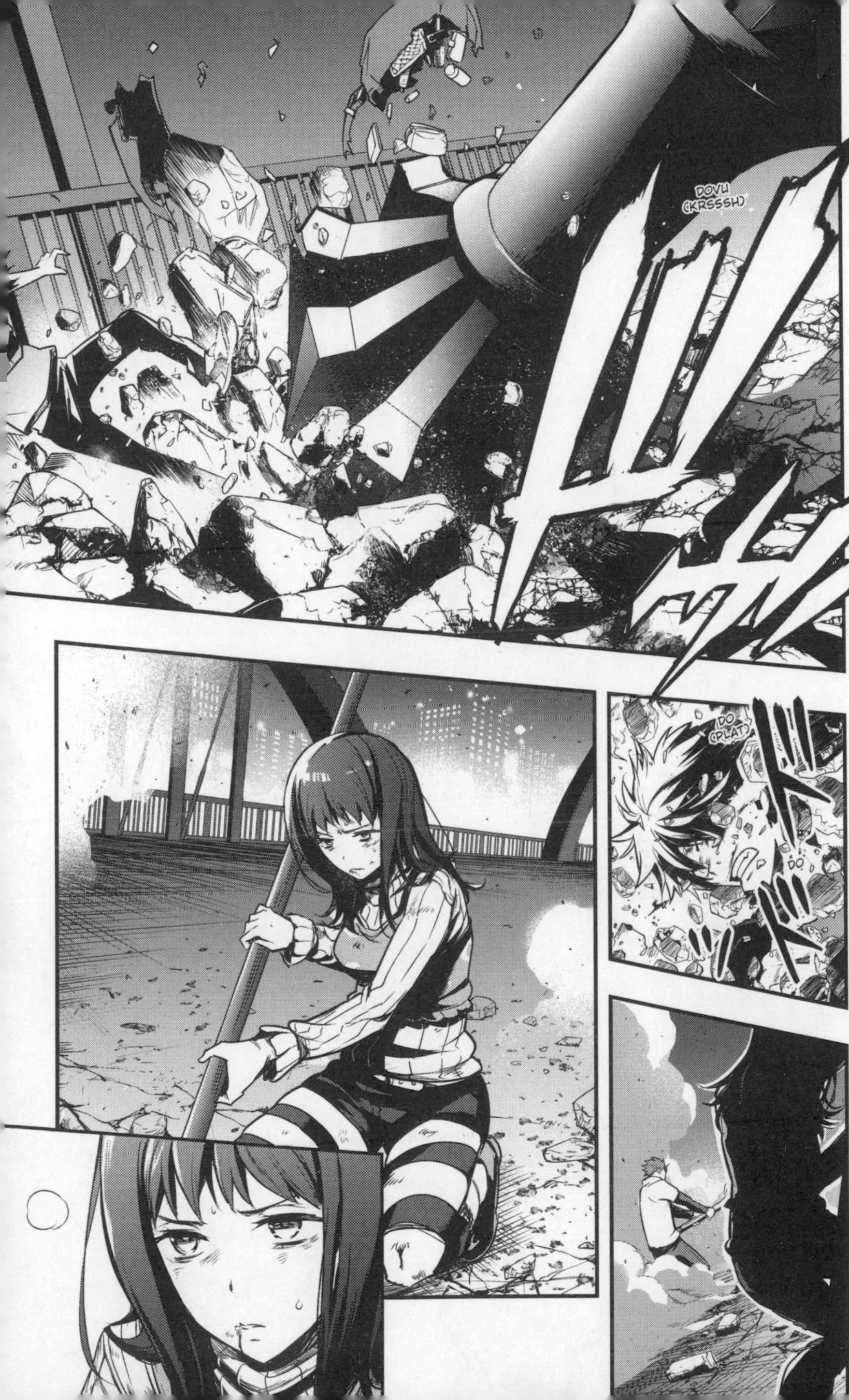
DOVU
(KRSSSH)
DO
(PLAT)
DO

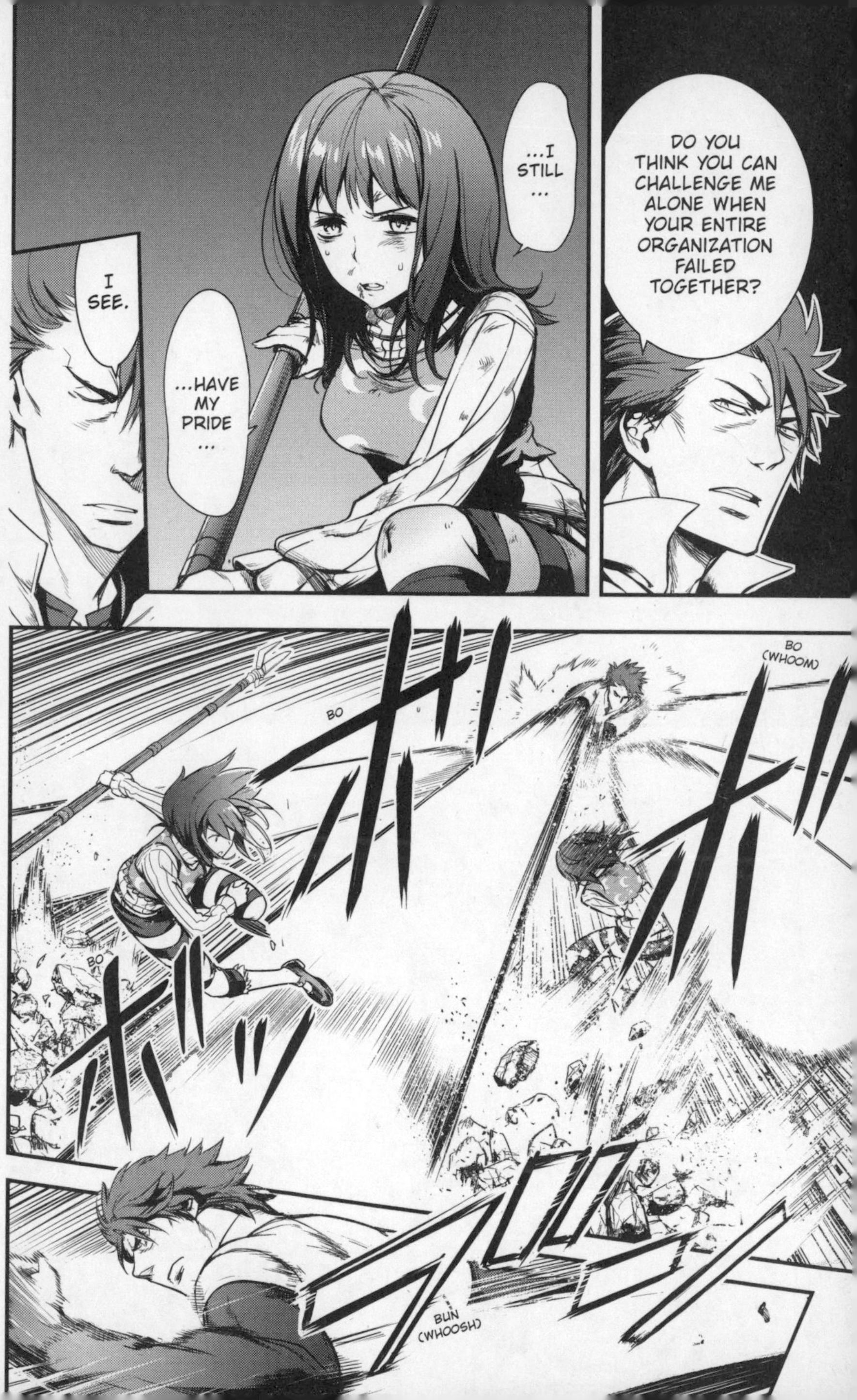
DO YOU THINK YOU CAN CHALLENGE ME ALONE WHEN YOUR ENTIRE ORGANIZATION FAILED TOGETHER?
...I STILL ...
...HAVE MY PRIDE ...
I SEE.
BO (WHOOM)
BO
BO
BUN (WHOOSH)

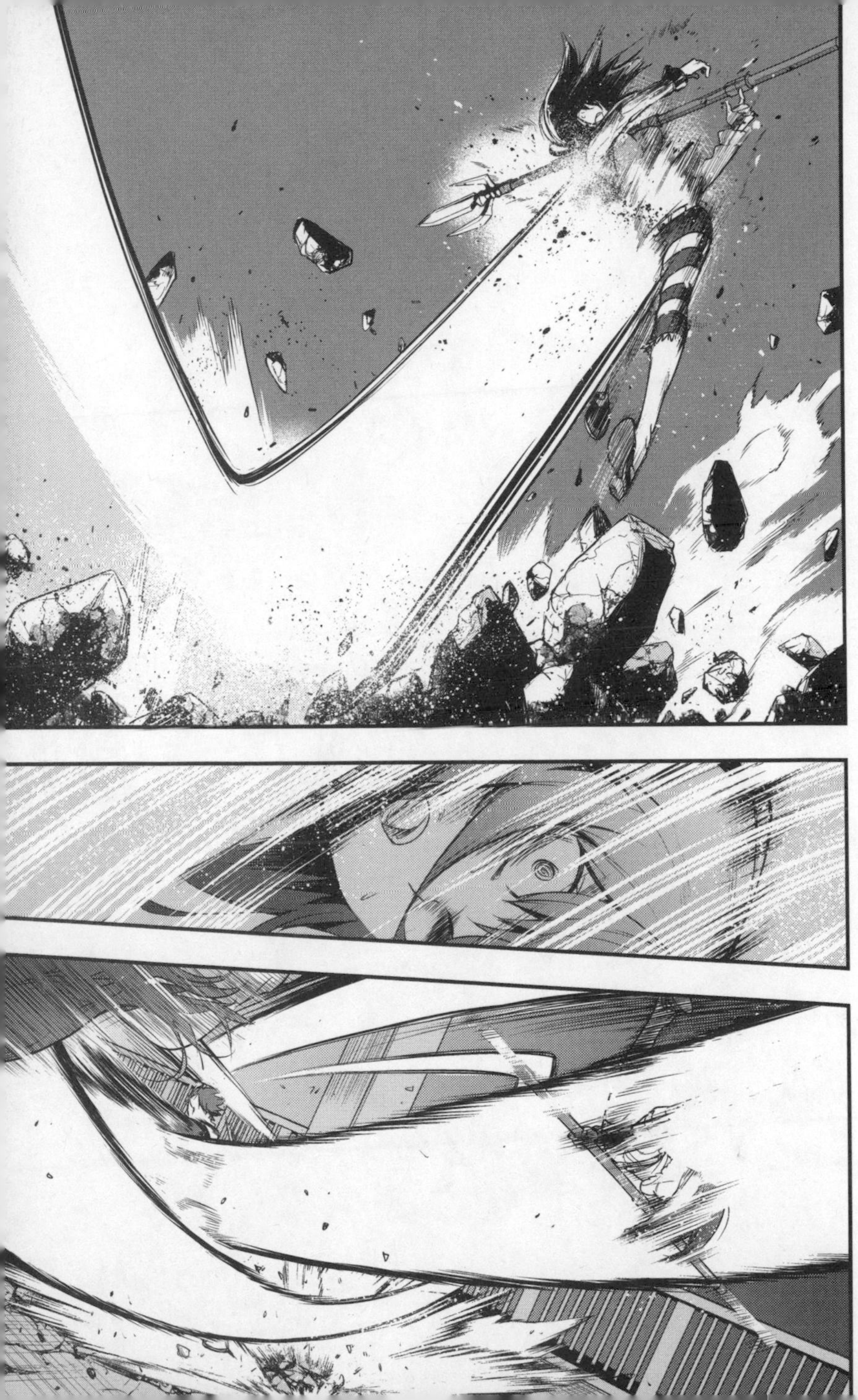

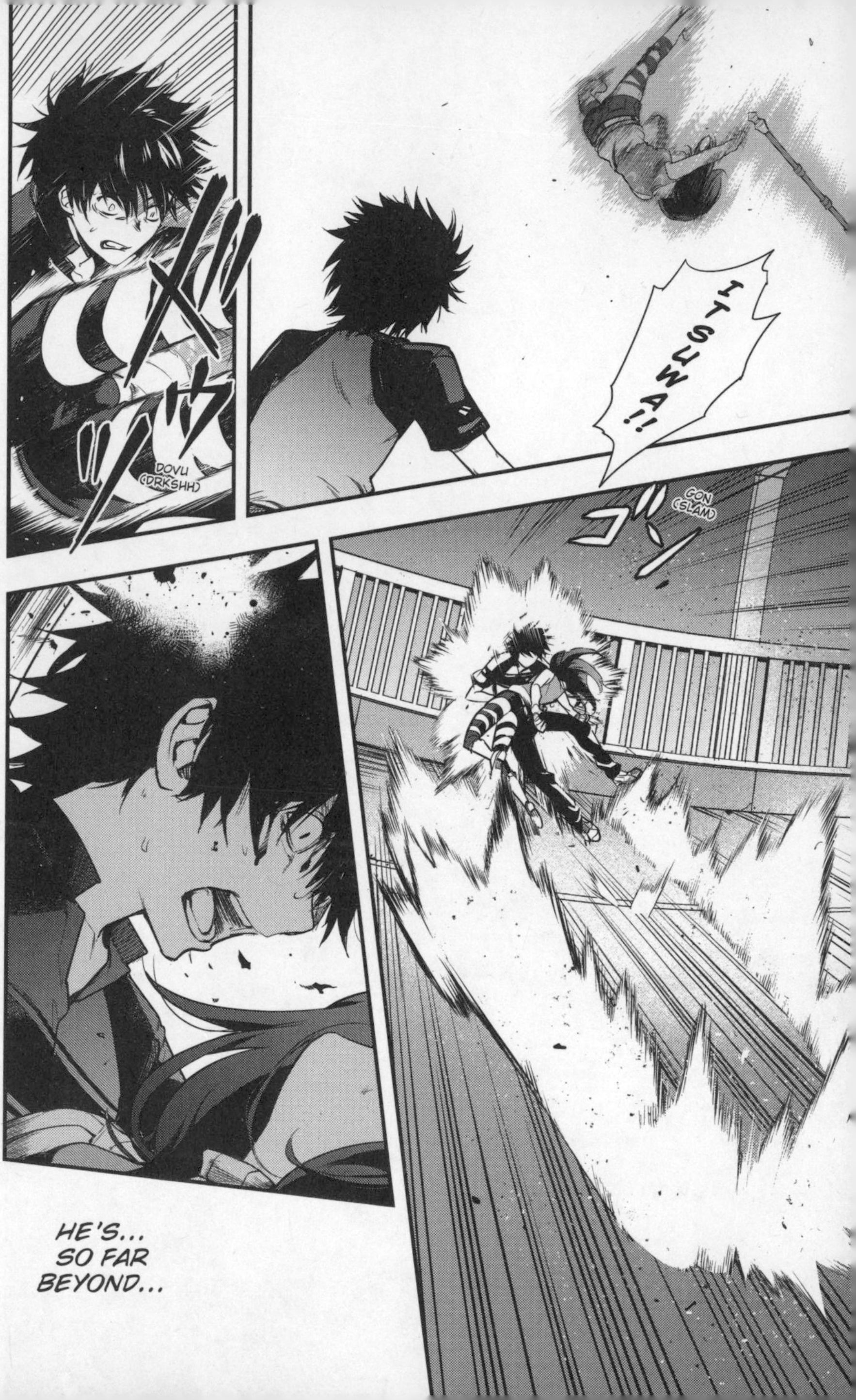
ITSUWA!!
DOVU (DRKSHH)
GON (SLAM)
HE'S... SO FAR BEYOND...

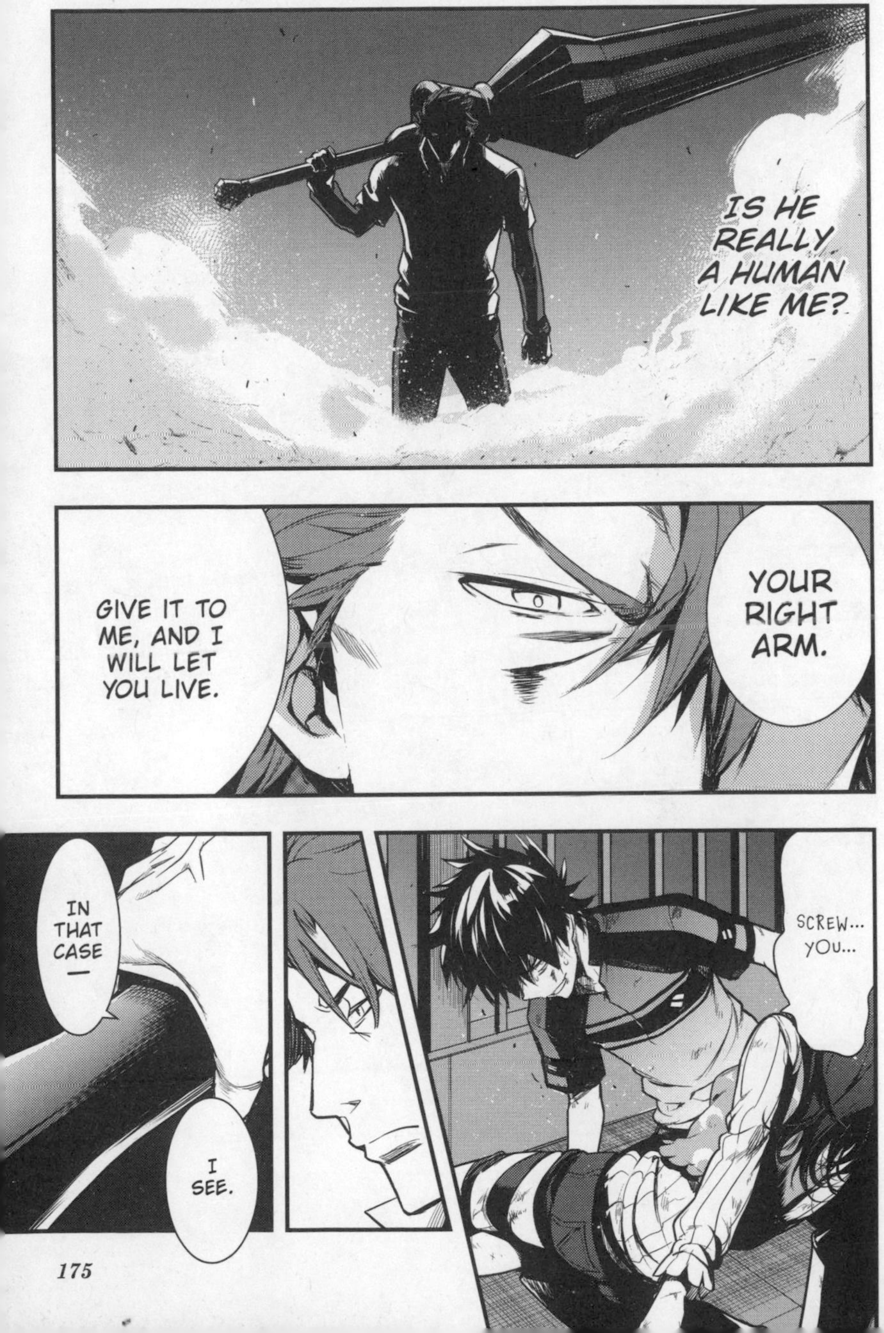
IS HE REALLY A HUMAN LIKE ME?
YOUR RIGHT ARM.
GIVE IT TO ME, AND I WILL LET YOU LIVE.
SCREW... YOU...
I SEE.
IN THAT CASE —

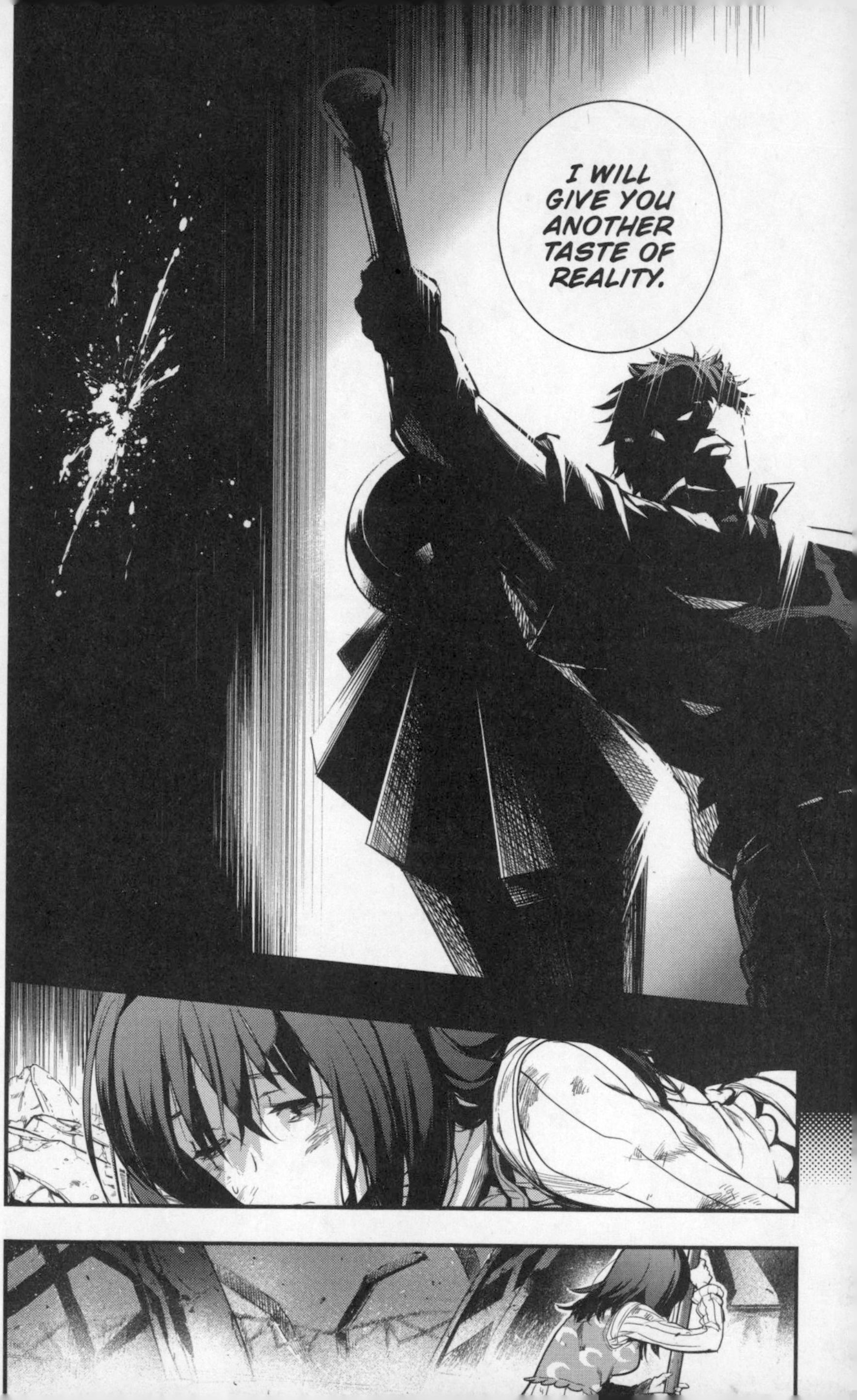
I WILL GIVE YOU ANOTHER TASTE OF REALITY.

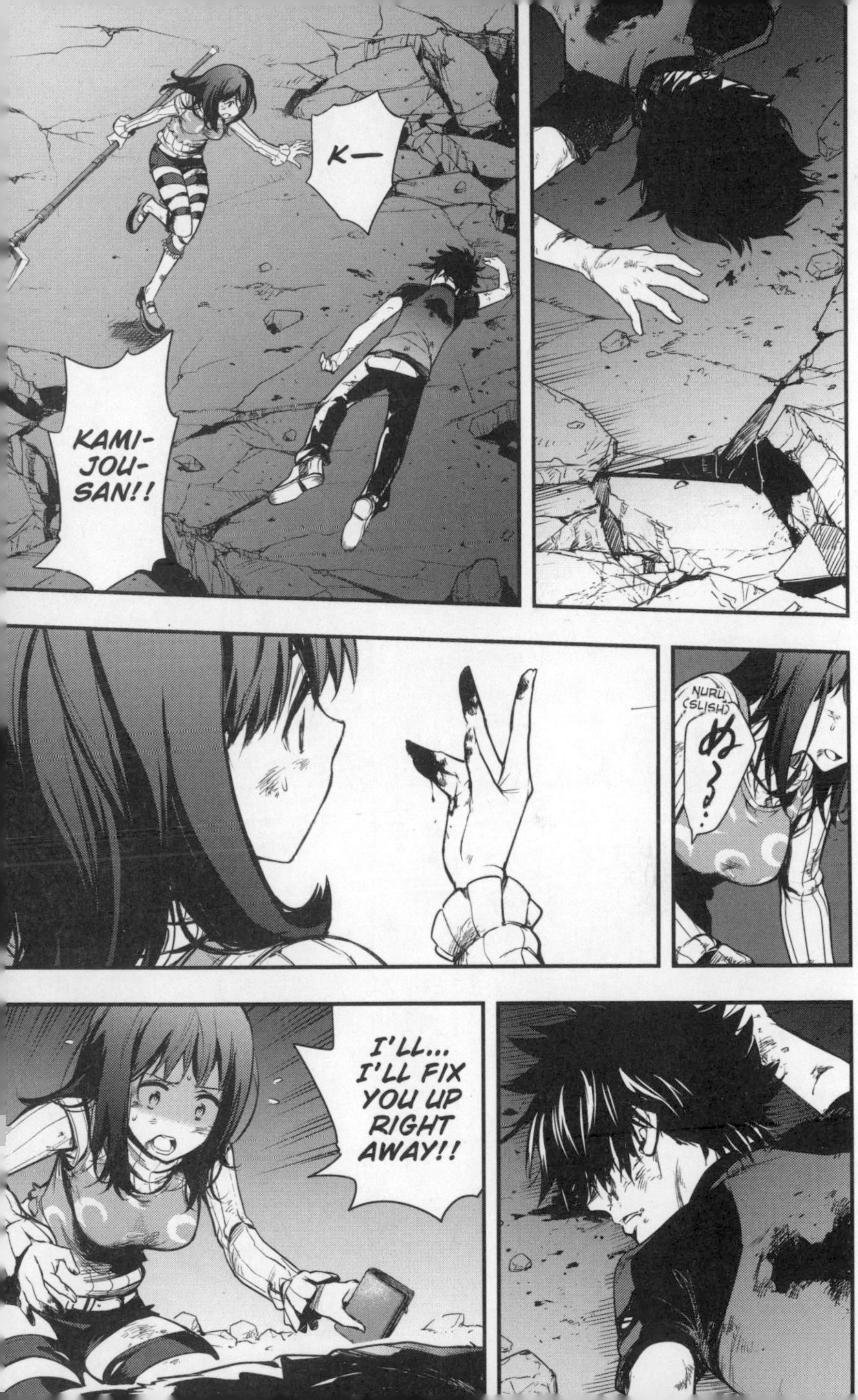
K—
KAMI-JOU-SAN!!
ぬる…
NURU (SLISH)
I'LL... I'LL FIX YOU UP RIGHT AWAY!!

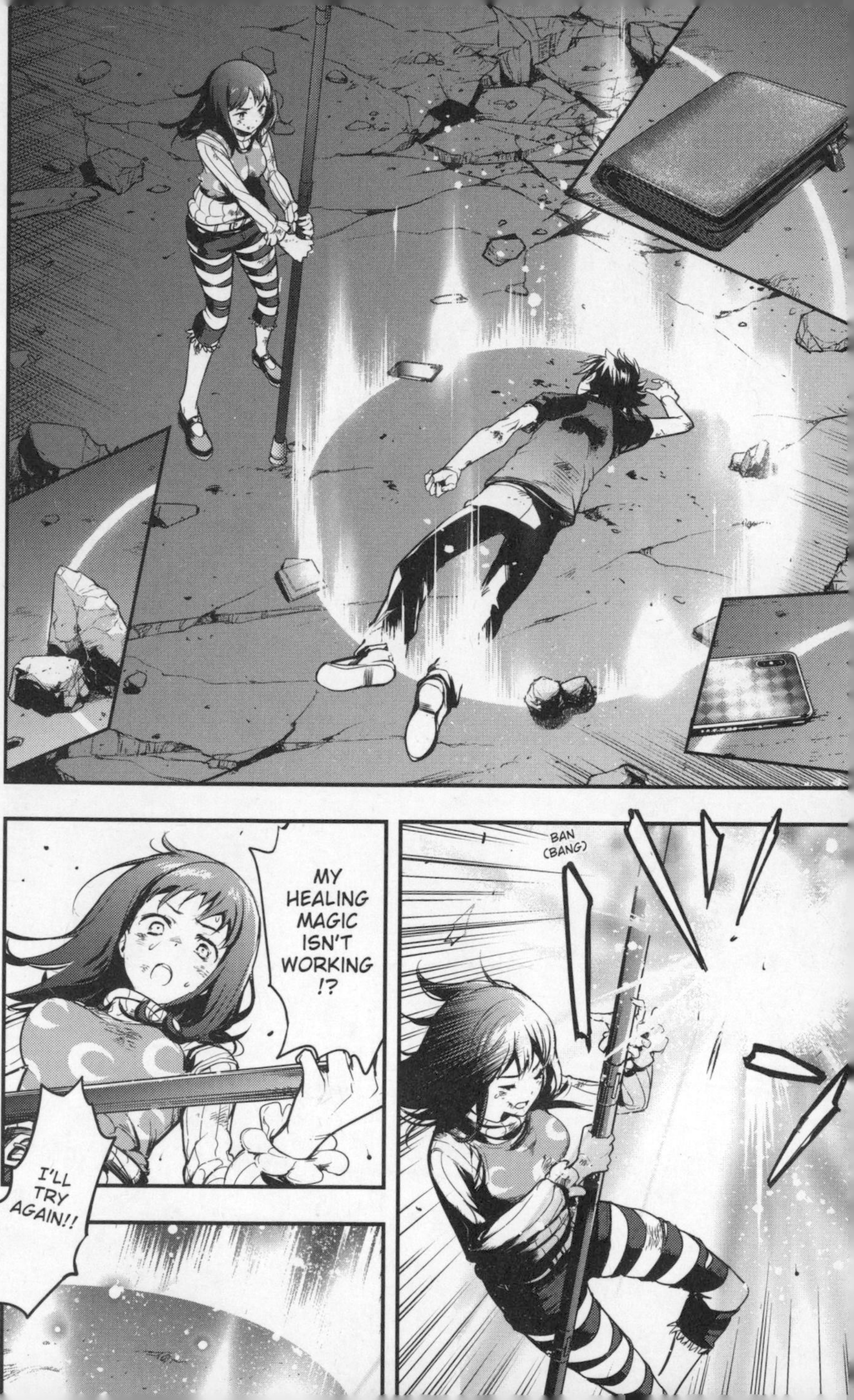
BAN (BANG)
MY HEALING MAGIC ISN'T WORKING!?
I'LL TRY AGAIN!!

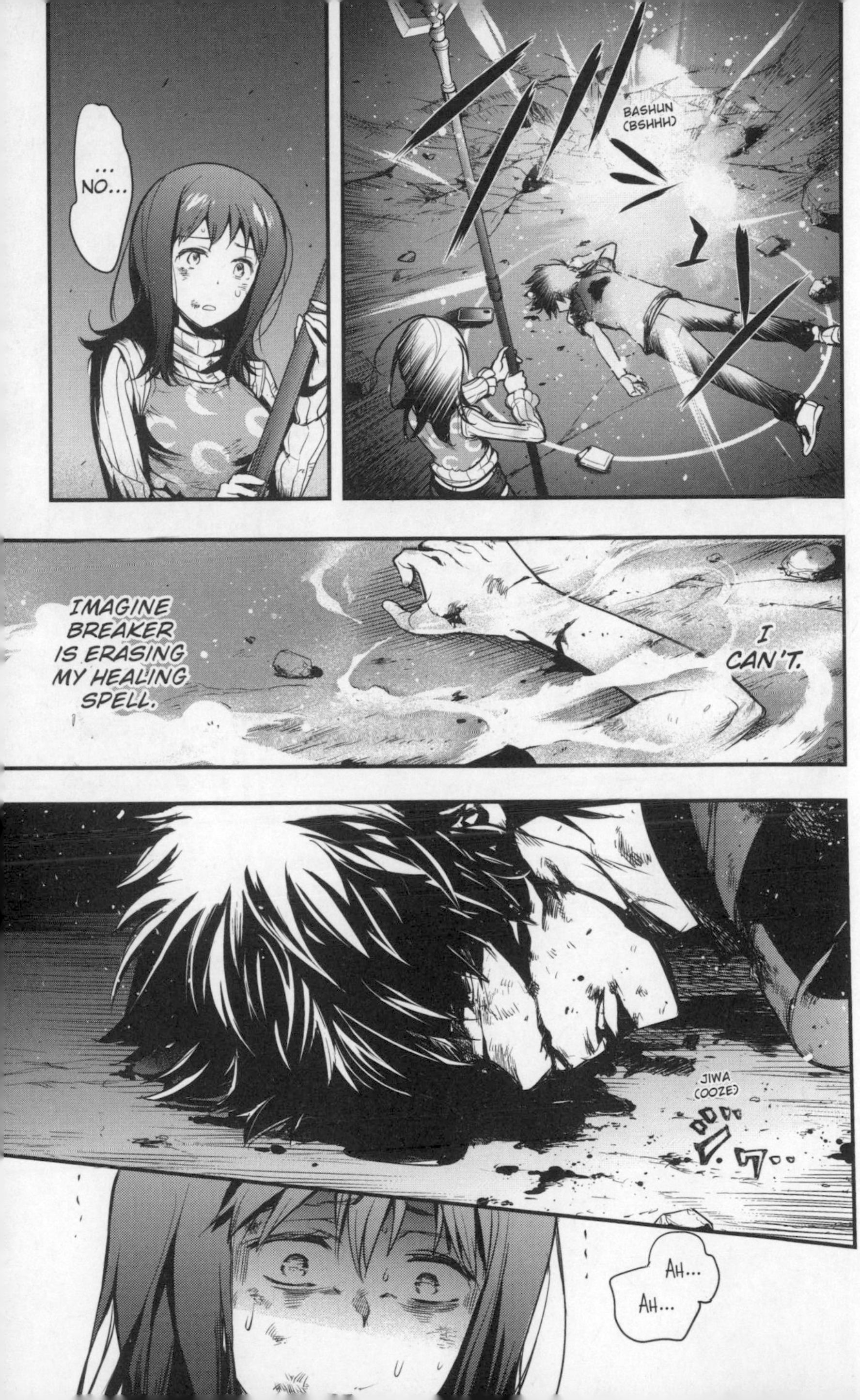
BASHUN (BSHHH)
... NO...
I CAN'T.
IMAGINE BREAKER IS ERASING MY HEALING SPELL.
JIWA (OOZE)
AH... AH...

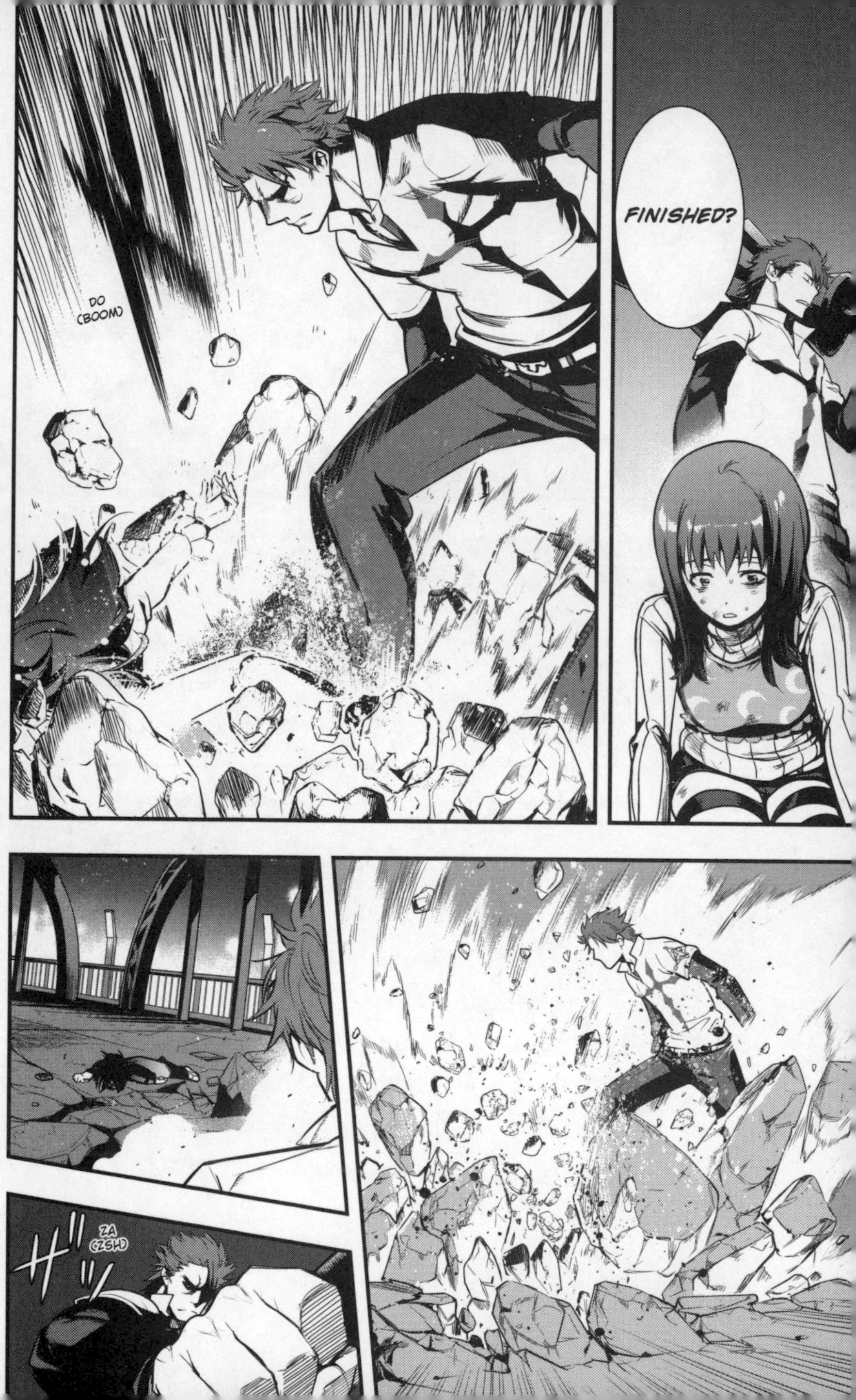
FINISHED?
DO (BOOM)
ZA (ZSH)

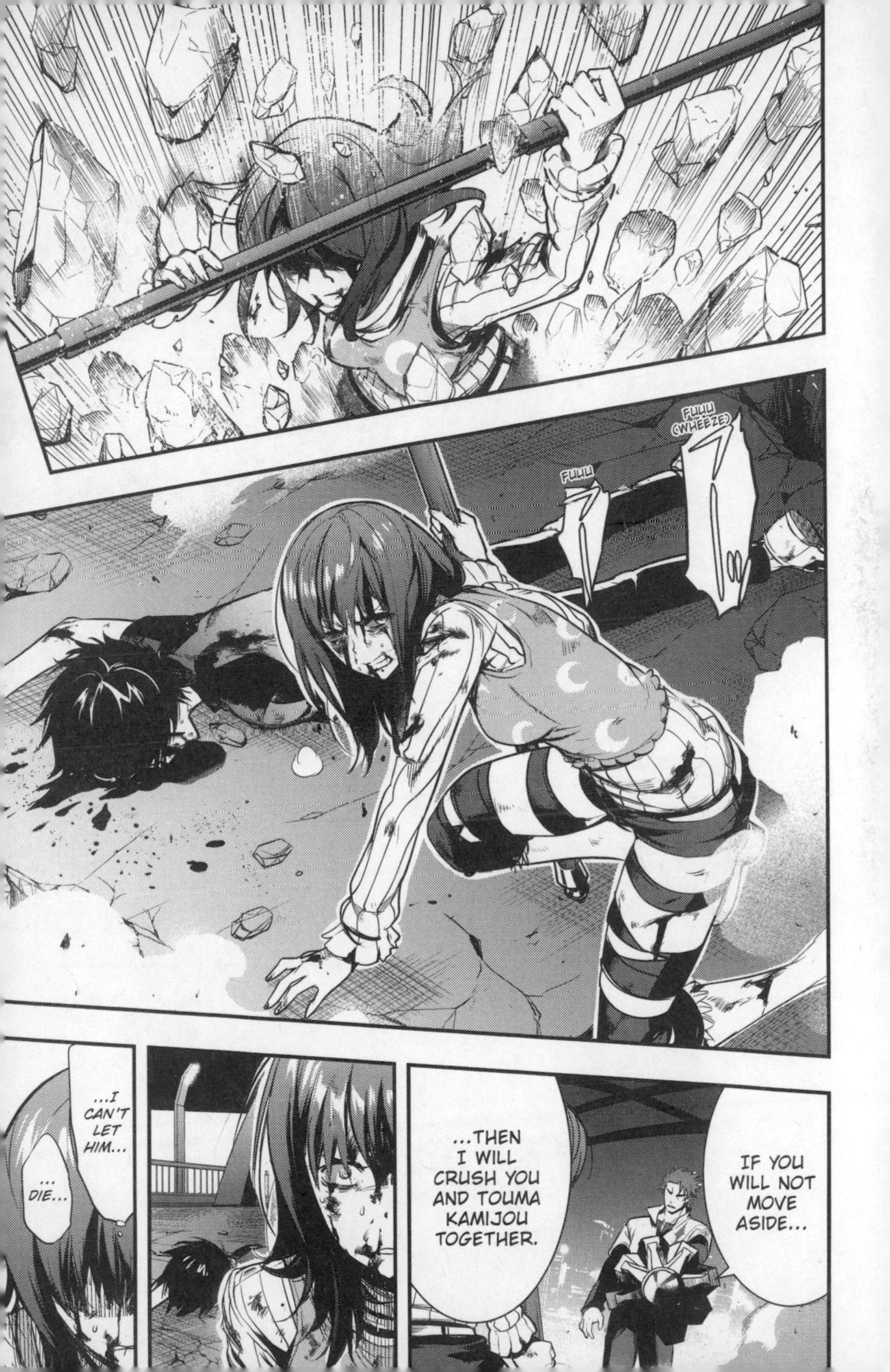
FUUU (WHEEZE)
FUUU
IF YOU WILL NOT MOVE ASIDE...
...THEN I WILL CRUSH YOU AND TOUMA KAMIJOU TOGETHER.
...I CAN'T LET HIM...
...DIE...

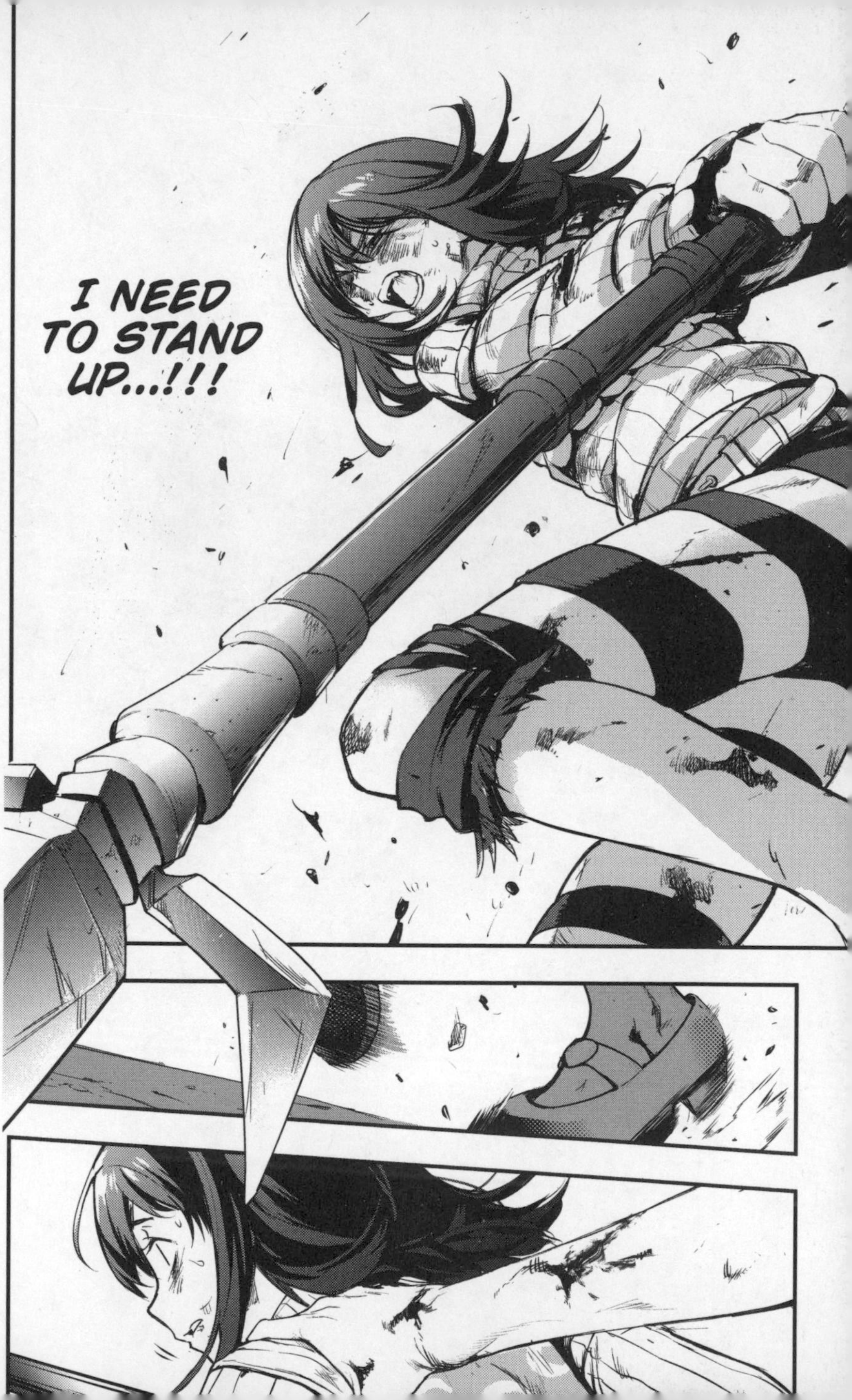
I NEED TO STAND UP...!!!

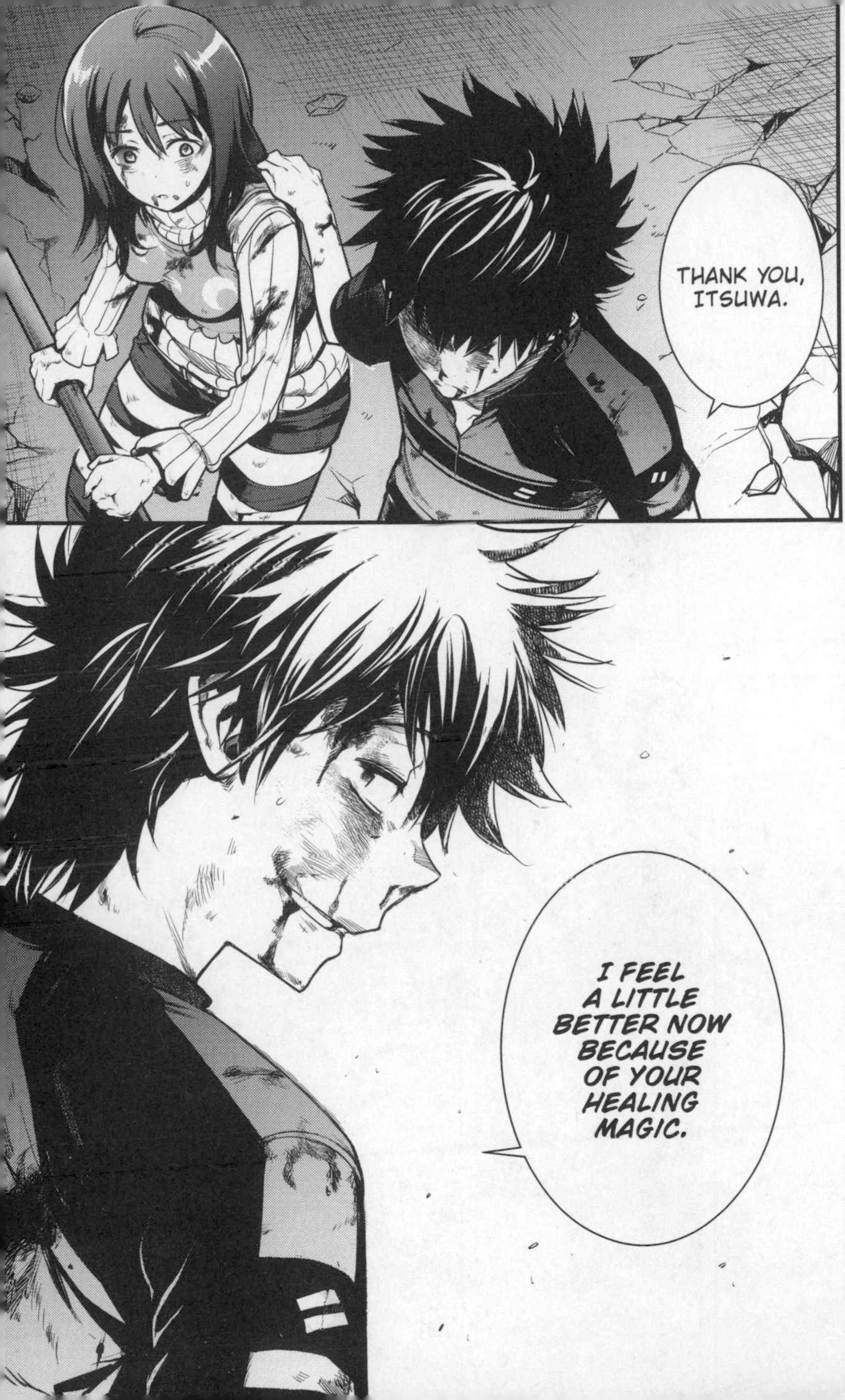
THANK YOU, ITSUWA.
I FEEL A LITTLE BETTER NOW BECAUSE OF YOUR HEALING MAGIC.

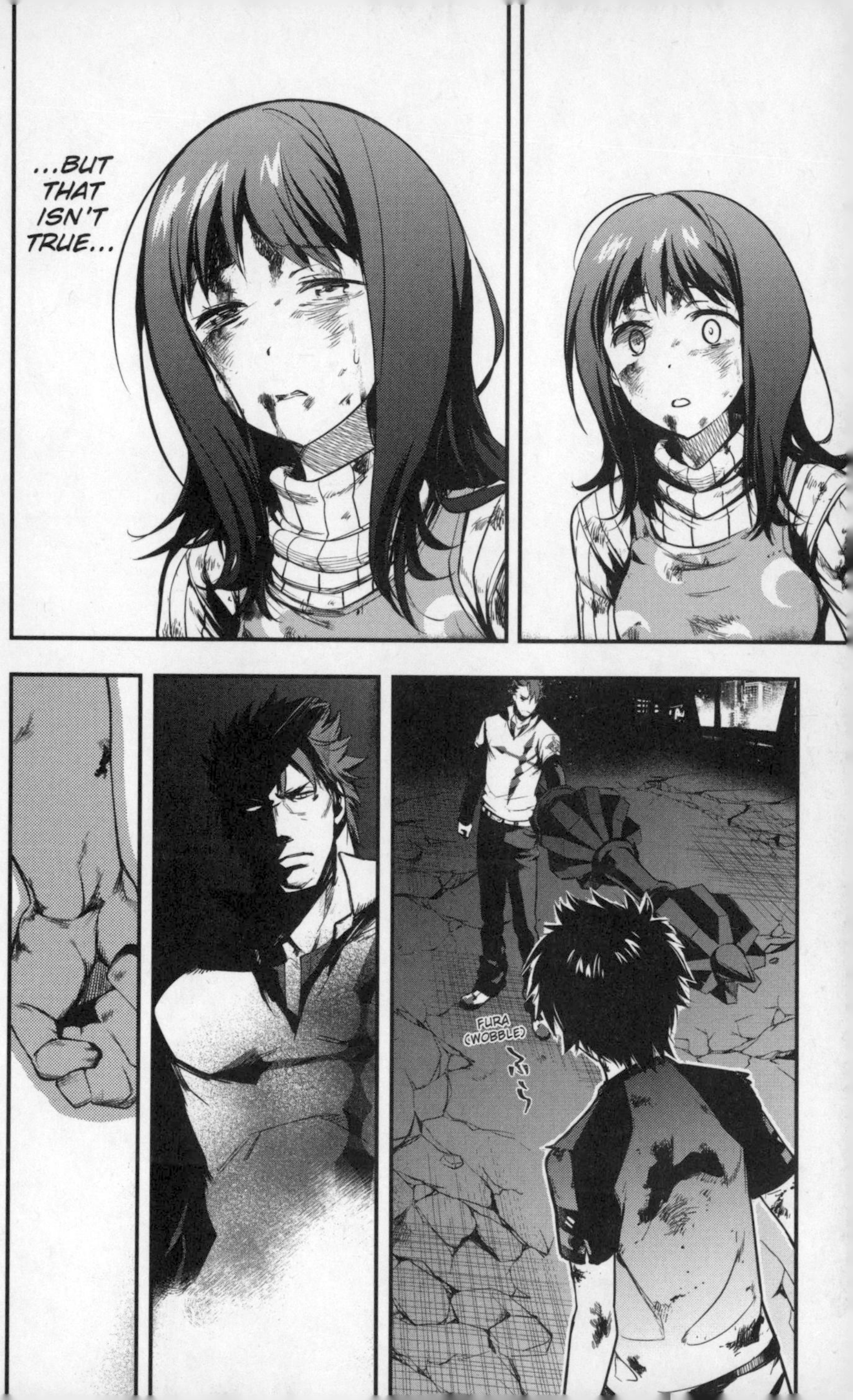
...BUT THAT ISN'T TRUE...
FURA (WOBBLE)
ふら

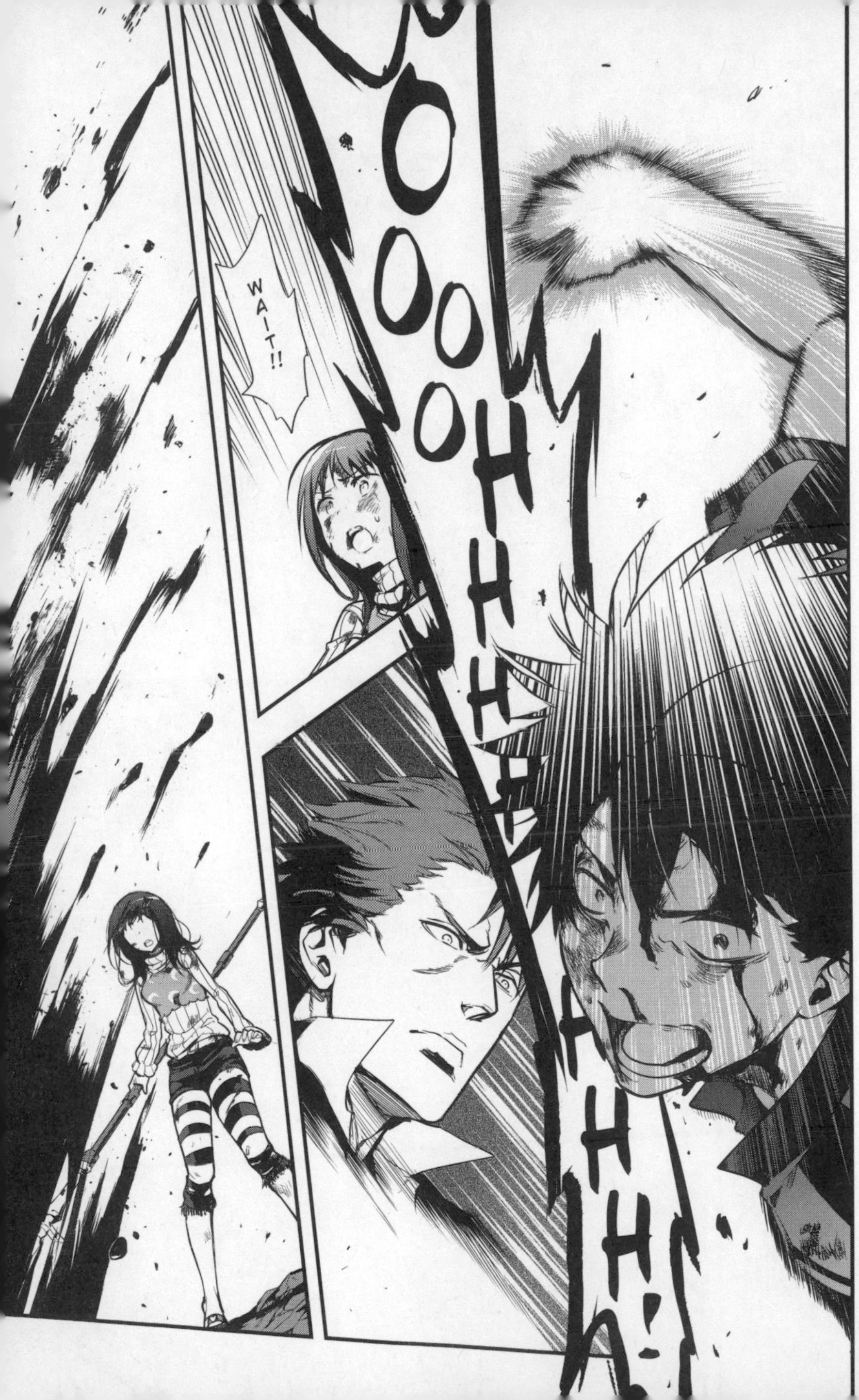
WAIT!!
OOOOOHHHHHHHHH!!

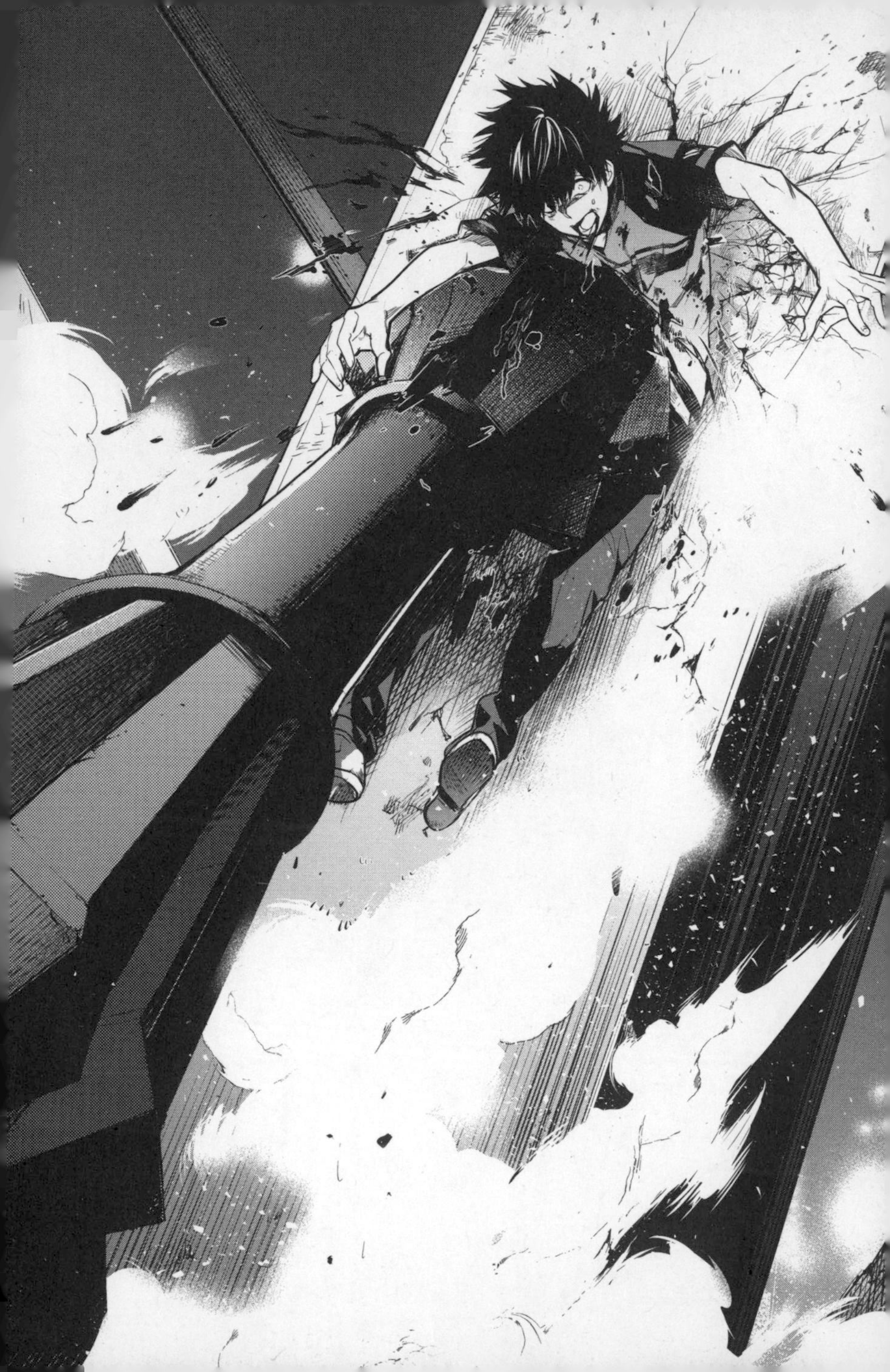

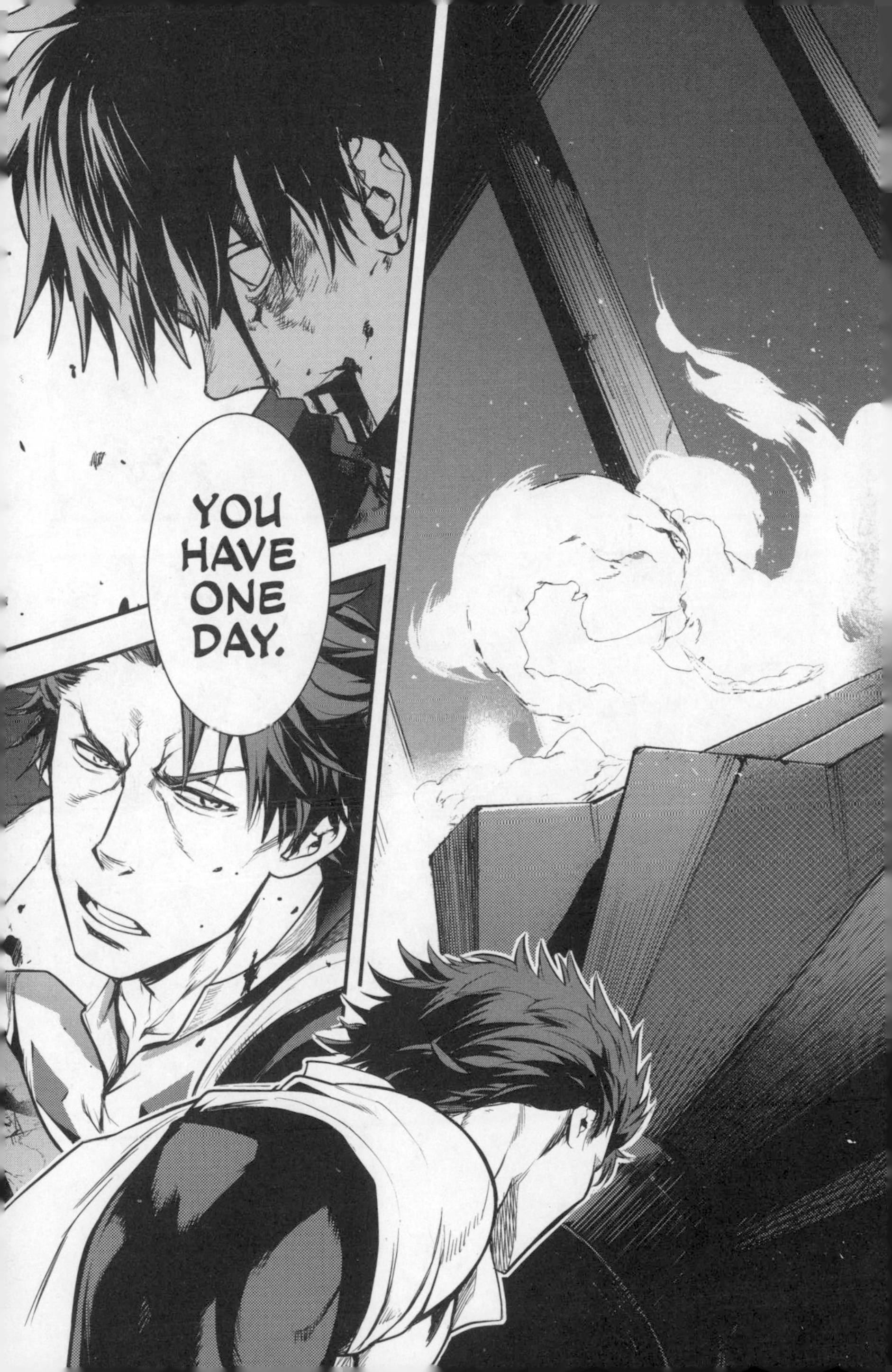
YOU HAVE ONE DAY.

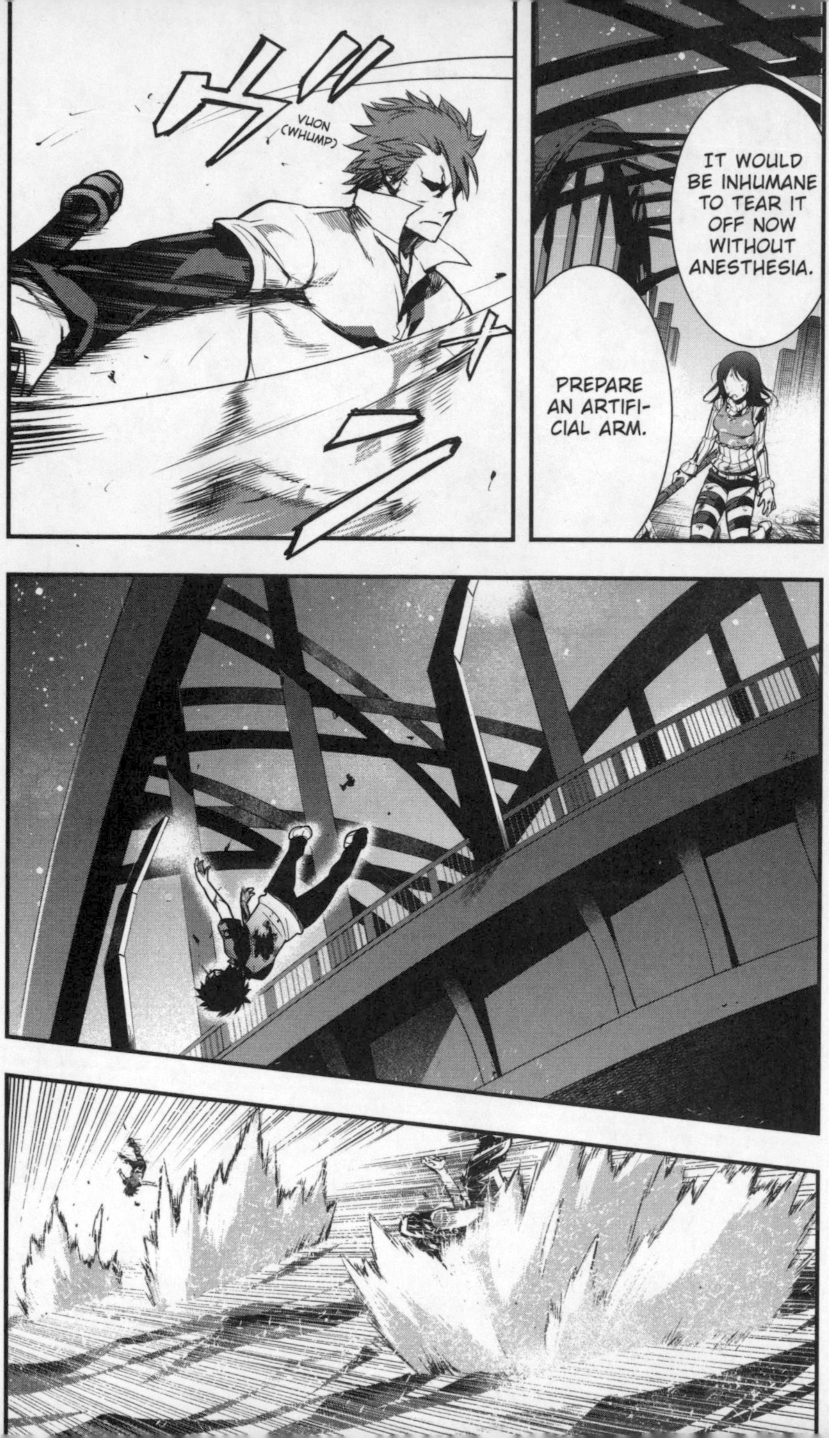
IT WOULD BE INHUMANE TO TEAR IT OFF NOW WITHOUT ANESTHESIA.
PREPARE AN ARTIFICIAL ARM.
VUON (WHUMP)

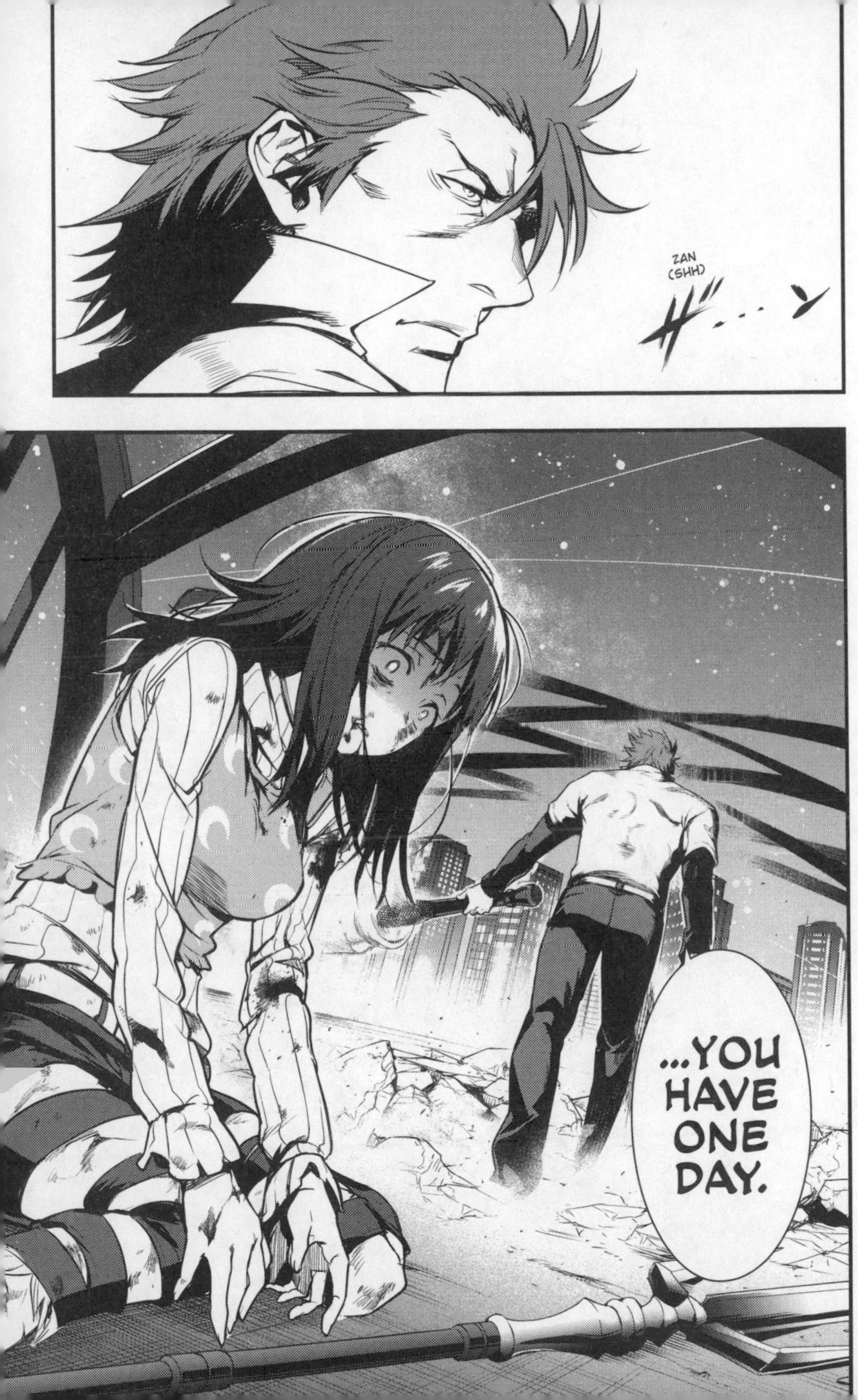
ZAN (SHH)
ザ・・・ン
...YOU HAVE ONE DAY.

A Certain Magical Index

#154 AFTER THE RAID

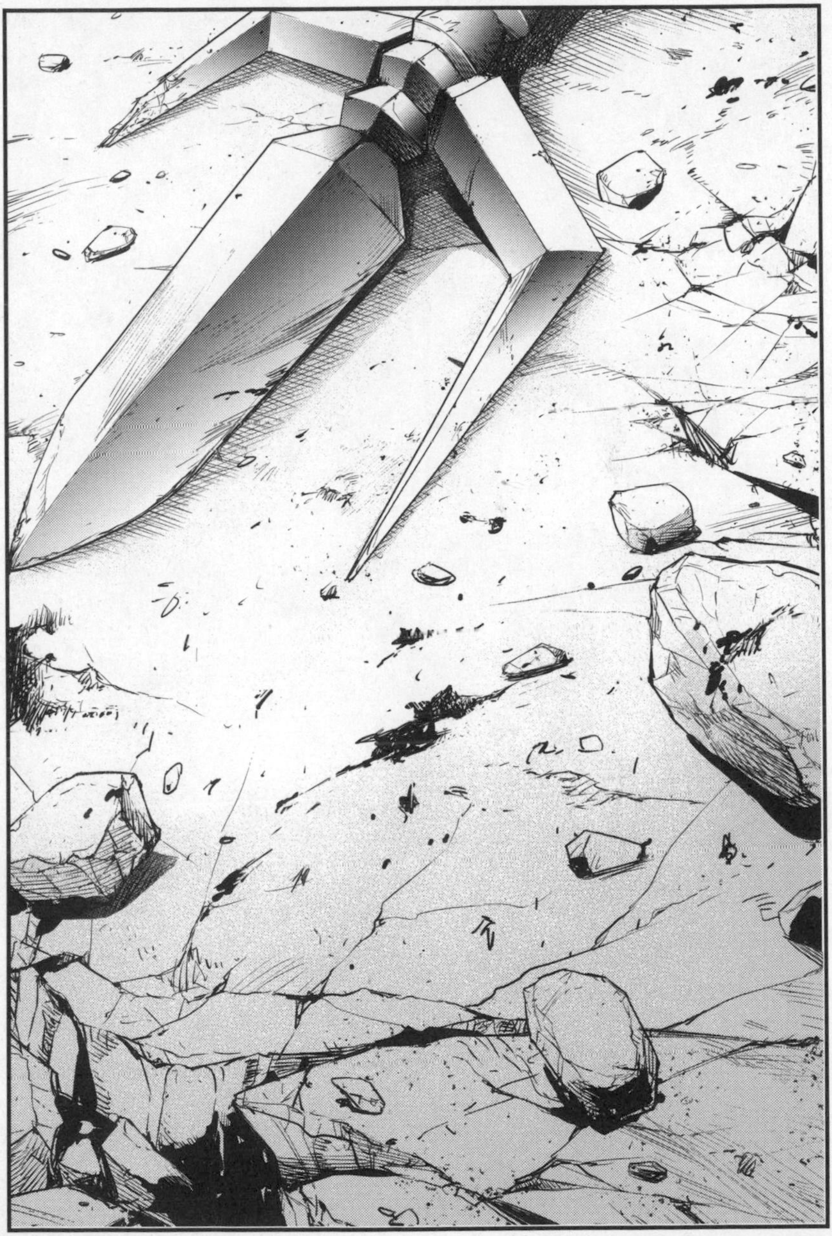

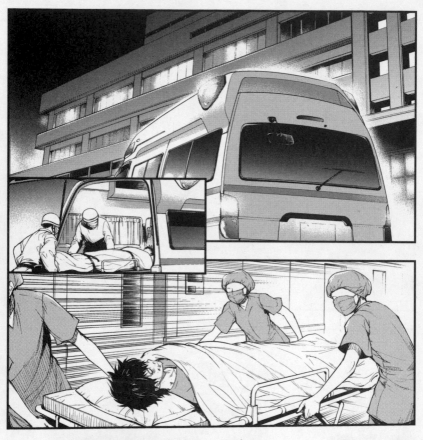

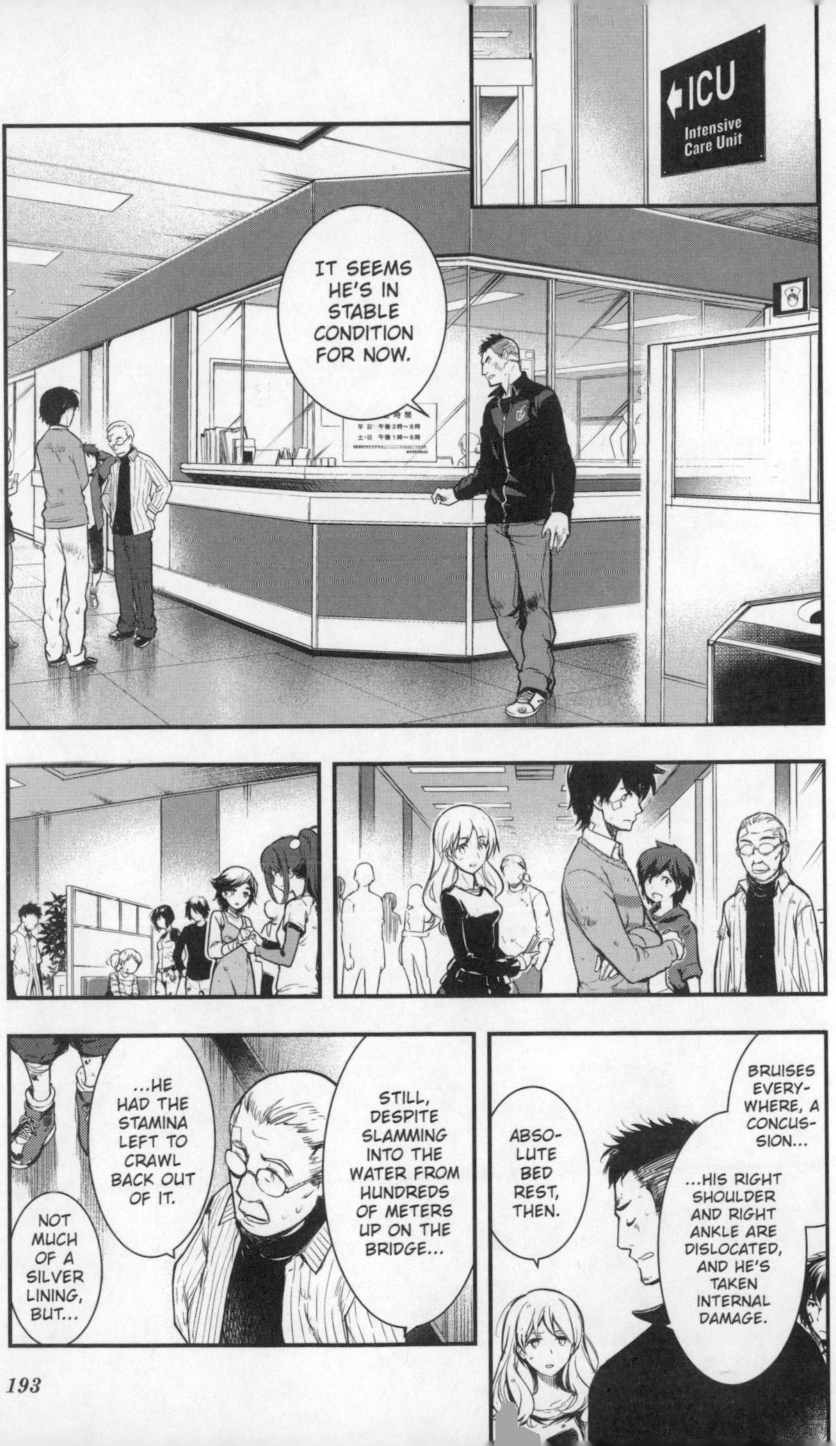

ICU
Intensive Care Unit
IT SEEMS HE'S IN STABLE CONDITION FOR NOW.
BRUISES EVERYWHERE, A CONCUSSION...
...HIS RIGHT SHOULDER AND RIGHT ANKLE ARE DISLOCATED, AND HE'S TAKEN INTERNAL DAMAGE.
ABSOLUTE BED REST, THEN.
STILL, DESPITE SLAMMING INTO THE WATER FROM HUNDREDS OF METERS UP ON THE BRIDGE...
...HE HAD THE STAMINA LEFT TO CRAWL BACK OUT OF IT.
NOT MUCH OF A SILVER LINING, BUT...

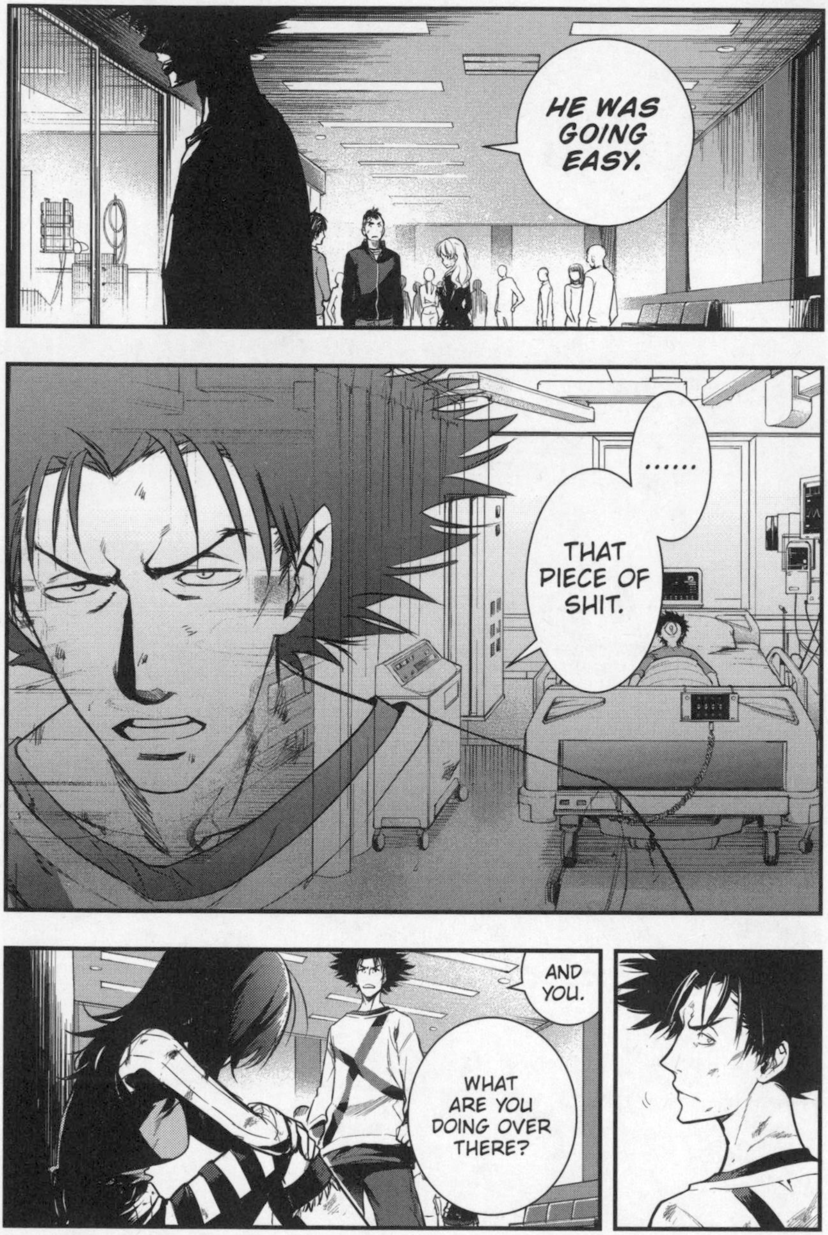
HE WAS GOING EASY.
......
THAT PIECE OF SHIT.
AND YOU.
WHAT ARE YOU DOING OVER THERE?

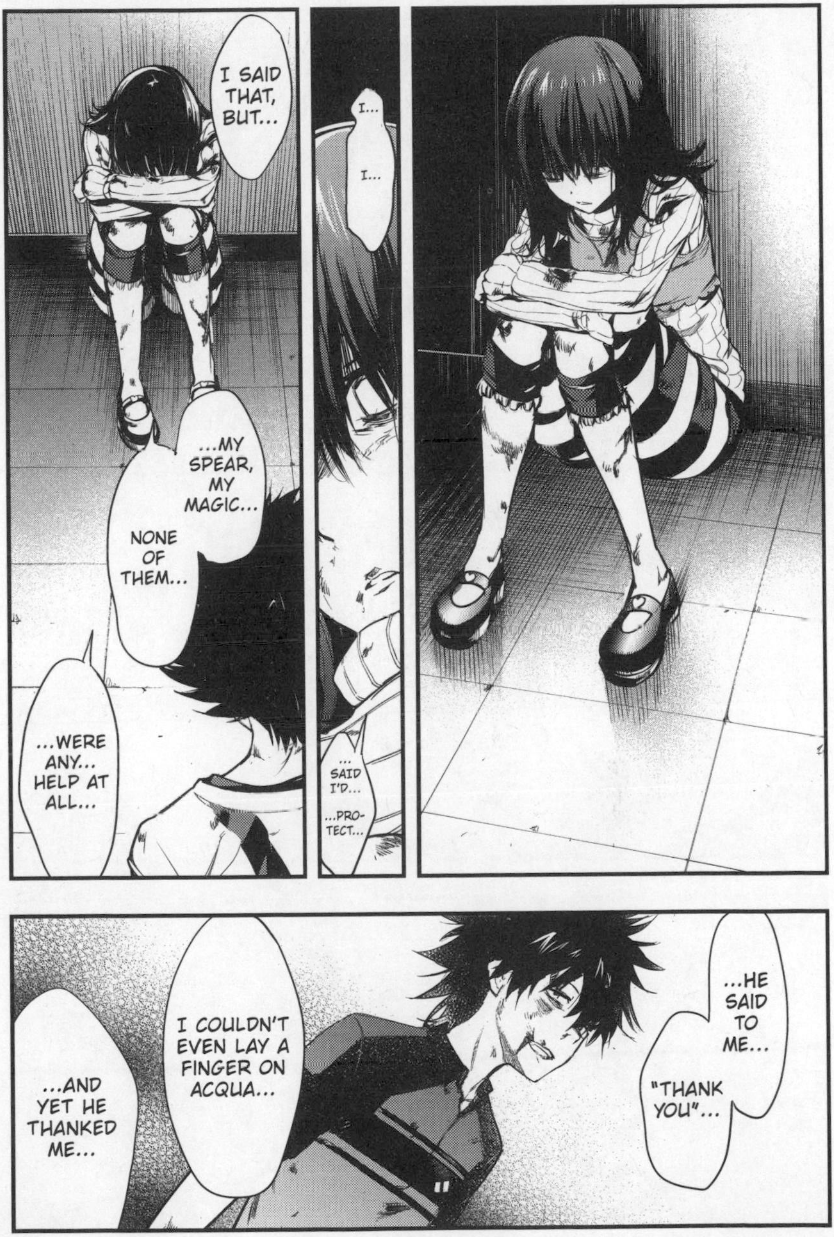
I...
I...
...SAID I'D...
...PRO-TECT...
I SAID THAT, BUT...
...MY SPEAR, MY MAGIC...
NONE OF THEM...
...WERE ANY... HELP AT ALL...
...HE SAID TO ME...
"THANK YOU"...
I COULDN'T EVEN LAY A FINGER ON ACQUA...
...AND YET HE THANKED ME...

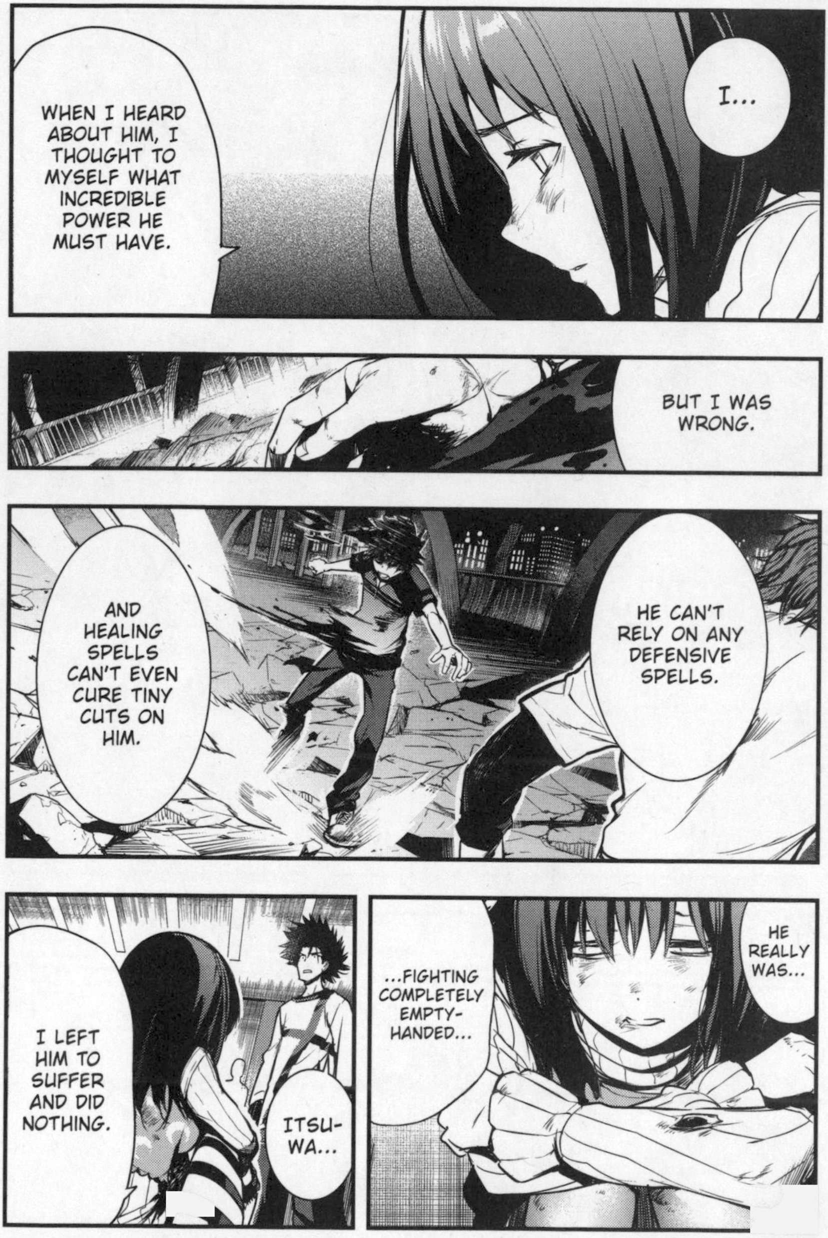
I...
WHEN I HEARD ABOUT HIM, I THOUGHT TO MYSELF WHAT INCREDIBLE POWER HE MUST HAVE.
BUT I WAS WRONG.
HE CAN'T RELY ON ANY DEFENSIVE SPELLS.
AND HEALING SPELLS CAN'T EVEN CURE TINY CUTS ON HIM.
HE REALLY WAS...
...FIGHTING COMPLETELY EMPTY-HANDED...
I LEFT HIM TO SUFFER AND DID NOTHING.
ITSU-WA...

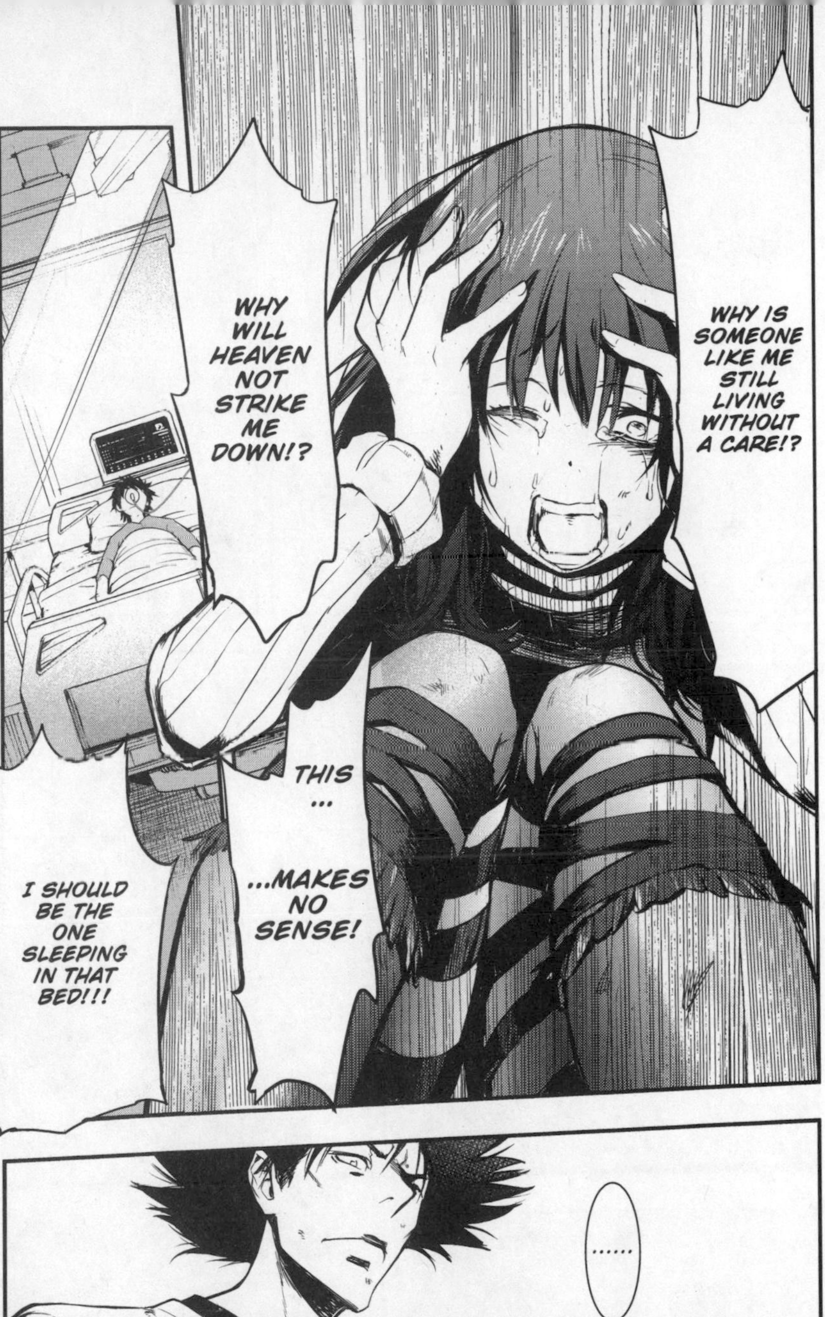
WHY IS SOMEONE LIKE ME STILL LIVING WITHOUT A CARE!?
WHY WILL HEAVEN NOT STRIKE ME DOWN!?
THIS ...
...MAKES NO SENSE!
I SHOULD BE THE ONE SLEEPING IN THAT BED!!!
......

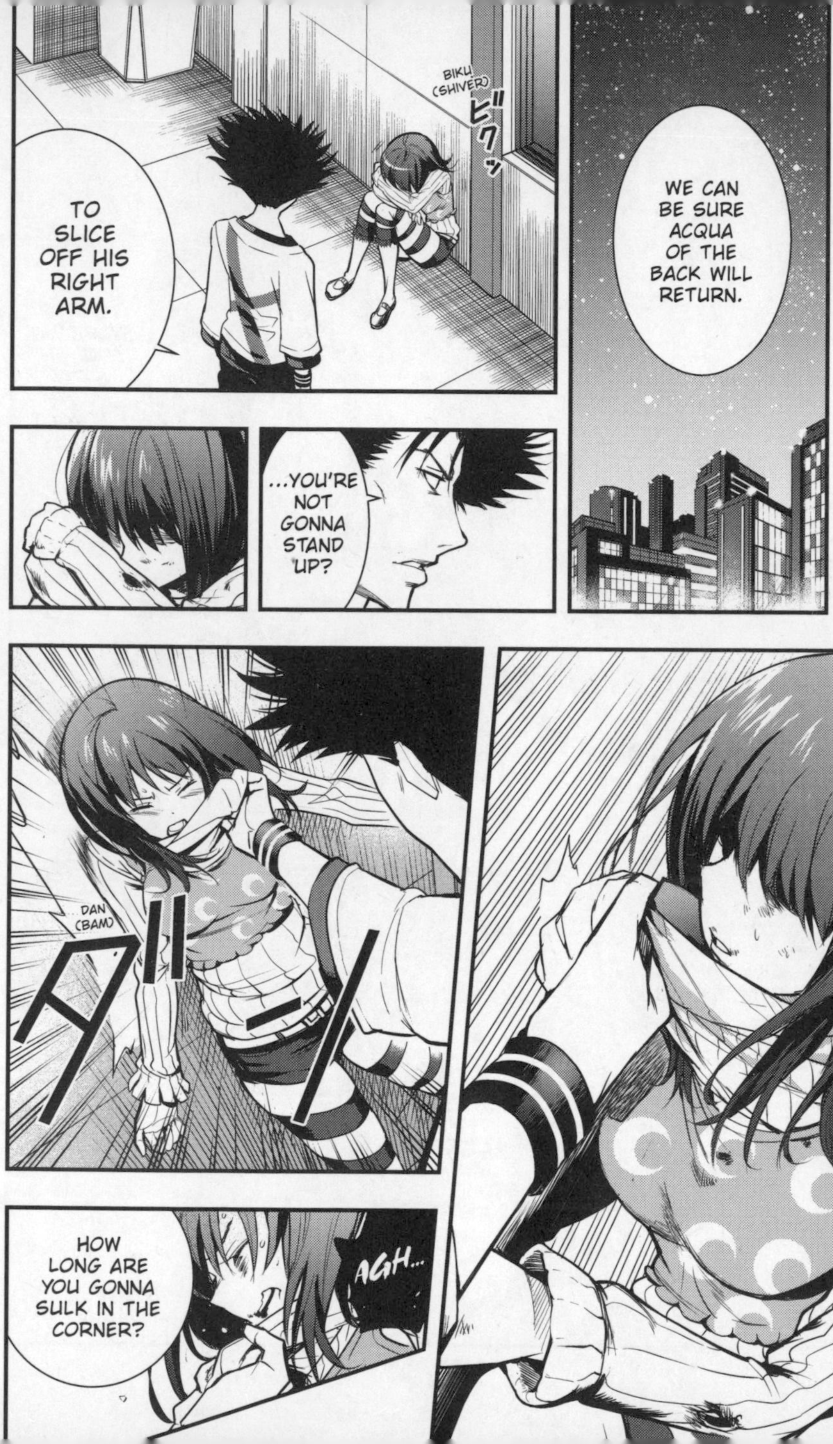
WE CAN BE SURE ACQUA OF THE BACK WILL RETURN.
BIKU (SHIVER)
TO SLICE OFF HIS RIGHT ARM.
...YOU'RE NOT GONNA STAND UP?
...DAN (BAM)
AGH...
HOW LONG ARE YOU GONNA SULK IN THE CORNER?

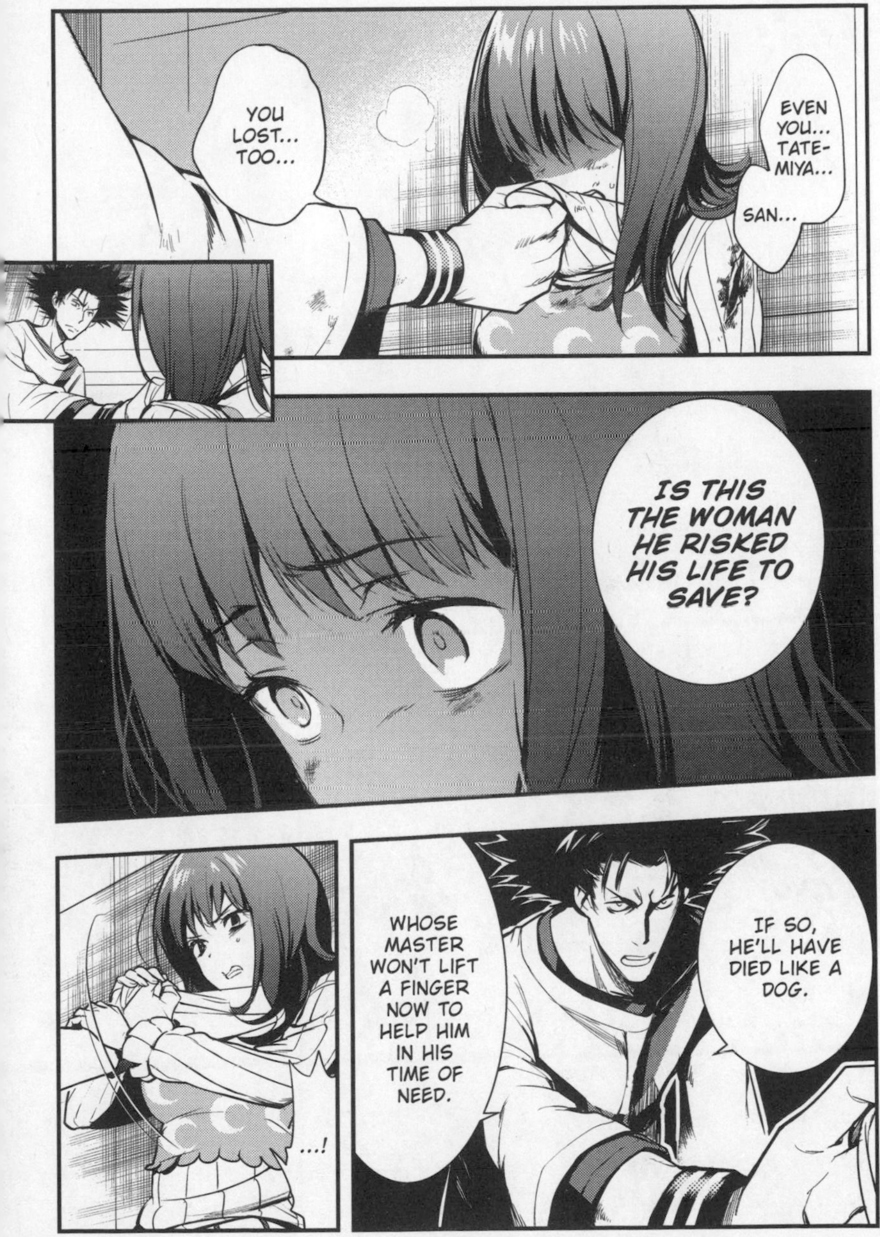
EVEN YOU... TATE-MIYA...
SAN...
YOU LOST... TOO...
IS THIS THE WOMAN HE RISKED HIS LIFE TO SAVE?
IF SO, HE'LL HAVE DIED LIKE A DOG.
WHOSE MASTER WON'T LIFT A FINGER NOW TO HELP HIM IN HIS TIME OF NEED.
...!

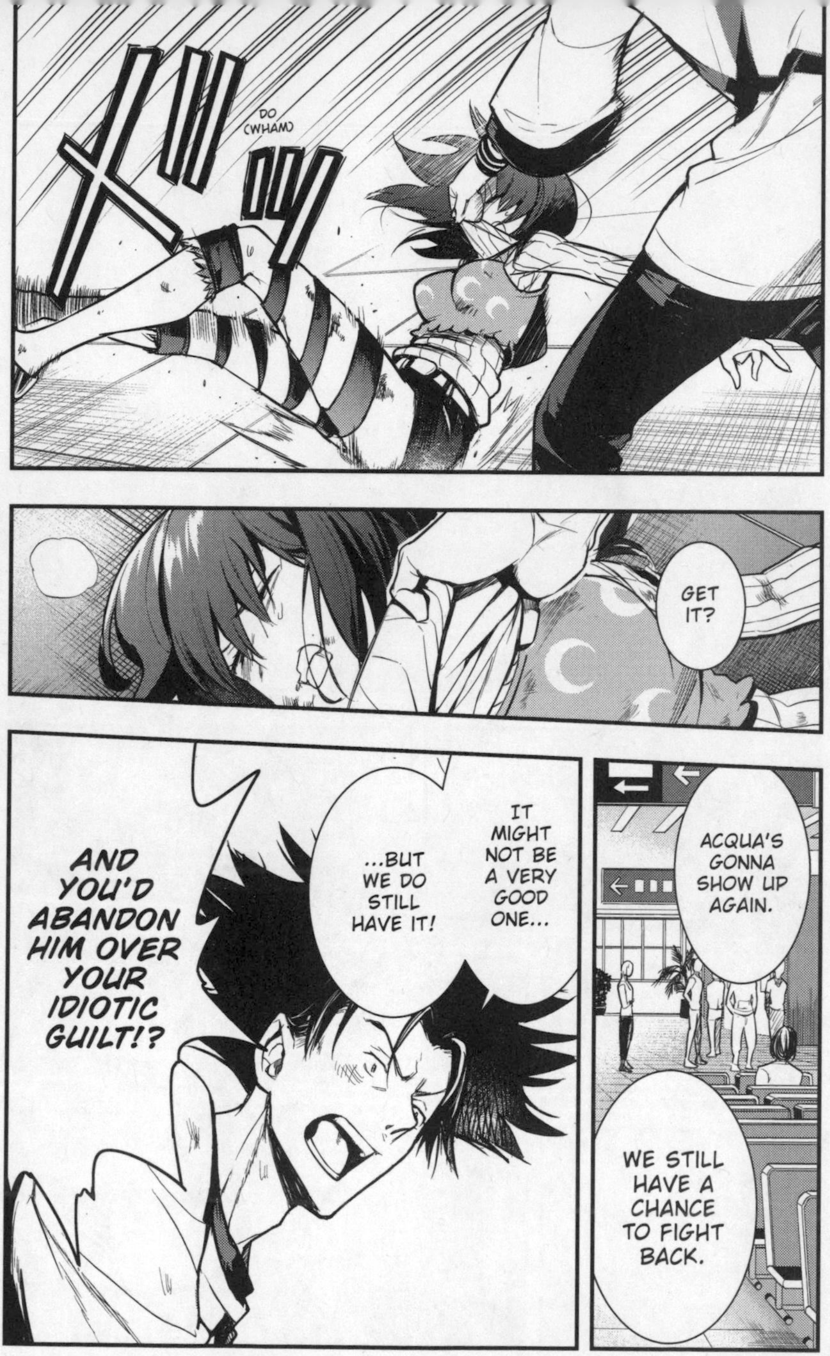
DO (WHAM)
GET IT?
ACQUA'S GONNA SHOW UP AGAIN.
WE STILL HAVE A CHANCE TO FIGHT BACK.
IT MIGHT NOT BE A VERY GOOD ONE...
...BUT WE DO STILL HAVE IT!
AND YOU'D ABANDON HIM OVER YOUR IDIOTIC GUILT!?

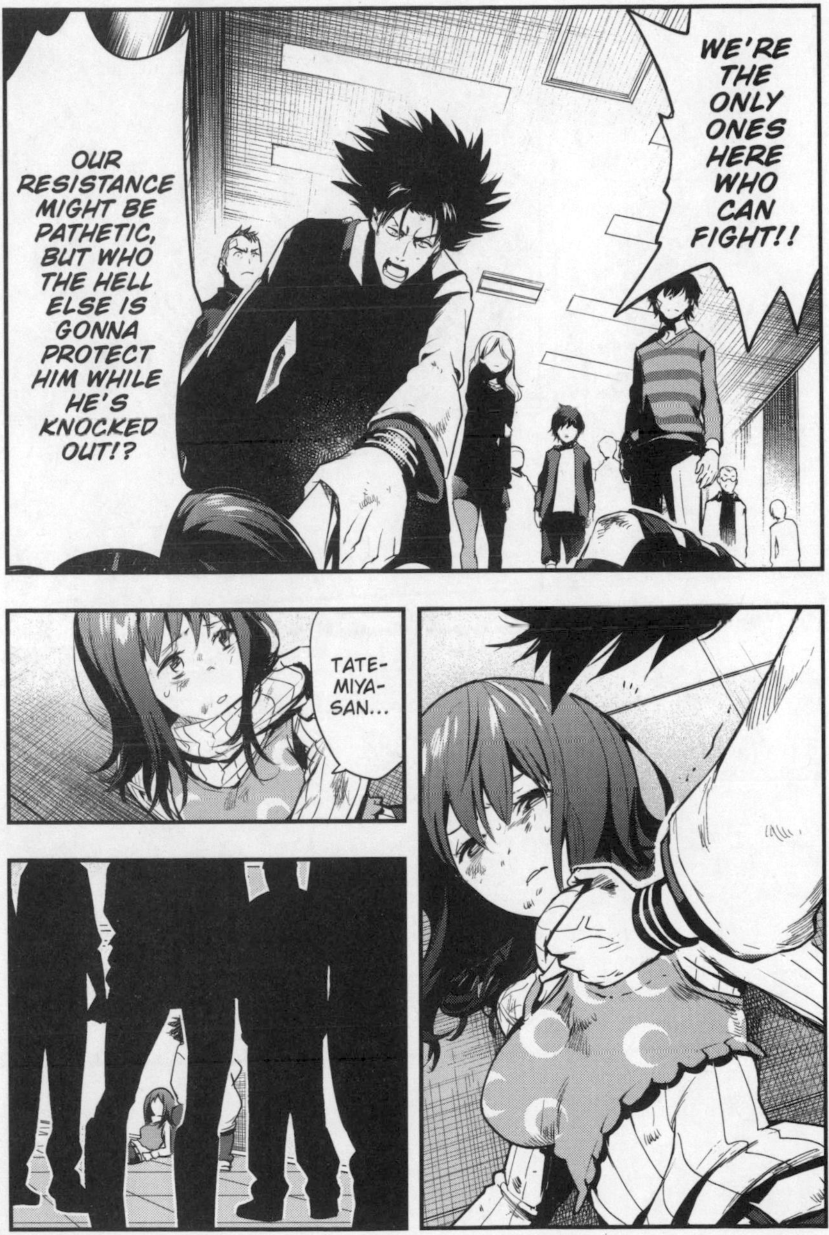
WE'RE THE ONLY ONES HERE WHO CAN FIGHT!!
OUR RESISTANCE MIGHT BE PATHETIC, BUT WHO THE HELL ELSE IS GONNA PROTECT HIM WHILE HE'S KNOCKED OUT!?
TATE-MIYA-SAN...

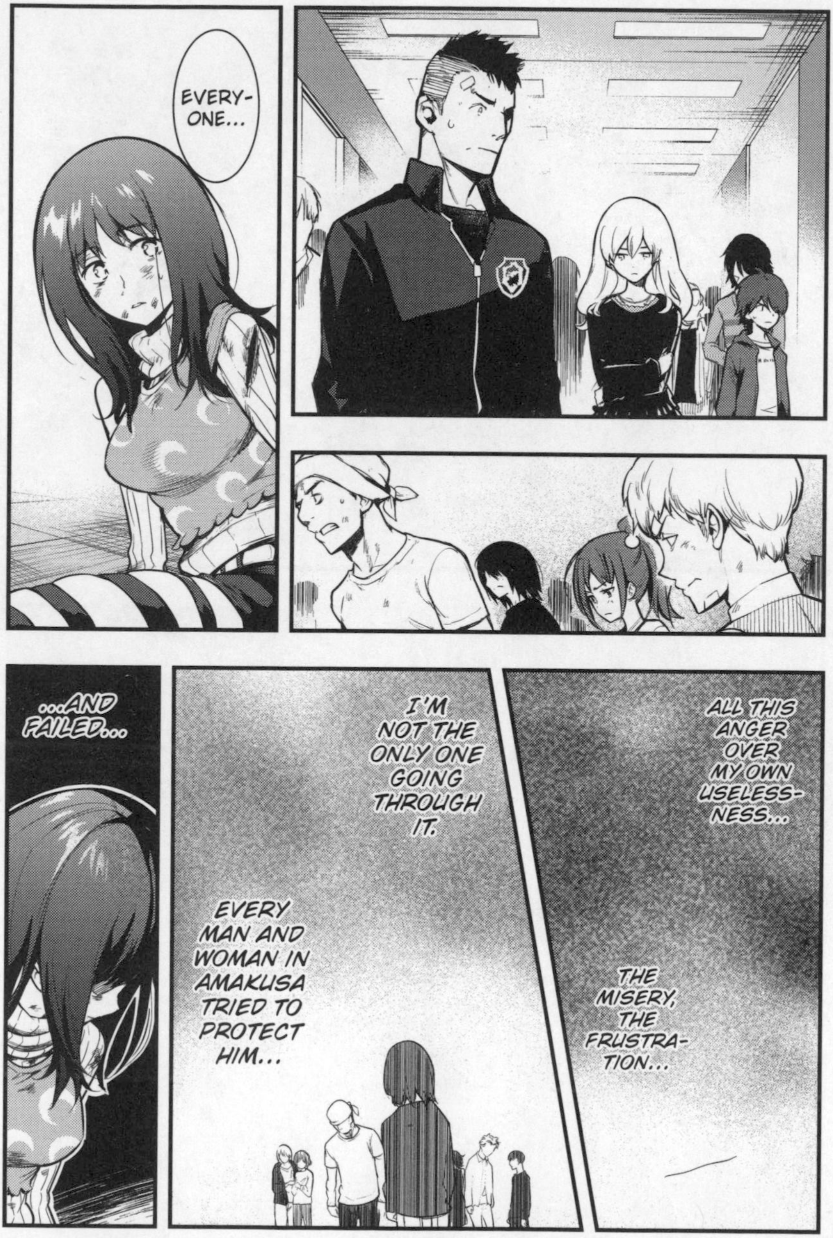
EVERY-ONE...
ALL THIS ANGER OVER MY OWN USELESSNESS...
THE MISERY, THE FRUSTRATION...
I'M NOT THE ONLY ONE GOING THROUGH IT.
EVERY MAN AND WOMAN IN AMAKUSA TRIED TO PROTECT HIM...
...AND FAILED...

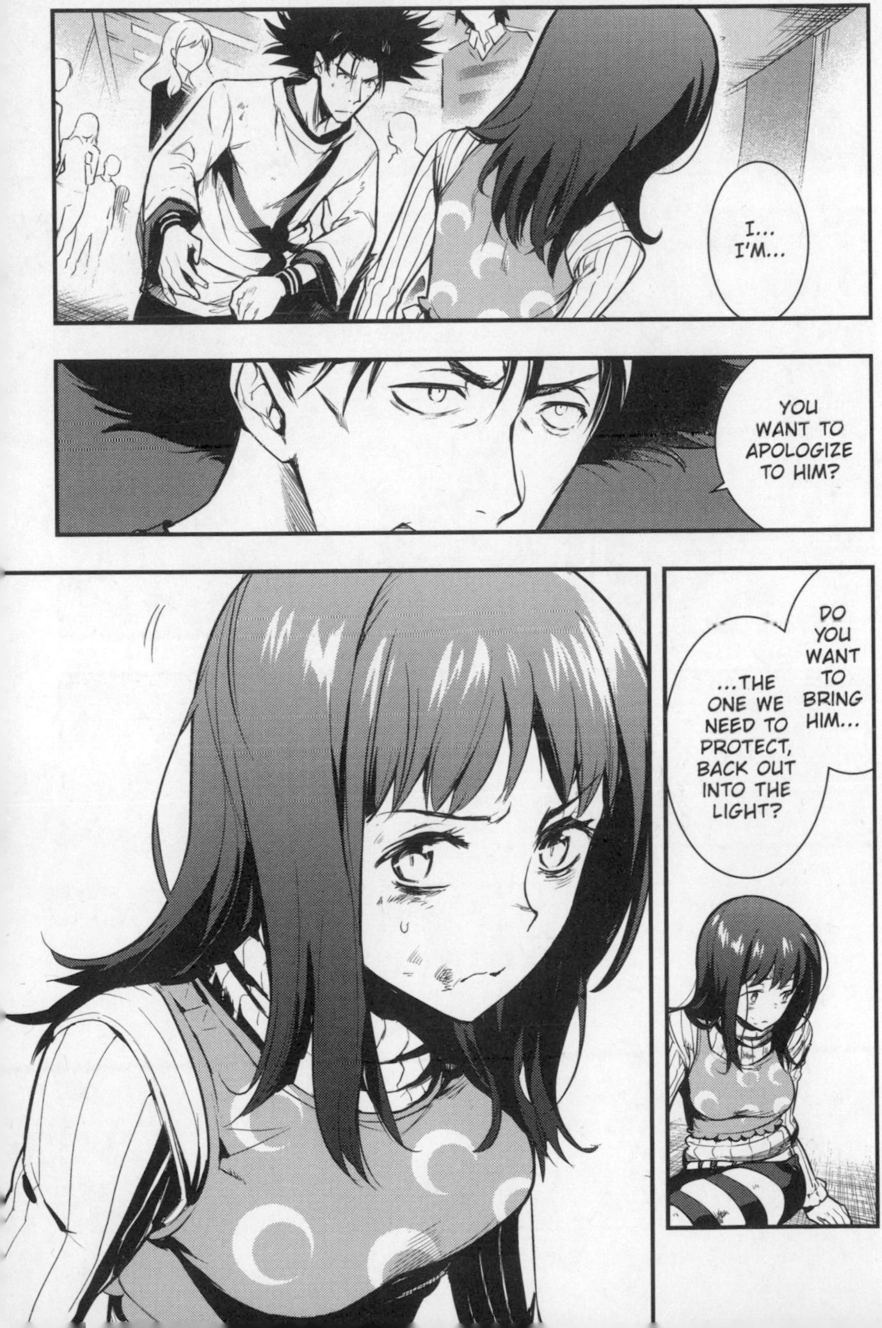
I... I'M...
YOU WANT TO APOLOGIZE TO HIM?
DO YOU WANT TO BRING HIM...
...THE ONE WE NEED TO PROTECT, BACK OUT INTO THE LIGHT?

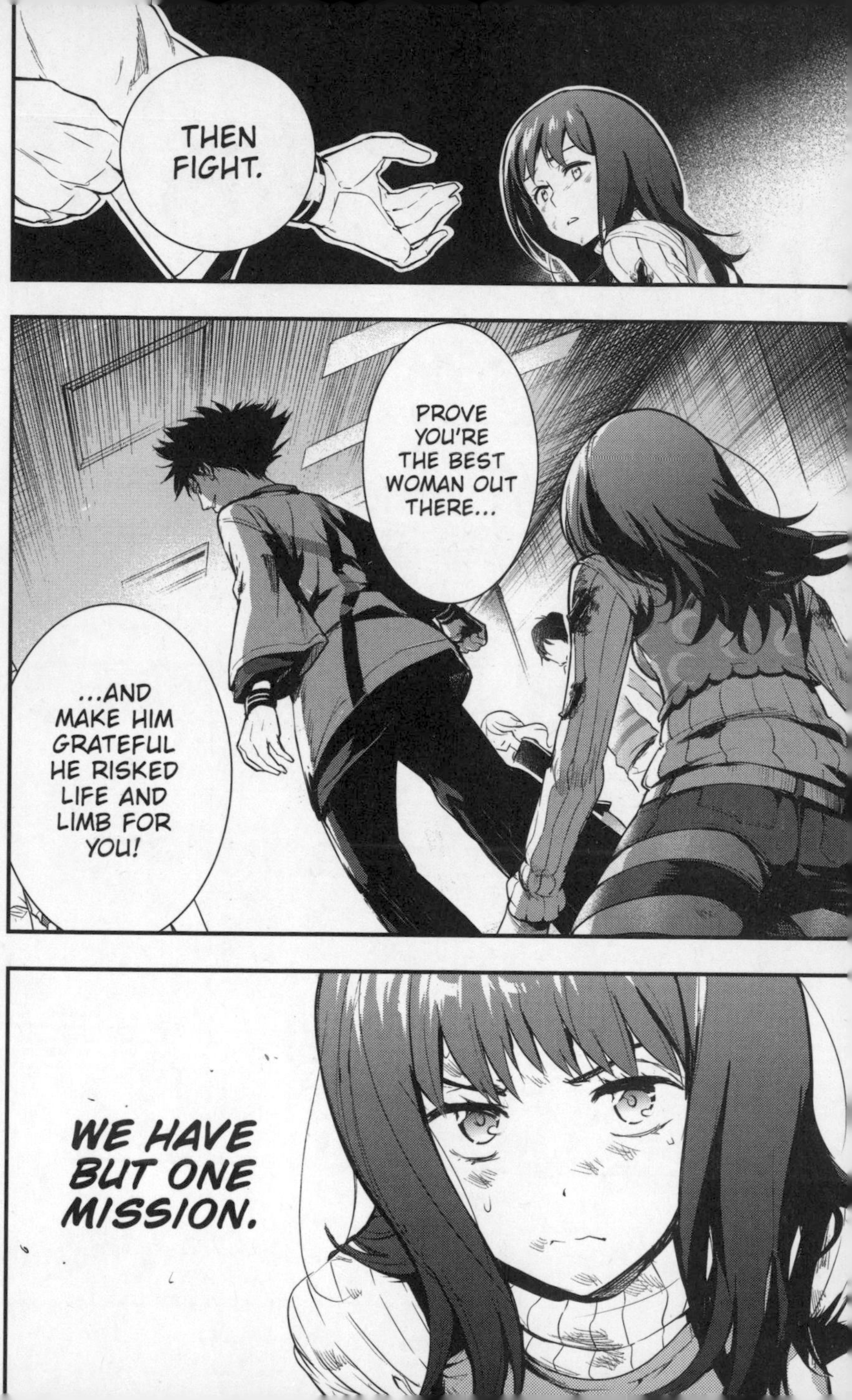
THEN FIGHT.
PROVE YOU'RE THE BEST WOMAN OUT THERE...
...AND MAKE HIM GRATEFUL HE RISKED LIFE AND LIMB FOR YOU!
WE HAVE BUT ONE MISSION.

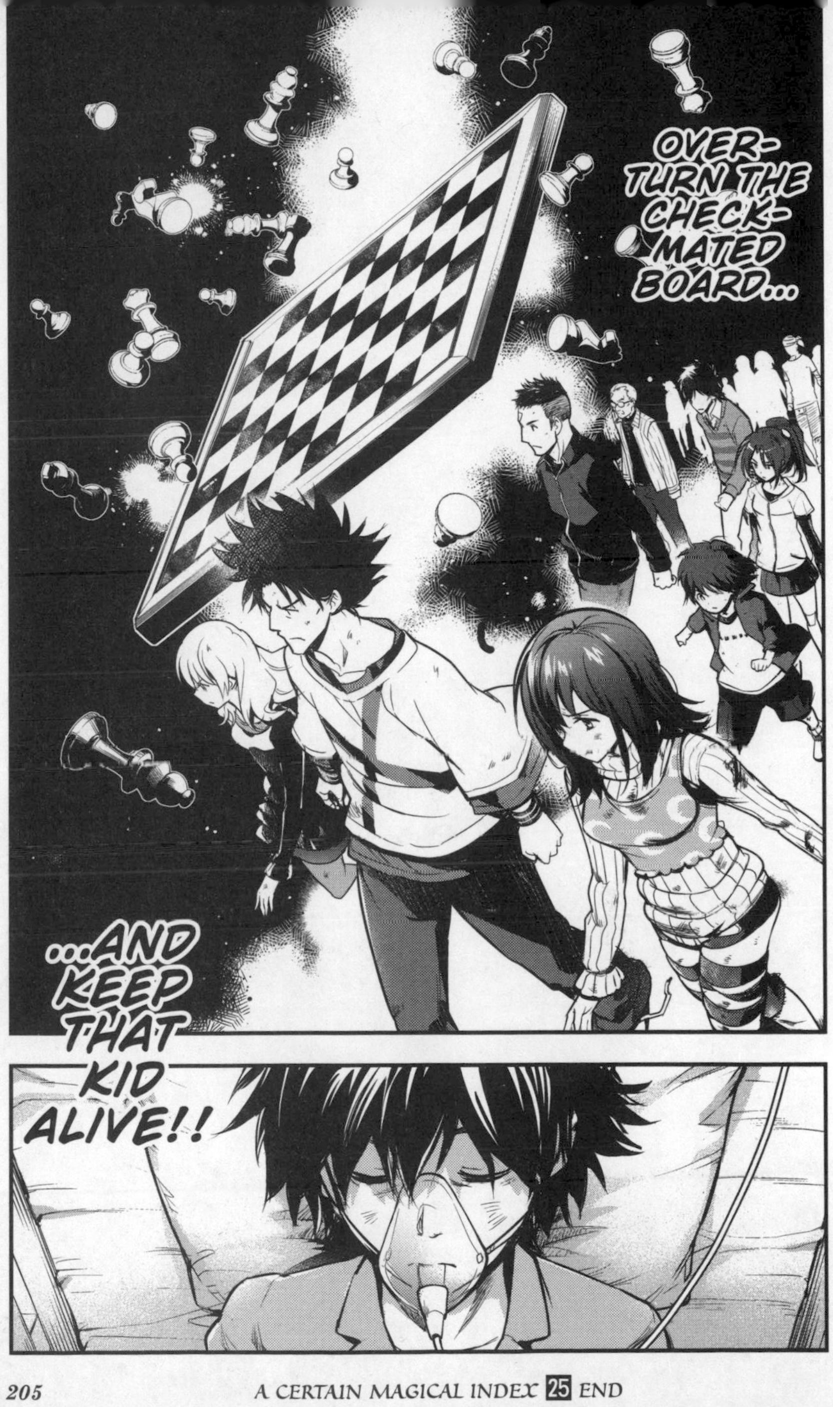
OVER-TURN THE CHECK-MATED BOARD...
...AND KEEP THAT KID ALIVE!!

The Phantomhive family has a butler who's almost too good to be true...

...or maybe he's just too good to be human.

Black Butler

YANA TOBOSO

VOLUMES 1-30 IN STORES NOW!

I've Been Killing SLIMES for 300 Years and Maxed Out My Level

It's hard work taking it slow...

After living a painful life as an office worker, Azusa ended her short life by dying from overwork. So when she finds herself reincarnated as an undying, unaging witch in a new world, she vows to spend her days stress-free and as pleasantly as possible. She ekes out a living by hunting down the easiest targets—the slimes! But after centuries of doing this simple job, she's ended up with insane powers... how will she maintain her low-key life now?!

IN STORES NOW!

Light Novel Volumes 1–11

Manga Volumes 1–8

NDEX ㉕

...na Kamachi
...ka Haimura
...uya Kogino

Translation: Andrew Prowse

Lettering: Phil Christie

This book is a work of fiction. Names, characters, places, and incidents are the product of the author's imagination or are used fictitiously. Any resemblance to actual events, locales, or persons, living or dead, is coincidental.

TOARU MAJYUTSU NO INDEX Vol. 25
© 2021 Kazuma Kamachi
© 2021 Chuya Kogino / SQUARE ENIX CO., LTD.
Licensed by KADOKAWA CORPORATION ASCII MEDIA WORKS
First published in Japan in 2021 by SQUARE ENIX CO., LTD.
English translation rights arranged with SQUARE ENIX CO., LTD.
and Yen Press, LLC through Tuttle-Mori Agency, Inc.

English translation © 2022 by SQUARE ENIX CO., LTD.

Yen Press
150 West 30th Street, 19th Floor
New York, NY 10001

Visit us at yenpress.com
facebook.com/yenpress
twitter.com/yenpress
yenpress.tumblr.com
instagram.com/yenpress

First Yen Press Edition: April 2022

Yen Press is an imprint of Yen Press, LLC.
The Yen Press name and logo are trademarks of Yen Press, LLC.

The publisher is not responsible for websites (or their content) that are not owned by the publisher.

Library of Congress Control Number: 2015373809

ISBN: 978-1-9753-3998-2 (paperback)

10 9 8 7 6 5 4 3 2 1

WOR

Printed in the United States of America